Blowing the Lid

Gay Liberation, Sexual Revolution and Radical Queens

Blowing the Lid

Gay Liberation, Sexual Revolution and Radical Queens

Stuart Feather

zero books

Winchester, UK
Washington, USA

First published by Zero Books, 2015
Zero Books is an imprint of John Hunt Publishing Ltd., Laurel House, Station Approach,
Alresford, Hants, SO24 9JH, UK
office1@jhpbooks.net
www.johnhuntpublishing.com
www.zero-books.net

For distributor details and how to order please visit the 'Ordering' section on our website.

ISBN: 978 1 78535 143 3
Library of Congress Control Number: 2015937455

A CIP catalogue record for this book is available from the British Library.

Design: Stuart Davies

Printed and bound by CPI Group (UK) Ltd, Croydon, CR0 4YY, UK

CONTENTS

To Twelve Gay Men and One Big Happy Family
and To All who Came Out in Gay Liberation

Abbreviations

AB The Angry Brigade.

BP Black Panthers.

CHE Campaign for Homosexual Equality.

CID Criminal Investigation Dept, a Division of the Police Force.

CND Campaign for Nuclear Disarmament.

CPO Compulsory Purchase Order.

C-R Consciousness-Raising.

CT *Come Together*.

DoE Department of the Environment.

DEP Department of Employment and Productivity.

FHAR Front Homosexuel d'Action Révolutionnaire.

FoL Festival of Light.

FUORI! Fronte Unitario Omosessuale Rivoluzionario Italiano. In Italian the acronym means Out!

GBH Grievous Bodily Harm.

GLF Gay Liberation Front.

GN Gay News.

HCA Hall-Carpenter Archives, the largest source for lesbian and gay activism from the 1957 Wolfenden report to the present. Archive Division, Library of the London School of Economics and Political Science.

IRA Irish Republican Army.

IRB Industrial Relations Bill.

IS International Socialists.

IT International Times.

Lily Lily Law: the Police in the gay slang of Polari.

LSE London School of Economics.

NCCL National Council for Civil Liberties. (forerunner of Liberty).

NFHO National Federation of Homophile Organizations.

NHCW Notting Hill Community Workshop.

NHHT Notting Hill Housing Trust.
NHPA Notting Hill People's Association.
NHSG Notting Hill Squatters Group.
NUS National Union of Students.
QC Queen's Counsel.
RAP Radical Alternatives to Prison.
RBK&C Royal Borough of Kensington & Chelsea.
S&M Sado-Masochism (ist).
SCUM Society for Cutting Up Men.
SB Special Branch.
SIB Special Investigation Branch, a unit of the British Army.
SN6 Stoke Newington Six.
SN8 Stoke Newington Eight.
TTA Trust Tenants' Association.
TUC Trades Union Congress.
ULU University of London Union.
WL Women's Liberation.
WLM Women's Liberation Movement.
WM Women's Movement.
WLW Women's Liberation Workshop.
WNCC Women's National Co-ordinating Committee.

Chronology

1954

June

8: The death of Alan Turing due to the horrendous side effects of chemical castration, the sentence he received for gross Indecency in 1952 after openly declaring to police during the investigation of a robbery at his home that he was having a sexual relationship with another man. 'The man who knew too much', had become a security threat to British and American interests during the Korean phase of the Cold War, and establishment panic following the defection of the spies Guy Burgess (who was gay), and Donald Maclean to Russia.

September

Sexual Behaviour in the Human Male (USA 1948) & Sexual Behaviour in the Human Female (USA 1953) by Dr Alfred Kinsey, known as The Kinsey Report, first published in the UK as *An Analyses of the Kinsey Reports on The Sexual Behaviour in the Human Male and Female.*

15: First sitting of the Departmental Committee on Homosexuality and Prostitution under Winston Churchill's Conservative government. Headed by John Wolfenden, it became known as the Wolfenden Committee.

1957

September

4: Wolfenden Report published by Harold MacMillan's Conservative government.

1958

March

7: *The Times* publishes letter signed by 33 eminent people including Isaiah Berlin, Bob Boothby MP, Julian Huxley, J.B. Priestley and his wife Jacquetta Hawkes, Bertrand Russell, and A.E. Dyson who organized the letter and persuaded a number of the signortories to found The Homosexual Law Reform Society, and its funding arm The Albany Trust, headed by Antony Grey, which also focused on Public Education, Research, and Counselling.

1964

October

7: The North-Western Homosexual Law Reform Committee held its first meeting.

15: General Election. Labour under Harold Wilson defeat Conservatives by a 4 seat majority.

1965

May

24: House of Lords votes in favour of Lord Arran's Sexual Offences Bill by a majority of 94 votes to 49.

1966

March

31: General Election. Harold Wilson increases Labour majority to 98 seats.

July

5: Leo Abse introduces the Sexual Offences Bill in the Commons. It is approved by 264 votes to 102.

1967

July

27: The Sexual Offences Act receives the Royal Assent.

November

18: Devaluation of Sterling. 'The pound in your pocket remains the same.' – Harold Wilson.

1968

March

The Western World's biggest economic collapse since The Great Depression.

17: The anti-Vietnam war demonstration in Grosvenor Square, London, ended with 86 people injured and 200 demonstrators arrested.

April

4: Assassination of Martin Luther King, Jr, prominent leader of the African-American Civil Rights movement.

May

2: Paris. The évènements commence with the closure of the University of Paris at Nanterre leading to mass uprisings of students and workers throughout France that lasted until the end of the month.

October

5: The Derry march of the Northern Ireland Civil Rights Association attacked by Loyalists.

1969

May

9: Scottish Minorities Group (SMG) formed.

June

27: New York. The police raid The Stonewall Inn, Greenwich Village. Drag queens and lesbians fight back. A riot erupts, followed by an uprising that continues until the following weekend.

July

The Mattachine Society New York meeting about the uprising turns into a walk-out of the newly radicalized members who move to the Alternative University in the West Village and form the Gay Liberation Front.

1970

February

27: The First National Women's Liberation Conference, Ruskin College, Oxford. 300 women were expected – 600 turned up.

April

24: *IT* publishes article by Jim Anderson of *Oz* Magazine in which the acronym GLF appears.

June

18: General Election won by Edward Heath's Conservative Party with a 30 seat majority.

August

9: Mangrove Defence and Black Panthers March disrupted by violent police attack in Portnal Road.

18: London office of Iberia Airlines bombed.

21: California. *Black Panther* carries a statement by Huey Newton supporting Women's & Gay Liberation.

30: The Commissioner of the Metropolitan Police's home is damaged by a bomb blast.

September

8: The London home of Attorney General, Sir Peter Rawlinson, in Chelsea is bombed.

21: Wimbledon Conservative Association firebombed.

26: Hampstead Conservative Association firebombed. Bomb explodes outside Barclays Bank, Heathrow. Simultaneous bomb attacks against Iberia Airlines in Geneva, Frankfurt, Paris and London airports follow.

October

The Women's National Coordinating Committee formed at Ruskin College, Oxford. The Four Campaigns formulated.

8: LSE students led by Bob Mellors and Aubrey Walter attack ULU and the offices of *The Sennett*.

Second explosion at Attorney General's home.

9: Simultaneous bomb attacks against Italian State Buildings in London, Manchester, Birmingham and Paris.

14: Bob Mellors and Aubrey Walter found the Gay Liberation Front at the LSE.
21: General Meeting agrees to go out advertising GLF with a leafleting campaign in the West End.
24: During a council workers strike a bomb explodes at Greenford Council's Cleansing Dept. Head Office.
26: Administration at Keele University campus is firebombed. Barclays Bank at Stoke Newington firebombed.
November
David Fernbach presents the GLF demands and the General Meeting votes to adopt them.
19: *IT* reports the conviction of its editors at the Old Bailey for publishing contact ads for gays.
20: A BBC Transmitter van parked outside the Albert Hall in readiness for the Miss World Contest is bombed.
21: Women's Liberation demonstration inside the Albert Hall disrupts the Miss World Contest live on TV.
25: General Meeting discusses ideas for a public demonstration.
26: Time Out states 'Gay is Good' in its Agitprop column and lists the GLF Demands.
27: The first public demonstration in the UK by lesbians and gays takes place at Highbury Fields, Islington, protesting police entrapment in general and the arrest of Louis Eakes for cottaging.
28: *The Times* reports the Highbury Fields demo.
30: Media Workshop begins duplicating the first issue of GLF newspaper *Come Together* 1.
December
3: Spanish Embassy in London machine gunned.
4: First GLF Disco held in the Students Union bar at the LSE.
8: Big demonstrations against the Tory Government's Industrial Relations Bill.
9: The DEP in St James Square, is bombed. Action claimed by the AB.

The GLF Principles drafted by Fernbach are discussed and voted on, section by section.
22: The first openly advertised Gay Dance, the 'GLF People's Ball' held at Kensington Town Hall.
23: GLF General Meetings move to the Arts Lab, Robert Street, Euston during the LSE Christmas holiday. *Come Together* 2 distributed.
27: The *People* feature the GLF Ball with interviews and a photograph.
30: GLF Street Theatre function group formed.

1971
January
Come Together 3 published. Article about GLF written by Andrew Lumsden is published in the *Spectator*.
4: Louis Eakes arrested on a charge of gross indecency with another man in the bandstand at Hyde Park.
12: Thousands of people strike and march against the Industrial Relations Bill.
The home of Robert Carr, Minister of Employment, in Barnet is bombed. Action claimed by AB.
13: General Meetings return to the LSE after the holidays.
16: The first GLF Think-In discusses structure and tactics.
17: *Observer* article with a photograph of GLF selling *Come Together*, outside *The Coleherne*, in Earls Court.
Agitprop commune in Muswell Hill is raided by Special Branch. Address books snatched.
19: Jake Prescott is arrested in Notting Hill on cheque fraud charges.
20: Prescott appears at Marylebone Court and is sent to Brixton prison on remand.
22: Police with a warrant for drugs bust the GLF Disco at the *Prince of Wales*, Hampstead Road, Camden.
25: Home of the Lord Provost of Glasgow bombed.

26: Street Theatre holds a costume parade around Trafalgar Square and the Strand.
30: GLF Dance at Camden Town Hall with the Pink Fairies and Hawkwind.
February
Come Together 4 published during first fortnight.
General Meetings now attracting over 200 people moves into the LSE Lecture Theatre.
GLF Office opened at 5, Caledonian Road, the home of Peace News and Housemans bookshop.
3: Prescott released on bail.
4: Four WL demonstrators arrested at the Albert Hall appear at Bow Street Magistrates Court. GLF Street Theatre perform The Miss Trial Competition on the pavement outside.
5: First British soldier killed on duty in the Northern Ireland 'Troubles.'
7: The women of Switzerland finally get the vote.
8: Counter-Psychiatry group demand publishers withdraw Dr Reuben's book – *Everything You Always Wanted To Know About Sex – but were afraid to ask.*
11: Prescott arrested and charged with bombing.
Habershon interrupts WL trial and takes four women defence witnesses to Barnet for questioning.
12: GLF demonstrate outside W H Allen's Offices and hand in petition demanding withdrawal of Reuben's book.
13: Leafleting and demonstrations against Reuben's book in Charing Cross Road, Notting Hill, Sloane Square and Earls Court.
Bomb Squad searches the homes of members of WL, among others, in hunt for explosives.
GLF women selling tickets in *The Gateways* for a GLF Dance are thrown out of the club.
17: Women call for volunteers to join their protest against the action of *The Gateways*.

20: GLF women enter *The Gateways* and demonstrate. 13 arrested including two passersby in the street.
21: GLF joins the massive demonstration against the Industrial Relations Bill.
24: Street Theatre perform a send-up of the elections held for the Steering Committee.
26: GLF Dance at Kensington Town Hall.

March

6: International Women's Day. WL march from Trafalgar Square to Hyde Park.
6/7: Midnight. A house in SW11 raided. Ian Purdie arrested.
9: WL and GLF Street Theatre in joint zap of all-male bar at Imperial College.
18: Ford Motors bombed during the nine week strike by AB.
1,800 extra troops sent to Northern Ireland.

April

Come Together 5 published.
1: Purvey of the Obscene Publications Squad arrests Richard Handyside, publisher of The Little Red Schoolbook.
7: The General Meeting moves to building site of former club *Middle Earth* in Covent Garden.
9: Ian Harvey, disgraced closet queen, ex-Tory MP and leading member of CHE attacks GLF in the *Spectator*.
11: GLF joins CND Easter Sunday Festival of Life at Alexandra Palace.
12: *Guardian* article by Jill Tweedie on GLF.
17: Rehearsal for first GLF Gay Day with Street Theatre teaching party games to the Action Group.
22: Committal proceedings for Prescott and Purdie opens at Barnet Magistrates.
23: Leafleting of Earls Court pubs, *The Coleherne* and *The Boltons* advertising GLF Gay Day.
25: First Gay Day takes place in Holland Park. 'Homosexuals Come Out!' stickers plastered all over London.

28: *The Times* receives a liquid bomb through the post with a message from the AB – the People's Army.
30: Dance at Camden Town Hall.
May
Come Together 6 published.
1: Biba, the fashionable department store in Kensington High Street is bombed. AB issue Communiqué 8.
4: A bomb is discovered underneath the car of Lady Beaverbrook, wife of the owner of Express Newspapers.
6: The GLF Communes Group holds their first meeting.
8: GLF Think-In at LSE abolishes Steering Committee in favour of a Coordinating Committee.
16: Gay Day at Primrose Hill.
22: Bomb attack on Scotland Yard Computer Room, British Rail, Rolls Royce and Rover offices in Paris.
24: Heavy police raid of Metro Youth Club, Notting Hill.
26: Metro Youth Club trial opens at Marylebone Magistrates.
29: GLF Women's Disco in basement of coffee bar at 470, Harrow Road.
June
6: GLF Street Theatre group take part in Bath Festival. The Theatre Group rehearse *Measure for Measure* in St. John's Wood.
11: A Red Lesbian Brigade zap spray paints the Stock Exchange.
19: First GLF National Think-In meets at Leeds University.
20: London GLF travel on to Edinburgh to attend the 'Traverse Trials'.
22: *Oz* magazine trial at The Old Bailey commences.
24: Aubrey Walter and Paul Theobald spray paint Harley Street.
25: GLF Counter-Psychiatry supported by Street Theatre, demonstrate in Harley Street.
28: At the Old Bailey three Black Panthers receive suspended sentences, and one is acquitted of riotous assembly during a police raid on Oval House, Kennington.
29: Trial of Richard Handyside, publisher of *The Little Red School*

Book opens at Lambeth Magistrates Court.

July

Come Together (Women's Issue) 7.

1: Handyside's book ruled obscene; he is found guilty of possessing obscene material for gain.

4: Agitprop move to shop at 248 Bethnal Green Road.

GLF Theatre Group gives up trying to produce *Measure for Measure*.

Freak Festival in Hyde Park. Rev.Fr. Fuck distributes communion bread baked with dope.

9: Occupying British Troops in Derry shoot and kill two rioters. Inquiry refused.

11: Gay Day in Victoria Park.

14: Metro Trial at Marylebone Magistrates.

16: Over 150 members of WL and GLF take part in joint demo against Wimpy Bars.

22: The home of Ford's Managing Director, and a transformer at the Dagenham plant bombed by AB.

23: Dance at Hammersmith Town Hall.

28: GLF moves to All Saints Church Hall, Powis Gardens, Notting Hill.

Oz Trial verdict; all three defendants found guilty on obscenity charges and sent to Wandsworth to await sentencing pending medical and psychiatric reports.

31: Secretary for Trade & Industry's home is bombed by AB who issue communiqué 11.

London GLF travel to Burnley to support CHE in their bid to open a gay club in the town.

August

Come Together 8 Youth Group Edition.

2: Intruders break into the country retreat of Judge Argyle of the *Oz* Trial and threaten him. Prescott & Purdie's trial date set. Police begin massive raids all over London looking for evidence that might support the defence.

Agitprop raided and material taken away.
15: Following announcement of Internment without Trial in N. Ireland, the Army Recruitment centre in Holloway is bombed by AB Moonlighters Cell.
16: Agitprop raided by police with an explosives warrant.
19: GLF demonstrate in Fleet Street against media prejudice and stereotyping of lesbians and gays.
21: Special Branch and CID raid a flat in Amhurst Road, Stoke Newington, and arrest four men and two women.
23: SN6 charged with possession of explosives, arms, ammunition, and causing explosions.
28: GLF Youth Group Demonstration against the Age of Consent begins with a Gay Day in Hyde Park and marches to a rally in Trafalgar Square. 30 Ejected from tea shop in the Strand because manageress objected to Claudia and Scottish Malcolm's drag. Dance at Fulham Town Hall.
29: Military wing of Edinburgh Castle bombed.
September
Come Together 9 published this month.
9: Festival of Light (FoL) inaugural meeting at Central Hall, Westminster disrupted by GLF.
16: Bomb discovered in officers' mess inside Dartmoor prison. News withheld for two weeks.
20: Support of Chelsea Bridge opposite Army barracks bombed by AB.
22: GLF find *The Chepstow* cordoned off by police, police vans and cars, and are told they are not welcome.
24: GLF members appear on Thames TV's Today programme.
Albany Street Army Barracks, near Bomb Squad HQ is bombed by AB.
25: FoL meet in Trafalgar square and march to rally in Hyde Park. 34 protesters and GLF banner arrested.
26: *Sunday Times* reports arrests, and Scotland Yard's claim that GLF is associated with the AB.

GLF Premises Fund holds a Benefit at *Theatre Royal* Stratford East.
28: On the orders of the police, more pubs in Notting Hill refuse service to GLF members.
October
At a General Meeting this month Andrew Lumsden brings up the idea of a national gay newspaper.
2: Think-In at LSE.
4: GLF Benefit Concert at Seymour Hall.
5: GLF Press Statement released warning police of non-compliance with their policy of apartheid in local pubs.
6: General Meeting demonstrates against the police ban on GLF members drinking in local straight pubs.
7: Notting Hill Police cave-in and abandon policy of threatening landlords who serve members of GLF.
Government order another 1,500 Troops to N. Ireland.
8: Paperback edition of Reuben's book issued by Pan Books.
9: Brighton GLF Gay Day on the beach during the Labour Party conference.
11: Media Workshop presented with 'Towards a Revolutionary Gay Liberation Front' by Andy Elsmore.
Strategy meeting in GLF Office regarding demo against Pan Books.
15/17: The second National WLM Conference, Skegness. GLF women takeover the microphone and lead a walk-out that puts lesbianism on the agenda.
19: Geoff Marsh found not guilty of throwing the proverbial half-brick at a police officer on the *Oz* trial demo.
Street Theatre performs The Court Room Charade.
20: Birmingham bombing claimed by Angry Brigade.
22: Think-In at LSE to discuss structure of General Meetings, new members and high turnover of visitors.
27: George Lennox, of the Ant-Internment League, urges GLF to join the protest march in London 31 October.

28: MP's vote 356 to 244 in favour of Britain joining the European Community. Most Conservatives were for the motion, most of Labour against.
30: Street Theatre demonstrated abortion, Reuben's style, in Foyles doorway, followed by trashing of Charing Cross Road bookshops.
GLF women and WL stage first demonstration outside Holloway on conditions inside the prison.
Antony Grey launches the NFHO. It involved paying money to be taken over by Grey's organization.
Post Office Tower bombed. The AB and IRA both claim and disclaim responsibility.
31: Anti-Internment demonstration marches through central London supported by GLF.
November
Come Together 10 published this month.
1: Army Tank HQ in Everton Street, London, bombed by AB.
5: Three members of GLF arrested at *The Chepstow* appear at Marylebone Magistrates.
6: GLF Street Theatre and WL Street Theatre perform outside the Albert Hall on the evening of the Miss World Contest.
Bomb attacks on British Embassies in Barcelona and Rome, Lloyds in Amsterdam, and Italian Consulate in Basle in support of the SN6.
9: Five policemen and one policewoman raid Women's Liberation Office with an explosives warrant.
10: FoL defendants from GLF and WL appear at Bow Street.
11: Angie Weir arrested in a raid on her home in Haverstock Street is charged with conspiracy to cause explosions, and remanded to Holloway.
13: Alan Wakeman plants a cross with his GLF badge pinned to it in the Field of Remembrance, Westminster Abbey. Questioned by a policeman, Wakeman whips out a notebook and pencil to take down the officer's remarks and is immediately arrested.

14: Remembrance Sunday. GLF present a triangle of pink carnations at the Cenotaph.

18: Paul Theobald, Martin Rowlands and two others appear at The Guildhall Magistrates.

Street selling of *Come Together* 10.

19: Sisters Disco at the *King's Arms*, Bishopsgate.

20: International Abortion Day demo supported by GLF.

22: FoL defendants at Marlborough Street Magistrates.

25: Bob Mellors founds Camden GLF, at The Foresters Hall, Highgate Road – the first local group in London.

29: Malcolm Bissett, John Church, Neville Smith and Les Tebb appear at Wells Street with their MacKenzies. Case remanded.

December

1: Jake Prescott found guilty of conspiracy to cause explosions. Ian Purdie found not guilty.

6: Media Workshop meeting at Barnes.

10: Demonstrators trash offices of Pan Books, paperback publishers of Reuben's book.

11: GLF Jumble Sale at All Saints Hall, Powis Gardens.

13: Jill Tweedie in the *Guardian* writes on sex roles of straights and gays.

14: Chepstow defendants at Marylebone Magistrates.

17: GLF Cosmic Carnival dance at Seymour Hall.

FoL defendants at Marylebone.

18: Think-In at LSE to consider structure of General Meetings and high turnover of new members.

Alan Wakeman gives a Christmas Party for children in Notting Hill using the name of GLF.

Kathy McLean arrested on charges of conspiring to cause explosions. She joins Angie Weir as one of the SN8.

20: Media Workshop meeting at West End Lane.

22: Christmas Newssheet gives details of availability, quality and price of LSD, hashish and grass.

23: Camden GLF Christmas party.

1972

January

Lesbian Come Together 11 published this month.

3: Committal proceeding for the SN8 begins at Lambeth Magistrates Court.

9: Miners go on strike.

10: Media Workshop at Marlborough Mansions, Cannon Hill.

12: Remembrance Day defendant Alan Wakeman at Bow Street.

14: Chepstow defendants at Marylebone.

15: GLF women and WL demonstrate outside Holloway Prison about the new psychiatric facilities and the conditions inside.

Conway Hall debate with Lord Soper on the Pauline Jones case.

18: George Lennox arrested at Earls Court while selling *7 Days* newspaper.

19: Chepstow defendant Peter Wells at Marylebone.

Newssheet announces the Action Group has collapsed.

George Lennox charged at Gerald Row Police Station with armed robbery at Victoria Station.

20: Number of unemployed goes over one million for the first time.

22: Britain joins the European Community, along with Denmark, Ireland and Norway.

25: Reporting restrictions lifted on SN8 Trial. Angie Weir bailed to her parent's home in Basingstoke, part of the prosecution plan to disperse defendants and make it difficult for them to prepare a defence. Those held on remand are placed in separate prisons or prison wings.

26: FoL defendant Nicholas Bramble at Marlborough Street. Police evidence of assault on officer 'cannot be found.' Case dismissed.

29: GLF Women's Think-In at All Saints Church Hall to discuss their situation and possibility of leaving GLF.

30: 'Bloody Sunday'. British Troops in Derry, N. Ireland, kill 13 civil rights protesters and seriously injure 27 more.

31: NCCL campaign to collect information on harassment of gays begins; GLF help to distribute the 10,000 questionnaires.

February

GLF join Bloody Sunday March from Hammersmith to Downing Street where 13 coffins are delivered to No. 10 and a riot erupts in Whitehall.

5: GLF Women's Think-In at All Saints debate their position in the movement.

9: Women of GLF walk out of General Meeting and declare they will work separately from the men.

British Embassy in Dublin burnt down by demonstrators.

11: Women's Gay Liberation Front formed at *The Three Wheatsheaves* in Islington.

16: Youth Group merge their political and education groups. Declare they are fed up with the situation in GLF.

19: National Think-In at Lancaster University.

South London GLF go on a recruitment demo.

The *Time Out* and *Other Cinema* conference on 'Freedom and Responsibility in the Media' at the Roundhouse is disrupted by WL and GLF who take over the platform having been ignored for the first half of the day. South London GLF Street Theatre performs.

22: IRA bomb kills seven people in Aldershot.

23: Agitprop raided for fourth time on an explosives warrant.

24: Camden GLF thrown out of Hampstead pub *William IV* for leafleting.

27: Media Workshop meeting at West End Lane.

March

Gay International News begins publication.

Come Together 12 (the rip-off edition) issued in the latter half of month.

3: West London Dance at Fulham Town Hall.

7: South London GLF demonstration and leafleting campaign outside *The Union Tavern,* Camberwell.

The Gay News Collective in discussions with GLF at *The Three Wheatsheaves,* Islington.

11: Think-In at LSE to discuss General Meetings and local GLF groups, and the discovery that the Office Collective are secretly producing an issue of *Come Together* without authorization.

19: Kilburn GLF founded. There are now GLF groups in Ealing, Harrow, and West London, as well as Camden and South London.

21: GLF members organized by Camden occupy *Time Out* to demand that gay contact ads be published and sexism in the personal ads should be edited.

26: Anti-Internment League March through central London.

30: British government dissolves N. Ireland Assembly and establishes Direct Rule.

April

Come Together 13 Camden GLF published this month.

5: Newssheet proposes people rip-off copies of the unauthorized *Come Together.*

11: GLF Benefit Dance at Fulham Town Hall for Trevor Woods, held in Italy on a drugs charge.

13: Newssheet reveals divisions within the Office Collective.

15: Think-In at LSE criticizes the politics of *Come Together* 12, finding it didn't advance the interests of GLF.

The all-London meeting is abolished and meetings at All Saints will be known as Notting Hill GLF.

22: Gay Day at Keele University attended by members from London.

May

5/7: National Think-In at Birmingham University.

6: GLF People's Dance at Digbeth Civic Hall.

Teach-In on homosexual liberation for people working in education and law takes place at the LSE.

12: GLF Dance at Fulham Town Hall.

14: Gay Day at Clapham Common.

17: School kids demo at County Hall, London, organized by Schools Action Union. Julian Hows arrested.
20: National Union of School Students founded.
21: Gay Day at Waterlow Park.
24: Appeal in Newssheet for spare paint to decorate the office.
28: Gay Days at Primrose Hill and Wimbledon Common.
30: Trial of the SN8 opens in No. 1 Court at the Old Bailey; the longest criminal trial in British history.

June

Cloud Downey and others establish Brixton commune in Athlone Road.
2-4: GLF Street Theatre perform at Bath Festival.
4: Gay Day at Finsbury Park.
11: Gay Day Parliament Hill.
12: Simmering discontent in the Office ends with the straight-gays claiming they'd been thrown out of the Office by the queens for not wearing drag.
14: House of Lords rule by 4 – 1 majority, Lord Diplock dissenting, to uphold the conviction of *IT* and confirm that gay personal contact ads are a conspiracy to corrupt public morals.
17: Radical queens paint office in runny, psychedelic colours in an effort to cheer it up before Gay Pride.
18: Straight-gays in Office collective reclaim the office walls and paint them white.
Gay Day at Alexandra Palace.
Jimmy Savile's *Speakeasy* on homosexuality excludes GLF. Other gay groups present collude with him.
Come Together 14 published by Birmingham GLF.
19: *Gay News* 1 published.
Spare Rib launched with a party at *The Place*. Controversy occurs over the queens' appearance and behaviour. *Sunday Times* and *Gay News* 2 make serious charges in their reporting of the Spare Rib party.
23: Dance at Fulham Town Hall organized by Youth Group. *Time*

Out reports poor attendance.
24: First Gay Pride Week begins, organized by GLF Youth and Education Group.
Fifty members of GLF selling *Come Together* are thrown out of *The Coleherne* and *The Boltons*. Others go to the King's Road and Piccadilly with more success.
25: Gay Days at Waterlow Park, Highgate and Battersea Park.
26: Street Theatre carnival and street selling of *Come Together*.
27: Street Theatre's Oscar Wilde Demonstration at American Embassy followed by Queens Pride March to Trafalgar Sq and Marble Arch before dropping in on *Gay News*.
South London GLF Fancy Dress at *The Windmill*, Clapham followed by torchlight procession across the common.
28: West London Disco at *White Lion*, Putney High Street.
29: Local Groups day.
30: Gay Pride Grand Ball at Fulham Town Hall. Local youths become aware of GLF presence. Trouble between *Gay News* seller and radical queens.
July
1: International Gay Pride Day. Carnival Parade from Trafalgar Square, 2:00 pm. via Waterloo Place, Lower Regents Street, Piccadilly, Shaftesbury Avenue, Charing Cross Road and Oxford Street to Speakers Corner for a Gay Day in Hyde Park.
Disco at Northern Polytechnic.
2: Gay Day on Primrose Hill. First UK Gay Pride Week finishes.
5: Athlone Road Commune invade Tulse Hill Comprehensive School in protest at attacks on their home.
7: GLF Dance at Fulham Town Hall. Tony Reynolds arrested after local youths cause trouble.
9: Gay Day at Bishops Park, Fulham.
16: Gay Day at Peckham Rye.
23: Gay Day at Turnham Green.

August

Athlone Road Commune leaves Brixton and go to stay with friends in Notting Hill.

8: Anthony Reynolds found guilty and fined £5 for using threatening behaviour at West London Magistrates Court.

42 Colville Terrace, Notting Hill, squatted by queens from Brixton and joined by other queens in Notting Hill to form the GLF Notting Hill Commune.

September

9: GLF Think-In renamed All-London Come Together, and agrees to hold meetings every month.

16: *Champion* refuses service to Radical Queens. Sit-in begins. Landlord calls police. Five queens arrested

21: Internment without Trial in N. Ireland is abolished.

24: Gay Day in Victoria Park organized by East London GLF.

October

East London GLF link up with Agitprop.

20: Notting Hill Housing Trust attempt to evict commune from 42 Colville Terrace.

24: *Champion* defendants appear at Marylebone Magistrates. Court. Lumsden and Reed found guilty of threatening behaviour. Bourne, Chappell and MacDougal bailed to appear on 14 December.

28: Notting Hill Commune moves to 7A, Colville Houses.

All-London Think-In hosted by Camden GLF.

November

2: Tim Bolingbroke, Sarah Grimes, Denis Lemon, Andrew Lumsden, and Michael Lyneham give evidence at the Old Bailey corroborating Angie Weir's alibi of being on the Fleet Street Demo of 19 August 1971, the date the prosecution in the SN8 Trial claim she was visiting France to buy arms.

Symposium on Aversion Therapy with Prof. Hans Eysenck and the London Medical Group disrupted by Peter Tatchell who challenged them to the point where they throw him out.

Newssheet announces end of Notting Hill & Kilburn GLF.
12: Remembrance Day wreath laying ceremony performed by CHE.
15: SN8 Defence Group urge picketing of Old Bailey as trial draws to a close.
18: SN8 Defence Group organize Demo outside Holloway for SN8 defendants and all other prisoners.
GLF members in drag attacked on Northern Line tube after GLF disco at *Bull & Gate* in Kentish Town.
19: First National Think-In for Jewish Gays organized by the Jewish Homosexual Liaison Group.
December
Come Together (Notting Hill) 15 issued in second week.
6: Trial of SN8 concludes. Angie Weir and three others acquitted. Four others found guilty of conspiracy to cause explosions are given 10 years. Jake Prescott's sentence reduced to 10 years.
14: *Champion* defendants summarily dealt with by Marylebone Magistrate; all three are found guilty.
18: Street selling of *Come Together* all over London.
20: Diplock Commission recommends suspension of trial by jury in N. Ireland.
22: GLF Christmas Party at Lime Grove baths.
25: 7A Notting Hill Commune hosts 84 visitors to 'Colevillia'.

1973
March
1: Bethnal Rouge Commune takes over Agitprop's lease of 248 Bethnal Green Road and open their own bookshop specialising in works on sexual politics.
3: Gay Marxist conference at Warwick University.
16: 7A join demonstrators protesting housing conditions and presence of RBK&C councillors in Notting Hill.
26: Noel Coward dies. The *Spectator* celebrates.
29: Last US troops leave Vietnam.

31: Local GLF groups and Homeless Action Campaign demonstrate at the Ideal Homes Exhibition, Olympia.

April

3: GLF Squat at 44 Parkhill Road forcibly evicted. Within an hour they find a house at Medburn Street, Somerstown, where they form a commune. Camden GLF take a room in the squat for their meetings.

6: Landlord with police assistance attempts to evict the radical queens from 7A.

7: GLF Counter-Psychiatry Group zap the conference of the British Psychological Society.

May

4/6: GLF National Think-In at Essex University organized by Marion Prince.

15: Radical Queens join NHPA and local people at All Saints Church Hall meeting with RBK&C housing officials about the Crick report on local housing.

29: Revival at the Conway Hall, Red Lion Square, Holborn, of the GLF All-London Meeting.

June

Come Together (Manchester) 16 published – the last edition of the GLF Newspaper.

7A Notting Hill Commune disperses.

5: Following the GLF All-London Meeting 40 members march on Fleet Street newspapers.

22: Bethnal Rouge Benefit Disco.

23: South London GLF Disco.

24: Gay Day in Hyde Park.

26: West London Disco at Fulham Town Hall.

27: Disco by the Bandstand on Clapham Common.

29: Gay Pride Rally in Hyde Park.

Bethnal Rouge Jumble Sale.

August

Peter Tatchell seeks endorsement of All-London meeting as GLF representative to the Young Communist League World Youth Festival in East Berlin.

25: 70 members from London go to support Hendon GLF and demonstrate against the *Hendon Times*.

September

29: *Gay News* host a meeting at *The Boltons* with representatives from 15 groups to discuss the idea of setting up a London Gay Switchboard.

October

2: All-London Meeting discuss moving the GLF Office to Bethnal Rouge, due to restricted opening hours and lack of volunteers at Caledonian Road.

3: Bethnal Rouge take the GLF paperwork from Caledonian Road to their centre in Bethnal Green.

13: National Think-In at Sussex University endorses Bethnal Rouge's takeover of the GLF office.

November

Falling attendance forces Conway Hall All-London meeting to move to All Saints Hall.

1974

January

GLF All-London meetings end.

Last Newssheet issued by GLF office gives details of the take-over of the office premises and telephone number by London Gay Switchboard.

February

Members of Bethnal Rouge attacked by Group 4 Total Security thugs at Goldsmiths Gay Soc Disco.

16: Seligman takes possession of former GLF Office.

28: General Election. The Labour Party under Harold Wilson form a minority government in a hung parliament.

March

4: London Gay Switchboard opens.

31: Bethnal Rouge collapses due to crippling overheads.
GLF groups that remained for a short while were located in Bangor, Birmingham, Blackburn, Bradford, Cardiff, Chester-le-Street, Coleraine (N. Ireland), Dundee, Durham, Lancaster, Leeds GLF Office, Manchester, Newcastle, South London and Sussex.

Acknowledgements

My first thanks goes to Lisa Power for permission to quote from her pioneering history of the Gay Liberation Front, *No Bath but Plenty of Bubbles,* which allows me to use her recorded interviews with all the main activists.

Supporting those stories are ones from my own contributors, Angie Weir, Elizabeth Wilson, Bette Bourne, Stephen Crowther, Dennis Greenwood, Cloud Downey, Michael James, John Lloyd, Allahn McRae, Mark Roberts, and Christopher Stockdale. My special thanks and gratitude goes to each one of you, for your time, hospitality, recollections, clarifications and considered opinions. My special thanks and gratitude also goes to Howard Llewellyn who kindly allowed me to use his previously unpublished photographs. And thanks to the staff at the Hall-Carpenter Archive for their cheerfulness and professionalism.

I wish to pay tribute to the memory of Mary McIntosh, the outstanding second-wave feminist and founder of the modern lesbian and gay movement in Britain who died in 2013. Her work in sociology and criminology paved the way to a new understanding of lesbian and gay history before the advent of GLF. Working with the Homosexual Law Reform Society led her to see that searching for the causes of homosexuality as an argument for reforming the law was useless without also examining the causes of heterosexuality. Realizing that this question opened an entirely new field of enquiry which could derail the work of the law reform movement, she decided to publish her new thinking in an obscure but influential American Journal 'Social Problems'. Mary McIntosh's contribution to the GLF *Manifesto* aided the entire community's understanding of sexism and sexual politics, as her further work on gender and sexuality influenced a whole generation of sociologists. Her political acumen in dealing with the parliamentary committee considering the lowering of the age of consent succeeded in the first change from 21 to 18. Unequal though it was, the Conservatives had been minded to make no change at all, until they were panicked by her caucus' proposing the age limit be lowered to 14. Mary McIntosh's kind permission giving me access to her papers held at the HCA was an invaluable help, and I would like to add, came with an eager enquiry about a book launch party.

Sarah Grimes to my surprise and delight, very generously volunteered to be my reader, patiently corrected my punctuation, told me when my arguments didn't work, and wisely remained silent at one point when I asked her what was going on in the GLF Women's Group; forcing me to think and make up my own mind. Her tact, intelligence, and faith in me have been my great support, and it is to Sara Grimes that I owe the greatest debt of gratitude and thanks for the kindly help she gave me when writing this book.

I wish to thank the following for kind permission to reproduce quotations: Georges Borchardt Inc., for permission to quote Michel Foucault; The History of Sexuality. Originally publish in French as La Volonté du Savoir. Copyright © 1976 by Editions Gallimard. Reprinted by permission of Georges Borchardt, Inc., for Editions Gallimard; Farrar, Straus & Giroux for permission to quote 'Notes on Camp' from Against Interpretation by Susan Sontag. Copyright © 1964, 1966, renewed 1994 by Susan Sontag; Millivres Prowler Ltd., www.millivres.co.uk for permission to quote from Gay News; Penguin Group UK for permission to quote; Susan Sontag, 'Notes on Camp' from Against Interpretation, Copyright © 1961, 2009; Michel Foucault, History of Sexuality: Volume 1, Translated by Robert Hurley (Allen Lane 1979) Translation copyright © Random House, Inc., 1978; Random House, Inc., for permission to quote *Thanksgiving for a Habitat*, copyright © 1963 by W.H. Auden and renewed1991 by The Estate of W.H. Auden, from *Collected Poems* of W. H. Auden by W.H. Auden. Used by permission of Random House, Inc; William Reed Business Media Ltd., for permission to quote from *Morning Advertiser*; The Wylie Agency (UK) Ltd., for permission to quote *Thanksgiving for a Habitat, Collected Works*, Copyright C 1976, 1991, The Estate of W.H. Auden.

Cover photograph by Pennie Smith.

Introduction

The Gay Liberation Front is the model of the first lesbian and gay sexual revolution in Britain. Along with Women's Liberation it was the most important social movement of the late-twentieth century. It was started in 1970 by two sociology students who invited gay men and gay women to unite around a simple set of demands. Among these were calls for an end to discrimination against homosexuals in employment, in sex education, in the age of consent (21 for gays, against 16 for heterosexuals) and, in being treated as sick by the medical establishment.

For gay men, there had been The Homosexual Law Reform Society (HLRS), and its funding, educational, and counselling arm, The Albany Trust, founded in 1958 by a group of prominent liberals. In 1964 another group formed that eventually became known as the Committee for Homosexual Equality (CHE). The work of the reformers culminated in the Sexual Offences Act of 1967. This went only partway towards decriminalising homosexual acts. It neither changed the way homosexuals thought about themselves, nor the way heterosexuals thought about gays. Lord Arran oversaw the passage of the Bill through the House of Lords. When it was passed he opined: 'I ask those who have, as it were, been in bondage and for whom the prison doors are now open to show their thanks by comporting themselves quietly and with dignity ... any form of ostentatious behaviour now or in the future or any form of public flaunting would be utterly distasteful ... [and] make the sponsors of this bill regret that they had done what they had done'.[1] The HLRS disbanded but The Albany Trust and CHE remained in place, the one to continue its educational and counselling service, the other to work for the idea of equality.

This was a time when psychiatrists still believed they could cure homosexuality with aversion therapy; the injection of drugs and electric shocks to the brain causing convulsions: blindly following the ancient, religious prejudices of patriarchy. Their heterosexist male superiority bolstering nineteenth century psychiatric views of homosexuals as sick pathetic victims held gays in a stranglehold. One of the first function groups to be formed in the Gay Liberation Front was Counter-Psychiatry.

It was just over a hundred years since the coining of the word homosexual by the Hungarian Dr. Benkert in 1865, and Carl Friedrich Westphal's article of 1870 on 'contrary sexual feelings'. In the early 1970s Michel Foucault wrote the following genealogy of male homosexuality from the end of the Renaissance:

> As defined by the ancient civil or canonical codes, sodomy [a term covering debauchery, sex with animals, the anal penetration of women, and the anal penetration of men] was a category of forbidden acts; their perpetrator was nothing more than the juridical subject of them. The nineteenth century homosexual became a personage, a past, a case history, and a childhood, in addition to being a type of life, a life form, and a morphology with an indiscreet anatomy and possibly a mysterious physiology. Nothing that went into his total composition was unaffected by his sexuality. It was everywhere present in him: at the root of all his actions because it was their insidious and indefinitely active principle; written immodestly on his face and body because it was a secret that always gave itself away. It was consubstantial with him, less as a habitual sin than as a singular nature. We must not forget that the psychological, psychiatric, medical category of homosexuality was constituted from the moment it was characterised – less by a type of sexual relations than by a certain quality of sexual sensibility, a certain way of inverting the masculine and feminine in oneself. Homosexuality appeared as one of the forms of

> sexuality when it was transposed from the practice of sodomy onto a kind of interior androgyny, a hermaphrodism of the soul. The sodomite had been a temporary aberration; the homosexual was now a species.[2]

Foucault places this description of the homosexual in the context of the eighteenth century, at a time when the discourse on sex was taken over from the church by the bourgeois State which was also wrestling with its new concept of 'population'. Population as economic and political; population as wealth; population as labour; population as increase for economic gain, at the heart of which was sex. The ideal of heterosexual marital sex that the church policed along with the discourses on the subject was then assigned to the medical profession, while the deviant remained subject to criminal justice. By 1865 religious morality, economics, politics, criminology and deviance had crystallized into the medical specialization of sexology, an agent of social control which viewed homosexuality as a condition, or as Foucault saw it, as a species.

Mary McIntosh writing in 1967 was unhappy with the conceptualization of homosexuality as a condition; it was freighted with religious morality and assumptions that there were just two kinds of people in the world, heterosexuals and homosexuals. To counter with bisexuality was no help either because it too was classified as a condition. Mary McIntosh:

> A second result of the conceptualization of homosexuality as a condition is that the major research task has been seen as the study of its etiology. There has been much debate as to whether the condition is innate or acquired. The first step in such research has commonly been to find a sample of 'homosexuals' in the same way that a medical researcher might find a sample of diabetics if he wanted to study that disease. Yet, after a long history of such studies, the results are

> sadly inconclusive and the answer is still as much a matter of opinion as it was when Havelock Ellis published *Sexual Inversions* seventy years ago. The failure of research to answer the question has not been due to a lack of scientific rigour, or to any inadequacy of the available evidence; it results rather from the wrong question being asked. One might as well try to trace the etiology of 'Committee Chairmanship' or of 'Seventh-Day Adventism' as of 'homosexuality'.
>
> It is proposed that the homosexual should be seen as playing a social role rather than as having a condition. The role of 'homosexual,' however, does not simply describe a sexual behaviour pattern. If it did, the idea of a role would be no more useful than that of a condition. For the purpose of introducing the term 'role' is to enable us to handle the fact that behaviour in this sphere does not match popular beliefs: that sexual behaviour patterns cannot be dichotomized in the way that the social roles of homosexual and heterosexual can.
>
> The current conceptualization of homosexuality as a condition is a false one, resulting from ethnocentric bias. Homosexuality should be seen rather as a social role. Anthropological evidence shows that the role does not exist in all societies, and where it does it is not always the same as in modern western societies. Historical evidence shows that the role did not emerge in England until towards the end of the seventeenth century. Evidence from the 'Kinsey Reports' shows that, in spite of the existence of the role in our society, much homosexual behaviour occurs outside the recognized role and the polarization between the heterosexual man and the homosexual man is far from complete.[3]

This history of GLF is the history of the attempt to discover, define, invent, enlarge, present and display the expansion of the homosexual role within society. The criminal label had been removed. Gay Pride vanquished the compromised sexologists, and homosexuals were free to begin the struggle to become themselves.

The gross inequalities enshrined in the Sexual Offences Act: the knowledge that what parliamentary democracy made legal one year could be made illegal the next, prompted GLF to reject formal campaigning structures – and with it the need for an organization with membership and fees. It saw itself as a gay peoples' movement, socialist by virtue of its demand for social change, and revolutionary by virtue of its recognition of the inter-connected struggles of other oppressed minorities fighting for their own demands. Stipulating as a precondition of attendance that gays cease to hide, wear a GLF badge and visibly 'Come Out' to the world by declaring their sexuality – was revolutionary. Nobody could claim to be ignorant of their existence anymore. Gays were out in the open; free to demonstrate against anyone who attempted to manipulate them back into the closet or frustrate their liberation.

People came along with ideas that were discussed at the General Meetings on Wednesday evenings, and when things worked well, they found a place in function groups – media-workshop, street theatre, youth group, etc. – each independently developing their own initiatives; places where different opinions were talked through and a consensus for action achieved through collective endeavour. At least that was the theory. A co-ordinating committee elected bi-monthly from members of the function groups took control of business and debates for the general meetings. When problems arose, especially with the direction that the movement should take, occasional Think-Ins took place on Saturdays to debate the issues.

The left was responsible for organising the structure of the movement, and for proposing the Demands and Principles which were adopted and published within the first three months. The left also introduced consciousness-raising groups, first evolved by Women's Liberation in California. Eight to ten people would meet weekly in a member's home to talk about the way their lives had been shaped by their sexuality, their feelings surrounding their sex roles and their experiences of being discriminated against and suppressed. They discovered their strengths through talking together about themselves. Within the intimacy and confidentiality of these groups, members were able to learn from each other and come to an understanding that many personal problems that made them feel bad were general ones imposed by prejudice. Through a reversal of perspective they understood that it was society that was sick, not gays. Just as slaves know everything about their master down to the state of his linen, gays discovered they knew more about their oppressors than their oppressors knew about themselves.

'Heterosexualism' is the politics of male supremacy, a notion so unstable it requires the continuous repetitive enforcement of its social ideology of masculinity in order to maintain the fiction. Differing forms of sexuality are a survival tactic and Man's natural condition, but crushed into an ideology which is completely contrary to his natural inclinations turns the best of men's energy to negative purposes, creating suffering not just for women, children, and gays, but for heterosexual males themselves, as well as the planet they also exploit.

Drawing on the experiences of living with the stigma imposed by heterosexualism and its juridical, medical, and mystical hierarchies of power – gay women and gay men – gays they called themselves in those days – developed a new vision of what being gay could mean, and a new view of their relationship with society: a sexual politics that was at one and the same time personal and universal, as exemplified in the GLF *Manifesto,* published in October 1971.

GLF demonstrations were opportunities to display the powerful sensibility of Camp. Irony born of adversity gave actions a mordantly witty edge that unbalanced police who were trained to confront left wing machismo spoiling for a fight. Not only were police thrown off kilter but also divided, as some officers saw the funny side of things. Women's Liberation protests were equally Camp: women's economic position produced a style of sparse simplicity with a wit that succeeded in getting across their message to the bystander in a nutshell. Both groups used satire to devastating effect.

As news of GLF activities spread through the grapevine, GLF groups spontaneously formed across the country, some meeting in local pubs, others started by students meeting in universities. The autumn of 1971 was the apogee of GLF activity. By that time the general meetings in London had become so unwieldy that local groups were formed in the inner suburbs; suburbs which had already witnessed a spring and summer of Gay Days in their larger parks. The move to local groups was also driven by the increasingly fractious nature of the general meetings as different views and interests coalesced, and as dominant ideologies began to compete, obscure and cover over new political ideas that challenged their old authority. The traditional straight male left saw Media Workshop, the publisher of the front's newspaper *Come Together,* as key to their takeover and control of the movement.

Throughout this book I've chosen to use the word heterophobia in place of homophobia because homophobia is etymological nonsense. Homo means same: what man is frightened of men? What heterosexuals fear is difference, the word for which is heterophobia, a word that is clear, precise, and unequivocal. Some may find problems with the implied binary, but the polarity between homo and hetro, between same and difference, is as the word difference implies, a matter of degrees.

To remain faithful to the use of the word transsexual in the articles published by the Transvestite and Transsexual Group of GLF reproduced in Chapter 12, and to avoid confusion on a very confusing topic, I use the same word and spelling throughout. Many different nouns have been used in the past to refer to trans people, much to their annoyance I'm sure, yet I have felt the need to add new ones in order to make sense of and clarify, I hope, the contested wish of male to female trans who demand to be treated as women by natal women.

For readers unfamiliar with the period I hope the following back story will be of help.

American influences

A search for social justice was in the air – the zeitgeist of America in the 1960s and of Britain in the 1970s. America was a seedbed of civil liberties activism, with direct action, grass roots organization, mass mobilization, nonviolent resistance and civil disobedience. In protests against the war in Vietnam, draft cards were burnt and underground railways and safe houses helped those who wanted to desert from the armed forces. An alternative counterculture evolved around the peace movement, with its own media and new music. The environment became a cause for concern. The notion of sexual liberation spread with the arrival of the contraceptive pill. It was a time when white activists joined the African-American Civil Rights movement by travelling to the Southern States to help the drive for black voter registration in the face of white supremacist resistance. Women activists, both black and white, went on to realize they had their own freedoms to sort out and founded Women's Liberation. Black activists formed the Black Panthers. Gay activists returned north to strengthen the homophile movement, primarily in California. And then towards the end of the decade – when all these new ways of organising and thinking (with the exception of Women's Liberation) had been suppressed by the violence of the US administration (by the assassination of black leaders and the shooting dead of student protesters) – drag queens, lesbians and gays erupted in *The Stonewall* riots of June 1969. Within weeks the first Gay Liberation Front was established in New York.

1968...

Here in Europe revolution came close with the May events in Paris. Predicted and encouraged by the genius of the Situationists, students joined with workers and engulfed the whole of France in confrontation with its government.

1968 was also a year of events and confrontations that shaped Britain for many years to come. There was the biggest economic crash since the Great Depression. At Derry in Northern Ireland the descendents of landless agricultural workers began demonstrating against the inequalities imposed on them by the Unionist government and their allies. The British Left was in growing crisis, continuously splintering and reforming, while students, emulating their French and American counterparts, attempted to take over their universities and build alliances with shop stewards and workers. In October, in a demonstration protesting the imperialist US war against Vietnam, militants broke away from the main march – led up the garden path by patriarchal leaders with more muscle than sense – ostensibly to shake their fists at the American Embassy in Grosvenor Square, but really to have a go at the police. Unacknowledged macho 'heroics' met a bloodbath, an all time low, haunting the left for years with a loss of credibility.

On the right, a major Conservative party figure – Enoch Powell – opened a campaign against immigrants with a racist speech that concluded with the image of 'the River Tiber foaming with much blood.' Ten years earlier Oswald Moseley's fascist electioneering in West London had led to the Notting Hill race riots and the murder of immigrant Kelso Cochrane. Moseley's agitation had been designed to spark racist hatred in the white working class – fears of black people taking jobs and housing, fears of black men taking white women.

1970: General Background...

The second-wave of feminism surged in February with the

formation of Women's Liberation at a conference at Ruskin College, Oxford. At a second conference in October women organized around four core demands: equal pay and opportunities; equal education and training; 24-hour nurseries; free contraception and abortion on demand.

The economic downturn of the late-1960s was producing increasing levels of inflation with the never before experienced combination of rising unemployment termed stagflation. Britain was fighting insurgency – a dirty war against the minority section of the working class in Northern Ireland. A failure to listen and respect civil rights demands – for equality in housing, education and employment – led to an aggressive war against republican communities. In mainland Britain, primarily in London, a series of bombs designed to damage property were exploding outside the homes of police chiefs and government ministers, set by a group called the Angry Brigade. The bomb squad were ripping up floor boards all over town, trampling on legal rights in a search for terrorists. Incriminating stories were planted with an unquestioning media – often designed to discredit Women's Liberation and the Gay Liberation Front by linking them to terrorism. In the face of rising white racism, the concept of Black Power – inspired by the Black Panthers – was educating immigrant communities. Black workers' rights and black youth's facilities were under attack. Police intimidation and terror was not a problem, as far as the establishment was concerned.

The Counterculture

The counterculture that developed in America around movements demanding peace, freedom, and civil rights came to Britain. In 1965 it gathered around the London Poetry Olympics and the first visit to London of Alan Ginsberg. Five years on it supported two large circulation underground newspapers and a monthly magazine. But this counterculture's alternative press – supporting the GLF, the Black Panthers and Women's Liberation (with some equivocation) – was already under attack, both for providing overt contact ads for gay men, never explicitly advertised before, and also for writing about drugs, youth, sex education, lesbianism, homosexuality and pornography. Powerful interests, working with the police and judiciary were conspiring to shut down these media, using conspiracy laws, assaults on witnesses, and the planting of drugs. One of the secret ingredients of GLF was its member's use of marijuana and LSD whose mind expanding properties organically deepened the perceptions of minds being expanded by political activism and a consciousness of new situations. (It was also, to use a hippie phrase of the time – a gas!)

The straight Left

Much of the British Left was unconcerned and unsympathetic to the minority working class of Ulster. Sharing similar values to Conservatives, they passed this conflict off as a religious war, when in fact it was a war between industrialist and agriculturalist cultures. A Troops Out Movement formed in mainland Britain, but it was supported by only a minority of left dissidents and by many of the Irish in Britain. Some New Lefts had decided to work to improve housing conditions – housing and race being major issues in Notting Hill, the inner-city district of London that would become home to the Gay Liberation Front.

Trade Union opposition to the Labour governments' Industrial Relations Bill – curtailing union power – was the issue that united the left at this time, and offered the first occasion for the GLF to join forces with protesting workers. There was opposition to the GLF presence on these marches from the International Socialists and other left groups who thought homosexuality was an aberration that the overthrow of capitalism would sweep away; for them lesbians were missing out on sex, while straight women should stay at home and act as wives and mothers.

The Gay Male Left

Mainly university educated activists, New Left Maoists and Marxist Socialists concentrated on early agitation, the GLF newspaper *Come Together,* and the Manifesto group. They later consolidated into the Gay Marxist Group which was not a function group but a covert one, studying and publishing various revolutionary theories when, in my opinion, the search was on for revolutionary tactics. For the New Left Maoists in particular, Gay Liberation was a brand: the real aim was to increase membership of a gay wing of some Marxist, Leninist or Maoist Party. Their ideology would not permit any deviation from party plans. Liberation for homosexuals, they claimed, could not be attempted for at least two hundred years. They were seriously proposing The Long March whilst others in GLF were for taking taxis. Despite claims to be internationalists, in my view English chauvinism prevented the Gay Left from learning new revolutionary tactics such as emerged in France during the uprising which would have aided the social revolution then underway in Britain. I would argue that their educational sources and dogged reliance on ideology made them as unchanging as the straight left itself, and eventually turned the Maoists into the resistance against feminism. I also argue that the Marxist opinions formulated by 1973 became the elitist ideology of a gay establishment. Queers and trans people would eventually pick up this political gauntlet of exclusion as well as the fundamentalism of some radical feminists, which has been the orthodoxy for over 40 years.

The Lesbian Left

Most of the first gay women who joined GLF were educated Marxist Socialists. The younger lesbians who entered later were mainly working class and identified with Radical Feminism. Nevertheless, the two groups would put their differences aside to work for women's issues. Although women members were in the minority, they held their own protests and demonstrations. The socialist women were among the brightest thinkers and tacticians, with interests encompassing Counter-Psychiatry, Media Workshop and the Manifesto group. Without their commitment and their compassion for the position of gay men, there would have been no dialectic and GLF would have been nothing but a small left wing group with Maoist notions. The fact that lesbians were in GLF to begin with was because of the euphoria and shared ideal of coming out, and their perception that Women's Liberation was for mothers and wives, with little sympathy or interest in gay women. Once the joy of coming together dissipated, they faced the same mysogynistic mind numbing humbug of male superiority and callousness that had distorted their lives from birth.

In my view many men rejected the women's complaints about men's chauvinist behaviour, misogyny and sexism; they refused to explore their gender roles and ideals of masculinity. They would not recognize that they were oppressing women with the same traditional values which oppressed and impacted on themselves. Amongst these men were the 'straight-gays' obsessed with discussing cottageing – a subject of no interest to the women, whose feelings were consistently ignored in constant attempts to initiate debates on the issue. Another group of conventional men, criticized for their misogyny, were the Maoists, who in denial and a swerve away from self-criticism started planning an all-male GLF, exploiting the women's divided ideologies as a way of getting rid of them. Fortunately the women had others to turn to. Invited to a Women's Liberation conference, they demonstrated their sisterhood by throwing out the Maoist men on its platform, changed the conference agenda to discuss women's sexuality, and returned to GLF as lesbian feminists. The men remained disinterested and unimpressed. The radical feminists formed a commune, instigated the split from gay men, and established Women's Gay Liberation. They too joined Women's Liberation, consolidated their graduated separatism and later cultivated a fundamentally separatist position. Eventually both groups of lesbians succeeded in having 'a woman's right to define her own sexuality' adopted as one of the demands of the women's movement.

Radical Queenery

One group of men with an interest in the counterculture were radicalized by direct action, and they came mainly from a non political background. They saw radical drag – men in frocks – not wearing falsies or imitating women, as more effective than badge wearing. Centred on the Street Theatre group and later described as the Monty Pythons of the movement, they helped turn Gay Liberation from an obscure left wing party into a national controversy. Radical queens were the first to demonstrate the issue of gender roles to the movement by challenging the men to take part in their gender-bending experiment. They experienced the same male chauvinism and sexism as the women, and supported trans people seeking shelter under the GLF umbrella. Like the radical feminists the radical queens were mainly working class, and for the same reasons formed their own communes, focal points opposing the other male groupings. I believe the queens' instinctive intelligence and freedom from ideology allowed them to discover tactics that had the makings of a gay revolutionary practice. Despite being perceived by the left as living in a gay utopia and despite having their politics denounced as no more than life-style choices, they were active within the general community around them. I suggest that the instinctive basis of their actions aligned them with the most advanced revolutionary thinking of those revolutionary times.

This history records the struggles of lesbians and gay men to make sense of and implement the ideas generated by a vision of gay liberation – the spirit that first arose in California at the end of the War in the Pacific when lesbians and gays were demobbed.

It challenged the redneck and diversified into race, gender and sexuality. It moved to San Francisco, then eastward through *The Stonewall* riots and New York GLF. It arrived in Britain with the agitation of the two Marxist sociology students who founded the movement in London.

Many older gay men have complained about how everything was wonderful in the gay world before GLF destroyed it all. It is, I believe, a mistaken idea based on the fact that in the main, as criminals, we looked out for each other. Indeed GLF can be seen as attempting to replace those intimations of community with something more tangible, progressive and enriching. From my experience it was the resistance of the ghetto to the sexual revolution that turned the ghetto into its opposite; from a united avant-garde to divided, exploited, camp followers.

Coming Out, and the resulting radicalization generated by direct action affected all who joined the Front. Some saw it as a project, some put their hearts into the struggle and it became their life. All who engaged found it turned their lives around. It began with a great sense of love and respect – solidarity between all members, and that vital energy sustained a hearts and minds campaign which succeeded in permanently transforming the face of this country. It was positive anarchy and it benefited everyone.

All history is personal; this is my memoir of events that I shared with the lesbians, gay men and trans people who joined in Gay Liberation. Sexism, heterophobia and misogyny remain, most painfully among the children of the ignorant and bigoted. The difference between now and then is that today we have words to explain the prejudice faced by lesbians, gays and trans people. The measure of gay and lesbian pride remains as it always was, achieved through undertaking activities that benefit the community as a whole, while remaining true to its socialist origins. Thanks to Gay Liberation and Women's Liberation – without which there would be no Gay Liberation – there exists today an out community of proud individuals, unfortunately divided by class and gender at a time when the right is increasing, unemployment rising and wages falling. A classic situation filled with a danger few LGBTQ people would fail to recognize.

Chapter 1

Coming Out

Revolutions should educate as well as entertain.
Abbie Hoffman – The Yippies.

On the 14 October 1970, Bob Mellors and Aubrey Walter, both in their early twenties, founded the Gay Liberation Front in a classroom on the upper floors of the Old Building at the London School of Economics (LSE), where Bob Mellors was a sociology student.

Three years had passed since legislation ended our criminal status. The more liberal sixties had enabled us to push the vicious law to the back of our minds; made it a badge of honour even as we got on with our lives, but the change of law had not brought acceptance, and the tolerance bestowed remained conditional on staying hidden and conforming to the perversity society continued to impose on us. In short, nothing had changed.

On the 8 October in a run-up to the inaugural meeting, Mellors and Walter organized a group of students at the LSE and held a demonstration against the University of London Union, (ULU) and the offices of the student newspaper *The Sennet* in the name of Women's Liberation and Gay Liberation.

> This was in response to an article which contained the myth that women attended college just for the purpose of fucking as many men as possible. There were also a number of slurs on gay people, referring to them as queers, and saying that first-year College of Education students became either 'missionaries, misogynists or queers.' The author of one of the articles claimed, that 'a friend was thinking of turning queer in desperation,' thus adding to the guilt feelings that society imposes on gay people.[1]

This group of gay freedom fighters marched to ULU with cans of gold and black spray-paint and began to decorate the inside of the building with the symbol for Venus signifying female, with a clenched fist painted inside the circle, and the symbol for Mars representing male, with a butterfly and clenched fist drawn within its circle. Another sign was of a prick crossed out to signify the end of prick power. Graffiti flowed over the walls on all six floors – 'Women's Lib & Gay Lib Unite and Fight Sexism' – 'Smash Prick Power', and, 'Ho-Ho-Ho Homosexual – The Ruling Class is Ineffectual'. A spokesman for the group said:

> We warn all those papers including *IT, OZ,* and *Friends,* and all student papers that sell on a basis of sex, tits and ass, that in future the struggle against sexism will be at a higher level and no-one will be immune from attack. We are not queer, but people who groove on loving someone of the same sex.[2]

Among these campus activists were Aubrey Walter's lover David Fernbach, and their friends who were also students at the LSE, Bill Halstead and Richard Dipple, a member of the Albany Trust. The one woman among them, Bev Jackson, later ran for LSE college office with the slogan, 'Bev the Lez for Prez'. All were present six days later along with a dozen other men at the first meeting of GLF. The following week more women turned up as well as men, and a leafleting campaign was organized. I joined a week later.

Bob Mellors and Aubrey Walter first met at the 'Revolutionary Peoples' Constitutional Conference' in Philadelphia in September. Both travelled to the USA that summer intrigued by the odd rumours and press reports from there about a new gay movement. Mellors became involved with New York GLF, while Walter visited a number of cities including San Francisco. The conference at which they met was called for and sponsored by the Black Panther Party. That August, Huey Newton, joint founder and Supreme Commander of the Black Panthers, made a remarkable and brave statement, given the confusion of fears and stereotypes existing between black men, gays, and women, in which he welcomed the women's and gay movements into the revolutionary ranks. Huey Newton's soul-searching embrace of revolutionary solidarity aroused considerable hostility and agitation among the Black Panthers, in fact his statement began the break with the violent, misogynist, needless to say, anti-gay Eldridge Cleaver, the Black Panther Minister for Information, that led to accusations, counter-charges and attempts to purge each other the following year.

Seeking to come to terms with the position of women and gays, Huey Newton addressed the Black Panthers:

> Whatever your personal opinions and your insecurities about homosexuality and the various liberation movements among homosexuals and women (and I speak of the homosexuals and women as oppressed groups) we should try to unite with them in a revolutionary fashion. I say 'whatever your insecurities are' because as we very well know sometimes our first instinct is to want to hit a homosexual in the mouth because we're afraid we might be homosexual; and we want to hit the woman or shut her up because we're afraid that she might castrate us, or take the nuts that we might not have to start with. Referring again to homosexuality ... there's nothing to say that a homosexual cannot be a revolutionary. And maybe I'm now injecting some of my prejudices by saying that 'even a homosexual can be revolutionary.' Quite on the contrary, maybe a homosexual could be the most revolutionary.[3]

Earlier in the year the London underground newspaper *IT (International Times)* announced the passing away of the old homosexual stereotype and the birth of a guilt free homoerotic masculinity in harmony with the new Age of Aquarius:

> So long Fag Hags. Sexual liberation means the merging of several sexual life-styles, and homosexuality will soon be a word without any particular significance. Instead of being the ultimate social scare word, it will simply mean the capacity to love somebody of your own sex. There are no homosexuals in the Underground, but there are a lot of guys who suck cock. It's not so much a question of who you make love to but how. It's time to be proud of making it with other guys, time to get out of the guilt ridden ghettos of the gay world. Until we do it in the road and get our fucks just like everybody else, we are all closet queens. Kiss goodbye to all those old classifications and fetishes. So long Bette, and Judy, and Marilyn, and Barbra. Girls are girls not mother symbols. So long Boys in the Band, you're stranded in the sixties. So long dinge queens, toe queens, leather queens, size queens, cottage queens, hair faeries, fag hags and chubby chasers. There is no need any longer to shriek and camp about like hysterical birds of prey, no need for that bitchy defiance. You can relax. The bum trip is over. Join the GLF. Carry a lavender banner, let it all hang out. Take it like a man. Suck and fuck for peace. The world in the seventies will be one vast erogenous zone with that most natural and persistent of sexual variations, homosexuality, an integral and vital part of the kaleidoscopic world of human sexuality.[4]

Jim Anderson was a gay journalist and editor of the underground magazine *Oz*. Here he shows off a hippy lawyer's rose-tinted idealism for what was happening in America, while satirising the price paid by an earlier generation of gay men, whose behaviour had been affected and distorted by the status quo they achieved with straight society in the fifties and sixties.

There were letters too from readers already living the alternative lifestyle.

> To All 'Gay Heads' Everywhere. We are a minority within a minority subculture and it's time for us to get an alternative thing to the straight gay scene – Earls Court is a far cry from Phun City. [Phun City was the first truly free Music Festival, with free food and free drugs, held that summer in Worthing, of all places.] We have read all the articles about Gayness and how there are no homosexuals in the Underground, well this means fuck all to us as we still have to use the straight gay scene for our basic needs.
>
> We don't accept the straight gay scene because it's just a fool copy of the straight system. It's a drag having to categorize but for a while it is necessary so that we can get together as brothers and sisters and work out an alternative. If you are a bi/gay head please write to me and send your ideas, scenes, and if the response is big enough then we can work toward something real. Peace and Love, Dave.[5]

Two friends of mine out shopping on Oxford Street were handed one of those leaflets produced at the second meeting and suggested to my boyfriend Roger Rousell that we go along and see what it was all about. On the following Wednesday night we found our way down to the basement of the LSE and entered a classroom filling up with lesbians and the kind of gay men I'd never seen before. By their clothes I could see they didn't go to any gay bar or club that I knew. Some of the men were our age, late twenties to early thirties, but most were ten years younger; students mainly, poorly dressed beauties with long hair, and some with beards. Others were hippies wearing afghan coats, beads, bracelets and even longer hair. Among the twenty or so gay women were a few teenagers, others in their early-twenties, but the majority were in their thirties, most with shorter hair styles and smarter trousers. There must have been fifty of us altogether, and the great thing was that everyone was warm and open, there was none of that uptight judgemental feeling you found in bars and clubs. Facing us behind a desk was Mellors and Walter, and as the evening progressed it was clear that everyone was extremely intelligent, politically educated and earnest. Politics for me was no more than Conservative, Liberal and Labour. My parents voted Conservative and I'd followed suit, but what I heard that night was something new and entirely different. What most impressed me was being asked to think about how our sexuality had affected our behaviour in the way we conducted ourselves at work. It touched the nub of my facade. That appeal and the general view that we were a minority group alongside women, children and black people, discriminated against by a white heterosexual world full of prejudice drew me in. That it was not us that was sick, but society with its hatreds and fears, opened my eyes to an entirely new way of thinking. I quickly learned Marx's rule that the categories of labour or class, bourgeoisie and proletariat, or wage labour, has equivalence with gender in a divided society (and race in Imperialist cultures), so bourgeois equals, Male, Heterosexual or White and Proletarian equals Female, Child, Homosexual or Black. We were encouraged to buy the GLF badge (badges were the cool fashion accessory of the time) and urged to 'Come Out' and show pride in being gay by wearing one. Someone said that despite the fact that there must be one gay person in every family, heterosexuals feared lesbians and gays because our invisibility had led them to believe that they didn't know any. By coming out, by being visible in the family and community, a lot of that fear and prejudice would be allayed. The heterosexual would see we were as human as everybody else, and that we counted and had to be reckoned with. I was fascinated, and ready to learn more. My friends, however, didn't want to know, and as it turned out, didn't want to know me anymore either. Roger and I, though still living together, grew apart as I engaged with these new ideas and became involved in rounds of evening meetings. Within a few months we separated.

Coming out is an experience unique to gay men and women. Coming out made Gay Liberation the only political movement to demand a process that only artists are generally caught up in, that of self-revelation. Perhaps that is why some claim it is liberating in and of itself. It is a surmounting of all the fears and inhibitions a dominating society had implanted in us, and it can truly be said to be an apocalyptic act and a major turning point in the discovery of ourselves as people. Those who cannot Come Out because of the life choices and benefits they are organised around are the closet queens, who mirroring the heterophobes are revolted by any sign of femininity in men, variants of those who cannot accept their gay sexuality, loathe themselves and their desires along with the heterosexual closet queens who repress their femininity and become prey to homosexual dreams and fantasies; men who are insecure about their sexuality and fear they might be gay. In drag or out of drag, as a queen I've never had any problems with 'straight men' – heterosexuals who are comfortable and confident in their sexuality. Which is not to say that straight men and out gays are not misogynist, but if the ultimate aim of the revolutionary struggle of gay men and women is the liberation of the homoerotic desire in every human being, then we must discover where heterophobia resides.

The next week I went to the general meeting by myself feeling free to talk to whoever looked friendly, and that was nearly everyone. After the meeting when people were milling around talking about the evening's debates I was invited to the pub to carry on the discussion. The pub was the place where new people in the intimacy of small groups could venture to ask questions, or even suggest things they were too intimidated to speak about at the general meeting. And after closing time if you were lucky, came an invitation to go back to someone's place for more discussions on how the world was opening out in new and unexpected ways, now that our opinions of ourselves and our position was changing.

At one of those early General Meetings a list of things we were aiming for were read out and we then had to vote on them. These had been drawn up by David Fernbach, Aubrey Walter's lover. Called 'The Demands', they were then made into a leaflet which read:

THE GAY LIBERATION FRONT DEMANDS . . .

- that all discrimination against gay people, male and female, by the law, by employers, and by society at large, should end
- that all people who feel attracted to a member of their own sex be taught that such feelings are perfectly normal
- that sex education in schools stop being exclusively heterosexual
- that psychiatrists stop treating homosexuality as though it were a problem or a sickness, thereby giving gay people senseless guilt complexes
- that gay people be as legally free to contact other gay people through newspaper ads, on the streets and by any other means they may want, as are heterosexuals, and that police harassment should cease right now
- that employers should no longer be allowed to discriminate against anyone on account of their sexual preferences
- that the age of consent for gay males be reduced to the same as for straights
- that gay people be free to hold hands and kiss in public, as are heterosexuals

GAY IS GOOD!
ALL POWER TO OPPRESSED PEOPLE!
COME OUT – JOIN GAY LIBERATION FRONT!

With this leaflet we went to Earls Court the following weekend and handed them to the guys outside the *Coleherne* and *The Boltons*. We met with a mixture of polite interest, outright hostility, and physical violence in one case, but the results were a definite increase in gay men coming to the next Wednesday's meeting. A couple of months later another version of the Demands was made up by John Chesterman.

We believe
That apathy and fear are the
Barriers that imprison people
From an incalculable landscape
Of self awareness
That they are the elements of
Truth
That every person has the right
To develop and extend their
Character and explore their
Sexuality through relationships
With any other human being,
Without moral, social or political
Pressure.
That no relationship formed
By such pressure, or not freely
Entered into, can be valid,
Creative or rewarding.
To you, the others, we say
We are not against you, but
The prejudice that warps your
Life, and ours
It is not love that distorts,
But hate.
On your behalf, and ours,
We demand:
The same right to public
Expressions of love and
Affection as society grants

To expressions of hate and scorn.
The right to believe, without
Harm to others, in public and
Private, in any way we choose,
In any manner or style, with
Any words and gestures, to wear
Whatever clothes we like or to
Go naked, to draw or write or
Read or publish any material or
Information we wish, at any
Time and in any place.
An end to the sexual propaganda
That disturbs the innocence of
Children, conditions their image
Of human relationships and implants
Guilt and nurturers shame for any
Sexual feelings outside an
Artificial polarity.
An end to the centuries of
Oppression and prejudice that have
Driven homosexuals from their
Homes, families and employment, have
forced them to cynicism,
Subterfuge and self-hatred and
have led them, so often, to
Imprisonment or to death.
In the name of the tens of
Thousands who wore the badge of
Homosexuality in the gas chambers
And concentration camps, who
Have no children to remember, and
Whom your histories forget.
We DEMAND honour, identity and
Liberation.

Back in April 1969 the Obscene Publications Squad, led by Det. Inspector Frederick Luff, raided the offices of the Underground newspaper *IT*, because the newspaper had started a personal column headed 'Males' to help gay men get in touch with each other. In the fifties and sixties the personal columns of *Films and Filming*, and *Dance and Dancers* had been the covert means of finding 'pen-pals', but the passing of the Sexual Offences Act in 1967, which for the first time legalized homosexual acts in England and Wales, but not in Scotland or Northern Ireland, or in the Merchant Navy or Armed Forces, and only between two men in private and over the age of 21, gave rise to the idea that subterfuge was no longer necessary. *IT* put a warning on their bold new column that homosexual practices were still illegal for under 21's and stated their right to refuse any advert thought to be from male prostitutes.

IT had a readership of 250,000, and using an obscenity charge against the publisher of a large circulation newspaper was becoming problematic for the Director of Public Prosecutions as the more liberal verdicts returned in the 1960s proved. Further debate in the press just three years after all the publicity about homosexuality leading up to the 1967 Sexual Offences Act was the last thing the authorities needed in their attempts to paint the picture of a free, tolerant, and liberal country. On the other hand, censorship of sexuality on the grounds of indecency and immorality would undermine support for gays; pontificating moral guardians and upholders of respectability would nicely obscure the insidious government policy of repressing minorities.

The choice of the charge eventually settled on showed how desperate the authorities were to inhibit our freedom – an obscure common law offence: conspiring to corrupt public morals, and conspiring to corrupt public decency. Totalitarian in its repression: there is no necessity under this law to prove the accused did anything. The only thing that needs to be proven is that all together they *thought* about something. Graham Keen,

Dave Hall and Peter Stanshill, as former editors and company directors of *IT*, were charged with conspiring to outrage public decency by publishing advertisements containing lewd, disgusting and offensive matter.

In a previous trial in 1960 for the same offence, the publisher of *The Ladies Directory*, Frederick Shaw, had been sentenced to two years imprisonment. By referring to that case, the prosecution of *IT* succeeded in completing a trope by linking prostitution to homosexuality, and from homosexual to pervert, degenerate, and dirty. Just how perverted, degenerate and dirty can be seen from the police and prosecution allegations suggesting that 'schoolchildren were being encouraged into sexual experimentation' – 'temptations were being held out.' The defendants were 'encouraging the promotion of homosexuality.' Seeing the advertisements, 'homosexuals who had repudiated their former life could be tempted back into wickedness', or 'that happily married men could be led into homosexuality by reading the columns.' The prosecutors seemed to believe that man's sexual instinct is weak, unstable and transient, when as we know it is the very core of who we are as people. All that was missing from this invective was the predatory homosexual himself, but as the men in the dock wrote about rock music, drug culture and revolutionary politics, they would do just as well.

At the committal hearing at the Magistrates Court, the men who had been rounded up as witnesses for the prosecution were asked about the replies they had received to their advertisements. Their answer was to tell the Court that they hadn't received any replies because the police had confiscated the letters. 'But a happy outcome was reported for two of the witnesses, who having met in the lobby of the Court while waiting to give evidence have been together ever since.'[6]

The case did not come to trial at the Old Bailey until 2 November, 1970, some three weeks after GLF was formed. The delay between the first raid on *IT* and the trial was because

Inspector Luff could not immediately find enough evidence, and so subjected the newspaper to a number of raids. Tarsus Sutton was one of the advertisers subpoenaed to appear for the prosecution. Asked by Judge Edward Sutcliffe what the phrase, 'well-hung' meant in his ad, Sutton serenely replied, 'It means I have no hang-ups M'lud.' *IT* editor Peter Stanshill considered the newspaper a forum for a number of minority groups, and that it was addressed to youth oriented people primarily under the age of 30. 'Our intention was to provide a forum in good faith for a minority of individuals who had been continually discriminated against, harassed and victimized. As a newspaper with some sort of social conscience we thought we could make a positive and practical contribution to the welfare of homosexuals.'[7]

The Judge in summing up 'likened *IT*'s position to someone who commits euthanasia: the motive was good, but the law was still being broken.'[8] This sarcastic comment was followed by a guilty verdict and fines of £1,500 plus £500 costs. On that note the farce concluded. The National Council for Civil Liberties (NCCL) described the punishment as savage.[9] When the case was appealed in the House of Lords the following year, the Law Lords upheld the verdict. The judgement implied that while it is not illegal to enjoy homosexual acts, it is illegal to bring about such acts.

Each week brought more people to the General Meeting, and by the last Wednesday in November we all agreed it was time to make a public demonstration. The perfect target would have been the Old Bailey trial of *IT*, but that opportunity came too early on, and indicates that members influenced by the counterculture had not yet found a voice. By now, however, I had gained enough confidence to have an opinion of my own, and disagreed with Andy Elsmore's proposal that we should picket the American Embassy to protest their visa restriction, banning homosexuals from entry into the States, thinking that was a matter for American gays to protest. I was sitting near Elsmore, and looking at him, I felt that I recognized a straight left proposal using us as tools for a revival of the anti-American, anti-Vietnam War protests that I imagined he would have been part of. He was big and loud in condemning America, I thought, making sure we all recognized that he was a real butch left-wing revolutionary. I voted instead for the counter proposal by Eric Thompson, lover of Anthony Gray, that we demonstrate at Highbury Fields, where Louis Eakes, Chair of the Young Liberals, was arrested for cottaging. I didn't know anything about Eakes, but I instinctively thought he was probably gay, though of course he'd denied it to the police. Similar thoughts crossed everyone's mind I'm sure, for we all knew the police used 'pretty policemen' as bait, as agents provocateurs in public lavatories throughout the country; the easiest way for them to keep us in-line, and increase arrest rates. So this was a real issue for gay men. The vote was overwhelmingly in favour of protesting Eakes arrest, and to do so on the coming Friday, 27 November, at the spot where the arrest had taken place.

Nearly everyone who was at the meeting turned up on the Friday night at Highbury and Islington Tube. It was so heartening to see my new sisters and brothers outside the station, under the streetlights, next to the pub – *The Cock Inn* – milling around, animated by seeing so many others turning up, everyone bright with excitement. Soon we moved off to find the cottage shouting 'Give us a G.' – 'G.' we shouted. 'Give us an A.' – 'A.' we answered. 'Give us a Y.' – 'Y', we cried. 'What does that spell?' 'Gay', we yelled. 'And what is Gay?' 'Good', we roared. We surrounded the cottage chanting, Gay is Good,' and then moved onto the fields shouting the slogans again and again. We walked along, hand in hand. Someone gave us balloons. This was fun. 'Where's the pretty policeman?' I demanded. 'Come out, come out wherever you are.'

We stopped where several paths cross, candles were lit and the GLF Demands read out for the benefit of the few newspaper reporters and the curious who had followed our progress. One of the reporters was overheard referring to us as poofs. He was quickly surrounded, roundly condemned and an apology demanded. To illustrate the protest and one of the Demands, we started forming couples and kissing each other which broke down into titters as we moved around trying to make sure we hadn't left anyone out. Then we all wandered off into the bushes which came alive with bursts of flame and the glowing tips of lit cigarettes used to attract attention and signal sexual interest with a beckoning – come over here – just as the police said Eakes had done when they saw him leave the cottage and go into the bushes.

Altogether I think there were about 80 of us who took part, though *Come Together,* the GLF newspaper states 150, but however many of us there were, by the time we entered *The Cock Inn* we had all changed. From the dark of the Fields to the light of the pub, we saw each other anew. We had shared our beliefs and convictions in public and acted them out in the world. We had made the first ever openly public demonstration in this country by homosexuals. Call it radicalization if you like, but to me it felt more like arriving at the Ball. Whatever barriers there were between us were let down that night. An emotional connection of solidarity and respect, for ourselves and each other was forged. It remains palpable to this day, and gave me at the time the confidence to talk to the men and woman I had been too shy to approach earlier.

One of the first things I did after joining the movement was to phone John Chesterman to tell him the exciting news, but he was in Formentera and didn't come back until late November. I first met John when I was 16 and he was 19 in the cottage near the Labour Exchange in York. Three months later, just before Christmas, we saw each other again in the Glass department of Rowntrees' store. He was with his family but managed to give them the slip long enough for us to make a date. We were together for four years. When he graduated as an architect from Leeds he found a job in Huddersfield; I followed and we lived there together for two years before we broke up and I moved to London.

My mother had discovered a love letter I had written to John and not sent, hidden in the pocket of a jacket hanging in my wardrobe. She found it after deciding to send the jacket to the cleaners, read it and gave it to my father. When I came home from work that day he confronted me in a fury, knocked me down and beat me up. Leaving home when the time came was not a problem.

In the summer of 1957 I played Pilate's son in the York Mystery Plays. One afternoon I caught John in bed in one of the backstage caravans with the handsome bassoonist we befriended from the LSO. I created such a scene, more so because I secretly fancied the man myself, an artist with a gym trained body like a Quaintance cowboy. John was amused at the drama, but gently wised me up to the fact that if we were going to stay together as a couple, then we had to be honest about our desires.

On 4 September the Wolfenden Report was published. We were both very excited at the prospect, imagining all the possibilities that could open up. We were now a well-known affair on York's gay scene, which met in the back bar of *The Punchbowl* in Stonegate. We weren't flaunting what we were, but we weren't hiding it either in that friendly smoke filled den of the criminalized, but being the young ones we wanted more than a change in the law, we wanted equality in the age of consent as well. On the day of publication we arranged to meet in the gardens behind the Minster at lunchtime, both of us having purchased a number of different newspapers from different newsagents so as not to draw attention to ourselves and our interest. The weather was beautiful; we dropped our bikes, sat on the lawn behind the Chapter House and started to skim through the reports and editorials, dividing the papers up into for and against. Soon the grass around us was covered in newsprint. Something distracted my attention and when I looked up, there were two older apprentices from work, cycling along the perimeter path, and I could see they had taken it all in. Sure enough by the time I returned to work the news was all over the factory.

The foreman who was a well known local jock, walker, runner, footballer and cricketer, did nothing about the hoots, whistles and jeers – neither did the shop steward, and within a week I was taken off the milling machine turning out precision parts down to five thousandth of an inch on piece rate – like really fast to make up a miserable apprenticeship wage – and put on a boring knurling machine alongside the factory dim-wit when there wasn't enough work for one. But the most hurtful abuse came from another apprentice I knew to be gay, whose derision was broadcast around *The Punchbowl,* and even continued years later in the *York Arms.* I could see I'd never be taught any more trade secrets, so I broke off my apprenticeship and got a clerical job with British Rail.

Chesterman was born in India, spawn of Empire, and at eight was shipped over here to Prep and Public School. His father was a Colonel in the Indian Army. His mother, from a medical family, was Australian, which is where I'm sure his warmth, wit and love of fun came from. His father served on the North West Frontier and made a name for himself in the army by inventing a way of accurately killing the tribesmen of the area. Beyond the territory he was defending he erected billboards at strategic points, on which were painted each location's exact range from his gun emplacements. The tribesman not understanding the purpose of the billboards, or the signage, ignored them; when they advanced they were efficiently mowed down.

After school Chesterman went to Bristol to do his foundation course in Architecture, existing for at least one term on nothing more than milk and cornflakes, before meeting a handsome Commodore in the Royal Navy who at weekends swept him up into the comfort of *The Dorchester*, and the best food that the restaurants of Soho could yield.

I had left school at fifteen and was forced into an engineering apprenticeship instead of going to Art School. Art and acting were the only things I was any good at, and also the two subjects that Chesterman and I always competed over. In every other way he was my tutor who taught me that curiosity and not being afraid to confess ignorance was the threshold to learning. He discovered that he delighted in passing on his knowledge, it was a role that became him completely, and one in which he discovered himself.

Some six months after we moved to Huddersfield the draft board finally caught up with John. No longer a student, he was liable to serve his two years National Service. To his pacifism he added the frustration of all those years of living on next to nothing as a student, and now with a salary and money to spend, he was even more determined to resist two further years of poverty. He went off to the medical examination board in Leeds ready to declare himself a homosexual. The trouble was, when he reached the induction centre he didn't know who to tell, so he had to go around declaring his homosexuality to every man in a white coat until finally one sympathetic doctor pointed him in the direction of the psychiatrist. He was declared unfit and sentenced to see a psychiatrist once a month for two years.

The success of the demonstration at Highgate Fields gave me a great feeling of confidence, as it did to everyone who took part. I'd talked in the pub afterwards to Bob Mellors, Aubrey Walter, David Fernbach, Mary McIntosh, and Elizabeth Wilson, and knowing that they were members, I thought I'd visit the Media Group, media being something I knew nothing about, except that they published *Come Together*. I imagine that my turning up at Walter and Fernbach's mansion flat in West Hampstead must have been a surprise to the others present, me, the manager of an employment agency in the City, of all things. I was taken into their library where the weekly meeting met. Pre-eminent on their bookshelves was a collection of green Moroccan leather bound volumes stamped in gold leaf, the complete set of Marx's *Das Kapital*. On the floor between us were piles of photographs, written articles, drawings, Letraset, and to one side a table with pots of paste, layout boards and a typewriter. I'd never been anywhere like this before. Everyone there was a Marxist. I was fascinated by the way they discussed and criticized the articles submitted for publication, and drawn in too, because I found that I could follow some of their arguments. But as for making a contribution I could see that the only thing for me to do would be helping with cutting and pasting, and there was already enough people doing that. And while the women were friendly, the men were rather hesitant and suspicious. Media Workshop I found was not for me.

The Demands had been a rallying call to the ghetto, which answered with an increase in attendance at the weekly meetings, giving everyone a real sense of purpose, and proving there was a large body of people out there ready to join the struggle. But the reassuring response and enthusiasm also made the more politicized members anxious about the goals they had envisioned, and they realized that a clearer definition of aims was needed if a sense of purpose was to be harnessed to positive effect. It is to David Fernbach's awareness and foresight that we owe the GLF Principles, which he presented to the General Meeting in early December, and which was immediately and overwhelmingly accepted, except for paragraph V.

> I. GLF's first priority is to defend the immediate interests of gay people against discrimination and all forms of social oppression.
>
> II. However, the roots of the oppressions that gay people suffer run deep in our society, in particular to the structure of the family, patterns of socialisation, and the Judaeo-Christian

culture. Legal reform and education against prejudice, though possible and necessary, cannot be a permanent solution. While existing social structures remain, social prejudice and overt repression can always re-emerge.
III. GLF therefore sees itself as part of the wider movement aiming to abolish all forms of social oppression. It will work to ally itself with other oppressed groups, while preserving its organisational independence.
IV. In particular, we see these groups as including:

(a) the women's liberation movement. The roots of women's oppression are in many ways close to our own (see II above).
(b) black people and other national minorities. The racism that these peoples are affected by is a similar structure of prejudice to our own, but on the basis of racial instead of sexual difference. They are socially and economically the most oppressed group in society.
(c) the working class, i.e. all productive manual and mental workers.

Their labour is what the whole of society lives off, but their skills are misused by a profit-oriented economy, and their right to organise and defend their interest is under increasing attack.

(d) young people who are rejecting the bourgeois family and the roles and lifestyles offered them by this society, and attempting to create a non-exploitative counterculture.
(e) peoples oppressed by imperialism, who lack the national political and economic independence which is a precondition for all other social change.

V*

VI We don't believe that any existing revolutionary theory has all the answers to the problems facing us. GLF will therefore

> study and discuss all relevant critical theories of society and the individual being, to measure them against the test of our own and historical experience.

Walter and Fernbach also made some organizational suggestions: (i) fortnightly general meetings: (ii) Groups based on a particular kind of work. For example: community work – anti-psychiatry – anti-repression and legal defence – media workshop – street theatre – office and organization – education group. (iii) Groups based on locality or occupation. Every GLF member should belong to at least one of the groups (locality, occupation, or task group). Many on these function groups came into being soon afterwards.

*Paragraph V was rejected by the General Meeting; it stated:

> Gay people cannot be indifferent to the worldwide struggle against capitalism and imperialism. This whole system is in an ever more acute state of crisis and all signs are that the capitalist ruling class will resort to any means necessary to preserve their power, including wholesale repression against all 'deviant' minorities. In Britain the failure of capitalism to serve the peoples' needs (housing, education, social services, etc.) has already led to black people being used as a scapegoat, with racist demagogues such as [Enoch] Powell playing on reactionary popular prejudices, and both Tory and Labour governments willingly conceding to racist demands (immigration laws etc). Now the ruling class is moving to legal repression against working class militants with the Industrial Relations Bill. Every historic example shows that repression of the working class, racism and attacks on gay people go together. They are all components of authoritarian capitalism or fascism (e.g.Nazi Germany, Spain, Brazil, Greece etc.) In Britain, gay people may well be the next victims of the policy of 'law and order'.

This paragraph with its left-wing views on capitalism, class oppression and dogmatic shibboleths did not fit happily with the oppression of gays that people had joined GLF to struggle against. It was enough that the link with women, black people and other national minorities was accepted, which aligned GLF with other revolutionary movements. As David Fernbach said, 'We didn't dig our heels in over the part of the principles that was voted down. It wasn't felt by people to be clearly enough connected to gay issues.'[10]

Aubrey Walter comments to the effect that although GLF now defined itself as 'part of the wider movement aiming to abolish all forms of social oppression,'[11] the Principles didn't explain where that oppression was located in the structure of society. The Principles indicate 'the structure of the family' but a theory of gender didn't yet exist which left us, as Walter has stated, with 'prejudice' as our only explanation for heterophobia. GLF had not yet made a critique of society where male supremacy and heterosexuality are bound together as in heterosexualism. These ideas were explored over the next year, resulting in the publication in October 1971 of the GLF *Manifesto.*

One of the things that GLF hoped to accomplish was the provision of an alternative social scene to that provided by the stone faced, tight-fisted pub, club, and brewery owners, behind which mask they greedily count their ever-increasing profit, acquired through a policy of overcharging their captive clientele. Having no money of our own and needing funds for projects, the best thing we could think of was to hire town halls for dances. This in itself was almost revolutionary at the time, to publicly announce and hold an openly gay dance in a civic building had never been done before. The dance scene in the ghetto was limited and the clubs were tiny. Before 1967, clubs where you could dance were very rare, illicit, and naturally didn't last very long. The only ones that lasted were coffee bars, like *The Calabash* which allowed linedancing, or *The Gigolo* early in the evening when there was room, but only as long as you didn't touch. GLF, by hiring town halls and having live music from Rock 'n' Roll bands, generally two, each doing a one hour set, together with a Disc Jockey, was offering something entirely new for the gay scene.

The first Gay Dance to be openly advertised was held at Kensington Town Hall on 22 December 1970. The ticket price was a democratic six shillings which translates to 30p. Called the GLF Peoples' Dance, it saw 750 lesbians and gays dancing together, the largest number of us ever to openly assemble in those days. Rumour had it that 500 people were turned away.

Mary McIntosh and Tony Halliday had volunteered as stewards for the dance, and rather nervously hung around the hall not knowing what to expect. In the event the only problem was people complaining that the band was super-straight and sexist, so it was the band that was hassled, except that Paul Theobald, who helped with the organising, copped off with one of the musicians, so they weren't all that straight. Both Elizabeth Wilson and Tony Halliday have told me with much amusement, that when the band started playing, no one would get up and dance, everyone just stood around waiting to see what would happen when someone did. Eventually Tony Halliday asked Elizabeth Wilson for a dance and the two of them walked out to take the floor, very aware of the irony of the situation.

For others the evening did not start off at all well. Angie Weir and her friends decided to call in at a pub on their way to the ball.

> *Angie Weir*: In those days it was unusual for a group of women in short hair and trousers to be together in any numbers: and men would scream at you and pick fights with you. That went on all the time – constantly – you went out with women who were harassed. I went to the Ball with my Women's Liberation Group which was centred around Grosvenor Avenue at the time, and we went to a pub in Church Street beforehand to have a drink, and this used to happen very regularly – we

> were just sitting there having a drink and all these blokes got very angsty and they ended up pouring beer all over us, and we were kicked and the police were called and we were ejected from the pub, and that's how it started. You were attacked with impunity by men, by police; you could be arrested and tried and put in prison. It's hard to imagine today that it would cause such a furore.[12]

> Once the night started, couples danced to the music of Hot Ice in the modern manner – not much physical contact, each 'partner' doing his own thing. Many wore dark suits, collar and tie. Others were more flamboyantly dressed – like the teenagers at any 'normal' dance. 'We want to fight against discrimination by coming into the open and saying, as it were: "look at me, I'm a homosexual and I'm no ogre!" There are homosexual policemen, homosexual MP's – even homosexual newspapermen.' Outside, hundreds of copies of the GLF duplicated journal *Come Together* and mauve GLF badges were sold. Inside the only discord was caused by the theft of the bar Christmas Box. The announcement was greeted with booing and followed by a collection.[13]

At Christmas the LSE closed for the holidays, so for that period the general meeting moved to the Institute for Research in Art & Technology, known as the New Arts Lab, in Robert Street where the Euston Tower now stands. There was a report about the success of the Christmas dance and what the money would be used for, followed by discussions on the need to provide more alternatives to the ghetto scene. It was Bette Bourne's first meeting accompanied by his lover Rex Lay who had inveigled him along by mentioning how much talent would be there. A bar queen near him was saying to the assembly, 'I don't see any difference between this meeting and the bars – everyone here's cruising, aren't they?'

> *Bette Bourne*: I shot out of my seat and said, 'If you think this is like a fucking cruising bar then you must be out of your box. Out of your mind! We're talking about our lives here; to each other; about our situation – in a public arena – we've never done this before. Since I was sixteen I've been going to gay bars. I've been to all the gay bars in the West End: we've never talked like this, ever! We've got a chance here; everyone wants to put their money on this horse – can't you see that you stupid fucking queen.' All this anger, it just came out. And afterwards this beautiful blonde called Aubrey told me he liked what I'd said, and would I like to join the steering committee. I'd no idea what he meant but I looked into his great blue eyes and said, 'I'd like that very much.' Next week I was on the committee.[14]

Later at the same meeting I heard an announcement calling for volunteers to form a street theatre group. As soon as the main meeting was over I joined. Then suddenly, who should I see but John Chesterman. He had finally got himself to Gay Lib and hadn't come alone, but brought his whole alternative family with him. I think the fact that GLF, in his eyes, had made it to the Arts Lab, a resource of the counterculture, meant he could take the movement seriously, and indeed he was grinning all over his face with excitement. He introduced me to Sue and Anne Winter, Tarsus Sutton, Geoff Marsh, Mitch Blunden and Angus Shields. We were joined by Paul Theobald and Trevor Wood, two of the beautiful hippies I'd seen every week since my first meeting, but never spoken to before. Chesterman was still a full time architect and also a member of the countercultural collective compiling *The Index of Possibilities: Power and Energy,* and had close connections with the underground newspaper *Friends* where Geoff Marsh was the typesetter. I was immediately welcomed into his circle, which was great for me because I hadn't really clicked with anyone else in the last couple of months, and as his enthusiasm was fired up, I knew I was in for some fun.

The first meeting of the Street Theatre Group was held the following Sunday at Derek Jarman's Bankside squat. I'd never heard of, or seen a street theatre performance before, but easy enough to figure out what it meant, until glancing through Jarman's bookshelves before the meeting, I was surprised to see a book entitled *Street Theatre In The Bauhaus*, and realized I might have let myself in for more than I'd thought. A group of about 15 people turned up, and apart from John Chesterman's family, who came without him, there was Roger Carr, Neon Edsel, Marshall Weekes an American, a teenage David, Marion Prince and Barbara Klecki. Sue Winter arrived with Howard Wakeling, a couple who seemed to know a great deal about street theatre and about 'The Media' and how to get media attention, and by being the loudest and most voluble they took control of the group. Sunday afternoon was agreed as the best time for all of us to meet, the only problem was that the use of Jarman's loft was just a one-off. For a couple of weekends we moved to different addresses until I decided to ask my boss if we could use the empty attic above his office in Fenchurch Street, to which he agreed.

Winter and Wakeling introduced us to a series of theatrical trust games. They would have us stand in a circle with one person in the middle with their eyes closed. The person in the middle would then fall, forwards or backwards or to the side, to be confidently caught before they hit the floor. Or splitting into two groups on opposite sides of the room and with eyes closed, we would crawl forward on hands and knees until an encounter occurred, and then explore the face and the body of the other to discover who they were. This turned out to be a very popular game. Then there was talking about one's worst fears and acting them out in front of the group. Week after week this went on with no end in sight until eventually I became critical.

Sue and Jane Winter were so obviously heterosexual – what

were they doing in Gay Lib. It was clear that neither of them were interested in getting it on with other women in the movement, either in the Woman's Group or generally. Apparently, Sue Winter had seduced Howard Wakeling away from Trevor Woods and was, I felt, a missionary lady. As for her sibling Anne, she was as single minded and implacable as a tank to any ideas but her own. She is recorded as saying about reporting back on our activities to the General Meeting, 'We used to make things up and lie outrageously about what Street Theatre had been up to,'[15] which goes to show how little she respected the members of the Front, and how much she underestimated our seriousness. I began to think that the Winter sisters were the kind of straights who were there to run the revolution for us because they thought we were far too dizzy to do it for ourselves. (There were quite a few men and women like that in the early days, which caused GLF to have a rule that no heterosexual could serve on the steering committee and everyone speaking for the first time at a general meeting had to declare their sexuality). I talked with the others in the group outside their circle of friends and found I was not alone. We ventured to suggest we'd like to do a gig. For some this was not love and peace, but squabbling and jockeying for position, so they dropped out.

The following week Winter and Wakeling came up with a plan. David, who worked for Bermans the Theatrical Costumiers, produced a collection of costumes he told us had been made for Fellini's *Satyricon*. They were in any case bizarre animal, bird and fish outfits complete with headdresses. With these we were going to parade around Trafalgar Square one evening. 'It was January,' I thought, 'it would be dark.' But with nothing better prepared and on the basis that we had to start somewhere, we all agreed.

On the day, we met in the late afternoon at Theobald and Woods' flat in King's Cross and changed into our costumes. Towards the end of the rush hour we walked to the underground in procession, and took the Piccadilly Line to Leicester Square, a journey without hassles, as most people in our carriage alighted at the next station, and the remainder being true Brits failed to notice us. We then progressed down St. Martins Lane and around an empty Trafalgar Square. Then for some unexplained reason we moved off along the Strand where Tarsus Sutton the 6'2" New Zealander, his long sinewy body encased in a bird costume and headdress made of orange and green chicken feathers, a large green beak, leggings and claw feet, broke ranks and started rushing backwards and forwards across the street, madly flapping his wings, dodging traffic like a demented psychedelic ostrich and nearly causing several accidents. The following is what he wrote of the event in *Come Together*:

At 7.10pm on a damp, cold,
Grey evening, a procession,
Of royalty, with fantastics
And aggressors in attendance,
Slowly filed down a narrow
Four-storey-high winding
Staircase in one of the more
Deliciously seedy mansion blocks
Of King's Cross, to the streets
And people of London.
Golden banners announced and
Leaflets proclaimed that the
Gay Liberation Front Street
Theatre were on the march into
The minds of all who beheld
And marvelled. Gorgeously
Bedecked in flowing gold and silver
Sparkling scarlet opulent
Feathers and jewels with
Beautiful sounds, harsh sounds,
Sharp sounds and the melody of

Human sounds
They went past and into
Unbelieving eyes and
Expanded minds of
Those that were bedazzled
By their splendour.

And that is exactly how it was, a surreal fancy dress party completely lacking any political content. Someway towards the end of the Strand we had a theatre ticket thrust into our hands. It was for a stalls seat at The Duchess Theatre for a show called *Isabel's a Jezebel*. How bizarre we thought, how did this come about? Thinking ourselves lucky, we continued on in all our tawdry glory and filed into the stalls of the theatre, to find only half the seats occupied and the rest of the theatre, the circle and balcony empty. We were in costume – were we expected to perform? We seated ourselves in the front stalls, and as we looked at each other in bewilderment, along the row came the startling information that Wakeling was in the cast of the show we were about to see. I saw at once that we had been duped and found myself quite angry at Winter and Wakeling's wheeze of using Gay Lib to promote his show, and hardly mollified when the curtain went up. The show was about a mermaid and her deep-sea lover forever making love, and then arguing about bringing children into a world that worshipped death. Charles Marowitz in his review of the West End Stage for *The New York Times* wrote, 'The composer is Galt McDermot the composer of *Hair*, but compared with the hirsute extravaganza of the original tribal romp, *Isabel's a Jezebel* suffers from Alopecia.'[16]

The Gay Liberation Front Street Theatre had been cynically used to further an individuals' own career. Time had been squandered without the slightest thought for our feelings, or regard for the need to advertise the movement to the best of our ability. Unfortunately it wouldn't be the last time street theatre would be manipulated in this fashion.

The first GLF Think-In took place on Saturday, 16 January, 1971 at the LSE. These were infrequently held general meetings held at the weekend to discuss ideas, policy and restructuring. Bob Mellors and Aubrey Walter took the format from one developed by Women's Lib in California: the large meeting is broken down into small groups of about eight members each, who discuss the agendas among themselves, eventually reporting back through one member of each group to the main assembly. It is a way of including everyone in the discussion and made for a more democratic base, although you could find yourself in a group with people who could dominate through their facility with language, or political experience and jargon, which is how I found it at the time.

The Think-In discussed ideas for making membership formal and adopting a straight structure like the closeted Committee for Homosexual Equality – with an executive making all the decisions – annual elections and membership fees. This proposal was put forward by Anthony Grey, head of the Albany Trust, who made several attempts to corral Gay Lib into an imitation of straight organizations like his, but soon learnt he could not work with GLF. His proposals were ignored; they came from a world we rejected, that of lobbying parliament for change by trawling the corridors of power in the hope of encountering sympathetic legislators. It was quite clear to us that what the law changed one day could be changed back the next. The things we did discuss were ideas for making attendance at consciousness-raising groups – awareness groups – a compulsory part of GLF membership, because too often the general meetings became a theatre for charismatic speech-making, which however fascinating, did not go anywhere. Along with that we also discussed the corresponding necessity to work collectively within the various GLF function groups, all of which made sense and was happily adopted. It was also proposed that a Discovery and

Research group should be set up, and that we should look for some central premises where we could have an office. This led on to discussions about finance and legality, and how to handle the press. It was decided that there should be no spokesperson for the movement, and if people did talk to the media they had to make it clear it was just their own opinion they were giving, and not an official statement. In discussions about an office worries were expressed about a build-up of power hungry ego-trippers, which was solved by the only other rule for GLF: that people must be in the movement for three months before joining the office collective, could only serve for three months, and must wait another three months before serving again. For the purpose of opening a bank account we had no choice but to elect a secretary and a treasurer.

The only problem with this method of procedure was that when the decisions made at the Think-In were announced at the General Meeting, there were objections from some who hadn't attended the Think-In, claiming the decisions made were an undemocratic imposition. The necessity for collective working in the function groups, and the rules dealing with the media, and working in the office were adopted, but the obligation to commit to an awareness group fell. People claimed that we weren't ready for them and were ignorant of the procedure. Aubrey Walter's response was to say, 'So what if we are ignorant of the correct methods, we must learn by our own mistakes and successes. If we have a real commitment, then we will succeed despite the warnings of the better informed. Mao says, '"Dare to struggle, dare to win". And we should follow this maxim.'[17]

For those who were interested, Awareness Groups exploring consciousness-raising began to form during December. It was another idea developed in the American women's movement, where 'raising the level of consciousness' was a first priority. Aubrey Walter informs us that the idea arose during the Chinese revolution, as witnessed by William Hinton whose book *Fanshen* records the revolution in a village where the poor landless peasantry were preyed upon by pitiless landlords and the bureaucratic class. It explains how the Communist Party urged the workers to talk about their lives until they understood that their individual misfortunes were connected and not their fault, that they were simply victims of the social system under which they lived.[18]

The model article below was reproduced by many American groups and by GLF in London.

> This article is a collective effort by a New York consciousness-raising group composed of nine GLF men. We have adopted the process of C-R from the Women's Liberation Movement. In our C-R group, we have been trying to step outside the straight man's myths and institutions, to suspend the limited ways we deal with each other, and experiment with new ways of relating. Everyone's feelings are considered … and instead of shouting each other down, consensus, a solution that is to each person's interest can be reached. If people are silent, they are asked to contribute. This is part of the collective process. We as men are struggling with our eagerness to dominate and ego-trip by being aware of the needs of others in the group, and struggling with our tendency to intellectualise by speaking from our experience. We are also learning what has been forbidden us – to relate to one another with respect and love ... We as gays must redefine ourselves in our own terms, from our own heads and experience, because no political philosophy designed by white heterosexual men can be adequate for us. Thus we use C-R to arrive at policy and positions, to plan actions and projects – to evolve a politics out of our experience.
>
> The format of the session consists of each person's testimony on a given topic and a concluding discussion. Notes are kept from week to week. The topic chosen must be

relevant to the members' life experiences and should be agreed upon by all. Usually chosen as a first topic is 'coming out,' one's first gay sexual experiences. When giving testimony a group member relates his personal experiences and feelings about the topic, avoiding any tendency to intellectualise or to draw conclusions. Each person speaks to the topic for as long as he wishes, and can only be interrupted for questions of clarification. The following is a list of some of the most important topics our group has used in the past month; Series: age 1-5 early formative experiences; grade school, acceptance or rejection of 'male role'; high school, pressure to conform to straight environment; college, post high school, sexual repression or expression. Series: on sexual relationships: coming out (first sexual experiences, acknowledging oneself as gay); sex roles; sexual objectification; cruising in bars; masturbation; sexual experience with women; S&M; sexual fantasies; monogamy; jealousy and possessiveness; domination or passivity in relationships; what kind of men we're attracted to; how do we approach men and how do we react to approaches from men; sex acts – sucking, fucking, being fucked, etc., experiences with and feelings about, parents, siblings, reaction to the term 'faggot' and 'queer'; relations with women; relations with straight men; racism; class background and prejudices; ageism – the pressure to be young; religious training and background.

The results of our C-R meetings have been many. While we began as nine isolated, alienated people, we have become a group politicised by the study of our experience. We found that our problems are not individual illnesses, but are generated by our oppression as a class. This discovery negated one of the most effective weapons of our oppressors, the false division between the personal and the political. Whether or not we'd had any previous political involvement, none of us saw homosexuality in political terms.[19]

Not everyone who came to GLF joined an awareness group, but for those who did it became an important development in their lives as they began to understand how they had unconsciously internalized the mores of heterosexual society, and its teachings on religion, medicine and law that alienates everyone with its notions of gender, masculinity, and sexual expression. Those who took the process seriously became core members of the movement that went on to change the social and political face of the country. It was, and remains, a vindication of the Marxist theory that consciousness-raising combined with activism are the first practical steps to a self-transformation that leads to the transformation of society.

Chapter 2

Have a Gay Day

'What's a revolution if it isn't fun?' said Kate Millett, talking of her gayness to the Daughters of Bilitis.

Bombs were exploding all over the country. In August 1970 the Spanish airline Iberia was bombed in protest at the fascist dictatorship of General Franco and his war with the Basque Separatists. At the end of August the home of the Commissioner of the Metropolitan Police was bombed, the news of which the government suppressed. The Attorney General's home was bombed in September, this too went unreported. In October his home was bombed a second time, the news again suppressed. The next day, bombs went off at Italian Government buildings in London, Birmingham, Manchester and Paris in response to the death of Giuseppe Pinelli, an autonomist anarchist thrown from a fourth floor window at Police Headquarters in Milan, while under interrogation as a suspect in the Piazza Fontana bombing. (His murder was the inspiration for Dario Fo's play, *Accidental Death of an Anarchist,* and the bombing was later discovered to be the work of Italian fascists pursuing their 'Strategy of Tension'.) On 26 October, Barclays Bank in Stoke Newington, and the Administrative Building at Keele University were firebombed. At 2.30 a.m. on 20 November a BBC transmitter van parked outside the Albert Hall was firebombed. On 3 December the Spanish Embassy was machine-gunned, and on the 9th, after a one day general strike protesting the Industrial Relations Bill (IRB), the Dept. of Employment and Productivity (DEP) in St. James's Square was bombed. On the day of the Trades Union Congress (TUC) rally at The Albert Hall, called to organize against the IRB on 12 January 1971, two bombs exploded at the home of Robert

Carr, Secretary of State for Employment. This bombing was finally reported in the media, and for the first time the public learned of a new enemy of the state called the Angry Brigade (AB). The attack on a Minister in Edward Heath's government was too close for comfort. Heath is rumoured to have told Inspector Habershon of the Bomb Squad: 'I don't care if you turn London upside down, just get the bombers.' A meeting that evening between Special Branch (SB) and CID resulted in random raids beginning at 6.00 a.m. the next morning on the homes of known left wing dissidents.

Jake Prescott was arrested on 19 January on cheque fraud charges. The next day at Marylebone Court he was questioned by Habershon of the Bomb Squad before being held on remand in Brixton, where he was placed in a cell with a 'Mr. A.' and a 'Mr. B.' On 3 February he was released on bail, then arrested again on 11 February and charged with the bombings.

Prescott's friend Ian Purdie was arrested at midnight on 6 March. Habershon said at Barnet Police Station: 'The raid was to find explosives and Ian Purdie. They are synonymous as far as I am concerned.' He admitted at trial that he had ordered Purdie to be arrested for questioning, which is illegal.

Some 18 hours after the AB firebomb exploded under the BBC transmitter van, a group of women from Women's Liberation protested the ritual degradation of the female sex at the hands of Eric Morley of Mecca Ltd., enacted annually at The Royal Albert Hall under a profit making excuse called The Miss World Contest.[1] The women disrupted the spectacle with football rattles, attacked the compère Bob Hope with flour bombs and stink bombs, and the whole demonstration was seen by the nation live on TV.

> 'And beauty draws us with a single hair,' Alexander Pope wrote several centuries ago. But happily he could not have envisaged the annual flesh fest the Miss World Contest, which

> Britain has added to the gaiety of continents.
>
> There was Bob Hope performing his routine cabaret turn when a sound of rattles and disturbances diverted attention to a group of women rushing down one of the aisles, sprinkling papers as they went.
>
> Sixty seconds noisy, smelly pandemonium reigned ... Bob Hope retreated unable to compete with this newer and frankly more interesting entertainment. Security officials seized the struggling women while an audience watched as outraged as if the minute's silence on Remembrance Sunday had been interrupted.
>
> Although the words 'cattle market' had been much invoked during the evening, it was only the mass rush of photographers at the end which gave a good example of animal behaviour. Otherwise the evening was as coyly libidinous as ever.[2]

Five women demonstrators were arrested and charged with a variety of offences, including threatening behaviour, possessing offensive weapons and insulting behaviour. Charges against Mier Twissle were dropped, but the most serious charge, assault on the police by Sally Alexander carried an automatic six-month prison sentence upon conviction. At the first hearing in December:

> Police Sergeant Geoffrey Bowers said Miss Alexander was one of two young women who ran towards the stage. He went on: 'I grabbed her as she climbed a barrier leading to the stage. She struggled violently and screamed. In her right hand was a lighted cigarette which she stubbed out on the back of my hand.' Miss Alexander was taken to Gerald Road Police station. Found in her handbag was a bag of flour, four plastic mice and an over-ripe tomato.[3]

But the way the four were treated by the police, you could be forgiven for thinking they'd been accused of blowing up the BBC transmitter van – they were certainly suspected of involvement.

The following is taken from the Women's Liberation booklet, '*We're not Beautiful. We're not Ugly. We're Angry*:

> After the ball was over, for a few of us came the decision as to whether we were going to defend ourselves in court, and explain why we had demonstrated, and what we were fighting. We were coming face to face with the law, and it looked like this...we were scared – scared to assert ourselves in the face of the law of the land. Why shouldn't we try and get off with a light sentence. Admit our guilt. A lawyer could defend us better than we could. What are we defending. We will be on trial. What for? Individual acts or Women's Liberation. All our lives we had been letting other people defend us, speak for us, lead us, apologise for us. This was a chance to change that, TO SPEAK FOR OURSELVES, break through our passivity and by doing that, challenging too the role that lawyers played in society.
>
> The Experts, well-oiled in legal jargon, ready to defend any persons' acts against the system, but never to step over that line and challenge the basis of the law. This was confirmed by various lawyers' reactions to us, like a woman Barrister saying, 'I can defend Women's Liberation, but not your actions.' Another, 'Be prepared for a psychiatric report.' And another, 'Just think of me as a mechanic with a garage full of legal information,' to which we chorused, 'OUT of the garage and into the STREETS.' And Women's Liberation Workshop said that this is the first trial since the suffragettes. 'You'll not be articulate or confident – you'll be smashed – and we don't want martyrs.'
>
> So we began to think, what do we want out of the Trial, and who are We? And by thinking of ways of challenging we began to feel the confidence that comes from working

> together, knowing that we can emerge from behind our conditioned responses, remembering the joy and strength of that feeling of togetherness in the Albert Hall, jumping from the seats, racing down the aisles, shattering the Spectacle of BEAUTY, and saying What the fuck is this all about. What is happening to Women?
>
> We wanted to go further than defending ourselves. We wanted to ATTACK. We wanted to break down the structure of the court itself and the isolation of being on trial as an Individual, feeling intimidated by the Court, the Law, the Science, the Mystery. That meant challenging the court at every point by speaking to each other in our own language that would be understandable to anyone. By speaking to our witnesses ourselves, as they were the women we demonstrated with, and explaining that way why we wanted to stop the contest, by using the court, to talk to other women and to create our own space in the court.[4]

Their case opened at Bow Street Magistrates Court on 4 February 1971. GLF Street Theatre received a request from Women's Liberation to perform outside the court on the first morning of the trial in order to show support and draw attention to their campaign against Mecca and the Miss World Contest. At last, Street Theatre had a real issue to work on, and with the top-down duo of Winter and Wakeling out of the way, the Think-In demand that we work collectively was put into practice. Everyone's ideas for this performance were discussed, and out of them developed The Miss Trial Competition, with contestants named Miss Judged, Miss Used, Miss Taken, Miss Behaved, Miss Conception and Miss Understood who were interviewed by a compère and told the story from the protesters point of view. We agreed that we would not have a director, and that we would ad-lib rather than have a script; we wanted to be spontaneous and 'in the moment'. Neon Edsel and I appeared wearing Felliniesque swimwear with padded bosoms and surrealist painted blue eyes for nipples. Ann Winter, Paul Theobald and Tarsus Sutton modelled evening wear, and Barbara Klecki, Marion Prince and Marshal Weekes modelled day wear. I wish I could remember the speeches but the tension was so great it was difficult to know whether my shaking body was due to nerves at being in drag for the first time, or dressed in just a body stocking and tights in February. I couldn't even recall what I'd said later the same day.

Again we all met at Theobald and Woods' flat to change and make up. Wrapping our fur coats around us, fur coats being very fashionable for both men and women in the Alternative Society at that time, second hand of course, we arrived at Bow Street at 9.30 a.m. relieved to find the supporters of the women on trial already there, dumped our bags, propped up our placards, threw off our furs and performed to the gathering. Passersby halted to watch, and the audience grew. Then the press arrived followed by a television crew from BBC2 who quickly pointed their camera at us. We were going to be on the telly. Then, just as we were taking our bows the police arrived. They made us move away from the Court entrance, so we retreated a few yards up the street to the wider area by the phone boxes where they left us alone because there were too many press photographers around for them to harass us any further. The anti-climax of police interference was a come-down, but we quickly recovered when the press asked us to pose for photographs, after which we decided to give another performance.

The second house gained a much bigger audience, but within five minutes some in the crowd were jeering and we found ourselves dodging tomatoes thrown by what looked like Covent Garden porters, and the police were coming back to support them. We faltered; we had no script, no structure, just our nerve. Another salvo and we lost it, grabbed our stuff and retreated back to the Tube and King's Cross. Once there, we turned on the TV to wait for the news, and celebrated our first real effort. But it was not a good day for news of us. Rolls Royce had collapsed; there was huge trouble in Northern Ireland and bad news from Australia about English cricket. We were left on the cutting room floor, along with any mention of the trial. But our collective way of working and the politics of Gay Lib had been demonstrated in support of our sisters in the Women's Liberation movement. That had been our aim, and it gave me plenty to think about.

A week later on 11 February, Inspector Habershon and the Bomb Squad interrupted the trial of the Miss World demonstrators, and amidst scenes of intimidation, false accusations, and attempted humiliation that brought the case to a standstill, they forcibly abducted four women defence witnesses from Grosvenor Avenue who were waiting to give evidence. 'Magistrate Rhees ruled that if they were the kind of person wanted by the police, then they were irrelevant witnesses to the case before him.'[5] The four women were taken in custody to Barnet Police Station, where they were questioned and denied all access to legal representation. Habershon revealed his true nature when he said to a senior partner of Birnbergs, the solicitors trying to get access to the four witnesses: 'I am not concerned with legal niceties.'[6] The solicitor took note, and charges were brought against Scotland Yard for assault of those dragged away from Bow Street and for their wrongful arrest and imprisonment.

But Habershon couldn't have cared less. He had succeeded with the assistance of the six SB officers present throughout the trial, and those in the shadows behind them no doubt, to link Women's Liberation to the AB. *The Times* on its front page the next day under the heading 'Police question Women'[7] published the smear, while both the *Evening Standard*[8] and the *Evening News*[9] reporting on the women's attendance at Bow Street, the bombing of the BBC transmitter van at the Albert Hall, their presence for questioning at Barnet and the police raid on their home in Grosvenor Avenue under the headline 'Carr Bombing'. A month later the *Evening Standard* repeated the calumny while reporting the bombing of the Ford Offices in Ilford, stating that 'detectives had visited a hippy commune and spoken to a number of youths and young women including members of Women's Liberation.'[10]

Before Habershon raided the court that day the defence had again been accused of obstructing procedure. Each witness was being examined four times because three of the women were defending themselves, whilst the fourth was defended by a lawyer. A legal precedent had been set in a divorce case, Mackenzie v Mackenzie, that allowed a person defending themselves in court to have a friend with them to assist. It also meant the accused could personally examine all the witnesses, particularly the arresting officer and other police witnesses. It could be a slow and ponderous process at times, especially in cross examination, unless you or your Mackenzie were quick witted, but the advantage was that the person in the dock was more in charge of proceedings, and if a slow pace of deliberation was purposely followed, matters could be stretched out over many weeks, with many adjournments, and it could begin to clog up the Court's calendar and the whole judicial system, especially if a number of people were being tried together. Angie Weir was one of the Mackenzie lawyers at the trial.

> *Angie Weir*: And it was a nightmare to get them all organised, because some of the more anarchic ones came with these reams of notes and paper and we'd try and get it all organized and she somehow resisted every attempt to do it. And then we actually had some members of the Bar, and there was a woman called Nina Stanger who was helping us, so it was also the beginnings of a radical movement in the Bar as well, and it was a very interesting set of circumstances.[11]

The reality in Court, unfortunately and only to be expected, was that witnesses testaments' were ruled irrelevant when they tried to explain their demonstration in terms of the cultural oppression and economic exploitation of women symbolized by the Miss World Contest. Some witnesses were not called and others had their evidence ruled out of order before they'd opened their mouths.

> Nina Stanger, defence lawyer was completely ignored and in general put down by Magistrate Rhees. In the afternoon after Habershon left with his four women defence witnesses, only men were allowed into the well of the court and at three-thirty, the court adjourned after refusing the women bail and ordering them to be held on remand in Holloway. Women's Liberation Workshop condemned this as a vindictive act.[12]

The next day the four women were given two minutes to sum up. Kathy McLean in her summing up said: 'While the prosecution had provided no evidence to suggest that the behaviour of the women insulted anyone, there had been plenty of evidence "from our witnesses that a large number of women were insulted by the Miss World Contest."'[13] Sally Alexander was found not guilty of assault but guilty of threatening behaviour. Jenny Fortune, Kathy McLean and Jo Richardson were also found guilty, with fines amounting to £80 and each bound over to keep the peace for two years or forfeit £100.

> *Angie Weir:* I was often a sort of cross-over between Women's Lib and Gay Lib, and that's how I managed to get myself to a Gay Liberation meeting. I was involved in the early women's group and we in our group became aware of gay liberation, and it was one of the first women's marches and, as I recall it, I went along to a meeting at the LSE *ostensibly* to rally support for the women's march. So I stood up and sought the support of our brothers and sisters in gay liberation, and then Warren Haig who was chairing, said we have a rule, (after my little spiel – I think he was quite appreciative), we have a rule here,

> anybody who speaks here has to say whether they're gay or straight. So I had to say – and that was my coming out moment.[14]

As Weir's approach was from Women's Lib, I imagine that she was able to make a more detached appraisal of GLF at the general meetings than the gay women already involved, and saw how useful it would be to have a women only meeting on a different night, and to establish a link with Women's Liberation. At first Elizabeth Wilson and Mary McIntosh were reluctant to go along with Weir's idea, as they saw feminism as being a movement of heterosexual women with doubtful sympathies to lesbians and gay men. To them, Women's Lib appeared focused on, and in many ways only endorsed the experiences of women as wives and mothers, but eventually they were won over to Weir's idea, as all three of them were socialists.

> *Weir:* Somehow I still have a letter from the Gay Liberation Women's Group applying to join Women's Liberation with a Postal Order for seven shillings and sixpence, and I had a letter back from this Maoist, Maysal Brar and her husband Harpul, and she said that we couldn't join because we were social deviants, and returned my Postal Order.[15]

At the Arts Lab after Christmas, they announced the formation of a women's group. There were a number of men who put up quite a resistance to this new development, some even demanding the right to attend such meetings. This called forth a thoughtful and prescient response from nineteen year old Tony Reynolds, very much in step with the women, and who must have recognized from his own perspective in the GLF Youth Group, of which he was the founder member, the difficulties – due to his age and good looks – of obtaining attention at the general meeting in any serious, meaningful way.

> As I felt the women in the meeting were yet again dominated by the men in the debate on whether the men should be in on their discussions, I think that example is in itself a good reason for the women talking on their own. I myself hopefully look forward to the emergence of a lesbian liberation voice. Unfortunately I feel bad about the fact that I'm a man putting forward a point that should be made by the women, but as was shown in the last meeting the women didn't get very far, and I think the point should be made pretty soon. The existence of a lesbian caucus in the New York Gay Liberation Front has been very helpful in challenging male chauvinism amongst gay men and anti-gay feelings amongst Women's Lib.[16]

From then on the GLF Women's Group met on a Friday night, and many who found it difficult if not impossible to speak at the general meetings blossomed in the intimacy of their own function group.

After the General Meeting a few of us in the Street Theatre Group usually ended up at Mitch Blunden & Angus Shield's bed-sit in West Kensington for a smoke. It was the first hippy home I'd visited, with mattresses on the floor covered in tie-dyed silks and Turkish carpets on the wall. Propped up by cushions, the fire blazing; shillings ready by the gas-meter; we were looking one night at the first edition of *Come Together*. What was missing someone decided was an Agony-Aunt column, somebody who could answer our questions on sexual politics. We gave her the name Doris Aversham, and started composing letters to her. Why, we wanted to know, were we expected to wait two-hundred years before we would achieve our liberation. Or, Dear Doris, What is the Marxist view on cottaging? When I heard the news that there would be elections held for membership of the Steering Committee (also known as the queering committee) I suggested that four of us should call ourselves Doris Aversham, and stand as one candidate, just to send up the whole election process.

By the time we had returned from the Arts Lab to the LSE after the Christmas break, so many people were coming to the Wednesday meeting that by mid-February it was attracting upward of 250 gays; gay women and gay men as we called ourselves in those days, and now took place, not in a classroom but in the elliptical, eau-d'Nil painted, wood panelled lecture theatre. On election night I wore a pale yellow cheongsam with my hair pulled back in a bun. Mitch Blunden was in a floor-length black velvet dress. I can't remember what I said in my speech, something worthy I imagine, or what Blunden or Sue Winter said, but I remember Roger Carr's speech. Everyone had to turn round in their seats and look up to see him because he appeared at the back of the theatre, at the top of the stairs by the right hand door, which was ajar. Carr, dressed in a Chanel style tweed costume, his long curly auburn hair piled up under a green Pill Box hat with a spotted veil partly covering his face. His lipstick was dark red, and under one arm he clasped a crocodile skin handbag. Smiling down at the saucer-eyed open-mouthed faces, this glamorous county lady declared: 'Brothers and Sisters! Power to the People! As a hard working member of the Street Theatre group I want to say that we have carefully examined the issues involved in portraying the ideology of GLF to the people, as you may have seen from our recent production in support of Women's Lib. By following the example of Chairman Mao's Permanent Revolution, we now feel confident that we can apply those skills, just as seriously, to representing your interests on the Steering Committee. Our plan is to commit –' He broke off, and turning to the open door said, 'Yes, thank you … Don't worry, I shan't be long.' Then turning back to the meeting continued, 'So Sorry – my chauffeur. With our experience of collective work we commit ourselves to following the instructions laid down in Mao Tse Tung's Little Red Book with the idea that if we are elected, the four of –' Turning to the door once more – 'Yes Gervais, I know the traffics heavy!', and to the meeting, 'I do beg your pardon. If we are elected, the four of us who represent Doris Aversham will follow the idea of the per – Of course you can Gervais. Just as soon as we get back to Guildford! ... Like the permanent revolution the four of us will rotate the position between us on the platform. Now please forgive me, but I simply must dash.'

Having given our speeches from where we were sitting, we had to move down to the front by the stage to face the meeting. Andrew Lumsden who was acting as the teller, and as surprised as everyone else by our appearance, came rushing over to me before the count to quietly ask if we were really serious; little did he know how serious we were.

Because it was a piece of theatre we hadn't thought about what would happen if we won, and I remember having a fright when the votes were announced, for we nearly got elected. It was the first time Street Theatre performed at a General Meeting, and the first time that drag, the power of which I felt when performing at Bow Street, was seen there. But more than anything it had been a fun thing to do, and possibly for that reason the implications and effect of our action didn't immediately become apparent to me, so I didn't pay much attention to the reactions of some of the men after the meeting who treated me as though I'd cheated or wasn't quite all there. I think for the Maoists and Marxists it was a bit of a jolt, a development they had not foreseen. To have humour used in politics was fine for Street Theatre – out on the streets – but the main meeting was supposed to be serious, and we may have been seen as taking their left wing authority too lightly. For the Trotskyites, whose method is to work within a system to bend it to their will, we presented more of a challenge; if they decided to infiltrate Street Theatre to bring us into line they might first have to join us out on the streets in drag. Not that anyone was claiming to be a member of any of those left wing groups; that went without saying, and at the time I wouldn't have known the difference between them anyway.

For gay men in London there were, at a fair estimate, around 30 pubs, clubs and coffee bars to go to. For women, after the closure of the short-lived *Robin Hood,* there was only one lesbian club to go to in the entire city, the long established *The Gateways* in Chelsea. Mary McIntosh, Elizabeth Wilson and one other sister were members of the club, so it was natural that they would wish to go there and sell tickets for the second dance at Kensington Town Hall on 26 February.

> *McIntosh:* We were having a hard time getting any interest and of course they didn't want us selling tickets to something else. Smithy [one of the owners] told us to stop, and Elizabeth and I got into a discussion with her on the door as she was throwing us out.[17]

First Smithy banned one of the women from the club for life. The other two were let off with a warning.

> *Wilson:* Because we are old and untroublesome members who had never necked in the lavatories or knocked anyone out, and also because it was our first offence as far as distributing GLF literature was concerned. Reading through the demands, Smithy said, 'When you come down to it we *are* abnormal. We're a minority … I think everything is beautiful the way it is – we have a lot of freedom – two girls can walk down the street hand in hand if they want to. No, I *don't* think men should be allowed to hold hands and kiss in public, I think that's *disgusting.* Men! – do you know why we won't have men down here? Because whenever we do, if you go out to the toilets you'll find two men out there having a quick bash, and the next moment they're doing it with a girl – they just don't care what they have, it's just quick sex, they can't have relationships, it's disgusting … I *don't* think the age of consent

should be the same for men – men are supposed to be three years behind girls anyway, aren't they? Do *you* think it should be legal for an old man to seduce a sixteen year old boy? I don't … well, I don't think a sixty year old woman should seduce a young girl either – would you like it if that happened to your sixteen year old sister? And I don't believe its legal either – no, it is not legal.'

An argument followed about what was the real age of consent, and Smithy, losing the argument, flexed her muscles and said, 'Well I'm a bigger lesbian than either of you will ever be'. She went on, 'I'm opposed to your aims because I don't think changing the law can alter attitudes. You won't change *anything,* baby – no you will not. You want to force it down people's throats – you want to change everything – the whole of society – but you won't – no – because people don't want to change – things are all right the way they are … I think the whole idea of kissing in public is horrible – why can't you do it at home, in privacy? If you have a steady girlfriend you don't *need* to kiss in the streets. Why parade yourselves?' Before ordering us out, Smithy said, 'I'd like to kick your bum up Bramerton Street, Elizabeth.' I don't think she'd ever addressed me by my name before. I didn't even know she knew it.[18]

McIntosh: We were just fascinated by it because it seemed to articulate everything; it made it clear to us what GLF was about, because we were opposed to all of that in ways we hadn't even questioned before.[18] So Elizabeth wrote it up for *Come Together,* because the whole thing seemed to be such a good way of stating the difference between us and a certain position out there. And of course *The Gateways* was absolutely outraged. After Elizabeth's article about it came out, *The Gateways* banned us – so the general meeting decided to have a demonstration against *The Gateways*. It was a build-up of confrontation.[19]

A plan for a demonstration was worked out and the flyer for the dance was amended to include on the front, a line saying: 'Do come along – and remember … Sappho was a right on woman.' On the back they printed a statement:

> The Gateways has made thousands of pounds out of women who come to the club (precisely how much money and publicity was gained from [using the club to film a scene for] *The Killing Of Sister George?*) yet the management of *The Gateways* considers lesbians to be sick. We are not sick and don't like people who condescendingly treat us as such – especially when they are making a living off us.[20]

As one GLF woman said, seeing the flyer for the first time in twenty four years, 'Oh, well, I don't suppose that would have endeared us to them, would it?' recorded Lisa Power in her even-handed well researched history and treasured oral testaments of the movement, *No Bath But Plenty of Bubbles.*

A call for volunteers for a demonstration against *The Gateways* was made at the Wednesday meeting which saw a number of men join with the women on Saturday night at Sloane Square Tube, who on their way down the King's Road, leafleted *The Queens Head, The Markham,* and *The Gigolo* coffee-bar.

> *Carla Toney:* I was a member at *The Gateways*. I remember the demonstration vividly. There was Angela Weir and Elizabeth Wilson, Mary McIntosh, Barbara Klecki, Barbara Cooper and Beverley and Marion Price, I think. There were a dozen women and we left the brothers, as we called them, outside the club to go down and leaflet and talk to women. The leaflet said 'Out of the closet and into the street' and we went in and did a spiel, talked to different women at tables and asked if they were out and why not, and of course the women in *The Gateways* were horrified at all these dykes coming in and

telling them to come out. Somebody at some point had asked me to dance and said, 'I can't tell by the way you're dressed whether you're a butch or femme.' So people were handing out leaflets and mostly talking to people about coming to the next meeting.

Gina used to have policemen come and drink in the club regularly, treat them to a drink, so she got on the phone to the police and they came promptly. In the meantime Gina dragged Marion Prince up the stairs by the hair. Barbara Klecki pulled the plug out on the juke box and screamed something like 'We're gay and we're proud,' and some of us fled as fast as we could. On the street, Mary O'Shea was there and Marshall Weekes and Pete McInally. The police told us move along and Mary, who was lovers with Lady Rose, told them to bugger off, so they snatched her and put her in the van. Marshall or someone screeched, 'Don't let our sister be taken away alone,' so about ten people leapt into the van to go with her. In the meantime, she'd crawled out over the front seat and disappeared down the King's Road ... and then they just started grabbing us and shoving us into the vans. By the time we got to the police station there were eleven of us, plus they'd accidentally picked up two passers-by from the bus stop who had never heard of GLF in their life.[21]

'In the van the police started getting very heavy. They hit one girl and she was poked in the arse with a truncheon.'[22] At the station no one was allowed to make a phone call, and no information was given to those not arrested who were waiting outside for news.

Carla Toney: Charlie Pig who used to paint a pig over his eye, went 'Oooh!' when they went to search him, like it really gave him a thrill. They really hated that so they locked him up in solitary.[23]

> They slowly released us over the night. Mary had disappeared and in court the people from the bus stop pleaded guilty and got a £1 fine, because their solicitor had advised them that if they pleaded not guilty the magistrate would assume they were with us and come down really heavy on them. All the people from Gay Liberation pleaded not guilty, and the two people who'd never heard of it pleaded guilty.[24]

Marshall Weekes was found to have overstayed his visa. He was given a 'supervised passage' back to New York where he continued his GLF activism.

The women's next action was with the Street Theatre groups of Women's Lib and GLF in a combined zap, an unannounced spontaneous demonstration against the male chauvinist students of the men-only bar at Imperial College. As a former engineering apprentice I was happy to join in. Some of the women and some of the men had to dress in drag. Two or three had a problem with that, but gave in so the plan would work. The men went to the bar first and ordered their drinks. Then the mixed party of kings and queens arrived and created uproar with the students bellowing, 'Close the Bar!' We ignored them and greeted each other with kisses in all sorts of combinations. Slowly the students began to realize some of the women were men, and then the penny dropped, those men must be homosexuals. We got all tensed up waiting for the attack, but it never came. When we looked round, silence fell; they were mesmerized. Then they opened a fire hydrant on us. We were heading for the door when someone said: 'Come on girls, it's only water, lets enjoy it' so we turned and stood there defiant. Our appearance was wrecked but so was the room. When they advanced we ran out of the door which they quickly locked behind us. Mad red faces glared at us through its porthole windows as triumphalist rugby songs seeped out with the water beneath it. We responded with chanting. Then they came out with baseball bats. We ran off down corridors, through endless fire-doors and down to the street. They tried throwing water at us from high up in the building but we saw them. For those without a car, two empty taxis appeared; we piled in, and were half way down the road before a police car passed us in the other direction racing to investigate. I was in the cab with Elizabeth Wilson and we were nearly in hysterics at the idea of being phantom fairies, creating havoc and then escaping by taxi into the night, 'leaving just a telltale wisp of perfume on the air.'[25]

Part of my re-education had to be Gay Lib's support for the people fighting the IRB that was to outlaw sympathy and secondary strikes and unofficial disputes, introduce a one month cooling-off period and a special Industrial Relations Court. My whole extended family had worked in the woollen mills of the West Riding as sorters, weavers and spinners. As an apprentice engineer I had paid my union dues, but the union was of no help when my sexuality was revealed. In clerical work there was no union either. The great transforming power of unionism, I thought, was past. Overseers for the bosses, they have a history of betraying autonomous workers councils. The TUC was now an authority arbitrating on behalf of proprietors and government, complicit with them in the idea that the possession of an address book and the ability to move goods should be rewarded a hundred times more than the hands that made the artefacts, or mined the coal. Nevertheless there were many gays inside the bureaucracies who could join us and hopefully fight for the changes we demanded the unions make regarding the employment rights of homosexuals and other minorities, so I found a few good reasons for being with Gay Lib on the Anti-Industrial Relations Bill march on 21 February.

For those meeting up at Hammersmith within sight of William Morris's house, the industrial workers of Britain got a shock when we arrived: long haired layabouts many of us must have appeared to be, carrying placards stating, 'Homosexuals Oppose

The Bill' and 'Poof to The Bill'. We handed out a leaflet explaining why we were there, called 'Homosexuals Are On The March', which startled recipients when we boldly thrust them into their hands. At Hyde Park Bette Bourne remembers seeing The Red Ladder Theatre Company manoeuvring their big red shiny ladder between the massed ranks, setting it down here and there so that a man with a megaphone over his shoulder could climb to the top and proclaim: 'We don't want a slice of the cake ... we want the whole fucking bakery.' As the seven mile long march moved off GLF was marshalled into position. The non-union marchers' place in the procession was at the back, but even so we were placed at the very back because the International Socialists (IS) could not be seen to associate with us, and started a general homosexual panic that swept through the left wing ranks, which they tried to cover up by claiming that our presence might distract from the protest. I thought bringing up the rear very appropriate. We gave a very vocal, colourful and uninhibited finish to the train, gays in the street joined in, and when we reached Trafalgar Square, protesters came up to ask for our leaflet. Many of them were miners, but who then could have imagined the magnificent solidarity of Lesbians and Gays Support the Miners in 1984.

The worry on the left that we might be a distraction proved true in a small but telling way that got our position across with humour thanks to the right wing *Evening Standard*. Their cartoonist Jak produced a drawing of the office of the TUC leader, showing all the newspaper headlines of the protest with their various estimates of the numbers of marchers pinned up on the office wall. Behind the General Secretary's desk sits Vic Feather surrounded by union officials, while another official gazing at the headlines says: 'Well Vic, I make it eighty to one hundred and fifty thousand, depending on whether you include the "Gay Liberation Front" or not!'

In addition to Tarsus Sutton's poem in *Come Together* 4 there are poems by Trevor Woods, a working class gay poet from Norfolk, and Howard Wakeling, the bisexual from a middle class more educated background:

Feel secure and comfortable
in the new womb-style sleeping
bags designed by Virginia pussey-
wobble.

Who are you?
I don't know, can you tell me?
Yes, coming back to my place for
coffee?
Instant?
Of course dear boy, you have a beautiful
smile, one of your most
noticeable attributes.

Why aren't you looking at me
when you say that?
I'm sorry dear boy, I was sent
adrift by your thick leather belt
that reminds me I used to be in the army once.

That's impossible, what as?
Oh, the camp sergeant. You see,
as a boy I always fancied myself
as one of the heroic lost,
In the battle of Waterloo.
That's how come I've see you down here
as often as I have.

I know a lot of people
from Waterloo. Most of whom I've

conquered at some point or other.
But unlike the real battle no blood
was spilled, only the jissomic over-
flow of Humanity fell to the floor
and was covered with small squares
of paper and engraved by footprints of
passers by.

Trevor Wood

Catch broken butterflies
And fold their wings.
Screw up your eyes
And think of things
That'll make you forget
That you're covered in blood
And caught in a net
And trapped by the flood.
Breakdown the barriers,
Throw down your gun
Catch broken butterflies and run.

Try to thread the beads of hope
On silken strings
Not on the rope
That whips and stings
And that's filling your head
With the torrents of hate –
How many dead?
And is it too late?
Catch all the butterflies – pull them apart.
Somebody's hate has found its mark.

Bathe in icy mountain streams
And catch the sun.
Naked in dreams
So hide and run
For a shiver of fear
Is a scream in your head
The stream is a tear,
The pavement's your bed.
Play with the butterflies – go for a ride.
Play on the mountain slope and hide.

Hear the screaming sirens song
And hold your breath.
Knowing they're wrong
You dream of death
For though freedom is just.
It's the world that's afraid.
There's no one to trust
So how is love made.
Catch all the butterflies
Climb on their wings
Find the reality
Love brings

Howard Wakeling

Here is poetry inspired by the meeting in Gay Liberation of middle class Wakeling and working class Woods. Wakeling: bisexual, full of anguish at his transgressive nature and feelings to conform, to avoid detection and hideaway, is tortured by the challenge to come out. 'Catch broken butterflies' harks back to 'Who Breaks a Butterfly upon a Wheel,' a phrase Alexander Pope used in his heterosexist attack on Lord Hervey, Pope characterized as 'Lord Fanny'. Woods, who has no conflict with his sexuality celebrates his promiscuous freedom. Both share the image of a pavement; for Wakeling signifying a loss of status and the site of fear, but for Woods and his street life represents a place for his sleeping bag. Woods' let-down is the mindless sexism of the unnecessary pussie-wobble. But it would be wrong to conclude that all middle class gays are tortured and all working class gays are sexist; it is just that in terms of sexual class, it's useful to treat male bisexuals as petit bourgoise because of their problems with masculinity. People say there were many bisexuals in GLF and indeed there were a few, but my experience of male bisexuals is that they are only in play for a short period in their sex lives, after which they choose the mono-sexuality that suits them best. The important thing to learn from bisexuals of either gender is: are they out to their families about their homosexual life, or is it that they are only out to their gay and lesbian friends?

At the next Street Theatre meeting after our Bow Street Demo, some of those who hadn't wished to work with us on that project, and failed to support us on the day, came back to the group. Wakeling never returned, but Sue Winter re-appeared and Chesterman made his first appearance. The two of them had not been wasting time. They explained that they wished to do a gay version of Shakespeare's play *Measure for Measure*. Winter said she had been to a party and met Charles Marowitz, the taboo breaking American director of the Open Space Theatre in Tottenham Court Road, and was convinced he would put on the production. Chesterman told us the Steering Committee had agreed that if Street Theatre were interested he could go ahead with his idea, but they would not at this stage give it official GLF backing. Both Chesterman and Winter repeatedly said this was to be a marvellous opportunity for all of us, a rare chance to show off our acting skills, and would really put GLF on the map. When I asked about Street Theatre, we were assured it would always be possible to do that. Auditions would be called, except

Tarsus Sutton was already cast as The Duke Vincentio, and Jane Winter would play Isabella, and would we agree that this project needed a Director, and that Chesterman was to take that role with Sue Winter as his assistant. The group would be known as the Theatre Group. Everyone agreed, including myself, that a Director in sole charge was vital, even though I was unhappy with the new situation.

With the announcement at the next Wednesday meeting of auditions for the Theatre Group, many new people came along. There was Michael Mason a former actor and young conservative, Carl Hill a well-to-do drop-out, Charlie Pig the artist and his friend Lala, Scottish Malcolm Bissett from the Youth Group and John Church, an actor who had just returned from five years on Broadway to look after his ageing mother. Chesterman recruited his friend Janet Phillips, and Claudia appeared, the first pre-op transsexual to join Gay Lib, whom Martin Corbett and I rushed out to visit at some council hostel in Cricklewood after he'd made a distraught phone call to the office for help. Gordon Howie joined, and Geoff Marsh brought along a video camera.

Once auditions were completed, Bette Bourne and his lover Rex Lay visited us at Chesterman's invitation to give advice. Bourne had been a player alongside Ian McKellan with the Prospect Theatre Company in a repertoire of Shakespeare plays in the West End a couple of years earlier. It was the first time I met him, and being Sunday in the City he correctly wore a smart tweed suit. Much to my secret delight he proposed that we do away with the idea of a Director; advice that was not adopted.

Sundays were now taken up by the stage production, involving a return to more theatre games and a new place to meet for rehearsals: the ground floor and very large garden of a big Victorian detached house in St. John's Wood next-door to Paul McCartney's. We were told the enormous house was a squat, though I never saw any squatters. It was not until I read Lisa Power's book *No Bath but Plenty of Bubbles* that I discovered the story was not true. Carl Hill, it appears, was in the know – '.....then I went along to Cavendish Avenue, the Astor place, where Princess Obolensky let me in. I had been a paying guest of her grandmother in the 60s (so I felt less isolated.) She and her brother owned the house, and lived at the top of it. I was in yellow dungarees and had long red hair. That was where the Theatre Group was but I was more interested in the Street Theatre Group.'[26]

At Easter Street Theatre took a break from Chesterman's rehearsals to appear at the Campaign for Nuclear Disarmament (CND) Festival of Life at Alexandra Palace. With no time to invent a show for the occasion, the Bermans costumes were tarted up allowing us to gambol around as friendly furry animals and masked fantastics, while distributing leaflets about GLF. Steve Swindell who was 18 years old and lived with his parents in Bristol hadn't found any young gay musician freaks to play with down there, but seeing the CND poster advertising GLF's presence, came up to London to find out more. He never went back. We discovered before putting our make-up on that there were many gay men and women there attracted by the posters, and the day was spent with us in those mad costumes trying to persuade people to take us seriously and come to a general meeting.

The Theatre Group with its focus on the production of *Measure for Measure* soon began to hobble the development of street theatre. We had been fortunate with the drag, but you can't build shows around costumes. It wasn't long before the situation was tested by an invitation to perform at the Bath Civic Festival, and calls from the Counter-Psychiatry Group who wanted us for their demonstration against the medical establishment in Harley Street. Since Bow Street, I had been putting together bits of dialogue from the Trial Scene in *Alice in Wonderland* and gave them to Gordon Howie who was keen to play at Bath. I didn't go there because of rehearsals for *Measure for Measure*, but those that did were trailblazers for provincial gays. They played at two venues in the city, one in a park and the other in front of the mayor and assorted bigwigs, and all had a great weekend apart from Carl Hill and Michael Mason who were attacked in the street for holding hands.

Out of our experience at the CND Festival came the idea of having Gay Days in London parks on Sunday afternoons. Holland Park was the first one we chose. The Action Group agreed to organize them, and at last we found a practical use for all those never-ending theatre troupe trust games, including one we played at Alexandra Palace called the kissing game.The games became a regular feature of Gay Days where 50 to 250 gays demonstrating affection for each other in public was an exercise that raised everyone's awareness, and sure enough it wasn't long before the whole country was saying to each other: 'Have a Gay Day'. Such are the results of hearts and minds politics that we had the country laughing, not at us, but with us; on our terms for a change.

> *Angie Weir:* I was at the Gay Day at Victoria Park in the East End. It was rather wonderful. I thought they were splendid occasions. We were all sitting in a circle and played that game where someone in the middle threw the ball and whoever caught it had to come up and kiss the thrower. There was a group of Hackney girls behind us who had come along to watch the fun. They were really interested in this game and thought it was a happening of some sort. That was the whole point about happenings, life had been so boring… The ball kept going man, woman, man, woman, so they didn't think there was anything peculiar about it. Then it went man, man and the first gay kiss and then there were some more, and I remember one girl turning around and saying, 'Cor, some of them are queer,' and then they looked around at this great big crowd and said, 'Ere, they're all fucking queer!' We talked to

> them about it all – it was a great belief you know, that you just went out onto the streets and collared the nearest person and explained your theory of life and revolution. We were very keen on doing that kind of thing. I remember that time because it was a lovely day and afterwards the women went up to swim at the women's pond. We were all slightly high.[27]

With the success of the public dances at Kensington Town Hall, the Action Group decided that future ones should be held in town halls in other parts of central London. They also organized a GLF Disco at *The Prince of Wales* in Hampstead Road. One Friday in January, Paul Theobald went there feeling 'out of love that night' and disappointed that the disco was the only alternative scene GLF had managed to organize. But his mood changed when he entered the pub and saw people he recognized, and many other friendly faces, especially a guy who offered him a drink who wasn't trying to pick him up. Theobald found that:

> Here were people. Happy, smiling, touching and talking, and not walking away with the impression of having talked to just 'nice-fitting pants' or 'pretty face'. Sure there were plenty of nice-fitting pants and pretty faces. I saw them. But I could also feel the vibes that came from these people. So together we danced, we talked, we touched and we dug it. We were digging it. [The police arrived. Stopped the music and demanded to know who was in charge]. 'No one's in charge, we've just come together TOGETHER.' 'Right, men over here. Women over there.' Everyone was searched, pockets, handbags, and hair, and nothing was found, not a nasty reefer in sight.[28]

But Theobald with his long blonde hair and stubble beard had been searched several times before, and so had a few of the other brothers, and they knew that the police were not being thorough, and with no women police on the raid the handbag inspection had been cursory. Dennis Greenwood remembers when the police ordered everyone out, 'We had to leave by the backdoor and go down this dark alley to the street with the police lined up on either side. That was the frightening bit.'[29]

> After the raid the police had a little chat with the landlord, intimidating him to the extent that we can no longer hold any functions at his pub. Up until this point the landlord, who was a really nice guy, had been very keen that we continue to use his pub. So we find another place. I'm sure we can see to it that it's bigger than the last and that more people will be able to get together and smile and dance and touch and dig it. Power to all oppressed People.[30]

The next big dance was held just a little further east along the Euston Road.

> *Jeffrey Weeks:* There was a dance in Camden Town Hall in 1971 and I remember vividly at midnight, all the lights went on and a number of people started protesting about the place being shut down and started calling the attendants, who after all were working overtime, 'fascist pigs' and shouting, 'Revolution now!' as if attacking the poor attendants was somehow going to bring on the revolution. That actually made me aware that there were different strands of GLF, there was the strand that supported trade union rights – that supported the workers – they had rights as well and they wanted to go home, why should they stay after midnight? And there was also a streak in Gay Liberation of pure individualism, whatever the language of 'revolution now', it was actually 'I want it and if so, I must have it.' I think those two strands are still with us in the sexual culture, between 'sexual' being about my right to do whatever I want, regardless of the consequences, and those who believe that my right to do something

> must always be tempered by the rights of others. That divide was there right from the beginning, between extreme libertarianism and a sort of liberationism which stressed solidarity and community and involvement with others.[31]

The writer Steve Mann was also present and described the same scene:

> There was David (the boss) Goodman looking demure (?) in a flowing white dress, Russell Hunter camping it up outrageously and looking sultry in a plunge neckline J. Ashworth original and Nik Turner trying to electrocute himself on stage.
>
> The occasion was the Gay Liberation dance at the Camden Town Hall; hundreds of freaks, gay, straight and just plain weird – cavorting merrily to the music of the Pink Fairies and Hawkwind in an atmosphere generally reminiscent of decadent Rome.
>
> Hawkwind opened, and provided the first moment of drama when Nik touched both mike and sax simultaneously, shorted something out and collapsed dramatically, returning later with a heavily bandaged hand and multiple curses. Despite the setback Hawkwind produced one of their best performances to date and added some meaning to the good vibes cliché.
>
> Due to the delay caused by Nik's accident, the Fairies started late, stormed into a tremendous, 'Tomorrow never knows', ordered the audience to 'do it' and were cut short somewhere in the middle of, 'Walk don't run' by the usual uptight management. 'But we've only just started, and we're booked for an hour,' stormed the Goodman. 'Don't care, council says it has to finish by twelve so that's it.' Cries of derision from the audience and the Fairies stomp on. 'If you're not out by twelve, we're locking the doors and you'll be here till morning,' bleated the man from the council to

roars of approval from the multitude. Then it really got farcical: the hall lights were turned out, power was cut off from the PA system, so a marathon drum battle started between Twink, Russ, Terry Ollis and anyone else who could get near a skin to bash, lit sporadically by a freak with a single flashlight from the floor, as the audience happily prepared to tear the hall apart.

A little man from the council tried to part Russ from his drum kit (no easy task) before finally the management stopped the imminent destruction of their beloved Hall by sneakily threatening to impound the band's equipment. Pink + Wind were gigging together in Swindon the following day, so reluctantly had to relinquish the hall to the council lackeys.

Despite the excellent performance of both bands, it wasn't the music that mattered, but the audience reaction. A few hundred Gay Liberation members and sympathisers managed to produce more community spirit, and a sense of totally unselfconscious enjoyment, than any number of 'liberated' freaks religiously digging the latest West Coast sensation at the Albert Hall or the Isle of Wight. Like the man said, lets have some phun![32]

Two versions of the same event underscores two different influences now at play in GLF: the Marxist and the counterculture, also known as the Underground or the Alternative society. The first is Apollonian, academic, cold, and authoritarian. The second, warm, spontaneous, uninhibited and Dionysian. I fail to understand how anyone could tease out tendencies and identify different strands in the mayhem of such an event. Hawkwind's groupies had among them many straight Glaswegians. Also present were gays from the ghetto bars who knew nothing of our politics. Given those facts, I think Weeks' attempt to identify opposing factions in the physiognomy of such a mixed crowd is like taking the dimensions of someone's skull as indicative of the danger they represent to the social order: moral opinions elaborated as sociological political science.

> Under the new conditions Individualism will be far freer, far finer, and far more intensified than it is now. [...] For the recognition of private property has really harmed Individualism, and obscured it, by confusing a man with what he possesses. It has led Individualism entirely astray. It has made gain, not growth its aim. So that man thought that the important thing was to have, and did not know that the important thing is to be. The true perfection of man lies, not in what man has, but in what man is. Private property has crushed true Individualism, and set up an Individualism that is false. It has debarred one part of the community from being individual by starving them. It has debarred the other part of the community from being individual by putting them on the wrong road, and encumbering them.[33]

To accept Wilde's socialist views on individualism could imply that Weeks, a Marxist sociologist, is trapped within and unable to think outside the fence of private property, however much he sincerely protests the rights of the workers. Weeks' opinions have been taken as facts for the last 40 years by his wide academic readership, but they are no more scientifically based than theology, as his 'vivid' memory reveals 24 years after the dance, when there had been plenty of time for him to review the evening, and his opinions and reaction to it.

Just four years after GLF collapsed, Weeks was writing in his book *Coming Out*:

> There were more men than women, [in GLF] as became typical in gay organisations (perhaps a ratio of 5 to 1), but certain women played a key role. Inevitably, most of the supporters were middle class, though often marginally or

> first generation middle class; but there were few working class gays.[34]

The overwrought qualifying of middle class membership says it all; fiddling the numbers of working class involvement: an antagonistic, class based bourgeois habit. In fact, dress was eclectic, hair was long; chins were worn very high. Regional speech was practically unheard of at the time, except in the regions. Beards were sported, and many working class gays followed the tradition of surmounting class barriers by changing their accents to hide their origins, myself included.

Marx based his scientific socialist thinking on material objects and mathematics, things independent of man's will and action, subject only to universal laws. One law he discovered through Dialectical Materialism states: *a change in the mode of production results in a change within society.* As homosexuals have always been discriminated against by Capitalists, heterophobia can be seen as the objectification of a sexuality that doesn't replace itself, a thing to be cast out to face death by starvation, but in the modern bourgeois economy assigned instead to the permanent pool of surplus labour.

In 1986 Margaret Thatcher's government deregulated the City of London financial markets. (leading directly to the financial crash of 2007/8). Called the Big Bang, electronic trading using computers was introduced, creating rapid movements of capital and thousands of new jobs to cover the new 24/7 market. For the first time ever, capitalism needed homosexuals for their ability to fill vacancies in the unsocial, un-familial, late and overnight shifts that the new mode of production and its extended market demanded. The capitalists' unspoken rule against the employment of homosexuals was broken by the autonomous action of capitalism itself and its relations of supply and demand.

When the numbers of suspected homosexuals working in the new financial markets was discovered, the Conservatives, to make amends for the inexplicable occurence – and as with all minorities – signalled to the privileged few they now relied on that they were not welcome members of the casino, while making trouble for the many; introduced Section 28 into the 1988 Local Government Act which prohibited the dissemination of information on homosexuality by local authorities and their schools. This directly affected sex education, the authenticity of lesbian and gay families and individuals, and caused the further oppression of homosexuals within society.

Socialism is a society of equals. At the basic level of men and women socialism is the balance of power between the sexes. It is here that lesbians and gays have a role to play. The sex-political struggle is the rebalancing of power between men and women skewed in favour of men, as we know, by their entitlement to property. Men do not need property, and their development, as Oscar suggests, has been crippled by it. Women, by their nature need a roof over their heads; men by theirs can happily sleep in the open air. By investing property in women, men will gain what they complain they've never had; freedom, while women will gain what they have never had; security. So socialism becomes a question of ending the economic and authoritarian enslavement of women and children.

> Not until that is done will the husband love his wife, the wife the husband and the parents and children love each other. They will no longer have a reason to hate each other. What we want to destroy is not the family but the hatred which the family creates, the coercion, though it may take on the outward appearance of 'love'. If familial love is that great human possession it is made out to be, it will have to prove itself. Compulsive morality as exemplified in marital duty and familial authority is the morality of cowardly and impotent individuals who are incapable of experiencing through natural love capacity what they try to obtain in vain

> with the aid of police and marriage laws. These people try to put the whole of humanity in a straightjacket because they are incapable of tolerating natural sexuality in others. It annoys them and fills them with envy, because they themselves would like to live that way and cannot.[35]

Homosexuals as part of a new social compact will have to offer the majority something they desire and can share with everyone if we are to be valued in the new society. I think we can offer homoeroticism, which will profoundly change relationships between the sexes, spells the dissolution of the authoritarian family structure, and as a consequence, the nature of capitalism itself. I also believe we have more to offer than sensuous pleasure.

Homosexuality has been subjected to Freudian psychoanalysis and Marxist social analysis, yet neither discipline can touch, composed as they are of concrete ideas, the intangible, yet steely essence another nineteenth century genius recognized in himself as reflecting the sensibility of many homosexuals; the Camp of the socialist aesthete Oscar Wilde.

One of the great cultural thinkers of the twentieth century Susan Sontag put it like this:

> The peculiar relation between Camp taste and homosexuality has to be explained. While it's not true that Camp taste is homosexual taste, there is no doubt a peculiar affinity and overlap. Not all liberals are Jews, but Jews have shown a peculiar affinity for liberal and reformist causes. So, not all homosexuals have Camp taste. But homosexuals, by and large, constitute the vanguard – and the most articulate audience – of Camp. (The analogy is not frivolously chosen. Jews and homosexuals are the outstanding creative minorities in contemporary urban culture. Creative, that is, in the truest sense: they are creators of sensibilities. The two pioneering

> forces of modern sensibility are Jewish moral seriousness and homosexual aestheticism and irony.)
>
> The reason for the flourishing of the aristocratic posture among homosexuals also seems to parallel the Jewish case. For every sensibility is self-serving to the group that supports it. Jewish liberalism is a gesture of self-legitimisation. So is Camp taste, which definitely has something propagandistic about it. Needless to say, the propaganda operates in exactly the opposite direction. The Jews pinned their hopes for integrating into modern society on promoting the moral sense. Homosexuals have pinned their integration into society on promoting the aesthetic sense. Camp is a solvent of morality. It neutralises moral indignation, sponsors playfulness.[36]

Masculinity, another sensibility gay men are obsessed with and oppressed by, leads them to believe that Camp is a weakness when it is our greatest strength. Because Camp dissolves morality, it plays an essential, joyful, unifying part in the sexual revolution, and the liberation of all. What oppresses men is a feudal masculinity nurtured for millennia on the ideals of military rulers. Masculinity needs new ideals. The nineteenth century gay socialist ideals were based on sandals, modern socialism requires a masculinity poised on high heels.

Chapter 3

Gay is Good

> We are a revolutionary group of men and women formed with the realization that complete sexual liberation for all people cannot come about unless existing social institutions are abolished. We reject society's attempt to impose sexual roles and definitions on our nature. We are stepping outside those roles and simplistic myths. We are going to be who we are. At the same time, we are creating new social forms and relations, that is relations based upon brotherhood, cooperation, human love, and uninhibited sexuality. Babylon has forced us to commit ourselves to one thing – revolution.
> New York GLF Statement of Purpose, 31 July, 1969, reprinted in *RAT*, 12 August 1969.

'Most of us are in the fortunate position whereby we can fight for freedom from oppression. Many of our brothers and sisters, however, are not even in a position to protest' wrote Martyn, a state registered mental nurse in *Come Together* 2.

> For instance, I remember only a few years ago, when I was working in a mental hospital, a young sixteen year old boy had been committed to us by order of the Courts, and was admitted to a locked ward, along with patients whom the hospital had found to be most disturbed or who were considered dangerous. When I asked about his diagnosis, I was told that he was 'another fucking queer'. Apparently he had been caught 'indulging in a homosexual relationship', and had previously been suspected of stealing some of his sister's clothes. Once in the hospital, he was subjected to the usual ridicule of the staff and was made to feel abjectly guilty

and despicable. One of his daily tasks was to clean the ward lavatories, this presumably being considered suitable 'occupational therapy'. The patients were woken at 6 a.m. Sundays and Christmas included, and his first job was to clean the toilets. This is not an incredibly unusual situation!

We are nowadays told that we are 'sick' and in need of treatment. The treatment consists of breaking down the individual's pleasurable response to someone of the same sex that he or she might feel drawn to emotionally and physically, and substituting an aversion reaction. This is achieved by means of electric shocks or emetic drugs, given when the patient responds favourably, so that the shock is associated with the photograph of the desirable person. I would like to emphasise that in-patient psychiatric treatment and private psychiatry often differ radically. If one is able to enjoy the benefits of private help, emotional support and sustenance is very likely to be offered. I have not seen this occur often in mental hospital treatment regimes. There are, and indeed have been, very many ethical objections to the use of such a form of therapy. However, my main concern at this particular juncture is that the person who administers the emetic drug or electric shock is almost invariably a psychiatric nurse.

I object strongly to this situation for several reasons. Not the least of which is that this is destroying a potentially supportive relationship. One may reasonably ask why nurses let themselves become involved in a procedure such as aversion therapy. Why didn't some of the nurses object to the locking up of a sixteen year old boy in an adult disturbed ward? The majority of psychiatric nurses are men. To challenge, question, or protest about the treatment meted out to a homosexual patient, renders one 'suspect'.

Men depend upon their jobs to earn a living, even male nurses. 'Suspected' men don't seem to get promotion, or alternatively seem to be prone to 'unsatisfactory' work records and dismissed. In the same hospital, a colleague of mine, a young, skilled and compassionate ward sister, was dismissed when it was discovered that she was having a love affair with one of the female student nurses. (After all, she might assault the patients.) Doctors and nurses are subjected to statutory disciplinary committees. They are liable to be deprived of their livelihood if found to be homosexual, even if no illegal activity has occurred.

The council have power to take disciplinary action against a registered nurse if it is brought to their attention (whether through the Courts, employing authorities, or individuals) that the nurse had been guilty of a felony, or misdemeanour, *or of any misconduct which warrants consideration as to whether her name should be removed from the register ....' (Functions, Procedure and Disciplinary Jurisdiction of the GMC, page 4.)*

What would you do? What *we* can, and must do, both for the protection of our brothers and sisters in the medical and nursing professions, and most important, for the patients, is this:

We must strengthen the position of the doctor or nurse, so that they will not be in a vulnerable position if they wish to object to 'treatment' policies. To achieve this, we must write to the appropriate statutory bodies and demand that no doctor or nurse be deprived of his or her livelihood because of their sexual orientation.

We must write to the medical and nursing press and make point 4 of our GLF demands quite clear – that we stop being treated as sick people. By changing the attitude of society at large, we will eventually modify the attitudes of potential medical and nursing students, and thus reduce the risk of patients being traumatised by psychiatric 'help'.[1]

Gay Liberation is generally dated to Friday, 27 June, 1969 when the drag queens and lesbians of the *Stonewall Inn*, on Christopher

Street, New York, physically attacked the police who had entered the bar and begun to harass them. Anger and disgust at the way the city treated lesbians and gays had been building for at least fifty-five years since the first police crackdown on the Greenwich Village gay and lesbian scene.

> As the police released the customers one by one from inside the bar, a crowd accumulated on the street. Jeers and catcalls arose from the onlookers when a paddy wagon departed with the bartender, the Stonewall's bouncer, and three drag queens. A few minutes later, an officer attempted to steer the last of the patrons, a lesbian, through the bystanders to a nearby patrol car. She put up a struggle, from car to door to car again, at that moment the scene became explosive. Limp wrists were forgotten. Beer cans and bottles were heaved from windows and a rain of coins descended on the cops ... Almost by signal the crowd erupted into cobblestone and bottle heaving ... From nowhere came an uprooted parking meter – used as a battering ram on the Stonewall door. I heard general cries of 'let's get some gas,' but the blaze of flame which soon appeared in the window of the Stonewall bar was still a shock. Reinforcements rescued the shaken officers from the torched bar, their work had barely started. Rioting continued far into the night, with Puerto Rican transvestites and young people leading charges against rows of uniformed police officers and then withdrawing to regroup in village alleys and side streets.[2]

On Saturday morning there was a message scrawled on one of Stonewalls boarded-up windows. 'THEY INVADED OUR RIGHT. THERE IS ALL COLLEGE BOYS AND GIRLS AROUND HERE, LEGALISE GAY BARS, SUPPORT GAY POWER.'[3]

By the following night, graffiti calling for 'Gay Power' had appeared along Christopher Street. Knots of young gays – effeminate, according to most reports – gathered on corners, angry and restless. Someone heaved a sack of wet garbage through the window of a patrol car. On nearby Waverly Place, a concrete block landed on the hood of another police car which was quickly surrounded by dozens of men, pounding on its doors and dancing on its hood. Helmeted officers from the Tactical Patrol Force arrived on the scene and dispersed with swinging clubs an impromptu chorus line of gay men in the middle of a full kick. [The chorines, hands on each other's hips, high kicked their way into the police lines singing, 'We are the Stonewall Girls / We wear our hair in curls / We wear no underwear / We show our pubic hair.'] At the intersection of Greenwich Avenue and Christopher Street, several dozen queens screaming 'Save Our Sister!' rushed a group of officers who were clubbing a young man and dragged him to safety. For the next few hours, trash fires blazed, bottles and stones flew through the air, and cries of 'Gay Power!' rang in the streets as the police, numbering over 400, did battle with a crowd estimated at more than 2,000.

After the second night of disturbances, the anger that had erupted into street fighting was channelled into intense discussions of what many had begun to memorialise as the first gay riot in history. Allen Ginsberg [the great American poet, out gay man, hero to dissenters all over the world] whose stature in the 1960's had risen almost to that of a guru for many counterculture youths ... arrived at the Stonewall on Sunday evening. [After surveying the scene] he commented on the change that had taken place, 'You know, the guys there were so beautiful', he told a reporter, 'they've lost that wounded look fags had ten years ago.'[4]

Sunday morning had seen a new sign at the Stonewall's boarded windows, 'WE HOMOSEXUALS PLEAD WITH OUR PEOPLE TO

PLEASE HELP MAINTAIN PEACEFUL & QUIET CONDUCT IN THE STREETS OF THE VILLAGE – MATTACHINE.'[5]

Sporadic uprisings continued until the next weekend, and by the middle of July the Gay Liberation Front had been formed. The ground, however, had been prepared earlier by the more intellectual muscle of the West Coast in San Francisco at Berkeley, and first of all in Los Angeles in April 1951, when Harry Hay, Bob Hull and Chuck Rowland founded the Mattachine Society, the first homophile movement in the US. Harry Hay had radically different ideas to the Mattachine message scrawled on the boarded up windows of the Stonewall 18 years later with those assimilationist pleas – 'we mustn't cause a nuisance', 'we mustn't rock the boat'. He based the organization on the communist structure of secret cells, in a pyramid of five ascending orders of responsibility, with one or two members of the higher orders in the lower ones. When the organization grew the cells divided. This gave protection to members from the witch-hunts fostered by McCarthyism emanating from Washington DC. The three used the Marxist theory of class politics which sees class as a socio-economic entity that can be agitated into consciousness of its own position and inherent possibilities, and with that new-found awareness demand political power. The early members posited that homosexuals treated as a class would fit the position of an oppressed minority. Unfortunately, in 1953 at a conference designed to bring the society out of the underground, having discovered that spies from the U.S. Senates' House Un-American Activities Committee was on its trail, the reactionaries within Mattachine who viewed themselves as no different to heterosexuals except in one tiny, unimportant detail, managed to take over the society and lead it down the road to respectability.

As the membership of the Mattachine Society waned, the Society for Individual Rights took over, established in San Francisco in 1965 with a more pro-active message. Its magazine

Vector promoted organized drives for voter registration and 'Candidates' Nights' in an attempt to get politicians to view the gay community as a political force. They also established a dialogue with the Police Department on its attitudes and policing of the gay community. 1965 also saw Konstantin Berlandt commence a series of articles in *The Daily Californian* student newspaper at Berkeley, the headline of the first being '2,700 Homosexuals at Cal'.

In 1961 Franklin Kameny started a Washington DC branch of Mattachine determined to pursue direct action. He rejected the integrationist policy in favour of the ethnic minority model of Harry Hays, and began to draw on the feminist and African-American civil rights experience. In 1964 Kameny took his beliefs to New York and made clear his views in a speech at the Mattachine Society convention. Revolted by the homophile search for the causes of homosexuality and their passive acceptance of the medical establishment's opinion that homosexuality was a mental sickness, Kameny asserted:

> We cannot ask for our rights from a position of inferiority, or from a position, shall I say, as less than *whole* human beings. I do not see the National Association for the Advancement of Coloured People, or the Congress on Racial Equality, worrying about which chromosome or gene produces black skin or about the possibility of bleaching the Negro. I do not see any great interest on the part of B'nai B'rith Anti-Defamation League in the possibility of solving the problems of anti-semitism by converting Jews to Christians . . . we are interested in obtaining rights for our respective minorities as Negroes, Jews and homosexuals. Why we are Negroes, Jews or homosexuals is totally irrelevant, and whether we can be changed to whites, Christians, or heterosexuals is equally irrelevant.[6]

In September of 1955 the women's homophile organization The Daughters of Bilitis was established by four lesbian couples in San Francisco, with Del Martin and Phyllis Lyon recognized for maintaining the society in its first few years, establishing and maintaining the magazine *The Ladder* with their own money and copy. It saw itself as a social club with the role of 'education of the variant, with particular emphasis on the psychological, physiological and sociological aspects to enable her to understand herself and make her adjustment to society in all its social, civic and economic implications.'[7] Barbara Gittings became New York President of the Daughters of Bilitis, and editor of *The Ladder*, which she used to champion a more militant position at odds with the founders. Meeting Kameny in 1963, she said that he was 'The first gay person I met who took firm, uncompromising positions about homosexuality and homosexuals' rights to be considered fully on a par with heterosexuals. He was more positive than any other gay activist on the scene.'[8] It was Frank Kameny who coined the phrase, 'Gay is Good'.

> Barbara Gittings: Psychiatrists were one of the three major groups that had their hands on us; they had a kind of control over our fate in the eyes of the public for a long time. Religion and the law were the other two groups that had their hands on us. So besides being sick, we were sinful and criminal. But the sickness label infected everything that we said, and made it difficult for us to gain credibility for anything. The sickness issue was paramount.[9]

The Counter-Psychiatry Group was one of the first groups to be formed in London GLF, and a great deal of GLF's political critique was developed within it. Among those with knowledge and experience were mental health nurses, as we saw above, and others who had considered subjecting themselves to aversion therapy.To the further benefit of the group and the movement as a whole, two of its members were not only qualified for the task of analysis, but committed socialists. Elizabeth Wilson and Mary McIntosh called the first meeting at their home in Haverstock Street, Islington. Wilson was a psychiatric social worker and knew from experience how heterosexist the psychiatric profession was. McIntosh was a sociologist and academic, who established the Leicester branch of the National Council for Racial Equality, and in 1968 published her influential article 'The Homosexual Role', which in addition to overthrowing psychiatry's obsession for discovering the causes of homosexuality, pinpointed the late-seventeenth, early-eighteenth century, when sodomites emerged as Mollies as the time when homosexuals first appeared in English history as a clear, distinct and identifiable minority.

The psychiatrist R D Laing in the sixties emphasized the importance of the role of society, as well as the family, in the development of mental illness; that individuals can often be put into impossible situations where they are unable to conform to the conflicting expectations of those dual pressures – leading to great mental distress. Laing thought that mental distress was a reasonable response to an unreasonable situation. He viewed psychopathology as being seated not in biological or psychic organs, but in the social cradle, the urban home, the web in which we are caught. That was at complete odds with the early-twentieth century opinion of sexologists, the medical establishment and police that we were sick and criminal, which the majority of us at some level had accepted because it suggested that we could not help ourselves, deserving pity rather than condemnation. With Laing's views bolstering the Counter-Psychiatry position that it was not us but society that was sick, GLF made a complete break with the medical view, its supporting institutions and the culture of gay martyrdom.

Elizabeth Wilson: We decided to go and spray the Tavistock [Clinic, where Laing had worked] which is actually where I was working at the time. So I stayed in the van, and I think I thought I can't do this, so that was Annie Brackx and Angie Weir mainly. Things were very fraught for me, I wasn't happy being a social worker anyway, and the atmosphere there ... it was more a women's issue than the gay issue; you assumed they didn't like gay people, that went without question, but they were so awful about women, they were so paternalistic and didn't think women should work. And the next morning I had to go in there, I was actually working in something called the Child Guidance Clinic, which was situated in the building but wasn't actually part of the Tav, and there was absolute mayhem. I can't believe how people could be so ... I was so naïve in a way, I couldn't believe people could care so much about this – it's amusing but they were going absolutely bonkers about it, and because psychiatry is such a long word when you're spraying, Angie had mis-spelt it, which was held against us. But it was very gratifying that everybody was so absolutely, so completely, sort of destroyed by this terrible, awful, awful thing that had happened. It was so terrible – 'That someone should have graffitied – Oh! The expense of getting it off, and the things they're saying – these people are mad!'[10]

The whole argument about homosexuality was the same: that originally it had appeared to be a move forward, that it was a product of your childhood rather than horribly sinful, but then the debate moved on to say it's not a sickness. So that was the central plank of the Counter-Psychiatry Group; that it was much worse for people to be sentenced to some sort of treatment rather than just be treated as a criminal, and in particular, there were horror stories about people being treated with electric shocks in aversion therapy. Someone came along to Counter-Psychiatry who had had aversion therapy, and it was still quite respectable, and one had to make an argument against it. I'll never forget Richard Dipple,

> who was one of our members, and somebody once said to him, 'Oh yes, I agree with you, there's nothing wrong with being a homosexual, it's just like having green hair or seven legs.'[11]

One of the attendees and long time members of the group had his own personal insights into aversion therapy.

> *Mickey Burbidge:* Aversion therapy, usually electric shock treatment was such a major issue because it was the publicly accepted way of dealing with homosexuality. I knew that I was gay in 1962 and decided that I didn't want to be. I read an article about a man who did aversion therapy for homosexuals and I wrote to him asking for therapy. He had a long waiting list, so nothing happened. Then I read a story in the paper about a man who had aversion therapy to make him fall out of love with the wrong woman and I suddenly realised that it was awful to think of switching off loving feelings by shock treatment. There had to be another way of dealing with it. That totally changed my mind and I decided that I wanted to be what I was, after all.[12]

The first thing the Counter-Psychiatry group did was to draw up a paper outlining their position and the issues they proposed to attack. Headed 'Interim Statement', it was handed out at the general meeting so that everyone in GLF was informed. One paragraph states:

> Psychiatrists themselves may not be aware that all their attempts to theorise about homosexuality are merely rationalisations: that they are simply reinforcing, under the guise of scientific objectivity, primitive Judeo-Christian morality. The only difference between now and then is that what was once regarded as a sin is today regarded as a sickness.[13]

That statement was soon to be proved in a challenge to Counter-Psychiatry, GLF and sexual minorities everywhere.

In the summer of 1970 a book was published in America that became a hardback No.1 best-seller. The author was Dr. David Reuben, and the title of his work, *Everything You Always Wanted To Know About Sex ... But Were Afraid To Ask.* In February 1971, Andrew Lumsden, who worked as a journalist on *The Times*, and first learnt of Gay Lib through that paper's reporting of the Highbury Fields Demo, was a member of Counter-Psychiatry. He discovered on the media grapevine that this book was to be published in London by W H Allen.

Gore Vidal reviewing the book wrote of Reuben, '[He] is a relentlessly cheery, often genuinely funny writer whose essential uncertainty about sex is betrayed by a manner which shifts in a very odd way from night club comedian to reform rabbi, touching en route almost every base except the scientific.'[14]

Reuben's style of writing consists of posing a question and answering it with trips into his own fantasy world to illuminate the point. Basically, everything in penis-vagina land is blessed. Every other form of sexuality is anathema, amusingly damned so as to titillate the sacred heterosexual and reassure them how much better off they are. To revive the dying embers of life-long monogamy he gives a psychiatrist's assurance that Sado-Masochist (S&M) practices are harmless indulgences for mature adult heterosexual couples. But for homosexuals it works like this:

> They specialise in luring homosexuals to their apartments, trapping them and torturing them. Fortunately the tortures are low-key and childish. Fear of arrest and punishment keeps them in line ... Occasionally the torturer gets carried away, the evening escalates and ends in mutilation, castration and death. Sadly, that's all part of the homosexual game.[15]

What do homosexuals actually do? [The first mention of

> homosexuality that male teenagers might read, says:] Because of the anatomical and physiological limitations involved, there are some formidable obstacles to overcome. Many homosexuals look upon this as a challenge and approach it with ingenuity and boundless energy. In the process they often transform themselves into part-time women. They don women's clothes, wear make-up, adopt feminine mannerisms and occasionally even try to rearrange their bodies along feminine lines.[16]
>
> Some gay guys write their telephone number on walls – in telephone booths, men's toilets, railway stations, anywhere other homosexuals pass ... They go home and wait for the phone to ring. It never takes very long. Another gay guy calls, they quickly exchange qualifications and make a date. A few minutes later there is a knock at the door, penises are produced, and another homosexual affair is concluded. Elapsed time from portal to portal, about six minutes.[17]

Dr. Reuben knows that the old jokes are best. He tells the story of a wise doctor who has seen it all before, and a trainee, who is shocked by his first experience of working the weekend night-shift in A & E and the sight of males bent double with pain, having to be helped up onto benches for examination. Sure enough, whisky glasses, torches and light bulbs are extracted from the patients' anuses; the torches are always lit, there is always light where no light should be. Reubens cannot resist the patriarchal temptation to be a nebbish.

According to this trickster, homosexuals are fascinated by food. Of the world's most famous chefs many are gay, and gays own the most famous restaurants. Homosexuals are also among the world's fattest people, though the reasons for that are too complicated to explain, he avers. Apparently the first problem for homosexuals wanting sex is lubrication, cooking grease, salad oil or margarine are preferred, but for gourmets the choice is butter or olive oil. A visit to the pantry produces carrots and cucumbers. Those who want to use their penis have to find an anus: 'Many look in the refrigerator. The most common masturbatory object for this purpose is a melon. Cantaloupe are usual, but where it is available papaya is popular.'[18]

What about Lesbians, Dr. Reuben? The problem is he doesn't know much about them, devoting just two-and-a-half pages to their existence in a chapter entitled 'Prostitution'. The agony of teenage girls does not trouble his malevolent derision:

> Since the majority of prostitutes are female homosexuals in their private life anyway, making it with another girl is like a bus man's holiday. Like their male counterparts, lesbians are handicapped by having only half the pieces in the anatomical jigsaw puzzle. Just as one penis plus one penis equals nothing so one vagina plus another vagina still equals nothing. All prostitutes have at least one thing in common—they hate men.[19]

Dr Reuben wants us to think he's a liberal. On abortion he writes: 'An African woman uses a stick ... her light skinned sister a coat hanger.'[20] As for the profiteers in human misery, 'Our old friend the coat hanger makes another appearance. After lying on the cupboard floor with muddy shoes for a year or two it does not exactly make the ideal surgical instrument. But among abortionists, who cares?'[21]

Not for this doctor the careful, empirical methodology of science when a sweeping generalization or a personal opinion will do: 'The bitterest argument between husband and wife is a passionate love sonnet, by comparison with a dialogue between a butch and his queen. Live together? Yes. Happily? Hardly.'[22] 'Orgasm among nymphomaniacs is as rare as orgasm among prostitutes'. Or doubtful statistics: 'Seventy to eighty per cent of Americans engage in fellatio and cunnilingus'.

The Counter-Psychiatry group prepared for a demonstration outside the offices of W H Allen, and called on Street Theatre for support. Andrew Lumsden wrote to the Managing Director the day before the protest. Here are two points:

> We are shocked to see a reputable publisher printing such pernicious and dangerous rubbish. The tone throughout is one of leering innuendo, the very tone of the 'locker room whispers' and sniggers you claim this book will end. We feel revulsion at Dr. Reuben's obvious contempt for those he claims he wishes to help.
>
> W.H. Allen is mistaken if they imagine that homosexuals are any longer a disorganized minority who can be insulted and vilified with impunity. We demand that this book be withdrawn from circulation immediately.

W H Allan & Co. Ltd replied in part:

> I am concerned of course, as far as I am able, to deal with the substance of your letter. You say that our claims for the book, which you describe as 'pernicious and dangerous rubbish', are unfounded. This is at most a matter of opinion. Personally, I feel strongly – and have some evidence to support my feeling – that the book serves a highly useful sex-educational function.
>
> What I will do – and gladly – is to show your comments to the author and ask him whether he wants to make any changes in a later edition.

The gentlemanly exchange of letters ceased, and a two page campaigning leaflet was printed for the demonstration:

An *Evening Standard* photograph showed Street Theatre at the protest.

> Members of the Gay Liberation Front – the civil rights group for homosexuals and lesbians – outside the office of W H Allen in Essex Street, Strand, demonstrating against the publication of a sex advice book … Mr Jeffrey Simmons, the firm's managing director, told them that he would approach author, Dr. David Reuben, about their feelings and ask him 'If he feels he wants to alter the book.'[23]

A photograph in *The Guardian* the next day shows in the background the large windows of the publishing house offices in front of which is Jeffrey Simmons open mouthed,

> … arguing with members of the Gay Liberation Front who protested in London yesterday about the firms publication of a sex manual. The delegation handed in to the firm's offices a letter objecting to the way homosexuality was treated in the book, which was written by an American psychiatrist. The letter was signed by 158 male and female homosexuals and is the work of the GLF.[24]

On the Saturday we leafleted Foyles and other bookshops in the Charing Cross Road.

Taking up the offer made by Jeffrey Simmons to send our objections to Dr. Reuben, the Counter-Psychiatry Group published a five page questionnaire for the General Meeting, giving us 35 statements from all sections of the book, out of which we had to choose 20 to be analyzed, and refuted. These were collected the following week and sent off to W H Allen. Nothing more was heard from them, of course.

In May the Counter-Psychiatry Group decided to hold a demonstration against the medical establishment. The group and many GLF members, about a hundred in all, met one lunchtime at the corner of Harley Street and Cavendish Square, together with Street Theatre.

> WE ACCUSE OF SLANDER THOSE PSYCHIATRISTS WHO CALL HOMOSEXUALS IMMATURE OR SICK. HOMOSEXUALITY IS NOT AN ILLNESS. IT IS NOT ARRESTED DEVELOPMENT. IT DOES NOT REQUIRE TREATMENT.
>
> Psychiatrists should not buttress the prejudices of a conformist society. They should, instead, support homosexuals in their battle to gain self-respect and freedom from guilt.
>
> 1. Check whether your own attitudes to homosexuality are rational.
> 2. Stop treating homosexuality with drugs, hormones, aversion therapy or analysis: stop treating homosexuality at all.
> 3. Campaign for sex education that deals truthfully with homosexuality.
> 4. Inform the public that homosexuality is as basic and as healthy a condition of existence for homosexuals as heterosexuality is for heterosexuals.
> 5. Send homosexuals to gay lib, stop growing rich out of their way of life.[25]

We were all a bit unnerved to find that the Harley Street pavements, doors and railings had been spray painted with 'Gay is Good' slogans, done by Aubrey Walter, Mick Belsten and Paul Theobald the previous night without telling us, which some thought a bit elitist. Their action certainly gave an edge to the demonstration.

Street Theatre dressed as doctors in white coats or patients in green gowns. Roger Carr had found some big old colanders onto which he'd fixed mattress springs. As GLF marched up Harley Street chanting, blowing whistles and handing out leaflets, the patients ran along behind them in terror, trying to hide in doorways or behind cars, hotly pursued by the doctors. Every patient caught had a colander placed on their head and would go into spasms from the electric shocks before collapsing to the ground with fake blood running from their mouths. The horns of the traffic jam brought faces to all the windows, and real doctors and nurses came out for a closer view, their faces a mixture of amusement, disbelief and contempt.

When they complained about the spray painting, we told them that that was just one of the prices they'd have to pay for treating us as sick human beings.

Chapter 4

Northern Exposure

> Agitators are an interfering set of meddling people, who come down to some perfectly contented class of the community and sow the seeds of discontent amongst them. That is the reason why agitators are so absolutely necessary.
> Oscar Wilde.

Jake Prescott and Ian Purdie were jointly charged with conspiracy to cause explosions likely to endanger life and cause serious injury to property between 30 July 1970 and 5 March 1971. Prescott alone faced three more charges concerning bombs: (1). causing an explosion at Monkeholt, Hadley Green on 12 January 1971; (2). the same on 20 November 1970 at Kensington Gore (The BBC Transmitter van); (3). on 9 December 1970 at the DEP. He also faced nine other charges concerning stolen cheque books and passing forged cheques. On the 22 April the committal hearings opened at Barnet Magistrates Court. The proceedings, spread over eleven days didn't finish until 27 May, when the magistrate, despite the paucity of evidence, took just 20 seconds to commit them to trial at the Old Bailey.

The day after our demonstration in Bow Street saw the death of the first British soldier in Northern Ireland. A month later the Government sent 1,800 more troops to the province. In response, the AB sent a note and a liquid bomb to *The Times*.

On the 1 May Biba the Department Store was bombed. Such a naff thing to do and a shame really – we all had some nice make-up and fabrics from there. The communiqué said:

> If you're not busy being born you're busy buying.
>
> All the sales girls in the flash boutiques are made to dress

> the same and have the same make-up, representing the 1940's. In fashion as in everything else, capitalism can only go backwards – they've nowhere to go – they're dead.
>
> The future is ours.
>
> Life is so boring there is nothing to do except spend all our wages on the latest skirt or shirt.
>
> Brothers and Sisters, what are your real desires?
>
> Sit in the drugstore, look distant, empty, bored, drinking some tasteless coffee? Or perhaps BLOW IT UP OR BURN IT DOWN. The only thing you can do with modern slave-houses – called boutiques – IS WRECK THEM. You can't reform profit capitalism and inhumanity. Just kick it till it breaks. Revolution. The Angry Brigade.

The message with its Situationist style text reveals the depth of anger that brought the AB to play with fire as the answer to their despair, a conclusion that would have appalled a real Situationist. Nevertheless, the Situationist communiqué agitating Biba consumers struck a chord with people living near the Bomb Squad headquarters, inspiring an authentic Situationist response.

> Forty girls and women from Barnet and north London schools, armed with stink bombs and flour, attacked Bus Stop, Biba and Mr. Freedom with count-down timing. Result: mass exodus of shoppers and a foul stench; followed by a *Communiqué* from the Slightly Annoyed Brigade, addressed to Fleet Street and Agitprop, saying, 'Just wait until we get Angry ...'[1]

Towards the end of May the computer rooms of Scotland Yard, British Rail and Rolls Royce were bombed. Agitprop bookshop, political information service, and community hub, was raided again. The AB Communiqué No. 5 stated: 'We are no mercenaries. We attack property not people.' And whatever one may think about the AB and their violence, it is important to remember that their way of operating was the opposite of British government policy.

Rehearsals for *Measure for Measure* went at a plodding pace. John Chesterman and friends, including myself, were turning up on Sunday afternoons for rehearsals after spending Saturday night on LSD or mescaline, and the grand house and garden in St. John's Wood had attracted visitors who came along just to hang out. Demonstrations like the one in Harley Street and against Reuben's book took time to arrange, and an ongoing protest against Wimpy Bars was being neglected because of the conflicting demands of Chesterman's production. I couldn't accept the situation any longer, and after talking to others I knew to be equally unhappy, we called a meeting to say that we were leaving to concentrate on street theatre. That spelt the end of the Theatre Group, and those who had bought the hype and thought they were on their way to a stage career, people like Michael Mason and Tarsus Sutton, were particularly bitter at what was termed our ego-tripping. The group tried to carry on, but within a fortnight or so the Steering Committee withdrew its support.

Chesterman and Winter saw things differently, blaming a poor rehearsal attended by Thelma Holt, the famous theatrical agent and Charles Marowitz's partner at the Open Space Theatre, as the reason for the failure. The truth is that neither Chesterman nor the Winter sisters had any idea of the enormity of scale, or the minute detail involved in producing a Shakespeare play. Led by Chesterman with his upper class ideas that anyone can do theatre because there is nothing to it, more people had again been taken up an empty, time-wasting dead-end. Chesterman was very good at the broad vision and what lay over the horizon, but his inability to grasp detail had badly let him down.

There was only one more attempt at a take-over of Street Theatre, which happened in August at the beginning of the planning stages for the demonstration against the Festival of Light. Chesterman, who by then had become the supremo of the Action Group, sent Denis Lemon his chief lieutenant to one of our Street Theatre meetings, now taking place in the GLF office situated in the basement of Housmans' bookshop at 5 Caledonian Road, King's Cross. Lemon came to tell us what the Action Group expected us to do. He was surprised to discover that we didn't take orders, but would discuss their 'request' and communicate our ideas just as quickly as we could. We told him we worked collectively as the best way forward for all of us in the group, and that we recognized the importance of the demo and were very keen to get it on. This was not music to Lemon's ear. It probably sounded like a petty quibble, but it was a line we maintained for the remainder of the collective's existence.

Chesterman didn't blame me for the collapse of *Measure for Measure*, so we continued to meet and rap out ideas. We were both still working, and with some cash to spare we were able to hire vans and take members to a series of meetings around the country.

By now there were GLF groups holding meetings in local pubs in Bath, Bristol and Cardiff, and others centred on local universities, like Brighton, Essex and Leeds. Leeds was one of the largest groups and organized the first GLF National Think-In so we could all make contact, exchange ideas and work out ways to co-ordinate our campaign strategies. Leeds also invited CHE. Originally the Committee for Homosexual Equality, they tellingly changed their name to Campaign for Homosexual Equality after the blatant appearance of GLF, but failed to re-examine their sixties policy of trying to influence change by standing backstage at Westminster, seeking legislators. GLF's rejection of parliament as a means to effect real change, its exploration of gay oppression, its insistence on coming out, its identification with the struggles of woman and other revolutionary groups was at polar opposites to CHE with its emphasis on respectable bourgeois values and demand for equality with the unequal. What Leeds GLF expected from this Clash of the Titans, this first meeting of these two opposed groups, I don't know, it was probably that in small cities people have to rub along together, and in Leeds CHE had more members than GLF, and Manchester had no GLF at all. Unsurprisingly it turned into a prickly confrontation.

On the Saturday morning Leeds GLF had arranged breakfast for everyone, laid out on the window ledges of the debating chamber at the university, and whilst we were munching away, Chesterman spotted some CHE types chatting up what looked like a journalist, so breakfast was hurriedly finished on the hoof as we made our way over. The greater part of the morning, once the setting up of a Northern News Sheet was agreed, was spent discussing ways of increasing the number of activists and how to appeal to the mass of homosexuals.

> It turned out that CHE were recruiting by advertising in newspapers. 'Are you ever banned,' asked GLF, 'Yes frequently. We have been thinking of complaining to the Press Council. Have we? No. We are going to complain. And we write to the newspapers several times, and sometimes they take notice.' 'We get our recruitment through action,' said GLF, 'when we started in London there was only a few of us, but after our first demonstration we had lots of people coming along'. CHE didn't think they attracted new members by action, 'Lots of people especially the middle-aged are frightened by action, it's not their fault; they are just conventional'. 'Yes', said GLF, 'we think there are lots of middle-aged gays out there who could spend the rest of their lives fearing exposure. The majority of men arrested in cottages are middle-aged. Did you know the Gay Guide to Europe lists more toilets as gay meeting places in London than any other continental city,' 'Maybe there are more cottages in London', suggested

> CHE. 'When we joined the TUC march in London against the Industrial Relations Bill, that showed where we were at, and brought people to us. And anyway it's more important to change the situation now so that young gays growing up have different attitudes, than to try and repair what's been done in the past', stated GLF. 'Exactly', responded CHE, 'that is why CHE is as necessary as GLF because we have different aims and can attract different people.' GLF pounced, 'It is not a question of attracting people. It's a question of attracting people who will Come Out!'
>
> 'You seem to think', said CHE, 'that the only way to Come Out is to wear a badge and militancy. I think it's down to each of us. From the age of sixteen it's been important to me not to hide it. I have told the people I live with, my parents, my friends, people at university, and if everyone did this there would be no need to Come Out.' 'If you can do that why don't you wear a badge?' 'I don't want to wear a badge.' 'But there's a basic fallacy here', countered GLF, 'to start with the people you have told are all those you had a prior relationship with. The issue is not whether your friends like you, but whether you have an acceptable position in the context of society.'[2]

Martin Stafford, the treasurer of CHE was the one who made the strongest attack on GLFs' position, whilst Warren Haig ridiculed the CHE policy of appealing to do-gooders and woolly-minded liberals. The arguments continued about coming out; criticism ran from complaints about conservative dress to long hair, freakish appearance, and hippie clothes with more point scoring, not just between the two camps but also between the GLF members, particularly Haig and Chesterman. 'The other major attack on the GLF slogan of "Say it loud. Gay is Proud" as being unsuitable for the average discreet middle class homosexual was rebuffed by Jeff Posner of Leeds GLF who felt an open proclamation could only have a liberating effect on the individual.'[3]

After a break for tea the two sides came together again. A woman from Manchester told of the *Rembrandt's* policy of running a men only bar. Various tactics and actions were discussed. The meeting also agreed to organize joint action on the heterosexual nature of sex education, books and publications. Gay Lib then announced that direct action was being planned against Dr. Reubens' book, which was shortly to be published in paperback, and invited CHE to join in. CHE refused to take part. Finally an agreement was reached to form a Liaison group with representatives from both organizations to try and work together where possible, and we agreed to disagree on the rest.

A party was held that night in the gay bar of the Great Northern Hotel. Chesterman and I hadn't been in there since 1960. How times had changed, they played music now and people were dancing to Tamla Motown. None of the London women had come to the Think-In except Lala, Louisa Hunt and Janet Phillips a straight friend of Chesterman's.

At about eleven o'clock the next morning the GLF convoy of cars and vans left Leeds and headed north for Edinburgh and the Traverse Theatre Club, where we were to attend what was called the Traverse Trials – debates held on a Sunday night on topical issues – organized by the theatre director Michael Rudman. The play that had been performed that afternoon was *Staircase* by Charles Dyer. Scotland was not included in the Homosexual Reform Act of 1967, and homosexuality there was still illegal.

Michael Rudman who met us on arrival had laid on drinks and a meal. Afterwards he took us down into the theatre where the platform was waiting to appear. We spread ourselves around the house, and then the doors opened and the place quickly filled to the rafters. Michael Rudman acted as Chair of the proceedings and announced that,

> This is another Traverse Trial. It divides itself into two sections. The first is as much like a trial as we can manage. We

> must entreat you to not interrupt until afterwards. Each advocate will introduce three witnesses, after which each witness is cross-examined by the other advocate. Finally they sum up and we take a vote. It sharpens the issues. Then we throw it open to questions and arguments. The motion is that all discrimination against homosexuals by law, by employers and by society at large, should end.[4]

The three witnesses for the motion were Ian Dunn – chair of the Scottish Minorities Group established in 1969 as a pressure group for the country's gay men, Tony Hughes of Edinburgh GLF and Louisa Hunt of London GLF. Against the motion were Councillor Antony Lester – an Edinburgh Conservative councillor, Dr. R.A. Parry – consultant psychologist at the Royal Edinburgh Hospital, and Prof. G.M. Carstairs – Professor of Psychiatry at Edinburgh University.

> The speeches of the witnesses for the proposal was listened to in polite silence which was shattered by Councillor Lester for the opposition who said, 'Homosexuality is a repugnant and undermining influence, particularly in these days when permissiveness is becoming the "in thing". It is corrupt and vicious and is undermining the root core of our society.' 'Right!' was the delighted reply from GLF. He continued, 'Perhaps I can be accused of prejudice, but prejudice after all is a basic emotion given to civilised people who rise above the beast, and it is by this emotion that we enjoy a higher standard of civilisation.' There was uproar throughout with loud bursts of laughter and rounds of applause. Dr. Parry took the predictable 'misery of homosexuals', line, 'With the increase in sexual permissiveness, all we have seen is an increase in national unhappiness. We have to seriously consider whether permissiveness does not stop here.' His colleague Prof. Carstairs played more sympathetic, he

claimed that he'd known other professors, clergymen and doctors who were homosexual, and he would not regard them as sick, adding, 'We saw in the play tonight, the longing that those two homosexuals had, and why they couldn't adopt a child.' 'Why not', shouted GLF. 'What a life that child would have had', he replied, 'with a bumbling womanish old queer, and another' – 'SHIT' replied Gay Lib, 'Right! Take that back! Withdraw that remark!'

When some order was restored the meeting was thrown open to the audience. Andrew Lumsden was on his feet. 'I want to object to "courtesy" and everything you have just said, and also to what you said about these people being a jury and listening to both sides of the case. This is a life and death matter to people who are homosexual. I am a member of the Gay Liberation Front ... Gay! We call it "gay" all over the world, and we object to the word faggot or queer, which were invented by people who don't like *me!* We don't like those words and we don't like this attitude of having a nice little liberal discussion and going away thinking it's alright: we voted in favour of it. Get on with it! Do something. Welcome homosexuality. It's not much in the population. Love it when it comes. Look at it. Greet it. Have homosexual children. You'll have a lot of heterosexual children anyway, so what have you to lose.'

A young Edinburgh man in his twenties stood up and told everyone that he was happily married with a two year old child and that he also enjoyed having sex with men. The only problem he had was that his wife's parents had found out and weren't speaking to him anymore. Bill Halstead pointed out that 'We've heard a lot of use of the word natural from these gentlemen, and I'd like to put the case that homosexuality is both unnatural and disruptive of society. Unnatural like houses, like culture ...' 'Like clothes', prompted Gay Lib. 'We heard that man talk about separating men from the beasts,'

Halstead continued, 'Beasts are heterosexual. They have to reproduce. It's what their sexuality is bound up with. But through history, evolution has allowed man to take himself away from nature and culture ... And he talked of protecting the family, the happy family where the women by the type of sexuality delineated for them, consider themselves dead objects by the time they are forty-five. A society whose sexuality is based on the aims of reproduction allows no alternative. That is why homosexuality is an advance on heterosexuality, in the same way that living in a house is an advance on living in a cave.'

'That typifies something that some people reproach against the GLF,' answered Dr. Parry, 'that they not only champion freedom from discrimination, but are actually saying, we are better than you – and someone up there said, "you persecute us and we'll persecute you."' 'He meant doctors', said Andrew.

Mick Belsten said, 'Look, I'm the eldest of nine children. I've had babies, plenty of babies. I don't want any more. I don't want any babies. I've a brother who's gay and a sister who's gay, and we're all very happy, and we don't want any kids. We're not missing out on a thing.' Aubrey Walter added, 'You say we miss out on things, and in a sense we do. Gay men give up the privilege of oppressing women.' Bette Bourne had a question, 'You have told us that the homosexual life is unfulfilling. Well I've fucked girls and I've fucked boys, and I know. How do you know, eh? How many boys have you fucked?' Councillor Lester was on his feet, 'What is repugnant to me is this statement here that this man had intercourse with a small boy.' 'He did not say that,' snapped Lala, 'he did not say he had intercourse with a small boy.' 'He did.' said the councillor. 'He did not,' said Lala, 'I trust that man enough to leave my son with him. He said he had intercourse with a boy, not a small boy. How could he have intercourse with a small boy? Show him your prick, man!' There was pandemonium. Councillor Lester, 'It was still a boy who came under the influence of this so called human being.' 'How dare you!' shouted Lala, [the only black person in the audience, as she moved towards the councillor] 'How dare you call my friend a so called human being! How dare you! I accuse you of not being a human being to say that! How can we be invited to an organisation that allows that man to say that?' The whole audience was now either shouting in protest, or laughing. GLF loudly, above the din, 'Why are you laughing?' to be answered, 'Because it's funny.' 'Is it so funny that we are angry,' GLF demanded; then answered themselves, 'It's funny if you don't have to live with it!' ... the shouting stopped and in the sudden silence a voice cried out, 'None of you have ever tasted bitterness.'[5]

The meeting ended in the small hours, going strong to the last. It is apparent that the public has not heard the last of gay people and their problems. It is also apparent that public silence has concealed a dramatic alteration in the way people are looking at their private lives.[6]

It was also in the early summer that the women's group began thinking of doing more actions on their own and decided a new name would make their position clear. 'Daughters of the Manifesto' was one of the suggestions before the clear winner was proposed.

Mary McIntosh: I remember Angie Weir suggesting that we call ourselves the Red Lesbian Brigade, and I was a bit shocked – it was a bit close to Angry Brigade. The group met in my flat in Arundel Square. It was very short-lived. It was just a meeting of the Women's group which decided to do some spray painting because we thought we should have some actions. We picked the name just in order to have a name and something challenging. I remember we spray painted the Maudsley Hospital over psychiatric treatment of gays[7]

Angie Weir: The Red Lesbian Brigade wasn't, really. Someone gave me a badge that said Red Lesbian. I remember we did a certain amount of spray painting.[8]

McIntosh: We painted the Stock Exchange, or as we called it, the Cock Exchange, that was what we picked, which was rather unfortunate because at the time it was in temporary buildings with hoardings up outside. We hadn't quite realized this, but hoardings proved very easy to spray on. I was doing the driving rather than the painting and we were pretty terrified.[9]

Across the front of the building they sprayed, Sod the Cock Brokers, accompanied by the intertwined symbols for women.

Obscene Slogans – Exchange is daubed over rights issue. There were fears today for security after a militant group daubed obscene slogans on the walls – under the noses of security guards. Two men and a woman – thought to be members of a group called Red Lesbians, drove past the guards in a green Morris Minor convertible. Then they walked past the main door of the building and sprayed slogans on the walls in three foot high red letters. They then painted an inverted sex symbol in black paint.

Security forces at the centre of Britain's financial world were checking to see if any attempt had been made to get into the building. The Red Lesbians are a militant breakaway group from the Gay Liberation Front – an organisation which wants social acceptance for homosexuals.[10]

Elizabeth Wilson: I always felt rather annoyed about the Stock Exchange zap because this woman turned up who was a journalist, a lesbian, and she really inveigled people into going and doing that, and of course it got into the papers. Marion and I and Angie and Mary, we went in Marion's ropey old van and we thought we'd all go down and spray paint the Maudsley, as being an oppressive institution, and I was actually a psychiatric social worker at the time so I was leading this completely schizophrenic life and we rattled down the Camberwell Road and we were stopped by the police, and we thought 'Oh! God, all those spray paint cans in the back and everything,' and they just said 'one of your wheels isn't quite right,' and they didn't look in the back or anything. So we carried on and sprayed the Maudsley. And once I remember a police car coming along when we were actually spray painting something and we weren't quite caught in the act, but we must have been looking terribly suspicious and they just slowed down and passed by.[11]

Dear Madam/Sir (are you sure?)
Further to our slogans painted outside, the enclosed explanatory material may be of interest to you. WE ARE NOT SICK - WE ARE NOT ABNORMAL - WE ARE NOT IMMATURE – Stop making a fat living out of saying we are. – WE ARE STRONG – WE ARE BEAUTIFUL – Power to the patients, we don't need you! In anger, Red Lesbian Brigade.

Alongside the item on the Stock Exchange raid, the *Evening News* reported: 'Lib girls go out with a Bang not a Wimpy', covering the story of Wembley Women's Lib storming a Wimpy Bar in Golders Green just after midnight, and insisting on being served a Wimpy and coffee. One of the ongoing campaigns of Women's Lib that GLF joined was against Wimpy Bars. A Wimpy was the English version of an American Hamburger, a mean, thin, grisly patty of dubious grey meat, topped with a teaspoonful of fried onions, served between two halves of a toasted bread bun. Tomato ketchup and Brown Sauce was provided, and it was presented with a portion of extruded potato-flour fries. The popularity of the Wimpy was that the Wimpy bar itself was open all night in some areas, and in others was open long after the fish and chip shops had closed.

'One of the very early first actions of Women's Lib,' said Angie Weir, 'was to occupy Wimpy Bars because no woman was allowed in after midnight as they were assumed to be prostitutes, and we had all these sit-ins in Wimpy Bars in Oxford Street.'[12]

There were at least ten joint demonstrations in London, and many more by Women's Lib against Wimpy House's policy of refusing service to unaccompanied women from midnight onwards. Actions commenced with leafleting and picketing and escalated to sit-ins. Letters were written to the head of Empire Catering protesting their policy, but the company hid behind the Late Night Refreshment Houses Act of 1969, claiming that they could be prosecuted for 'knowingly permitting prostitutes, thieves or drunken and disorderly persons to use their premises.' As Women's Lib pointed out, this was a strange interpretation of the law, implying that men are not prostitutes, thieves or drunk and disorderly. In the face of such weasel attitude, Women's Lib wrote to the head of Grand Metropolitan Hotels, owners not just of Empire Catering but also owners of Mecca who ran the Miss World Contest. But despite sending the letters by registered mail, they never received a reply.

Eventually on 7 October, the loss of business resulting from the campaign forced Empire Catering to call a meeting with members of Women's Liberation Workshop (WLW) to announce it was abandoning its policy 'of treating women as Cinderellas who turned into undesirables at the stroke of midnight.' According to a report in *The Times* the next day, Wimpy Bars alleged that five years earlier they had been prosecuted for serving food to a prostitute, which had formed the basis of the ban that was now lifted.

A few weeks after the visit to Leeds a request came from Allan Horsfall the long-time campaigner who in 1964 founded the North-West Homosexual Law Reform Committee out of the N.W. Homosexual Law Reform Society. In 1969 the group's name was changed to the Committee for Homosexual Equality, and then in 1971 as mentioned earlier, they substituted Campaign for Committee. Following on from the Leeds Think-In agreement to co-operate, Horsfall wrote to GLF asking us to support his plan to open a gay social club in Burnley by attending a public meeting at Burnley Central Library to discuss the project. Burnley was the first attempt by Horsfall to persuade CHE to open its own social clubs called *Esquire* throughout the country. He had found the ideal premises, a former Co-op restaurant, coming up for let and applied for the lease. Talks were completed and an agreement reached just before a local radio interview with one of his supporters, which alerted a Catholic and an Anglican priest to this new development in town. Joining forces, the priests called a hastily organized meeting, formed the Burnley and District Christian Group, and succeeded in forcing the Co-op to back down on its offer just hours before the lease was due to be signed. The Co-op was supported in its retraction by a motion from the Labour controlled Council who also petitioned the chief constable of Lancashire, warning him of the threat to extend dangerously, and unnecessarily, the limits of an encroaching permissive society.

'A weekend in the country?' – 'What could be better?' 'Another little demo on the side?' – 'Perfect.' We whizzed up the motorway and found about 300 people meeting in a large room of the Art Deco Burnley Public Library. On the platform with the novelist Ray Gosling as chairman sat NCCL officer Ivan Limmer, Ken Pilling – chairman of the committee for the proposed club, and Manchester University lecturer and member of CHE executive committee Michael Steed. The town's senior policeman was in the audience, town councillors were dotted about and so were several JP's, one of whom found himself sitting among twenty or so members of GLF. There were also two clergy present, a subdued band of skinheads and a hall full of curious citizens.

Limmer in his opening remarks said: 'It is a general principle that any group of people meeting together to do something that is not against the law should have the right to do so. Using pressures to repress minorities is the way Fascism starts.'[13] The issue had raged with passion and bristling hostility for some time, so the opening remarks were completely ignored by both sides; this was the first direct confrontation between the entrenched protagonists and a great slanging match immediately broke out. When some order was restored to the hall, others on the platform made their own impassioned attacks on the unchristian, illogical and illegal activities of those opposing the opening of the club. 'Pilling accused Alderman Tom Gallagher, leader of Burnley Council, of inciting local youth to violence against homosexuals when he said that skinheads would come to the club and attack its members.'[14] He also refuted Alderman Gallagher's claim to be speaking on behalf of 90 percent of Burnley's ratepayers in opposing the club.

Supporting the platform, several townsfolk spoke of the shame they felt at the unkindness of their fellow citizens. Pilling then claimed that the opposition was whipped up by the local Roman Catholic Church, and said that Father Neville's so-called Christian group were an unrepresentative minority. The meeting boiled over again, arguments were interrupted, debate descended into epithets and insults: 'misuse of sexual appetite', 'disgusting', 'perverted' were heard above the clamour, all interspersed with 'Sit down Fascist,' and 'You're going to have trouble in Heaven, man,' and lots of play on 'the smallest minority of all' – self imposed celibates, until Andrew Lumsden intervened in the only way possible by asking every homosexual in the meeting to stand up. At least a quarter of the audience did so with sobering effect.

But the two clergy who had formed the Burnley & District Christian group aroused the greatest dissention, and even the chair had to complain about too much 'priest bating' from the floor. The Roman Catholic priest as spokesman for the Christian group denied stirring up opposition, and using the oldest ploy in the book claimed that the protest arose out of immediate action by a group of women, and it was the women's agitation which resulted in the formation of the committee. He stressed of course, that it was the club and not homosexuals that he was against. 'I have fought just as hard for homosexual rights on other occasions, but a true homosexual wants integration and to take part in the normal community facilities.'[15] A remark which met with feigned laughter, jeering and further uproar.

The most valuable contributions were from the people of Burnley who attacked the hypocrisy of the authorities and declared their own feelings of a need for a proper meeting place. One young gay man stated that he had tried three times to commit suicide.

> One woman declared it would be a good thing for her children to meet gay people, and if they turned out gay themselves to be able to get it together with people in a place where they could feel fine and be themselves. This is the crux of the importance of the Burnley fiasco. It does not represent a struggle against the roots of sexism, but is the first stage in what for most provincial gay people is a struggle for the elementary needs for survival.[16]

No motion was put, but it was clear, despite the police, the councillors and the Christian Groups' claim that most people were against the club opening, that the majority in the hall, like the majority who had written to the local paper, were in favour.

'Asked if he was happy with the results so far, the priest replied, "Only public opinion could have stopped the club opening." The group will stay in existence to counter any further moves to get premises.'[17] Just before we left the hall that evening, the police outside swooped on the skinheads and took away the umbrellas they were clutching.

In spite of threats by CHE to put up independent candidates at the next council election with the aim of making their main policy the right to open a gay club, the Co-op Society would not change their minds about the lease, and the campaign in Burnley failed. Moreover, the Co-op with its origins in socialism and connection to the Labour Party turned vindictive, and gave instructions to all branches not to let out empty properties to homosexual organizations. Subsequently the *Esquire Club* initiative failed countrywide, and the report in the CHE Bulletin of the public meeting at Burnley makes no mention of GLF support.

About three weeks after the event, the *Daily Mirror*, owned by ex-MP Robert Maxwell, fraudster and millionaire running a newspaper designed for consumption by the working class, ran a story on the Burnley meeting by journalist Colin Dunne. Dunne attempts to treat it as a wildly funny farce in which 'the citizens came out branded as Fascist pigs,' GLF were all nancy-boys, while the bigoted Frederick Evans, secretary of the Christian group, appears as a knight on a white charger, and the skinheads are credited with good behaviour and a sense of humour when they 'restricted themselves to a sly "Whoops, dearie" when the police weren't looking.'[18]

Considering the censorship when the subject is mentioned, and the corrosive reflux of bile that jets from every newspaper in Fleet Street when writing about homosexuality, it was surprising that GLF hadn't demonstrated against their institutionalized mania before the 19 August Fleet Street Demo. The leaflet produced for the protest was addressed to all newspaper workers:

GAY LIBERATION FRONT IS ALIVE AND WELL, AND WE WISH WE COULD THANK YOU FOR IT, BUT WE CAN'T. BECAUSE THE PAPER YOU WORK FOR DOES ITS BEST TO PUT US DOWN.

Here are a few recent examples:

What pansies want is a lecture on self discipline ... these creatures who children should be warned against (*News of The World*)

It is editorial policy never to write about GLF (*Sun*) nor to accept any advertisement containing the word Gay (IPC)

No letter mentioning homosexuality may be discussed on the advice page (*Sun)*

Aristocracy pervaded with fornication, sodomy and drunkenness (*Morning Star*)

The Times and *Guardian* frequently print without comment items on 'chemical castration'. They don't print without insulting comment any activity of GLF, nor report on the work of the Counter-Psychiatry Group.

Spectator published celebrations of Noel Coward's death.

In spite of this revolting nonsense, we are glad to be gay and nothing will alter that. But many of our sisters and brothers are very isolated, and they are especially harmed by the press.

DO YOU REALLY WANT GAY PEOPLE TO BE DESCRIBED IN THESE WAYS?

'Is that how you feel about your gay colleagues, your gay daughters and sons, your gay brothers, sisters, aunts, uncles, neighbours?

'We think you could help to change the way the press insults and abuses all gay people.

By challenging the instruction. By asking why. By complaining to union or management. By getting something favourable published. By not using gay to abuse, humiliate, insult.

There are many ways you can help. Here is one way a group of workers did help:

Labourers today banned all work on the half-finished university at Sydney because a student was expelled when he said he was a practicing homosexual (*Evening Standard* June 2nd)

We're not asking you to risk your jobs. Just to think about it and do what you can.

We try to think about your problems, especially those of your work. GLF has always supported your struggles against management. We marched with you against the Industrial Relations Bill.

We'd like you to think about us. London Gay Liberation Front.[19]

John Norman Lloyd: There was a decision we would have a demonstration in Fleet Street. There was something that the *Mirror* printed, I believe, that triggered it. It wasn't that well organized, I don't think. Anyway, I was to produce some placards and there was the Action Group which met in the GLF office to produce these placards, and I think ... some of the things on the placard were rather fey, things like Gay is Beautiful, or gay is something like that, and somebody said, 'No! Let's say Gay is Angry.' So we made all these placards and Andrew Lumsden was going to produce the hand-out which we would take to each paper and put on their desk for the editor. It was a Press Release. We were to rendezvous on the steps of St. Paul's. Glenys Parry was there; Angie Weir and Aubrey. Denis Lemon and Michael James were there, I remember because I went to the office to collect the placards and Michael was there, and Denis turned up and I think it was the first time I'd seen him, and he said he was going to demonstrate and we'd get there by taxi. So we all got in a taxi and I was the one who was working so I was the one who

> paid, and I think Denis said it was the first demonstration he'd been on.
>
> There were about thirty people who turned up, and we walked down Ludgate Hill and up Fleet Street shouting, and the police arrived and they weren't too heavy. We marched into every newspaper office in the street, chanting and waving placards and we went down Bovary Street where the *News of the World* was, and spent some time there with people shouting 'News of the Screws.' Now the *Mirror* is not in Fleet Street but in Holborn Circus so we trudged round there and we got in the building shouting, and handed in the press release and someone at the desk said, 'Hang on, why are you doing this?' And we said, 'Because the *Mirror* printed this article about us.' So they said, would we like to send a delegation up to see somebody, not Capt. Bob by the way, so a few of us went up. I went up and Glenys Parry went up and she did all the talking. And they were quite – they were okay – whether it made any impression: it must have made some impression. Then we took a taxi back and the whole thing was about an hour and a half – two hours. I'm not sure what publicity it got, but for the people involved in it – it was evolving in the right direction.[20]

Around this time I had the idea of advertising Gay Lib with a sticker displayed in cottages. My design included an official looking crown I placed above the warning 'Police Entrapment Practised Here', and below that in smaller type, Gay Liberation Front. Chesterman liked the idea and arranged the printing. Michael Mason, owner and editor of *Capital Gay,* appears to have got it all wrong in 1995 when he claimed, 'The police entrapment sticker was produced with the idea of deterring cottagers, not protecting them. Cottaging was objected to because objectification was a big sin, as was, "owning" someone, i.e. monogamy or coupledom.'[21]

Trying to stop cottaging? What a futile campaign that would have been. It suggests GLF was out of touch with the real world. In fact there was no line on cottaging; a male activity in a male dominated movement: no man was going to limit himself by banning it. The problem was not about cottaging, it was about the number of talks *on* cottaging that certain uptight men were having at the General Meeting. It was a subject entirely without interest to the women, yet one that was being continually inflicted on them. The reoccurring discussions endlessly churning the matter was a refusal by those men to regard and respect a very basic difference in sexuality between women and themselves.

Michael Mason making nonsense out of GLF ideas makes me think he is trying to cover-up the women's criticism of the cottaging debate, and disguise a gay misogyny fuelled by fears that lesbians were attacking gay men's sexual behaviour. The cottage, a symbol of rampant encounter for an urgent male sexuality, became a very sore point in relations between gay women and conservative gay men.

GLF did condemn compulsive monogamy however. Problems with couples were encountered in consciousness-raising groups when participants faced questions of clarification about their sexual experiences, difficulties and fears. With couples it's automatic for one partner to come to the rescue of the other who refuses to consider alternative interpretations to personal problems. Couples begin to police each other's responses, bat away questions and attempt to dominate the group to protect their joint mythology. The distrust of couples in awareness groups spread out into the movement where some exclusive couples felt challenged because the more radical couples had decided to put their own relationships under the microscope, looking for reasons for possessive behaviour they wished to overthrow. Some of these couples had already decided that monogamy didn't work, and reached an understanding that the best way to protect their relationship was to have an open one that celebrated man's sexually promiscuous nature. They were trying to move away from the heterosexual model of monogamy, which for gays seemed an eminently sensible thing to attempt.

In a society ruled by the fetishized object, sexual roles modelled on the dominant images supporting the hierarchy of power are reified, and the stereotypes fetishized. But unlike the social stereotypes dominating the economic and cultural hierarchy of power, sexual stereotypes have no power over us unless we find them attractive to what we feel in ourselves to be sexy. If they fail to arouse us then those images are nothing, or nothing more than an irritation or a joke feeding off a sense of order. This sense of order was I think behind the condemnation of sexual objectification that radiated from Counter-Psychiatry and some awareness groups that encapsulated it as 'those elements in homosexual life which above all create and sustain the role-playing that cripples the ability to form balanced relationships and that destroy the emotions in wasteful fantasy.[22]

This condemnation can also be seen as a call for sex to be more playful, an eroticising of the whole body instead of concentrating on the penis. As this questioning of sexual role play spread through the movement, some men tried to break down their role-playing by switching roles, others attempted to give them up, and although these tactics may not have worked in the end, the experiment confirmed their real desires. Some on the left chose to condemn fucking. A cat never allowed out of the flat of one set of Marxist-Leninists men, escaped one day for a few hours. Nine weeks later the sky fell in. 'Our cat's been raped – Raped!' they cried, 'Males! All they can think of is penetrative sex.'

I think most gay men, women and queens are fundamentally circumspect about the sex roles they inhabit and are able to hold them at arm's length, putting distance between the role and the self: a space of free play that can be filled with humour. Roles are also a disguise and 'a man is never more true to himself than when he is wearing a mask.'[23] Once we can see that all roles are ridiculous, I think we are on the road to transcending their power, discovering our real desires and fulfilling our humanity.

Chapter 5

The Permissive Society and its Enemies

> There is more to be learned from wearing a dress for a day, than there is from wearing a suit for a lifetime.
> Larry Mitchell, *The Faggots & Their Friends Between Revolutions.*[1]

What was gay in my thinking and what was straight – I for one, wanted to find out. If my sex roles were fixed, my gender role obviously wasn't, so it seemed that the best thing I could do would be to follow the line of least resistance and see where that led me. It wasn't long before I began to meet others who were having similar thoughts.

Walking down Portobello market one Saturday in the early summer I saw Charlie Pig from the Street Theatre Group ahead of me. He was wearing a blouse, an ankle length denim skirt, and sandals. As I got closer I had a strange feeling that this was going to be another coming out moment. Reaching him I saw that he'd completed his look by painting his eyes with kohl and purple eye-shadow. He looked great. We kissed and sauntered on together. I was bowled over by his nerve, but as we chatted, I felt a rising sense of panic at the reaction he was receiving from the crowd, which I was catching in their second glance. I began to feel embarrassed by association, the force of which shocked me, and I tried to cover it up by redoubling my efforts to appear cool and calm. At the same time another part of me was appalled and disgusted with my reactions. When we went our separate ways at the bottom of the hill, I was left with a great deal to think about.

The distressing feelings generated by that encounter left me surprised and sad. I couldn't go on with my Gay Lib ideas and then react like that to a friend and brother, who had simply got out of bed that morning at Lala's, and not having any clean clothes of his own to put on, wore some of hers instead. What was I to do? Dressing up in drag in Street Theatre had not been a problem – that was larking about – but going out on my own in drag, that was serious and scary. That was right up against all those beliefs implanted in me when I was growing up. And yet it made things crystal clear. I thought about my first sight of drag queens in 1962, a dozen of them in stylish coats and hats sitting around a table in the forecourt of a pub on Albert Road Silvertown, beneath the George V Graving Dock wall, the scene backlit by the lights of the cargo ships moored in the basin above – all looking relaxed and enjoying their night out, and my thinking that they're the real basis on which our lives are built. I reminded myself that I laughed at one of the GLF Demands – the right to hold hands in public – because I had been doing that already with my boyfriends, admittedly only around the King's Road in the late-sixties, and how I had enjoyed making the point to people on the street. And I remembered being at a public dance in 1961 in south London and dancing openly with my boyfriend of the time, and apart from an initial frisson, the atmosphere picked up and everyone started beaming. I also knew that no amount of thinking or talking was going to get rid of fears buried deep within, and recalled, perhaps a Jungian idea I read somewhere, that if you can't get over a thing, then the only other way is to go through it. So I stepped into the looking glass and emerged in a puff of smoke, with eye-make-up, varnished nails, and a more androgynous look to go with my long hair.

Up until then, on the streets, on public transport, in the shops, if people spotted your GLF Badge and asked what it meant, the explanation always tended to be in terms of a movement, a joining together, the demand for an end to discrimination against us, a fighting for our rights. Sarah Grimes: 'Once when I was on the Tube a man sitting opposite to me said, "You're wearing a gay badge but you look depressed! Cheer Up."'

My new appearance said it all. On stepping out of the door it was, 'Hey Man! Why are you wearing make-up?' I quickly learnt to respond with, 'Hey Man! Why are you not wearing make-up?' It was immediate, personal and confrontational. Even among some friends, but especially with many of the men in the movement, the change of appearance was even more challenging, and their reactions were more aggressive and complex. Every man in GLF when confronted by a man in make-up or drag had to ask themselves why they rejected the challenge of a gender-bending experiment. It called into question their gender stereotyping, ideals of masculinity, male superiority and self-repression that had been troubling me.

Within Gay Lib it would seem that I had gone from coming out, to transgressing to far out. I was no longer a gay man but had transformed myself into a stereotype fairy, faggot, transvestite, a thing to be avoided. I found myself being patronized, treated as second rate, that what I had to say was not important, of no interest. I wasn't even listened to. I began to realize that I was being treated the way a heterosexual male treats a homosexual, but now by gay men, who like all gay men, must have experienced the same attitudes from straight men at least once in their lives already. I had presented myself wearing make-up, looking a bit femme, and was now being treated as inferior, not because I wanted that, but because from my appearance they thought I was asking for it. And because that excuse made it convenient for them to patronize me, they did so. I had become one less man, one less rival to worry about. It was then that I realized the positive to these situations: the chance to feel, through their negation, what it might be like to be a woman in such encounters. That perhaps these experiences were an indication that this was the right direction towards comprehending and maybe even breaking down my gendered thinking.

What I slowly began to understand over the following months was that there were large numbers of gay men who were not prepared, or felt themselves unable to question their personal ideals of masculinity. Sincere as they were in looking for change, they sought it by challenging the prejudices of straight society, believing that therein lay the whole of their oppression. They refused to accept that society's repression of homosexuality, through its constant re-enforcement in all areas of our lives, was ultimately internalized and became self-oppression. They refused to see that their ideals of masculinity were heterosexist because they knew themselves to be homosexual. This denial of self-oppression allowed them to ignore their male superiority and blinded them to the alternative, the feminist point of view. Consequently for them, the struggle was a simple matter of civil liberties. That there would be no gay liberation without women's liberation was therefore a revolutionary idea they could not comprehend, and so could not consciously work towards, no matter the lip service they gave to the axiom.

In an article written just over a year after GLF started, Jill Tweedy of the *Guardian* arrived at the following when meditating on the homosexuals' perception of the heterosexuals' masculine role:

> Because homosexual men do not play out the normal 'masculine' role they are forced to question the results that come of heterosexual males playing heterosexual male roles and they see, more clearly than most, the shortcomings, the disadvantages, the downright tragedies brought about by social ideals of 'masculinity'. They develop willy-nilly, an understanding of how women are oppressed by such males, they have recognized (through their own initial mistreatment of their gay sister) the same tendencies in themselves and have become concerned to root them out.[2]

Jill Tweedy's reading is only faulted because she saw all gay men in the movement as one. What was beginning to appear were two kinds of men: those who stubbornly ignored their oppressive behaviour towards women and those who wanted to rid themselves of such behaviour.

Not conforming to my stereotype appearance inevitably led to further problems: I was accused of being aggressive and violent. One of the main prejudices held by gay men against drag queens and lesbians is that they are violent. But anyone who knows drag queens or lesbians can see that they never go out looking for trouble, because they know that in a conflict no one will support them and that in most senses they have everything to lose.

I was being neither aggressive nor violent, but I could see my presence did engender that in others, which they in turn perceived as their own reaction to my alleged violence. It was as though I had become a blank canvas onto which they painted their picture of me, one based not on life and observation, but copied from their tainted idea of the effeminate. There was a total refusal to see their own attitude as at all sexist, or that they should question their way of thinking. Their defence against self-examination was to turn the argument round and claim it was me who was sexist because I had turned myself into a sex object, ignoring of course their own consciously crafted image.

I began to think of these reactionaries with their heterosexist ideal of masculinity as the straight-gays. If I stood among them in a room or pub, no matter how packed in we might have been, there was always a clear space at least two foot wide all the way around me, and wherever I moved that space moved with me.

At the beginning of April the LSE gave notice to GLF that we could no longer meet on their premises. Andrew Lumsden, who was a member of the Steering Committee, found himself with the job of finding a new home. He fortunately knew Anthony Blond, the publisher who casually mentioned that he'd taken a lease on a property in Covent Garden that had been a famous night club, and maybe he could swing something, but as usual with those kinds of conversations nothing definite was fixed. Then came the last meeting of GLF at the LSE, and Lumsden had to say something, so he coolly announced, without having the owner's permission, that the General Meeting the following week would be at *Middle Earth*, 46 King Street, Covent Garden. And it was as though the waiting was down to the wire. Lumsden had the keys to the basement, half nightclub, half cavernous building site, given to him just two hours before four hundred gays came looking for their new home.

One new member to arrive for the first meeting at *Middle Earth* was Michael James, who stood in the street confused by the address he'd been given, turning out to be a building site, until he saw a man in a green velvet suit, and watched Bette Bourne, whom he recognized, negotiate his way around piles of sand, cross some planks and disappear down a tunnel. Assurance restored James followed suit.

> *Michael James*: It was quite a silly evening, going into this place with no light, it was like a gloomy cave. It was all pillars and things and there was some sort of meeting being convened down the end, it was like a set for *Phantom of the Opera* really. There was a little blue light down the end and there was Carla and Warren Haig and someone else, Aubrey probably. I lurked behind a pillar and then at one stage they said, 'We're going to have a newcomers meeting, so anybody that's here for the first time, come along,' so I went into this other room. The place was like a big room with coal bunkers, but divided by very wide [half] walls. There was Warren Haig standing in the middle of this maze-like pattern of coal bunkers and we were all standing with this big gulf in between us. He gave us this political harangue and I guess with everything that I had gone through, the arrest and everything, it just all suddenly fell into place.
>
> It was the road to Damascus experience. I just saw it in my head, I'd never had drugs or anything, but I was so excited and so attracted by this … I couldn't wait for the following

> week, to see all these wonderful lesbians and gay men again. And the following week I didn't wear a suit, I wore some jeans ... it was obvious it was a whole new fashion look. They asked for volunteers to do the teas in meetings so, as I had a café, it was straight up my street and I volunteered ... but I guess I didn't want to be a tea-lady all my life and I got into the Media Workshop.[3]

A few weeks later I saw Michael James for the first time as he was serving tea from the kitchen in *Middle Earth* assisted by Bette Bourne; they had some kind of routine going and were having a laugh in the middle of all the serious political stuff. Then I saw James working in an antiques shop at World's End, just round the corner from my squat in a block known to local queens as Gibraltar because of the number of Spanish restaurant workers living there. One day when I passed the shop James was there alone, so I popped in to say Hi, and we immediately clicked. So much so that within a week he'd flitted from Lots Road where a summons for an unpaid fine for soliciting in Half Moon Street Piccadilly was due, and installed himself in my spare bedroom. Also living with me was Nicholas Bramble who I'd only met the month before when he came to a Street Theatre meeting. James soon took us to visit his friends Peter Flannery and Mick Belsten, who had a first floor flat in a house surrounded by gardens, near the river in Barnes.

After Chesterman and I returned from Burnley, I spent the rest of the summer with Michael James going to Barnes once or twice a week at least. Bette Bourne was often there, sometimes with Rex Lay, and there was Gordon Howie, Frank O'Looney and Roger Carr, John Church, Andrew Lumsden, Nicholas Bramble and many other visitors, including Mick Belsen's gay brother and his lover. All of us were queens. There was a marvellous cross fertilization of all our different interests and involvements in the movement, as the weed expanded our minds, deepened our focus and tickled our funny-bones. The Media Workshop collective met at the flat, and Belsten for our benefit, would analyze the politics of all the different left-wing participants pushing their agendas. He would mull over the politics of Warren Haig, the Canadian activist previously involved with gay groups in North America. Haig's counter-cultural ideas combined with a talent for oratory, thinking on his feet, and sensitivity to his audience made him the dominant speaker at the Wednesday meetings. Haig was a gay hippie whose great concern was liberation, and the first eloquent counter-culture figure to state that gay liberation was as much for the individual as it was for the masses. That notion infuriated the Marxists and Maoists at one general meeting, who claimed it would be two hundred years before individual liberation could even be attempted. Replying, Haig wagged his finger at the organized left on the steering committee, accusing them of devious manipulations, before turning round and warning the rest of us against the red menace. Haig was labelled the ego-tripping super-star by the left-wing wannabe ego-tripping superstars who wilted in his shade.

We talked too about that Maoist's claim. Why wait 200 years? Why couldn't we start now we asked each other; why do we have to sacrifice our own attempts for some queens in the future; who may or may not be in a better position than we are? We understood that liberation meant the liberation of all, but that had to start some time, and it had to start with a group, somewhere or other. Why sit around waiting for everybody else to catch on, that would be a waste, and what was the movement to do for the next two centuries when the ground was being ploughed now? Was our new desire to look for our own liberation, in leftie language elitist and vanguardist, individualistic and purely selfish? Most definitely yes, would be the answer of those organized around an ideology who felt that their authority, their way of thinking was threatened by former street and bar queens. Was that the Marxist plan, to turn Gay Lib into a disciplined party that would put the lid on liberation until they decided that the conditions were right, then take their shiny new theory to the IS and spend years trying to tell a bunch of programmed heterosexuals that we gays had the answer? What a disaster that would be, spying, policing, judging, ensuring members toed the line, in a word – tribalism. No, Gay Lib started after two individuals, Bob Mellors and Aubrey Walter, had been out in the world informing themselves, and acting out of instinct as much as forethought, called a meeting. 'Put some music on darling, call me selfish if you like, but I'd love to hear Janis Joplin sing "Get it while you can."'

I remember arriving at Barnes one evening, just after their consciousness-raising group had finished meeting. Peter Flannery opened the door for me and apologized all the way upstairs for the state of the flat. When I reached the top I could see why. Apart from a pathway from the kitchen through the living room to the bedroom beyond, the floor was covered in Porn magazines. Flannery explained, 'We were just having a last look before we burn it all.'

> *Lumsden*: I first took acid with someone after we'd gone to the Royal Court Theatre to see a play and we were in a taxi going back to Barnes where Peter Flannery and Mick Belsten lived. He said, 'Try this.' We got back to the flat in Barnes, which was like the first salvo of what became 7a [the radical drag commune], it was very similar inside in atmosphere.
>
> So everybody was lying around and then a French deserter came to the house, just at the point when everybody was simultaneously peaking. I didn't know the ins and outs of it – I was told there was an underground railway for deserters from various armies and this was one of the safe houses. And that evening, Peter Flannery had decided that if he took some shaving foam and piled it on the top of his head, he could shape it like Marie Antoinette's hairdo. He'd got it about a foot

> in the air and spectacularly shaped – he was a big man anyway – and we suddenly became conscious that the doorbell was going.
>
> As anyone who's been in the middle of an acid party knows, getting to a front door downstairs is a tremendous difficulty. Peter finally managed to get a dressing gown, some flamboyant silk thing, round him and got down the stairs and even remembered when he got to the bottom of the stairs, why he was going to the bottom of the stairs, which was also often a problem. And he opened the door. And this French deserter, who did spend the evening with us, who was a little late adolescent with no English, was confronted on the doorstep by an enormous drag queen in a Chinese silk dressing gown and a high coiffure of shaving foam.
>
> Also of course, when you're on acid if you do manage to get something together you're very punctilious about it. I could just hear Peter saying to this young man as he walked him up the stairs, 'Mind your footing, that stair there isn't all the good. Have I asked you if you'd like a cup of tea? Oh no, you can't speak any English, can you?' and so it went on. And I had enough French to have been able to say something to him, only I found that I couldn't remember any French at that particular point, at all. So this unfortunate man spent the evening with a lot of people tripping. Maybe he knew, but if he didn't he must have thought the English were just as eccentric as all the French had always said we were.[4]

For all of us, Mick Belsten and Peter Flannery's flat in Barnes became our melting pot. Over the summer our friendships matured through the conversations we had about our lives and experiences before coming out and since. Looking back, I can see I was moving away from the big picture and the grand visions of what gay liberation could be, to the more personal situations I found myself in. Belsten's socialism and our shared counter-cultural ideas supported, illuminated and warmed our relationships.

British Imperialism was in retreat. Sensing its weakening power, and fearful of losing control, it began to flail its subjects. 1968 was a pivotal year. Catholics in Northern Ireland protesting against discrimination in education, housing and jobs by the Protestant majority resulted in the Government's criminally insane decision to send troops to the province, arm protestant loyalists and instigate a vicious, sectarian dirty war in order to quell a few hundred civil rights protesters. Its support of America's war in Vietnam had it unleash terrible police violence on anti-war protesters trapped in Grosvenor Square. A generation of youthful dissidents inspired by new ideas of freedom and social justice were being brutalized. For conservative reactionaries, the permissive society became the scapegoat for every misfortune that besieged the nation.

In May 1970 *Oz* magazine presented a bare and shameless cheek to authority. Spread over its pages was the thinking and artwork that came from the unprompted minds of schoolchildren given a chance to show-off work usually confined to the back of the classroom, but thanks to *Oz* 'The Schoolkids Issue' circulated all over the country.

Smarting from criticism that *Oz* had lost touch with youth, the editors Richard Neville, Jim Anderson, and Felix Dennis advertised an invitation for school 'kids' to edit a run of the magazine which became *Oz* 28. About 20 students aged between 14 and 18 answered the call, The most salient and salacious piece in the production was a cartoon depicting a sexually rampant Rupert Bear, created by 15 year old Vivian Berger, who stuck the head of Rupert onto the body of a cartoon character by Robert Crum, a misogynist cartoonist and favourite of the underground press, making it appear as if Rupert is raping Gypsy Granny, who looks to be enjoying the experience. The issue also featured articles on corporal punishment, school exams, drug use, sexual freedom and pop music. The cover was a drawing of two naked women with their genitals artistically hidden.

The police raids on *Oz* were headed by Det. Inspector Frederick Luff using the same archaic conspiracy laws he utilized when leading the raids and prosecution of *IT*. The editors were charged with 'conspiring with other young persons to produce a magazine containing obscene, lewd and indecent and sexually perverted articles, cartoons and drawings with intent to debauch and corrupt the morals of children and other young persons and to arouse and implant in their minds lustful and perverted ideas.'[5]

The case came up at the Central Criminal Court on 22 June 1971 before Judge Argyle. John Lennon and Yoko Ono made *God Save Oz* for the *Electric Oz Band,* and marched in the protest demonstration through London, together with many members of GLF and the readership of the underground press.

Richard Neville defended himself. Barristers taken on for Jim Anderson and Felix Dennis returned their briefs just days before the trial commenced, which was very unusual. At the very last moment John Mortimer QC, the novelist and barrister arrived and offered his services. The prosecution was led by Brian Leary, who stated that 'the case concerned homosexuality, lesbianism, sadism, perverted sexual practices and drug taking.'[6] Mortimer announced that 'the case stands at the crossroads of our liberty, at the boundaries of our freedom to think, draw and write what we please'.[7] For the defence, this specifically concerned the treatment of dissent and dissenters, the control of ideas, and suppression of the messages of social resistance published in *Oz* 28.

From the very start of the trial Judge Argyle made his prejudices clear. Every time he intervened, and he did so frequently, he attempted to score a point for the prosecution.

The trial lasted 26 days, and by a 10 – 1 majority, Neville, Anderson and Dennis were found guilty on four obscenity charges, but not guilty on the very serious charge of conspiracy to corrupt morals. Argyle remanded the three in custody saying that he wanted social, medical and mental reports about them before pronouncing sentence. Neville, Anderson and Dennis were taken down and sent to Wandsworth Prison, where immediately upon arrival, and despite the fact they were on remand and not yet sentenced, their long hair, the most potent symbol of their identity was shorn off. Argyle sentenced Richard Neville to 15 months imprisonment and six months to run concurrently. Jim Anderson got 12 months and six concurrent, and Felix Dennis nine months and six concurrent. The Company (the defendants were the Company) was fined in total £2,250. At the Appeals hearing in August the sentences were overturned because Argyle was found to have grossly misdirected the jury. It was also revealed that Vivien Berger, whose appearance as a witness had been under a police subpoena, was harassed by officers numerous times, and on one occasion assaulted by two constables.[8] The real obscenity in the cartoon depiction of Rupert Bear was that Gypsy Granny was depicted as enjoying the rape, and that the editors published a stereotypically sexist fantasy image. When the women, the Marxists and queens of GLF were called on to support *Oz,* that iconography was central to their objections. In *Come Together* 8 Mick Belsten wrote under the headline, 'About Oz, About GLF, About Freedom.'

> A great deal of heated discussion has taken place recently within GLF as to whether or not we should support the '*Oz* Trio' in the recent prosecution. The objections (which were many and strongly held) sprang from what many of us thought was the blatant sexism in *Oz* magazine's treatment of women (and also gay people) as sex objects, subject to male superiority, inferior tools of male pleasure, objects of ridicule. Others in GLF either could not see the sexism in *Oz* or felt that if it was sexism, it was something which GLF should deal with

at a later date. GLF support for *Oz* had already been published, which rankled many sisters and brothers, who felt that such decisions should not be made without discussion. Hopefully we learn from such mistakes, and will fully discuss all such issues and declarations before making public statements in future. At any rate, no decision (fait accompli or not) was, in fact, arrived at, though the general feeling was probably sympathetic to *Oz*. This sympathy it must be stressed, came principally from the men in GLF, not generally from the women, who were the most critical.

Supporters of *Oz* had stressed that what was happening to *Oz* could and would happen to us. That this was a 'first freedom' which was being attacked, and that we were as much the victims as Jim, Richard and Felix. Their view was that *Oz* needed all the friends and supporters who could be mustered. In the event, the sentences were announced and the reverberations of shock hit GLF immediately. It seemed to come together in its true proportions. We did feel attacked, we did feel victimized, and our intelligence was insulted by the brutal, sadistic, bigoted and repressive sentences. We were angry.

We already find ourselves, in GLF, being censored. The workshop which produces this magazine has had to make a decision. We received an article written by a GLF member, which, for its deliberately ambiguous approach to a vital subject of interest to all gay brothers, for its high literary quality and its controversial nature, we all felt strongly should be published. But although we admired it, and wished to print it, we knew that it undoubtedly would be a provocation to the enforcers of the so-called obscenity 'laws'.

Had we the right as a group within GLF to put at risk the whole organisation, with the expenses involved, the possible imprisonment of gay activists, and the loss of a whole edition of *Come Together*? We discussed this problem in great and sometimes agonising depth. The possibility of having it approved or not by the coordinating committee of GLF, or even a members' meeting, would not be possible for such a piece of writing, we decided to shelve the problem.

Angrily and bitterly, we decided not to include it in this issue. We became our own censors. The *Oz* trial pigeons began to roost. What shall we do, brothers and sisters? What shall we *do?* Mick.

(The article that Media Workshop felt unable to publish was 'Shirley Temple Knows' by Rex Lay, which was eventually published in *Come Together* 12 in March 1972.)

Lisa Power in her book records Chesterman claiming 'I was a Trotskyite,'[9] which I just couldn't believe at first, but now see as fitting his personality with his cultivated air of mystery, his take-over of projects and independent actions. Of all people, it seems to me that he was the one who had most to gain by delivering the statement to the underground media that GLF supported *Oz,* and also the one to trivialize its sexism as something that could be dealt with later.

Whilst the spotlight was on the *OZ* trial at the Old Bailey, another equally important trial commenced at Lambeth Magistrates Court, similarly concerned with obscenity and schoolchildren. Mr John Mortimer again stepped in at the last moment to act as defence counsel, managing to negotiate a commute between the two Courts. *The Little Red Schoolbook* was a translation from Danish of a guide for schoolchildren written by Hansen and Jesper Jensen. In simple factual language that children could understand, it gave information on sex, and highlighted the inequalities and injustices of the education system and how children could organize and influence changes that would improve their position. It was published in London by Richard Handyside of Stage 1.

The publisher's offices were raided by Purvey of the Obscene

Publications Squad on 21 March and 1 April, 1971. Richard Handyside was charged with two counts of possessing obscene material for gain, namely 1,136 copies of the book stored at his offices.

At Lambeth Magistrates Court, where the trial commenced on 29 June, Detective Chief Inspector Purvey described the books as hard-core pornography. He also defended his department by telling the Court that they were already looking into the matter before Mrs Mary Whitehouse (self elected moralist and religious fanatic) started campaigning against the book's appearance in this country. John Mortimer said it might have been better if Mrs Whitehouse had appeared as a witness for the prosecution. Mr. Michael Corkery for the prosecution said she would not be appearing. Nevertheless she was present in court throughout the proceedings, and two prosecution witnesses stated that they were friends of hers.

The Magistrate refused to admit that the book was an entire book, a complete concept, one in which the part dealing with sex could only be regarded in context with the whole. This allowed the prosecution to concentrate on 23 pages out of a total of 208. As John Mortimer said, '... it is characteristic of those seeking censorship to concentrate on sex.'[10] Needless to say the wording of the Obscene Publications Act presumes from the beginning that books can have a 'tendency to deprave.' The law does not respect scientific or psychological truth, and there was no necessity for the prosecution to define what 'corruption' or 'depravity' means. John Mortimer summed up:

> Most legal cases deal with hard facts. This case differs from them in that it deals not with facts, but with opinions. The court has heard two totally conflicting sets of opinions, and the result of this case will be in essence an opinion. No one will ever be able to establish a danger of corruption or depravity, and it is very difficult for a court to try such an

> issue. There is the danger of the court finding itself with two legitimate but conflicting points of view, and being tempted to join the side with which it feels in sympathy.[11]

The magistrate took less than ten seconds to announce his verdict and convict Richard Handyside with a fine of £25 each on the two counts of publishing an obscene book, awarding a derisory £110 towards his considerable costs.

The first casualty of the police failure to convict the three defendants in the *Oz* trial was Det. Inspector Luff, whose drunkenness on duty and criminal methodology (he planted dope on Richard Neville) had become an embarrassment even by the dubious standards of the Obscene Publications Squad from which he was retired.

After the prosecution of both *Oz* and *The Little Red School Book* the knock-on effect of the squad's concentration on the underground press, while leaving the well known porn merchants of Soho alone, prompted criticism of the Home Secretary, Reginald Maudling, who was forced to institute a secret inquiry. Det. Chief Inspector George Fenwick, head of the 'dirty squad', tried to turn the evaluation round by stating that pornography was not displayed and on open sale in Soho, an argument which disturbed inquiry officials. At the same time, Lord Longford's unofficial inquiry into pornography led by Matthew Oliver made allegations against seven porn merchants, whom he had discovered, had a country-wide network of senior police officers on their payrolls.

Further inquiries got nowhere until early 1972, when it was discovered that one of the seven porn barons, James Humphreys had spent a two-week winter holiday in Cyprus with Commander Kenneth Drury, head of the Scotland Yard Flying Squad. The explanation proffered by Drury was that they were looking for Ronnie Biggs the escaped prisoner from the Great Train Robbery.

But investigations ordered by the new Met commissioner, Robert Mark, finally unveiled the systemic corruption at the heart of the police. Four years later Mr Justice Mars-Jones named Fenwick as the 'chief architect' and sentenced him to 10 years' imprisonment.

Secret home office papers show the public backlash to the savage sentencing of Richard Neville and the editors of the hippie magazine helped precipitate Scotland Yard's biggest ever anti-corruption drive in which 400 officers, including a deputy assistant commissioner, were imprisoned or left the force.[12]

Chapter 6

Revolution in the head ... and/or in the World

> I say that it is time to open the closet door and let in the fresh air and the sunshine; it is time ... to discard the secrecy, the disguise, and the camouflage; it is time to hold up your head and to look the world squarely in the eye as the homosexual that you are, confident of your equality, confident in the knowledge that as objects of prejudice and victims of discrimination you are right and they are wrong, and confident of your rightness of what you are and the goodness of what you do; it is time to live your homosexuality fully, joyously, openly and proudly, assured that morally, socially, physically and psychologically, emotionally and in every other way: Gay is Good. It is.
>
> Frank Kemeny.

At the end of July, and with just a week's notice, the Wednesday General Meeting had to move again, this time to All Saints Hall, Powis Gardens, Notting Hill. Nobody missed the dank oppressive atmosphere of the former *Middle Earth* once they stepped into the light of the large community hall. There was a stage at the far end of the hall that was democratically shunned, and the meetings continued as they had been in Covent Garden, with the steering committee in the middle, and everyone forming a circle around them. Sometimes there were chairs so the committee and inner rows could be seated, and stacks of tables against the wall that could be pulled out by those at the back to sit on. This move from the impersonal West End to a multiracial neighbourhood was to have a profound effect on the movement.

Housing and race were the two defining issues of life in

Notting Hill. The district was home to immigrant communities from republican Spain, Portugal, Italy, the sub continent, the West Indies and Ireland. The cheap rents in the dilapidated properties also attracted artists, lesbians and gays, hippies and middle class drop-outs, all scattered among the working class poor, who were mainly employed in service industries. For the black inhabitants of Notting Hill the fifties had brought racism from Oswald Mosley and his British Union of Fascists Movement with their public meetings and agitation of the white working class, resulting in the murderous race riots of 1958.

Interventions by the New Left Club supporting local Tenants Associations culminated in the formation of the London Free School in 1966 by a temporary coalition of individuals grouped around the idea of a counter-culture based on community action and Carnival roots. This gave rise to *IT* and its information arm BIT, a local paper *The Grove,* the Adventure Playground under the new Westway motorway, and the first outdoor Carnival, led by Trinidadian musicians who had been jamming Sunday lunchtimes at the *Coleherne* since the fifties. (Black history hasn't yet acknowledged the fact that the only pub in the whole of West London where black musicians found acceptance and sympathy for a shared experience of hatred and prejudice was gay.)

A year later, former New Left individuals, notably Jan and John O'Malley formed the Notting Hill Community Workshop (NHCW) to co-ordinate the work of local people organized around neighbourhood issues. The NHCW established the Notting Hill People's Association (NHPA) and the People's Centre, with sub groups covering housing, education & youth, playgrounds, police, claimants unions, the Notting Hill Press, and a weekly newspaper, *People's News.* Two years later they formed the Notting Hill Squatters Group (NHSG) and the North Kensington Neighbourhood Law Centre giving free advice to local citizens.

To the south of our new meeting place was the bed-sit land of

Bayswater with its famous gay bar the *Champion*. Just to the north was All Saint's Road, well known for its drug dealers and used as a honey trap by Notting Hill police. Also in the street was the, by now famous, Mangrove Restaurant, and a few streets away a youth centre called the Metro Club.

Transplanted GLF could not have found better soil in Notting Hill. Locating itself in the midst of Britain's social engineering, it burst into flower.

For over two years racial tension had been rising due to the policing of the area. One issue was the existence of the Mangrove Restaurant. The other more recent event began on the evening of the 24 May 1971, when two young men were in the street outside the Metro Club playing at sword-fighting. One of the young men was holding a piece of wood the size and shape of a drumstick. Two policemen arrived in a Panda car, one of whom made a sudden grab from behind for the arm of one of the lads, who broke free and with his mate ran into the club. This short scene was witnessed by one of the white workers at the club who asked the police what they wanted. He was told that the youth had to be arrested for possessing an offensive weapon, and would he let them into the club. The youth worker declined, and suggested he would phone a senior officer at Harrow Road Police station. But in the one or two minutes of this exchange the situation changed dramatically; five Special Patrol Group Transit vans, seven squad cars, and four Black Marias, in all seventy policemen, plus dogs, arrived to arrest the two sixteen year olds.

A siege commenced. Absent members of the management committee and a solicitor from the Neighbourhood Law Centre arrived. Despite repeated requests for a senior police officer to come and mediate it was two hours before one arrived. By then a large crowd of local people were watching. Among them were members of the NHPA, who had left their weekly meeting having been requested over the phone by club management to witness the situation. A camera belonging to the NHPA was smashed by the police in a scuffle, and two arrests were made before anyone had left the club. All along the police continually demanded to be let into the club to arrest the youth with the playstick.

A Chief Superintendent and his sergeant eventually arrived on the scene and demanded the teenagers file out one by one, past the two constables from the Panda car so both youths could be identified and arrested. The young man whom the police snatched was known to have spent the whole evening playing table tennis. He was dragged to the police van despite calls that the police had the wrong man. There was then an attempt to block the police van; the pushing and shoving led to blows, the police retaliated and fights started. When the police appeared to turn on the crowd there was a rush to seek refuge in the club, but it was sealed off by a line of officers. Twelve people were arrested. One club member suffered broken ribs and a punctured lung. One was seen at the station with a battered bleeding face. One seventeen year old was run over by a police car, severely beaten and knocked senseless in the police van, and attacked again at the station. A woman bystander was arrested and suffered an injury to an already slipped disc. All the arrested were taken to Harrow Road, where medical assistance was denied to everyone except the injured who had first been taken to St. Charles Hospital.

All the youths were charged with assaults on police officers and possession of offensive weapons; one with a mysterious metal bar which was never identified, and two with dustbin lids they had used to protect their heads from the rain of blows by police truncheons. The eleven were kept another night in police custody before appearing at Marylebone Magistrates Court on the 26 May. At the hearing two youths were remanded in custody, the rest granted bail.

That morning a crowd of about one hundred people, family, friends and supporters gathered outside the court before moving inside to find places in the public gallery. The police agreed to allow fifteen people into the public gallery, but only six were actually let in. The sound of arguments in the corridors over entry into the public gallery was so loud that a Magistrate ordered the building to be cleared:

> Twenty policemen filed in from the Gaoler's room, adjoining the lobby and formed a cordon 'ushering' the crowd along a corridor to the street entrance. At once people began to push against police lines and fights broke out. One girl screaming, 'My baby, my baby!' was knocked to the ground; another about seventeen was grabbed by a burly officer not by the arms but with two hands locked around her throat,[1] another held her and a third kicked her.[2]

At a series of trials spread over the summer, with the youths broken up into different groups, all were found guilty, including the woman bystander. Sentences included heavy fines, imprisonment, and incarceration in detention centres. The one arrested for being the youth with the stick was acquitted, as police were unable to provide any evidence.

As an act of solidarity and to announce its presence, GLF distributed the following leaflet:

> THE GAY LIBERATION FRONT
> SUPPORTS THE METRO CLUB
> STOP PIG BRUTALISATION OF BLACK PEOPLE
>
> Brothers and sisters, we are united against police brutality. But, even more, what lies behind this. We know that the Metro was bust because it was a black club, and because the forces of repression realize that they can no longer contain Black people in Notting Hill Gate by isolating them in one club – the Metro. They have seen the Metro people becoming more aware of their collective strength, and of how they are being robbed by white racist education committees and councils. They have seen the Metro people get more angry, and now they want to

close it. But their attack on the Metro has been an attack on the whole community.

We, as homosexuals, are also fucked about by society. It is illegal for us to contact each other, to show any signs of affection in public (they call it soliciting and importuning). If we're under 21 it's illegal for us to exist. Straight society thinks of us and treats us as sub-human. 'Queer' bashing and 'queer' baiting are some of the pigs' oldest pastimes. And, as we start to organise, to find a sense of solidarity, our dances and demonstrations are systematically busted.

There are gay people everywhere, black and white, male and female. The usual gay person is shown as being fairly well off; a person who, because of his position in society, can 'buy' his pleasures. In whatever way he or she manages to buy this 'consumer sexism', society will not usually put them down, unless they need a scapegoat. For thousands of working class, and black people, it is not possible to come out in this diseased way. We don't have money, influential friends, or social position. (Ted Heath can never 'come out', because to do that he would have to desert the ruling class that he belongs to and upholds, and lose its perks and privileges). We can't and don't want to come out in the 'middle class' way, to 'buy' the privilege to be ourselves. Our only choice, if we want to be free, is to confront and attack the society that oppresses us.

So we support the sisters and brothers from the Metro who have been falsely arrested, brutalised and intimidated for the crime of wanting to be free.

POWER TO ALL OPPRESSED PEOPLE

For GLF the summer and early autumn of 1971 was to be the most vibrant, unified and engaged period in the existence of the movement. The Youth Group were one of the main instigators of events with their own edition of *Come Together* 8, carrying the

Youth Group Declaration of Rights and Demands, and an article on The Age of Consent by the group's founder, Tony Reynolds. Whilst working on *Come Together* 8 Tony Reynolds was also planning the first and the biggest central London demonstration GLF had yet attempted, the 28 August Youth Group Gay Day in Hyde Park, followed by the Age of Consent March from Marble Arch to Trafalgar Square, headed by the *Ginger Baker Band*.

Alaric Sumner's mother heard of GLF and told her teenage son to join.

> *Sumner*: The demo and the *Come Together* were being done at the time when I arrived, so there was a time when I was being assessed if you like, to see if I would become part of the inner circle, but not in an organisational way – Youth Group people were working out what I would do in relation to them. I was at the front of the Youth Group demo but I don't recall doing much organising for it, though I did do leafleting … Leafleting the Boltons was just before the age of consent demo. I don't remember much except that one of the people we leafleted kept on telling us that he knew what we really needed, which was to go to bed with him. The whole youth group had gone to do Earls Court; we were trying to get the scene people out and we did that at the *William IV* too. There were people in there who said, we don't want the age of consent lowered because then the older men will go for you lot instead of for us. Which made me feel a bit disgusted.[3]

The pamphlet produced for the demonstration read:

> We are stardust – we are golden. We are fifty million year old children. And we've got to get ourselves back to the garden.[4]
>
> Love is eternal. Love is natural. Love is golden. Love is God. God is homosexual. God is negro. God is a Jew. God rapes children. God is the Archbishop of Canterbury, the Pope,

Edward Heath, the Queen and you all rolled into a ball. A cosmic ball. Essence of porphyry. Magic mushrooms, LSD, pot, cocaine, heroin and Tia Maria. These things too are part of our natural environment. As are Homosexuals under the age of 21 who want to make love to each other. What difference does it make to you, Mrs Smith, if two boys make it in a room? Does it offend you while you sit watching Coronation Street to think that somewhere somehow two males under 21 are screwing the daylight/moonlight/love/fuck/ass/cocksuck/want it want it want it out of each other while the world outside continues unperturbed. Do you really believe that it does the world harm when two people make love. Or when three people make love. Do you really believe that it harms the people who make love. Do you make love?

When my son asked me what homosexuality was, I made love to him. If your son was homosexual wouldn't you prefer him to know where homosexuals meet rather than hide away, ashamed of his supposed guilt, mentally dented, incapable of decision, afraid of love. Homosexuality is natural. And Love is the greatest force for Good. In the present conditions of social unrest we need all the love we can get. So do you. So does the world. Turn on, tune in, turn over. Make this Help a Homosexual week. Give your bedroom to two guys for a night. Preferable two guys under 21. Then walk the streets and see the ways that society forces gays to meet – in public lavatories, in bushes, in shady groves. Then decide which way you would like your son to make it if he were a homosexual.

COME OUT
SUPPORT YOUR GAY HUMAN COMMUNITY
WE WILL NOT CORRUPT YOUR CHILDREN
BUT THEY'LL BE DAMNED GLAD WE'RE HERE IF THEY'RE HOMOSEXUAL
AND STATISTICS PROVE THAT THEY MIGHT BE

> Gay Liberation Front Demonstration. Aug 28th. Lower the Age of Consent.
>
> Lower your threshold of prejudice. We love you.[5]

I remember little about the Gay Day in Hyde Park. A lot of those Gay Days have run into one another in my mind, but I do remember setting off from Marble Arch behind the lorry carrying *Ginger Baker and his Band*. The front of the lorry carried the GLF banner, flapping in the breeze, and each function group had their own banner and placards, making it look like a proper march. We moved directly into Oxford Street with a mass of shoppers frozen to the pavement for a moment before the ridicule and taunting began. The parade was a mesmerising novelty for the bystanders, as it was in its own way for us, with thousands of eyes watching as we held hands, hugged, kissed, boogied together, whistled, and shouted slogans. We had been on other people's marches, but this was our parade and everyone really let go. I was nearly hoarse with shouting by the time we were half way down Regent Street. The police, as usual, over-reacted in strength of numbers, but with manly restraint, and the usual whiff of disdain beneath their nostrils, didn't stop an hilarious conga-line as the carnival reached Piccadilly, where the rent boys under the arches, their punters fled, joined the party as we swung past Eros blowing kisses, and streamed down the Haymarket to rally beneath Nelson's Column.

Tony Reynolds' speech in Trafalgar Square was similar in content to the leaflet headed *Why we're Marching,* which he helped to produce.

> After the 1967 Sexual Offenses Act, a homosexual act is only legal if performed in private between no more than two consenting adults over the age of 21. It is still an offence to commit a homosexual act, if one or both of the participants are under 21.
>
> We are marching against this act, which forbids a person

from loving another of the same sex. Also we are marching against an attitude of society which tells us we are sick.

Gay people are an oppressed group in Britain and the World today. We have been forced into ghettos, the only place where we can find one another, and into the few jobs and professions where we can get by. We often have to meet in dehumanizing gay bars, or on the streets where we are arrested by plainclothes police who entrap us. Often we never meet but if we do come out to each other, most of us are compelled to lead double lives.

We hide and feel guilty because this society says we are 'sick' and to varying degrees we are fool enough to believe it.

The Gay Liberation Front has been formed all over the country to fight against the lies and myths perpetrated by this society, we are following the examples of Third World and Women's Liberation movements by rejecting what we are told we must be. We are not sick. We are making love with people of the same sex. We feel good and whole about our love and we want to remain gay.

Gays will no longer tolerate the oppression and attitudes British society puts on us. We are uniting to fight for a free society. We will join with all oppressed people in the fight against this sexist, racist, imperialist country, because we know that we can be free only when all people are free.

Homosexuals are being imprisoned, fined and sent to mental hospitals by an Act which forbids one person from loving another of the same sex. The official estimates are 1 in 10 people in England are homosexuals. So of a population of 56 million in England, there are 5.6 million gay people continually living under the threat of the courts and prisons.

Arrests and convictions for buggery, attempted buggery and indecency by under 14s, 14 to 17 year olds, and 17 to 21 year olds [show that] in 305 arrests of under 21 year olds there were 305 convictions. There were four cases discharged, 31

> conditional discharges, 105 probation orders. 46 were fined, and 52 sent to prison, borstal, remand homes and mental hospitals. This oppression must end now.
>
> Homosexuals are standing up and fighting back against a Government which defines for us what we can and cannot do. We no longer will tolerate such an archaic form of oppression.[6]

Ian Dunn, who organized the Scottish Minorities Rights Group in his parents' living room in 1969 was the next to speak.

> Many of my brothers and sisters have bled and fled and are now living in London. The Wolfenden reforms do not extend to Scotland. Technically we still suffer under the draconian Victorian act of 1885. Yet we want no part of your reforms, and even the moderate Scottish Minorities Group has expressed its opposition to the English act. Why is this? It is because young people are being put down by an Act of Parliament which denies them basic civil rights and invades their privacy.
>
> In my country Scotland, the age of consent (in practice, not law) for men loving men is 15. In another country or another time, this would be a beautiful thing – but Scotland doesn't yet love her gay people. Together we must demand our rightful parity with our straight cousins. I declare before you all that I fully intend to continue sleeping with my seventeen year old lover. If you believe it – and you do believe it, join me in a great and general love-in. Love (with sex up to you) is stronger than fear, stronger than hate, stronger than war. Love will overthrow the hateful 1967 act, but it must be determined, even angry love.
>
> One, let us strike non-victim crimes, such as laws against young gays, from the statute books. Two, the State has no business in the bedrooms of its citizens. Three, let us claim our basic rights as human beings.[7]

After the Youth Group speeches, the microphone was taken over by Michael Mason and Martin Corbett, and the day's enjoyment took an embarrassing dip when the two started publicly casting about, looking for a woman to come to the microphone to support the male platform on the male issue of the age of consent. Carla Toney, who rightly complained later about being a token sister, said of the event:

> I started hearing 'Where's Carla, where's Carla', and I turned to a friend and said, 'I can't go up there alone'... I grabbed Rosie's hand and dragged her up to the plinth with me and we stood there holding hands, and all I could think of to say was, 'I'm gay and I'm proud' or something, and Rosie and I put our fists in the air and I heard this cheer from the crowd, and when I got down there was this young girl just in her teens who said, 'I want to be a lesbian when I grow up' and I said, 'Well, you just need courage.'[8]

Warren Hague in his speech reminded us that although permission had been granted from every conceivable department of government in order that we could have our march, and the police were on their best behaviour, as soon as it was over the same shit would come down on us as usual.

Afterwards about twenty of us went to JoLyons cafe in the Strand, where half way through our tea, the manageress threw a fit at the sight of Claudia and Malcolm Bissett in drag. The first we knew of it was when two policemen clumped down the stairs followed by a grim faced manageress pointing out the pair. We immediately stood up and surrounded their table. Ted Walker-Brown held up his camera and John Chesterman his video camera. The police ordered us out. Andrew Lumsden persistently demanded to know the reason for the police action. One of the pigs pointed to Claudia and Malcolm, 'That object there and that object there, and that thing there, and that thing there ...' The other pig interrupted, 'It was only this table, so what were you all doing coming over to join them?' 'Because we're all Together! And if you want us to leave we'd like our money back because we haven't finished our food.' The manageress ignored us, the police said, 'Outside!' Tables were cleared and a tray of ice creams, cakes and cups of tea were carried up the stairs to a chorus of, *I like a nice cup of tea in the morning, and a nice cup of tea with my tea, and around about seven it's not my idea of heaven to take tea at JoLyons.* Warren had been right.

Numerically there were fewer women than men in GLF, but a body-count did not come anywhere near to indicating their contribution to debates or activism. In function groups such as Anti-Psychiatry, the Manifesto group and Media Workshop where they were well represented, the balance between the sexes still left them in a minority, but all in all, they were taken more seriously, because the men in those groups were to some degree conscious of their own chauvinism, or at least aware of the issues women had with men. *Come Together (Women's Issue)* 7 published in July 1971, was the first to be edited by the women's group. The introduction was unequivocal.

> We share the experiences of our gay brothers but as women we have endured them differently. Whereas the men in GLF partake of the privileges of the male – you have been allowed to organise, talk and dominate – we have been taught not to believe in ourselves, in our judgements, but to act dumb and wait for a man to make the decisions. As lesbians, 'women without men', we have always been the lowest of the low. Only through acting collectively can we overcome our own passivity and your male chauvinism so that together we – the whole of GLF – can smash the sexist society which perverts and imprisons us all. WE'RE WOMEN. WE'RE LESBIANS. WE'RE OPPRESSED. WE'RE ANGRY.

Sarah Grimes: Media Workshop had a weekly meeting and there were usually about half a dozen people there. Mick Belsten, Bill Halstead, Aubrey Walter, Annie Brackx – she and I were the only two women who stayed, other women used to come and go, and that very sinister man in black, John Chesterman, was around sometimes ... Mostly we'd write a lot of the articles ourselves and we'd agree what would go in the issue and each article would be read out to us for discussion. We put it together ourselves as well. It was all a bit *ad hoc*. We started hanging out in various lefty publications like *Time Out* and *IT* and *Frendz*. We'd go in at night and use their typesetting machine, so the paper got slightly smarter as it went along, and a good time was had by all. It was all real amateur stuff, but they look quite good really when you pull them out now, all the illustrations and the care and things. Not so much the design and typography, but the imagery.

Mick Belsten was particularly warm. It wasn't until I read his obituaries that I realised his background, with the merchant navy and everything, so he was a bit older than most of us, most of the Media Workshop were in their early-twenties. We would meet in his flat in Barnes, it was a lovely place. I don't think he did an awful lot of the writing but he was a great facilitator, he could put people at their ease and get discussion going. He had a great kindness – he never got overwrought – so he could sort things out with the printers and so on. We used the International Socialists' (SWP) press in Shoreditch to get it printed, but they charged us commercial rates, not the left political reduced rate. That was pretty annoying for us, and an exposure of their limited political outlook – then we took it to the community based cooperative Crest Press in Ladbroke Grove]. We got people writing things, like for instance from the Youth Group, the declaration of rights, and there was quite a lot of submitted stuff.

There was a sort of Puritanism – there was one article I

really hated which criticised something Pat Arrowsmith had written in the women's issue about butch and femme roles – this was another article saying how awful that was. So there was a sort of hidden political right-on-ness that certain gay lifestyles were out of the question.[9]

Mary McIntosh: I remember doing the first women's issue, the one with photos of us in drag. It wasn't anti-men, we just wanted to do something on our own and didn't feel we had much influence on the regular issues. And we wanted to have some fun together, which we did. We did it in Sarah Grimes' flat. You can tell who did it by the pictures. Carla Toney, Annie Brackx, me, Elizabeth, Angie, Barbara Klecki and Sarah.[10]

Sarah Grimes: The handwriting is all mine, I did the layout and graphics. I wrote *Hold Your Head Up High, Love* which was a personal confessional piece. I was thinking about why it had been so hard to come out before GLF and it was to do with the image of lesbians, of not having any charisma, any glamour, any creative ability or genius. Lesbians were silly, crass. There wasn't a role model equivalent to Oscar Wilde. There were two counterpoised articles – *Revolution in the Head … Or in the World*. That was two different points of view which we allowed to coexist, individualism and internal revolution versus seeing that as just the first step to external revolution. We didn't try to assimilate the views or allow one to overcome the other, there was no power-struggle over it, and there was the dressing up, which was great fun. It was at my flat in Notting Hill, and my brother lived upstairs and we raided his wardrobe. I don't know who had the idea of dressing up but it was a very good tactic – it brought us together as a group, like one of those exercises at a strategy group to put people at their ease.[11]

Hold Your Head up High, Love

The first major disappointment in my life took place when Greta Garbo changed into women's clothes toward the end of *Queen Christina* and took a fancy to John Gilbert. It was the first of a long line of betrayals, most of them inflicted by myself on myself in an age-long comedy of double-think which aimed to destroy the soul's integrity.

In the first act one might deny to oneself one's emotions absolutely; this is easily done in the general confusion and flux of awakening sexuality, in the unnatural setting of single-sex schools where delightful crushes flourish in hot-house claustrophobia and the gloom of the dawn of self-awareness. That is all just the prelude however. The action proper only begins in the second act, when the protagonist awakens, rubs her eyes, and sits up. In a delicate romantic haze she wanders alone, idealising the tender and beautiful women she sees and then recreates, and all the time remaining blind to one thing – that her emotions are good and valid, that they can be expressed in a shared, loving life. My goodness no, I have to remain blind to that because that has a label, that is called lesbianism: and who could accept for herself the image of a pathetic cold coarse unattractive creature who denies her nature and tries to be what she is not? The butch, the tweed suit and heavy shoes? The travesty of heterosexual domesticity? The situation catches me up in a vicious circle: if I had faith in my feelings I could use them as the standard by which I might measure the stereotype and the cowardly mockery that it is, and reject it; but the stereotype itself, reinforced by the conventional attitudes to sexuality which engendered it, destroys all possibility of faith. So our protagonist is unique, and cannot ever seek fulfilment for her emotions. Not recognising herself in any public image, she is thrown back into her private world. Isolation is forced upon her, and isolation she takes to herself, extols self-sufficiency as an ideal, adopts the role of a solitary. At this point the play becomes rather boring, I admit: nothing happens; nothing happens. The promising dawn gives way to overcast skies. She shivers in the cold of arid introspection and the loss of all warmth from without, trembles in the inadequacy of fantasy which seems to offer so much yet finally cheats and frustrates. So total is her self-mistrust that all achievement becomes inaccessible as inhibitions descend.

It might seem incredible that anyone could give up hope so easily, but perhaps few straight people realise that the labels they impose on us are not merely insulting, but also shattering in their effect on the way we look at ourselves. All labels are at best merely ill-fitting public clothes to our individuality, but those which carry with them a stigma can cause a barren loss of confidence if we reject them, thus depriving ourselves of an external description, or, if we accept them, an equally barren self-contempt, since in accepting the label we also inevitably accept the values assigned to it, the stigma.

Therefore, after sampling methods of escape other than solitude – hilarious forays into heterosexuality (a humiliating failure for me, painful for him) and suicide (literally painful to me and distressing to family) – the realisation and acceptance of my homosexuality, which occurs in the next act, brings little relief. I thought to dispel self-deception and find that, although some of the inner conflict and repression is resolved, concealment from others causes self-concealment, however strong the belief that one is facing up to oneself. Hence I still cannot live myself fully, and the dead weight of inhibition still flattens all creativity. Why do you conceal from others your … what shall we say, your propensities? Guilt. Guilt in the face of conventional values. Guilt destroys the last traces of self-respect and rampages through the unprotected soul. Guilt resigns you to unhappiness, leads you to expect nothing else as your due. Guilt puts you always in the wrong, always at a disadvantage; it draws its strength from the timidity it creates, it mocks and questions not itself ...

(The above was, of course, written after the annihilation of these horrors. For only then, in the freedom of self-respect, could I see the pattern and unity of my past and thus recognise causes. Act four took place in the afternoon, with the sun trying hard, and sometimes succeeding, to break out and brighten Parliament Hill. Act five takes place in the clear evening, and the night).

Revolution in the Head ... and ... or in the World.

[The first states] Revolution in the second part of the twentieth century is not an action. Revolution today is a *state of mind* that manifests itself through its bearer's way of acting. Revolution isn't something that happens on the 4th or 14th of July or in February or a specific year – where it is real, it happens every minute of the day, and starts every morning over and over again! This state of mind does not express itself particularly in so-called 'revolutionary actions' such as demonstrations, etc. It can be seen in every movement, it speaks through every word and commands every gesture of the 'revolutionary'.

The seed of freedom sleeps in every contemporary human being, but it does not grow out of its own nature – it has to be planted in a conscience. If consciousness does not throw light and water and warmth on this seed, it is bound to die. And so within most people the seed of freedom is killed by absent-minded survival – by things, careers, time-passing amusements or freaky, trendy, 'spontaneous' conformity. Within people who in one way or another are extraordinary – the outsiders – there is a more fertile condition for a revolutionary potential to become a real, alive quality, partly because society makes it painful and difficult for them to live, and partly because they often have an inner need to think about their existence, since they don't fit into a well-known, too well-known, pattern that one learns by heart when one learns to walk. These people bear, by necessity, a longing towards something other than the existing world order, towards other laws, other habits, other imperatives. A gay person is one kind of outsider.

Only during the last few years have gay people – as a more or less coherent group - expressed some other social ambition than being gay. This social ambition – in many cases one could even say: this desire! – brings gay people together to work for a new way of life. A life more in accordance with a wider kind of human being than the limited inhabitant of the world today; a human being who realises life not mainly as a struggle to survive but as something joyful, something magnificently rich and affluent, full of different forms and modes of manifestations.

[The second piece argues] The revolution in our heads, our changed consciousness, which is partly a psychological change, *can* help gay men and women. It can make us proud to be gay instead of apologetic and ashamed: it can increase our self-respect. But this increased self-respect will lead us to question and reject society's view of us as sick, perverse and inferior. If we say 'Gay is Good', *why* does society say we are bad? There must be a reason for society to keep us down, to indoctrinate us with a belief that we are sick, and to perpetuate the myth that we are inferior, unnatural and unhappy. There must be something wrong with a society that tells lies about us. Our new pride does *not* of itself make a revolution. On the contrary it could lead to greater oppression – and indeed this has already happened. When GLF tried to organise socials and discos in ordinary pubs in order to come out of the gay ghetto, police pressure put an end to our efforts. Individual self-liberation may change our minds and those of a few of our friends, but it cannot change the law that oppresses our brothers. It cannot do away with oppression.

Consciousness-raising is only a first step in the real revolution. It offers a changed conception of the oppression and how it relates to other oppressed groups – ultimately how sexual oppression of all kinds relates to the economic organisation of society – this leads us *away* from the view that it's all in our heads and towards the realisation that society is unjust and that therefore we should demand and work for change. The individual cannot alone and unaided bring about social change, and therefore the next step is for us to band together, because if we unite we are strong. To say that revolution takes place entirely inside the individual is itself a counter-revolutionary statement. It is part of the ideology of our present society that the individual is himself responsible for all that befalls him: if he gets in the shit it's his fault. We see this in the prevalent belief that a man on the dole is likely to be a scrounger – when it is far more likely that the current economic fuck-up has made it impossible for him to get work.

To say that the revolution is in our heads would mean that the individual could be 'free' in prison, in the harem, in any situation of objective unfreedom. No. One might be inwardly at peace there – but to deny the outward reality of an oppressive life imposed from without is to be a quietist, a conservative and ultimately a theologian or psychoanalyst concerned only with the state of one's own spirit or psyche. Revolution is not just about feelings. It's about power – who has power over us to direct our lives into distorted patterns and hidden paths, and how we ourselves can achieve the power to alter this.

Chapter 7

Freaking Out the Fundamentalists

> Religion is the sigh of the oppressed creature, the heart of a heartless world, and the soul of soulless conditions. It is the opium of the people.
> Karl Marx. *German-French Annals,* 1844.

John Chesterman was one of the first to be alarmed by the rise of Christian fundamentalism. Evangelical sects, chapels and churches were banding together to fight an overwhelming tide of filth they were led to believe was sweeping the country, conjured up by two missionaries: a married couple recently returned from India who were horrified at what they perceived to be the slide of the nation into moral pollution. This pair of sincere, arrogant, interfering troublemakers formed the Festival of Light (FoL) organization, designed to raise moral standards and pressurize the government into backing their crusade against abortion, sex before marriage, pornography and homosexuality.

When the FoL announced plans for a national rally and a march through central London, Chesterman began single-mindedly planning a GLF counter demonstration. First he took over the Action Group, and not wanting any further misunderstandings between them and Street Theatre after Denis Lemons' clumsy attempt to give us orders, he made sure that when he and I now met, Lemon was part of the company. I remember tripping with Chesterman, Lyndsay Levy, and Lemon in the white carpeted sitting room of his rich sugar-daddy's luxury flat in Faulkland Mansions. Lemon had been out of the room for a while, when suddenly he came back in with a face full of fury, his belligerent eyes flashing daggers at me as he strode forward. I raised myself off the floor and stared back at him, sure he was going to strike, but he pulled up short. Slowly his looks hollowed into confusion, he turned and left the room. After that display, whatever his problem was – I'd seen enough.

Chesterman named his anti-FoL campaign, Operation Rupert, and Lemon became his gofer in the Action Group. I feel sure it was an experience that gave Lemon the skills to be a facilitator and manager of people and their ideas. With his sex-appeal, and backed by Chesterman's plotting, he was a potent spokesman at the General Meeting, urging us all to sign up for the demonstration. Chesterman's friendship with Geoff Marsh at *Frendz* was Lemon's introduction to the underground press, whose readership was being invited to join the GLF campaign.

Immediately after the Age of Consent March Chesterman went into overdrive, having just ten days to organize and co-ordinate the 15 independent groups he successfully persuaded to unite with GLF against the right-wing religious fundamentalist threat. Key to the whole operation was Chesterman's friend Janet Phillips. He persuaded her to pose as a committed Christian and apply for a job with the FoL and she succeeded beyond his wildest dreams, appointed to a job in the office that was organising their whole campaign.

Janet Phillips was soon feeding Chesterman the plans for the inaugural event at the Methodist Central Hall Westminster, and details of the meeting in Trafalgar Square followed by a mass rally in Hyde Park to be held two weeks later. She acquired a selection of tickets for various parts of Central Hall, the mailing lists and all the literature. People were being bussed in to London from all over the country to attend the mass rally, so at the very last moment Chesterman arranged for new instructions to be mailed out, some with false parking arrangements miles outside the West End, whilst others were told that due to the numbers attending, the rally in Hyde Park would be delayed until 6.00 p.m. which was in fact the official finishing time.

Individuals in *Frendz, Oz, IT* and *INK* newspapers formed

groups. The White Panthers, Women's Liberation, their Street Theatre group, and all the GLF function groups broke down into individuals, couples and groups, each deciding their own form of protest inside Central Hall. Participants were sworn to keep their details secret. Only Chesterman knew what each act would be. Once he had the full picture he ranked them in order, and a few days before the Inaugural Meeting he gave out a number to each group, and told them what the group before them would be doing, so that each group in turn knew that the end of an action they now had knowledge of, was the cue to choose their moment to demonstrate.

Our rendezvous point was Cleopatra's Needle some distance from Central Hall. We were all wearing ordinary clothes in an attempt to look respectable and pass scrutiny, a very casual scrutiny it has to be said because many of those outer garments were made lumpy by the costumes worn underneath. The atmosphere was very downbeat as we all looked so different and drab, in plain scruffy old mackintoshes or not so modish suits found in the backs of wardrobes, the exceptions being Bette Bourne and John Church dressed like a pair of tweedy buffers, and Tony Salvis the dodgy Gay Lib secretary done up in a dog collar, purple shirt and immaculate suit, like a sleek and well fed bishop. Just as we were getting a little apprehensive, Chesterman arrived on his ticket distribution rounds to us and the other groups assembling elsewhere in the area.

Once we had our tickets we went off in ones and twos to Parliament Square, only to meet up again, tickets at the ready, pretending not to know each other (gays are good at that), outside the doors of Central Hall, and to piously shuffle past the Festival stewards and into the enormous chapel. Frank O'Loony, Tim Bolingbroke and I were part of a Klu Klux Klan group with seats in the balcony. We found our places midway up the steeply raked tiers and seated ourselves in the middle of a row to be joined by the others in our party, and soon enough we merged into the mass of the faithful who came to surround us. On the opposite side of the balcony I could see Michael James and Peter Flannery way up in the very back row. In the centre at the front of the balcony were members of the Youth Group and some rows behind them were Bette Bourne and John Church, but looking down into the body of the Hall it was difficult to recognize anyone else as we sat there thumbing through our hymnbooks. Had the others managed to get in we wondered.

High up beneath the great organ, a choir in scarlet velvet capes filed in from behind a matching curtain and moved to their places on the tiers below. Beneath them was a long dais raised above the floor, filled with dainty chairs and a stand of microphones. Stewards in their mid-twenties, early-thirties, cricketers, sportsmen, the kind of men so beloved of the Methodists, dressed in their Sunday best, the enamel badge of the sacred lamp glinting in their lapels, directed the last of the congregation to their places.

The scarlet curtain parted again and the organist appeared above the choir, seated himself at the console and began to play a murmuring undertone accompaniment to the chattering faithful. Skilfully the music grew louder and the audience quieter. A door opened behind the balcony and out came the organizers of the FoL: the missionary Peter Miller and his wife, followed by the more famous moral leaders of the nation, Lord Longford, Malcolm Muggeridge, Mary Whitehouse, Cliff Richards the pop-star and notorious closet case, Bishop Trevor Huddleston and various minor characters like Judy Mackenzie, a folk singer, a Danish evangelist Johannes Facius, Joan Gibbons, and a cockney, Ted Lyon, to reassure the working classes. At the peak of the applause the organ thundered, the choir rose, the congregation stood, the first hymn was sung, and during the last verse the organizer of the rally, Nigel Goodwin, slithered to the microphone – 'cloaked in the greasy aura of his onetime boss, David Frost: "Hi everybody, and hi to all those lovely people who are praying for us right now. I hope you pick up some good vibrations here tonight." He then introduced the first speaker, the organization's missionary secretary Peter Miller.'[1] When the ecstatic applause that greeted him subsided we heard controlled, defiant, slow hand claps that disturbed the worshipers. The missionary raised his hands for silence, but had to pause before he could tell of his shock at the moral degeneracy and utter godlessness he had encountered on returning from his missionary work in India. But, he confided that he had received a revelation from on high; a vision of tens of thousands of young people rising up in protest against the permissive society. He had spoken with God the Father, swearing to do his bidding, and The Almighty himself had confirmed him in his resolve to make this campaign the spearhead that would return the nation to the path of righteousness. This was what the audience had been waiting to hear and they responded with wild applause which gradually fell away to expose slow, disapproving, measured claps, once more disrupting the elation. With his wife by his side the missionary told us how heartened they were at the response from the others on the platform to their appeals for support. They too had done god's work in making this great campaign possible. This drew another great round of applause, but again the clapping died to a slow, censorious, provocative beat, and heads started turning in all directions. '"On September 23 beacons will be lit across the land to warn of the approaching tide of pornography, just as beacons warned of the coming of the Spanish Armada. The Royal Navy has entered the spirit of the occasion by agreeing to lend its searchlights at Plymouth Hoe, and Calor Gas is marketing a do-it-yourself gas beacon."'[2]Jubilant applause at that announcement faded once more to slow hand claps; deliberate, menacing, mocking. The faithful were incensed. Now everyone was furiously turning around trying to locate the source of what had to be a disruptive element in their midst.

The Bishop of Stepney, Trevor Huddleston took the microphone and we all listened to him respectfully because of his anti-apartheid stance when working in South Africa. He was old now, and considering his history obviously misguided in supporting this platform, so his speech was met with polite applause, leading many to think the disturbance was over.

The Dane was next to take the stand, and told us how his country had been flooded with pornography since the censorship laws had been rescinded. Suddenly there was a piercing scream from the main floor, followed by another and another, with people jumping up in their pews with snorts of disgust, while others began mimicking them in panic, all of them looking down at the floor or trying to push their way out along the pews, panicking their neighbours. GLF had released a battalion of mice. The woman conductor moved to the rostrum with a determined stride, the choir stood and sang out a hymn. All the heads of those seated on the dais inclined together, turning this way and that. The Dane was withdrawn before finishing his speech and was replaced by the cockney. Ted Lyon of course was there to tell us how he had been in a bit of bother but had found Jesus and wasn't getting into trouble no more, and if some people here were protesting it was a shame, because the majority was all good, honest, decent folk. Ted urged us to 'have a go for Jesus, he's a wonderful saviour, thanks.'

As the meeting settled once more, nuns in blue habits and white wimples filed out of their pews to stand in line abreast across the central aisle, before moving solemnly to the front of the hall. The pious sisters turned to face the congregation, lifted up their skirts and Can-Can danced their way down the aisle. There was pandemonium. People were utterly staggered. They couldn't believe their eyes; nuns going mad, exhibiting themselves in public. Corybantic banshees screaming with laughter at the worshippers, and one of them looked like a man. The choir mistress wasn't to be seen, she must have left the stage. The organist ordered a chorister to go and search for her. In the body of the church the stewards had to tackle the nuns but there weren't enough of them, and some of the nuns slipped past and carried on the Can-Can to the end of the aisle before being caught. As the multitude fought for breath the Youth Group at the front of the balcony chose that moment to drape a great white sheet over the edge, daubed in big red letters with 'Cliff for Queen'. The worshippers rendered witless by the nuns now looked up in fearful alarm at this further sacrilege, this desecration of the temple. The choir didn't know what to do, while up on the balcony the stewards were moving as fast as they could, clattering down the steep wooden steps to remove the Youth Group and untie the banner, but the rows they were sitting in had first to be emptied of all the innocent on either side before the guilty could be apprehended. The organist could wait no longer and thundered out 'How Great Thou Art'. Valiantly the audience rose and sang as though an act of godly worship would end the torments of the devil.

Joan Gibbons was the next to stand before us. She had been a sinner she said, and had been married several times. Until she was 51 she had led a life of depravity among the jet set while working for an English millionaire in New York. 'Fuck me, what were you doing there', interrupted her speech. She tried to reason with us by saying she understood that there might be some homosexuals in the meeting, and it was such a pity that they had chosen to be disruptive because she had homosexual friends too, and she knew how much happier they were, when like her they had found Jesus, and renounced their former life. The temperature shot up with suppressed rage. Clouds of talcum powder suddenly filled the air, and down from the sides of the balcony were hurled religious pamphlets which opened up to expose pornographic pictures tucked inside. The stewards came clattering down the stairs again to haul this group away, while down on the ground floor a great groan rose up at the sight of same sex couples, who had stood up, and started to kiss each other. Up went the baton and 'How Great Thou Art' trumpeted forth again. The tawdry life-story of Joan Gibbons was cut short.

Next was Malcolm Muggeridge, who came forward and took the microphone to great applause, for the congregation now knew they were in safe hands. Muggeridge started his talk by quoting something he'd read by the editor of *The Humanist*. A voice from the audience retorted: 'I am the editor of The Humanist, and I said no such thing.'[3] Muggeridge didn't stop to check the veracity of that. Raising his voice he said, 'It has been fashionable for the last fifty years for sociologists to tell us that the plight of the homosexual is the' – 'You don't like homosexuals do you Mr. Muggeridge?'– John Church's great baritone voice rang out. 'No,' he snapped back, 'I don't like them at all!' at which Cliff Richards leapt to his feet and jumped up and down with glee. 'Then you won't like me,' shouted Simon Benson from just below the pulpit, 'because I'm both homosexual and Jewish.' Bette Bourne's voice rebounded off the ceiling: 'How can I pray, how can I concentrate when I am surrounded by violence? There is violence in the air.' John Church agreed, 'I too can feel the violence in this assembly. It is all very disturbing.' Bette Bourne continued, 'I cannot pray in this violent atmosphere. There is violence in this house.' The man in front of Bourne turned round and stared at him. 'I can see the violence in your eyes', said Bourne. 'No, no', the man replied, 'It's the light of Jesus.' Without intro the organ broke into 'How Sweet The Name Of Jesus Sounds' the choir stumbled to their feet to join in, the stewards had once more to empty the pews to get at Bourne and Church, who were hauled to their feet and propelled to the nearest exit.

Muggeridge stayed in place, and at the end of the hymn asked his fellows in Christ to note how those who denied the light behaved, how they refused to listen to anyone except themselves; this blind, vulgar, brutish dis… – there was a wild shriek from high in the balcony and a voice cried out 'Ahs'a seen the face of the Lawd! Ahs'a been saved! Lawdy, Lawdy, ahs'a been saved! Glory, Glory, Hallelujah, ahs'a seen the face of the Lawd!' A woman in a coffee coloured lace dress with dark shoulder length hair stood with arms raised and a face full of rapture, praising her saviour in the southern accents of down home Alabamie. It was Michael James. He had managed to take off his trousers, smooth out his dress, step into his heels, apply eye make-up and lipstick, taken off his jacket, and put on a wig as those either side and in front of him were standing up singing. The worshipers were transfixed. The Methodist Central Hall was silent but for his cries. The entire congregation held their breath and for a moment or two believed that what they heard was true. Then came doubt, but oh how ardently they tried to suppress it, wishing it really was true. They were yearning for a miracle and it was being withheld.

Then, by some silent and mysterious command, the worshipers sharing the same back row as James stood up as one and fled into the aisle. The stewards advanced as Flannery, wardrobe mistress with the carrier bags, and James still proclaiming hosannas, descended the stairs, reached the central aisle before them and continued down to the front of the balcony, declaring 'Lawdy! Lawdy! Ahs'a been saved!' before being grabbed 'centre stage' and dragged off, testifying to the last. 'How Sweet The Name of Jesus Sounds' tried to calm nerves and steady the faithful, but many were too emotionally strained to give voice.

It was now the turn of my group and as soon as Muggeridge mentioned the word homosexual again, we removed our coats, displayed our Klu Klux Klan uniforms, donned the hat and stood arms raised, shouting, 'Yes burn them like faggots! Hangings too good for them! Bring back the birch! Jail them for life! Crucify them!' The stewards arrived, dragged us from the pews, and two-apiece manhandled us through the nearest exit and into the stairwell, where they landed a couple of punches to our bodies before we wrenched ourselves free, ran down the stairs and escaped into the night. Muggeridge despaired, 'I think it's a waste of time to try to develop any sort of cogent thought in the presence of such yahoos,'[4] and finally he gave up by quoting the bloody red hand of Ulster himself, the Rev. Ian Paisley, 'Let us put on the sword of strength, pick up the armour of righteousness, and come out into the light.'[5]

Fleeing from the arms of the church militant, we went round the corner to the pub where all the others who'd been thrown out were waiting. We were swapping stories when news came that some of the Christians wanted to talk with us about our reasons for the protest, so a few of us left and went back into the vestibule, but nobody from their side came forward. Some worshippers were leaving as we waited around, and most of those coming down the stairs from the balcony, looking over the balustrade and seeing us, made the sign of the cross with their forearms held in front of their faces, like we were vampires. Others raised their right arm, as many had done inside the hall, in a gesture reminiscent of the fascist salute.

What we missed by being ejected from the hall was the last planned event of the demonstration, carried out by the Action group themselves. Martin Corbett, Chesterman and others, disguised as workmen, succeeded in getting inside the relay room in the basement and threw a number of switches that plunged half the hall into darkness. As the *Guardian* headline next day put it: 'Darkness in our Light.'[6]

Two weeks later, Gay Lib Street Theatre, together with Women's Lib Street Theatre, were two of only three groups who decided to protest against the FoL rally in Trafalgar Square. The third group were a small number of volunteers from the Action Group on a separate mission. The rest of GLF and the libertarian groups had decided to demonstrate at the mass rally at Hyde Park.

Just as we did two weeks earlier, we passed through the West

End and into Covent Garden looking ordinary and respectable, with our costumes hidden under our outer clothes or in carrier bags. We thought there might be people on the lookout for us now that our faces were known, and a little discretion might get us through. Covent Garden in the seventies, before the neighbourhood was destroyed and the district redeveloped into a consumer spectacle, was very quiet at weekends; it was near to the square, and a place where you could find old shop doorways set back from the pavement. We all arrived at Henrietta Street at the same time. One minute we were hurrying along alone or in couples, the next moment the street was empty as we all dived into shop doorways. Then elbows poked out, legs flashed. Pairs of hips jostled. What looked like trousers flew upward and disappeared into a carrier bag. A pair of women's shoes appeared on a doorstep and a pair of large feet were crammed into them. Slowly we appeared on the street again. Some of us were dressed as nuns, others like the riot police. A school mistress, her hair in a severe bun, raised a cane at her children. A choir mistress wearing fifties upswept spectacles and a sensible two-piece outfit checked the choir girls in red tissue-paper capes assembling a coffin made of cardboard, with a note on its side saying 'The Coffin of Freedom'. A young man with a violin joined the choir. The Spirit of Porn, with shoulder length blonde hair, a short black skirt and fishnet stockings, like a cigarette girl, carried a tray of masks for sale of Mary Whitehouse and Lord Longford. A bearded man wearing a loin-cloth and a crown of twigs carried a cross. Women with painted beards dressed in men's clothes, clinging to feminine looking women, started to chain and padlock themselves together like heterosexual couples. They were joined by two women pushing toy prams with dolls inside. Together we filled the street with laughter at the sight of each other. The chorus mistress lined up the choir, the coffin was shouldered, the schoolmistress gathered her children, and a procession was formed that slowly moved west towards

Trafalgar Square led by the man with the cross.

The plan was to join the march to the rally as it left the square, heading west for Hyde Park, but when we entered the square it was immediately obvious that we would never reach the other side. The crowd to the north in front of the National Gallery, facing the speakers on the plinth of Nelson's Column was solid with religious devotees waving banners and roaring approval at the speeches being broadcast overhead. In all directions we were surrounded by the most ordinary looking suburban families standing there rocking backwards and forwards shrieking 'Jesus Saves!' 'Jesus Saves!' Their suppressed fury at the ungodly, unleashed by licence from their religious leaders on the plinth, fuelled by their secret love of acting that lies at the heart of fundamentalist worship, and the fact that they were away from home for the day, enveloped them in a frightening hysteria. Alongside the berserk, the odd spouse and some of the children joined in with reluctance, cringing at the mad fervour of their wide-eyed, tunnel-visioned family.

There was no choice but to turn south and edge along the boundary of the crowd. Carefully we picked our way between the ranting mass of families and the bystanders at the side, and by keeping an eye on each other reached the sanctuary of the steps to St. Martins-in-the-Fields, which quickly emptied at the sight of us. Excited by that reaction we mounted the steps and regrouped, taking full possession of the elevated position. We had planned to sing a hymn when walking to Hyde Park, but here we were in front of the portico of the great church, in the perfect architectural setting for a performance.

The choir mistress organized her charges to form up on the first row of steps. The schoolmistress placed children either side. The nuns appeared behind the choir one step higher. The riot police stood either side on the next step. The coffin of Freedom was held high. The bearded man stood in the centre of the step above draped around his cross, the violinist raised his bow, and under the baton of the choir mistress everyone broke into the Hymn, 'All things bright and beautiful.' The crowd in front separated. The self-righteous fled in terror at this vision from hell, while the bystanders burst out laughing, and gave us what can truthfully be described as a standing ovation.

> *John Norman Lloyd*: My job again was to provide smoke bombs for Trafalgar Square. Denis Lemon found out where to get them from, it was some place not far from Lambeth Palace and a friend drove me down there and I bought twelve, which must have cost quite a bit because they were quite big. The whole campaign was called Rupert, and I remember Peter Tatchell phoning me up and he said, 'This is Rupert speaking,' making it sound like espionage. He wanted to know if I needed any help in making banners with this idea, it wasn't very good, to associate the rally with fascism. I was going to dress up, I had a cap on and a little moustache and I was to hold up a banner saying 'Mein Kamp!', with a swastika on it, and I made a few of these and I turned up with these banners and the smoke-bombs. Behind St. Martin's-in-the-Fields I gave out the smoke-bombs, I gave one to Tony Halliday and his went off I know, only two or three did go off in the end, but the thing about them was they got on television. I thought that was wonderful, it showed this pall of smoke all around the plinth.[7]

After the hymn singing it was decided to continue going around the square to try and move off towards Hyde Park, so we set off in line down the side of South Africa House. About halfway along we stopped and bunched up when we saw ahead of us a line of policemen stretching from one side of the road to the other. Suddenly the crowd in front of us vanished and there we were, face to face with rank upon rank of lilies, who were not pleased to see us: they had been expecting us somehow, and had definitely determined not to let us pass.

We explained why we wished to go around the square. We explained why we were dressed as we were. We told them of our right to demonstrate. They were impassive. Then from the rear of the police lines a Deputy Commander of Scotland Yard stepped forward, walked up to the centre of the group, mostly women at that spot and told us to disperse. When we asked why, he answered, 'You're the Angry Brigade'. He stood there accusing us of being the mad bombers. We were shocked to the core. When we yelled out 'What do you mean?' he replied, 'That you are suspected of being associated with the Angry Brigade.'[8] The police then manoeuvred, drove a wedge between us, splitting us in two. On the square side the police line pushed us slowly round and backward, towards the crux of the lion plinths, and further and further they forced us, until our backs were pressed against the plinth of Nelson's Column itself, from where the only escape was up. So up some of us went. The choir mistress, the schoolmarm and several nuns somehow scrambled to safety up the black granite side of the monument. There below at the side of the plinth, their anxious faces turned upward, searching for their mistress was the choir, still resplendent in their red tissue paper capes. Seeing them down there the choir mistress raised her baton, and the choir once more sang out the hymn.

On the North side of the plinth the Festival organizers stood listening to the preacher and gazing at the immense crowd in front of them. Those at the corners, having glimpsed or sensed something odd happening behind them, came round the side of the column to investigate, and were aghast to discover the Alternative Mary Whitehouse, in her trade mark upswept glasses conducting choristers in a hymn, while the real Mary Whitehouse stood on the north side, holding herself and her beautiful morals aloft for the adoration of the congregation in front of her.

The police, finally realising they would have to exert

themselves, hauled their lard arses up onto the plinth, and then found they would have to climb onto the topmost ledge, in order to push those on the plinth back down. We queens of course scattered round the sides so that the police manoeuvre didn't work, forcing them to regroup and descend as a body on all three sides to surround us. The schoolmarm Michael James was the first to be picked off. Encircled by six or more policemen standing shoulder to shoulder they made a grab at him. We watched in horror as James's green and yellow patchwork wedgies and then his legs appeared high above the policemen's helmets – kicking air. They were holding him completely upside down. Still kicking wildly, lilly started lowering him headfirst over the side of the plinth, bumping his back on its edges, sea-sawing him over in their brutal efforts to get him to the ground. In the scrum at the base of the monument James's remaining wedge finally connected with a policeman's balls. Two Nuns restricted by their habits were also grabbed, the rest fled before the pigs returned. Somehow we got down off the column and away across the square and into the Mall, while the choristers disappeared into the crowd along with Richard Dipple who abandoned his cross.

Half way down the Mall we escapees began to meet up and calm down, and stopped to wait to see how many had got away. Five of us were left, The Spirit of Porn, two Nuns, a riot policemen and the Alternative Mary Whitehouse. United we started off again for Hyde Park and the mass meeting. All along the Mall and up Constitution Hill more of the barking mad stood on the pavement shrieking 'Jesus Saves.' What a relief it was to enter the Park and find some peace as we headed for Marble Arch. Striding out from beneath the trees our group reached that great open plateau of springy turf where we could see in the distance the huge crowd assembled. Streams of people flowed towards the gathering from all directions. Priests with banners led parishioners forward. There were whole convents of real nuns, and faintly on the breeze the sound of hymn singing. Where was GLF we wondered, scanning the distant view and looking for our banners as we strode towards the crowd in line abreast.

Our party were jerked backwards to a halt. It was so violent we felt sick with the shock and the sight of them. The police had swooped so cleverly we hadn't been aware of them at all. Silently the constables had run over the grass behind us. Grasping hands slid down to pinion our wrists, push our arms up our backs, and force us round and forward to a waiting police van. Fortunately the van door wasn't big enough to allow the police to throw us in, so we managed to regain some dignity and clock our captors as they hustled us onboard. A priest ran up and asked why we were being arrested. The door was slammed shut in his face, and off we bumped over the turf to the road leading down to the woodlands which hid Hyde Park Police Station. It was a short journey, but long enough for us to ask the arresting officers why we'd been arrested. Why had you behaved like that, we demanded, we haven't been causing trouble. We were making a peaceful protest. 'Don't you know that violence only leads to violence? 'Cat got your tongue? Shy are you? Do you prefer boys or girls, officer?'

The van drew into the yard and up to the main door of the station. There to meet us was another bunch of police, a smirking reception committee. Now the officers had to get us out of the van in front of their colleagues, so they all started shouting out orders, making it look good, and pushing us forward out of the van, face to face with the welcoming party while twisting our arms up against our backs again. The reception committee joined in by pushing our heads down and two-apiece frog marched us into separate cells. Those pigs loved it, they'd never seen anything like it. What a fucking laugh.

The cell door banged shut. The smirking policemen and the sneering one had gone. I stood looking at the bars on the window high up, the glazed brick and the scratched graffiti when suddenly the door opened and there they were again, in a bit of a cod panic. 'Are you wearing a bra?' they leered at me. 'Yes' I replied, thinking 'The only time I've ever worn one.' 'Take it off!' 'Why?' 'Because you might hang yourself, now get it off.'

We were held in solitary confinement for four or five hours, presumably until word arrived that the last Christians had left the park, before the cells were opened, and we were told to stand in line by our doors. Half way down the corridor, on the other side to where we were standing was the charge-sergeant sitting at a desk in a corridor at right angles to ours. In that other corridor were the arresting officers, stepping forward to claim their prisoner as we appeared from behind the sergeant, having moved down our corridor, u-turned at the end and come back down the other side. I was the last in the line, and when I drew level with the desk it was Nicholas Bramble as the Spirit of Porn who was being charged. I heard the sergeant say to Bramble's arresting officer, 'Are you sure? Are you sure you want to charge him with assault'. 'Yeah, I am,' he answered. 'Well if you're sure ...' said the sergeant looking at the officer and shaking his head, 'what happened?' Like the others, he had approached from behind to grab his victim's arms, but although Bramble was small he was deceptively strong from his Royal Ballet training, and reacted by locking his arms. The policeman's hands, meeting much stronger resistance than he anticipated, overshot, and he ended up cutting his little finger on Bramble's diamante bracelet. The colour drained from Nick Bramble's face as he was charged with assault of a police officer, a conviction for which carries an automatic six month jail sentence. Chris Blaby and Tim Bolingbroke who were the nuns, Paul Theobald the riot policemen, and myself as the Alternative Mary Whitehouse, were charged with Disturbing the Peace.

Outside, on the grass, in the warmth and soft light of the evening was dear Andrew Lumsden, who hearing of our arrest came to wait for our release. As Nicholas Bramble said, 'Where were the Marxist men, it was them that got us into this in the first place.' Where too was the support from the Action Group, we wondered. What we didn't know, was that those arrested in Trafalgar Square had no one there to support them either. Women's Lib theatre's pretend heterosexuals all chained together, were all too easily arrested soon after they unfurled a banner proclaiming, 'All God's children got Nipples'. Nuns Michael Reading and Douglas MacDougall and Riot Policeman Carla Toney were also grabbed in Trafalgar Square.

The Action group, the straight-gays who organized and co-ordinated the demonstration had made no arrangements for arrests in Trafalgar Square: there were no observers in place, no lawyers on standby, as there were for 19 others arrested in the park. That failure to support the women and drag queens was the point at which a line was drawn. We felt it was class betrayal. At the next general meeting, Bramble, on bail and facing a possible jail sentence, demanded an explanation. They had none to give.

The other police action in Hyde Park was to arrest and take away the big black, red and purple GLF Banner with the inter-linked female and male symbols. Attempts were later made to retrieve it but police claimed it was lost. We tend to believe they held a ceremony and burnt it.

But in the end Operation Rupert was a great success and only half of the 70,000 expected for the rally in Hyde Park turned up. The FoL was so blighted by GLF's campaign it withered away and there have been no more mass rallies by fundamentalist Christian groups. The threats to civil liberties caused by the repression instigated by the FoL was taken up by libertarian groups in a serious way, and all because our sense of humour trumped the religious extremists, entertained press reporters, and invited the country to laugh at an organization that couldn't face down a bunch of lesbians and gays.

Police retaliation for our attack on the FoL was swift. Members going for a drink after the next General Meeting found *The Chepstow* barricaded in by police cars, Black Marias, and a force announcing that the landlord did not want us in his pub. Pretending that GLF was associated with the AB, the Metropolitan Police were attempting to impose apartheid; forcing us back into the ghetto where their agents, the landlords, could control our access to the community.

After the first General Meeting in All Saints Hall back in July, 400 thirsty men and women had fanned out into Notting Hill looking for refreshments. The nearest gay pub, the *Champion* in Bayswater was nearly a mile away. Somewhat nearer was *The Chepstow,* which had been gay for some six months during the late-sixties (in the Paddington Police District gay bars have never lasted longer), with drag shows in the upstairs room organized by the landlady whose daughter had reputedly married a son of Alan Ladd, the fifties Hollywood movie star. Many went there because of its previous reputation, and it was these two pubs that first began to discriminate against people wearing GLF badges. The nearest straight pubs were *The Colville* in Talbot Road on the corner with Portobello, or in the opposite direction *The Artesian.* There was also the *Pembridge Castle,* the *Duke of Norfolk, The Alma,* and if you were heading to the Gate up Portobello Road, *Henneky's* Wine Bar. After the meeting, all those pubs were suddenly swamped by gay libbers, long haired bearded students, colourful hippies, men and women in denim and slacks, all wearing the same badge, and all doing a lot of hugging and kissing, mostly with people of the same sex. The landlord of *Henneky's* having taken everyone's custom, closed the bar, ordered people to drink up and called the police.

The next Wednesday night those pubs were again overwhelmed, and again the landlord of *Henneky's* took the money then stole the pleasure with a repeat performance. About sixty Gay Libbers then went to the *Pembridge Castle* and the *Duke of Norfolk* where they were turned away, the bar closed and the police called. Andrew Lumsden with backing from the Steering Group contacted the press.

> Mr. Andrew Lumsden, a Front Member, complained yesterday of clear discrimination, and said, 'landlords were encouraging a return to the days when homosexuals of both sexes were forced into "ghetto" pubs as the only places in which they could behave naturally ... if people kissing one another was not offensive to regulars at the pub we used for three months in Covent Garden, why should it be assumed to be offensive to the public in Portobello Road? It seems that the community is afraid of us. This is an important matter of principle and it could get worse.' The Front was likely to distribute leaflets to public house customers in Portobello Road on a Saturday in their campaign to establish the right of homosexuals to kiss in public. *Henneky's* said, 'two or three' Front couples had been seen kissing in the bar on the first Wednesday. The landlord did not want a build-up of people, whose behaviour was suspect, taking over one of our houses. 'Fellows kissing each other and holding hands is not what we want in what is a mainly family house on weekdays. I am not talking about homosexuals but the difficulties of running a pub. A canoodling courting couple would be just as objectionable.'[9]

As news of Gay Lib's move to Notting Hill circulated the grapevine and was then broadcast in the press, the meetings grew more crowded than ever. After the publicity, *Henneky's* became the frontline pub of choice for some members, but again they found their money exchanged for drinks they were not allowed to enjoy for long. Again the manager rang the police, who this time must have been waiting for the call, because as members left the premises and started walking back down Portobello towards the other pubs, the police were waiting and grabbed John Church, Malcolm Bissett, Neville Smith and Les Tebbs, pushed them into a police van and rushed them off to Notting Hill Police Station. The four were charged with obstruction, but before Malcolm Bissett was charged, the police stripped him to his underpants and forced him to stand on a table in a room full of uniformed officers, who jeered, mocked and threatened him with violence. The institutional humiliation of nineteen year old Malcolm Bissett was terrifying – his forbearance truly heroic.

When the details were reported at the next general meeting on the 18 August there was uproar. The four declared they wanted to defend themselves, and appealed for volunteers to act, as MacKenzie lawyers prepared to take over the court and invent delaying tactics so that the hearings could be stretched out as long as possible in the hope that this would discourage the police from making more arrests. It was overwhelmingly agreed that the Action Group must plan a protest.

Behind closed doors the Action Group debated and thought through ideas for a demonstration. New to the group and GLF was Phil Powell, a left-wing polytechnic lecturer, who proposed and oversaw the plan, together with Chesterman. First they drew up a leaflet appealing for support from the local community. Addressed to the people of Notting Hill it reminded them of the fun everyone had at the Carnival, and invited them to boycott *Henneky's, The Colville* and the *Champion.*

Matters settled down in the following weeks, price rises were noted along with other restrictions that occurred as the police tightened the screw and tried to provoke some kind of confrontation on the streets. The continuous harassment made everyone calmly decide to have a demonstration on our terms. Things were clear and out in the open. In October, the Action Group were ready and called on members to help distribute a leaflet they had prepared, addressed to the straight-gays on the scene.

PISSED OFF

WE'RE PISSED OFF BEING OVERCHARGED, HERDED TOGETHER IN A SMALL NUMBER OF OVERCROWDED

GAY GHETTO PUBS AND COFFE BARS WHICH EXPLOIT GAYS AND GIVE LITTLE IN RETURN – no holding hands, no close dancing and behave or you're out.

WE'RE PISSED OFF being barred for expressing our sexuality.

WE'RE PISSED OFF being beaten, and hustled and pushed around on the street for simply being ourselves, gay,

AND, ABOVE ALL, WE'RE PISSED OFF with not being allowed to talk as we want, be what we are, act as we want.

YOU KNOW THAT HOMSEXUALS ARE DENIED FULL CITIZEN'S RIGHTS and it's getting worse not better.

SO, WE'RE DOING SOMETHING ABOUT IT – THAT'S WHY WE'RE TOGETHER

And that's why, next Wednesday, we're going to some Notting Hill pubs that the police and landlords have barred us from WE'RE GOING TO DEMAND FROM LANDLORDS AND POLICE EQUAL RIGHTS FOR ALL OUR HOMOSEXUAL BROTHERS AND SISTERS – the right to drink where we please.

If you think our problems are your problems – join us

7.30pm, next Wednesday, All Saints Church Hall, Powis Gardens, Notting Hill.

GLF is a lot of different people from different places with different ideas.

That's why some of us turn you off sometimes.

BUT – we have the one thing in common that really matters – our homosexuality – that's why we ask you to join us.

Join us this Wednesday – in a place where gay people are getting together as people and not as consumers. Are you gay during licensing hours only?

Come and see what it's all about. Get us to listen to you. We must learn from each other to work out a better style of life.

In GLF we are developing real relationships, real warmth,

real love.

The politics is only one aspect of a way of life that is allowing gay people to stand up to say and mean and *feel* that *Gay Is Good.*

Gay Liberation Front. 5, Caledonian Road. Tel. 837- 7174

Meetings Wednesday s, 7.30 All Saints Church Hall, Powis Gardens, W.11.

GAY IS GOOD [10]

To remain within the law and challenge the authorities, the following letter was sent.

To: Superintendent, Notting Hill Police.
Copies: Commissioner Metropolitan Police. Press.
Re: harassment of gay people in and around Notting Hill pubs.

The members of the Gay Liberation Front intend, on Wed., October 6th, evening, to exercise their right as citizens to purchase drinks in pubs of their own choosing.

We shall respond passively to any hindrance or violence, whether by publicans or police. Any assaults that occur will be on us not by us.

We will not be dissuaded by any means that are available to you from our purpose of securing the right to equal treatment whilst wearing a badge that expresses our identity as people.

We may, as we see fit, file a complaint relating to police threats to publicans who serve people wearing GLF badges, which complaint would be backed by signed affidavits.[11]

A message of a similar nature was sent to all the pubs in the area and their breweries. An invitation to the press to witness the demonstration followed; another attempt to use the media instead of being used by them.

Press Statement, October 5th Police Harassment of Gay Liberation Front

On Wednesday, October 6th, 300 or more members of Gay Liberation Front are prepared to be arrested, if necessary, to secure the right to drink at pubs of their own choosing. They are pissed off at the continual harassment which has prevented them from exercising that right.

After a meeting of GLF at All Saints Hall, Powis Gardens, W11 on Wednesday Sep 22nd, members went to the Chepstow Public House in Chepstow Road, where they had been warmly received by the landlord and his wife on the two previous Wednesdays.

They found the entrance barred by a large number of policemen, some apparently drawn from other areas of London. In the road outside were a black maria and various other police vehicles. The police informed us that they had been called as the landlord no longer wanted to receive our custom.

On going to The Artesian (corner of Chepstow Rd and Talbot Rd) we were told by a barman that we could only be served if we removed our badges as THE POLICE HAD TOLD THE MANAGER THAT RENEWAL OF HIS LICENCE WOULD BE OPPOSED IF HE SERVED GLF CUSTOMERS and that THE SAME THREAT HAD BEEN MADE TO OTHER PUBLICANS IN THE AREA.

Members then visited other pubs, including the Colville, the Alma and the Duke of Norfolk, in all of which we were refused service.

This harassment by police of GLF was raised by one of us on the Thames TV Programme 'Today' (Friday 24 Sep) during which Lord Longford offered to go with us to the pubs in question.

After considerable evasion LORD LONGFORD HAS NOW AGREED TO MEET A REPRESENTATIVE OF GLF, TODAY

(Tues, 5th) WITH A VIEW TO ARRANGING THIS VISIT. WE EXPECT LONGFORD TO FULFIL HIS PUBLICLY STATED PROMISE AND TO BE WITH US ON WEDNESDAY NIGHT. [He didn't and he wasn't: just cynically media savvy]

Scotland Yard has demanded a transcript of the television programme.

This act seems particularly significant in view of the brutal police behaviour towards GLF demonstrators when they arrested several of them in Trafalgar Square and Hyde Park on Saturday, Sep 25, during the Festival of Light. So violent and brutal were the police that a number of Festival of Light supporters have offered to testify in our defence and pay our fines. The events were reported in the Sunday Times.

As a non-violent organisation, GLF particularly resents the statement by a police inspector, reported in the Sunday Times (26th) and witnessed by several of us, that he knew 'the GLF is connected with the Angry Brigade'. This accusation has no possible basis in fact; but it is one that the police seem to be using against an ever increasing number of groups, in order to give an air of legitimacy to what is a crude attempt at the repression of various legitimate minority groups.

It is impossible to view the events of the past fortnight without reaching the conclusion that the police are mounting a campaign against GLF members, with the object of driving them back into the ghetto.

In an attempt to verify this, a few GLF members with independent observers visited public houses in the Notting Hill area on Tues, 28th. The answers were oddly evasive (perhaps the landlords had received a second visit from the police?) but in several cases landlords remained adamant in their refusal to serve GLF members.

It is in this context that GLF has decided that it must assert its right to equal treatment in the pubs.

We will, on Wednesday, 6th, leave our meeting at All Saints

Hall and seek as a group to purchase drinks in the pub or pubs that we choose.

We shall respond passively to any hindrance or violence whether by publicans or police. Any assaults that occur will be on us, not by us.

We will not be dissuaded by any means that are available to the police or publicans from our purpose of securing the right to equal treatment whilst wearing a badge that expresses our identity as people.

We will leave our meeting after 8 pm.

Further we do not intend to tolerate other forms of discrimination against our sexuality. The price of a pint of bitter, in The Colville, went up from 13 to 14p to 20p during the period when our money was welcome.

We have had enough; we will fight back; and there is every indication that our fight is supported by a massive number of gay people throughout London and the country.[12]

At the meeting prior to the demonstration a leaflet was handed out to everyone, on the reverse of which was a map of the area with the hall and the pubs marked out. 'THE RIGHT TO DRINK WHERE WE CHOOSE' detailed the reasons for the demonstration and how we were to behave, offering only passive resistance. We were instructed to always move in groups so as to prevent the police from picking us off individually. It called for volunteers who were prepared to be arrested and advised the remainder to stay close to their convenors and to always obey police instructions. It assured us that lawyers were on standby, reminded us of our rights and what to do when arrested, told us that the pubs had all been leafleted, and the press, television and local MPs informed.

Often when a demonstration is planned people say they will come and then never turn up, but there were at least 350 of us for this one, a great show of strength that made everyone feel proud.

As we left the hall we gave our names to the convenors to say we were willing to be arrested, read our instructions, wrote the lawyers telephone number on arm or wrist, and with excitement mounting, quietly departed. Some had brought balloons, someone else produced clouds of soap bubbles. The street was empty with not a policeman in sight, and five minutes later we were walking into *The Colville*. It was immediate and total capitulation by the Landlord; pints were being pulled as quickly as the pumps allowed.

About half of the demonstrators stayed there to drink, but once a sizeable number had been served, point made, it was on to *The Chepstow*, which we thought was going to be more difficult given the big police presence there the previous month, but when we came around the corner at the bottom of the street, again there wasn't a policeman in sight. Despite the victory at *The Colville* we approached *The Chepstow* just as quietly, for if they heard us and shut the place we wouldn't be able to demonstrate effectively. But it was open and we were in there like a shot.

'A pint of crème de menthe please.' The first in lined the bar, proffering their pound notes and trying to give their orders. 'You've already been told you're banned. If you don't leave right now, I'll call the police,' the purple nosed publican announced. Those at the front politely continued to ask for drinks, but gradually people started sitting down, on the chairs, the banquettes and the floor, until there was just no room to move. The sullen staff found chores to do, whilst we all chatted and joked and waited for the police to arrive. The landlord anxiously huffed and puffed, ignored by everybody.

> Two hundred members of GLF descended on a pub demanding to be served. They created such a disturbance, screaming and using obscene language that the licensee was forced to call the police. Despite repeated calls the police did not arrive. In desperation the licensee phoned Scotland Yard

> who sent the Flying Squad. He has appealed to his local Licensed Victuallers Association St. Marylebone for help. A special meeting is to be called to discuss the threat. He is also complaining to his brewery that the local police ignored his call for aid. 'If they come in we are not going to serve them. Some of them were in here two or three weeks ago kissing and cuddling in the saloon bar. I can't have men making love to one another in my pub.' Many of the regulars had complained about the behaviour, he stressed. Representatives of the flamboyantly dressed GLF group apologised to the pubs regulars for the inconvenience, 'This pub is one of the last bastions of reaction and prejudice for us.'[13]

After waiting about an hour, the police eventually turned up and after surveying the scene, ordered us out, 'Come along ladies and gentlemen, you've been told to leave.' But we didn't move. The press were there as well as the NCCL, and Chesterman with a borrowed video camera with a label stuck on the side that read GLF TV, gave the nod to Geoff Marsh to switch on a pair of impressive looking lights whilst Chesterman panned the scene. The camera was in fact empty as he couldn't afford the then expensive video tape, but the trick worked well. The police were immediately on their best behaviour, and knew the drill. First the landlord had to ask the individual sitting nearest the front door to please leave, and when the demonstrator refused, two of the policemen could then pick that person up and carry them out to the pavement, and place them back on the ground. Gradually as space opened up inside the pub, more police were able to enter, but it was a slow process with everybody having to be asked personally by the landlord to leave the premises, before police action could be taken. As time went on the police realized that their hard work was not producing visible results. Many who had been deposited on the pavement outside had not remained there, or strolled off, but like me, nipped down the mews and got back in the pub by the side door.

> The following day the Chepstow agreed to serve GLF members. By Monday, all pubs in the area had backed down: GLF members are promised service in any pub they choose.
>
> OUR ACTION ON THIS ISSUE WAS COMPLETELY SUCCESSFUL.[14]

There was one casualty, Mark Roberts an eighteen year old from South Wales who had arrived in London the day before and was on his first demonstration. He was the first to be ejected and with no witnesses around placed in a police van and charged with assaulting an officer. Fortunately at trial the magistrate did not believe the police, and the charge was reduced to obstruction for which he was found guilty and fined £10.

Chapter 8

Ideologies Clash

> The suffering of women is the history of the worst form of tyranny that the world has ever known. The tyranny of the weak over the strong. It is the only tyranny that lasts.
> Oscar Wilde

Throughout the summer and autumn of 1971 raids by the Bomb Squad on the homes of dissidents increased exponentially as the police trawled through the address books seized from every house they searched. If you heard that a house had been raided and knew someone who lived there and had your telephone number in their book you could be sure you would be turned over.

As the Bomb Squad raided homes in London and Essex, bombs exploded in protest at the Government's closure of Upper Clyde Shipbuilders and the introduction of Internment without Trial in Northern Ireland.

On 21 August, a house in Amhurst Road, Hackney, was raided by Special Branch and CID. Jim Greenfield, Anna Mendleson, John Barker and Hilary Creek were arrested. The four were taken to Bomb Squad HQ in Albany Street, where the two men were subjected to savage beatings with the aim of extracting confessions. In the afternoon, Stuart Christie was arrested when visiting the house. The police then planted two detonators in the boot of his car. Chris Bott was arrested an hour later when he visited the address. Both were taken to join the others at Albany Street Police Station. All of the arrested were verballed.[1]

On 23 August the six were charged at Albany Street Police Station with:

1. Conspiring to cause explosions between January 1 1968 and August 21 1971.
2. Possessing explosive substances for an unlawful purpose.
3. Possessing a pistol without a firearms certificate.
4. Possessing eight rounds of ammunition without a firearms certificate.
5. Possessing two machine guns without the authority of the Secretary of State.
6. Possessing 36 rounds of ammunition without a firearms certificate.
7. Greenfield: attempting to cause an explosion in May 1970.
8. Greenfield and Mendleson: attempting to cause an explosion in Manchester, October 1970.
9. Christie: possessing one round of ammunition without a firearm certificate.
   (This was dated back 2 years when a bullet was taken from his flat. No charges had been proferred against him at the time.)
10. Barker, Christie and Greenfield: possessing explosive substances.
11. Barker, Creek and Greenfield: receiving stolen vehicle.
12. Christie: possessing explosive substances. (The two detonators planted by the police).
    All were refused bail and remanded in custody to await trial.

Despite the police claim to have arrested all of the AB, seven bombs exploded nationwide in the following two months, one was even discovered in the officers' mess inside Dartmoor prison, and communiqués continued to be issued. On 30 October the night before the big Anti-Internment March through London that GLF was joining, the Post Office Tower was bombed, which the IRA and the AB both claim and both disclaim responsibility for, whilst outside London the AB bombed *The Cunning Man* pub,

Reading, that refused to serve workers from the M4 road building site. Agitprop suffered raids at least once a fortnight.

> *Tony Halliday*: I do not think that anyone at Agitprop had any connection with the Angry Brigade: had there been even the remotest evidence that they had, it would have been very much in the interests of the police to arrest someone from the collective as it would have lent credibility to their activities. Police attention directed at Agitprop was clearly intended to spread paranoia amongst the extra-parliamentary left in general, and, to judge by what happened in GLF, it was not ineffective in that respect.[2]

It was during this period that I learnt that some in Gay Lib suspected that others might know someone in the AB. Many people were telling their friends that they had come across individuals they suspected were plain clothes policemen, or policewomen, or informers at the general meetings. We began to believe the office phone was tapped. Andrew Lumsden was told by a school friend that a class mate of theirs, who worked for the Secret Service, had come across his file, and that could only have come about through his GLF activity. General meetings now began with the announcement that people should be aware that the Special Branch might be present.

The left was another covert operator, always sneaking into each other's meetings, but fortunately our sexuality protected us from any approaches by them. They saw us as degenerates and perverts, and in any case the organized left were into organization, and with no structure to our movement there was nothing for them to latch onto. The often chaotic and anarchic general meetings sometimes made headway difficult, but the compensation for that was that the left could not get a grip on proceedings. The problem was the AB. As we have seen, they targeted the Miss World Contest indicating that they supported the sexual politics of Women's Lib. Whether they saw us as recruits to a gay wing is impossible to know, but they must have been aware of the gay ability to lead successful double-lives, and may have considered us to be suitable material for clandestine work.

> *Carla Toney*: Barbara and I were invited to become involved in something more radical, quite loudly, by Andy Elsmore. He said, 'Do you want to join the Angry Brigade?' – on top of a bus – with other people listening – and I thought, 'You asshole.' I think I looked out the window. They were such assholes, so stupid about it, and I thought, 'These guys are going to get busted', and of course they were. They were all middle class, and as middle class people are wont to do in Europe and America, while the working class are too busy earning a crust of bread, the middle class people go out and bomb.[3]

> *Elizabeth Wilson*: I think Andy wanted to pose as Angry Brigade. I don't think he was anywhere really, but he thought it was tremendous to be associated with it.[4]

Shortly after the GLF Manifesto was published, and in response to its findings, Media Workshop was presented with an article for publication in *Come Together* written by Andy Elsmore. Its title was: 'Towards a Revolutionary Gay Liberation Front'. It fell like Thor's hammer on the rigid tensions within Media Workshop, fracturing the surface unity and exposing the separate ideologies that lay beneath. When the dust settled, everyone in the collective could agree on only one thing: the article was badly written and needed more work on it before being reconsidered for publication. Elsmore agreed to the deal and was given assistance by Walter, Fernbach and Powell. With a week to think about Elsmore's article, some members of Media workshop like Sarah

Grimes, Anny Brackx, and Mick Belsten, who recognized how much of a threat the article represented to their politics and view of the development of the movement up to this point, were concerned enough to privately discuss and ready themselves for the second meeting.

The amended version was headed with this note:

> The original version of this article was submitted to Media Workshop to be put in *Come Together* two weeks ago. It was criticised for its style and attitude towards GLF and was rejected. Three members of GLF, including the original author, all of whom feel that it raises very important questions about GLF, revised it in the light of Media Workshop's criticisms and resubmitted the following Thursday. There was a long and heated discussion, and it was rejected again: Media Workshop thought that the matter should be taken to a general meeting, so here it is. The authors feel that both the article and its rejection from GLF's newspaper are very important issues and must be discussed by as many members as possible. So we have duplicated the article together with a complete list of objections taken down at Media Workshop on Thursday. Sisters and Brothers, let's have some feedback on this so that Media Workshop can function as a truly representative mouthpiece of GLF.

TOWARDS A REVOLUTIONARY GAY LIBERATION FRONT

History:

[1] GLF has been going for over a year now. Yet in spite of a lot of actions and discussions, how many of us have attempted to analyse how we are oppressed, who is responsible for the oppression and how we are successfully to fight back and smash the oppression? Probably most of us still see the immediate enemy – the most apparent enemy, i.e.,

'straight society' – as the main enemy, and often the only enemy. We're really into recognising and attacking sexism, but only in isolation. We do pay lip service to other forms of oppression (racism, capitalism, etc) but the main enemy is sexism; all other forms of oppression are secondary, and therefore do not concern us.

[2] Thus most of us saw the Festival of Light only as an attack on gay people, and its more sinister aspects – i.e. its parallels with Hitler's fascism and all that that implies – are ignored. Only 'gay' issues affect gay people.

[3] Thus it could be said in *Come Together* No. 5 when talking of GLF's presence at an anti-IRB march '... many, in fact most, of the people on the demo were real male chauvinists themselves, and therefore our enemy ...' Surely this is a confused idea of who in fact our main enemy is and who we should be uniting with on a critical basis? But is such confusion surprising in view of the way we have separated sexism from related oppressions?

[4] When people are told of a gay group in California who are going to take over a small county (with no respect for the people already living there, no attempt to explain gay feelings to them, and every intention of setting up the whole oppressive structure of our society, complete with pigs and property rights) there is an automatic 'right on' – after all they're sure to be sexist pigs, so what the fuck. When we talked about Jake Prescott and Ian Purdie, who have been in solitary confinement in Brixton prison for eight months, the first question is 'are they gay' – and sure enough it was only if they were gay that GLF would be interested enough to hear about them. So we seem to be into supporting an oppressive society if it is run by gays, but not supporting those who are fighting oppression in our own society.

And Now?

[5] We must ask ourselves: how do other people see

themselves in this system, how can we unite with those who also are oppressed by this Capitalist/Imperialist white, male dominated system? How do we smash this system and start to build systems based on love and trust, one where people can live as people and not be oppressed and exploited at every turn? These are the questions we should be considering in relation to that of sexism

I was a soldier
A cockney soldier
A man that was born to die
Only cockney blokes get killed
Stuffy officers stay back safely.

I was a soldier
A cockney soldier
Before I died on the hill
With a bullet in my heart
I clawed my way to hell

My brother was a soldier
A bloody good soldier
He was also born to die
But he died by being shot
Climbing over the wire
back to our trenches
We both met in hell.

This poem, written by a young Stepney boy, sums up, from long and bitter experience, what his position in this society is – cannon fodder in the wars between land grabbing Imperialists. But he's sure to be a sexist – after all, I doubt that anyone has ever told him what sexism is, but by our history we would put him down as an enemy. That unfortunately, is where most of us in GLF are at, at the moment: even the Manifesto talks about gay people being oppressed only in terms of sexism, and even then the discussion of sexism seems isolated from any broad view of society's structure. Where does it tie in with other forms of oppression? How can we fight it effectively? Even the section headed 'Why we are oppressed' does no more than talk about 'straight society' and yet 'the first class antagonism which appears in history coincides with the development of the antagonism between man and woman in monogamous marriage and the first class oppression with that of the female sex by the male.'* So if this was the first class antagonism it leads one to think that there are other class antagonisms and oppressions and that we could unite with other people being oppressed and fight those responsible for the oppression. The monogamous marriage is related to the development of private property and the development of the second class antagonism, namely that between those who have stolen property to become the ruling class and those whose property and/or labour has been stolen thus forcing them into becoming a lower class. The first class antagonism cannot be solved without also solving the second, and vice versa. Thus it is useless to discuss class struggle in isolation from the struggle against sexism, as do most Marxists, and equally useless to discuss sexism in isolation from class struggle. *Engels; *The Origin of the Family*.

[6] Moreover, the Manifesto simply reflects the class basis of GLF – an essentially middle class base, with plenty of ideas about male chauvinism, but so far, no understanding of the need to fight its own class chauvinism. For example, only two gay days in working class areas; a Benefit which cost one pound a head and which was so much into the star system that it had to be cancelled when the star backed out. We must avoid the 'Gay Nationalist' attitude that only gay problems affect gay people and concern ourselves with all oppressions.

We cannot be free until everyone is free.

So Where do we go from here?

[7] GLF can and must change, the Manifesto must be open to change, we cannot be contented with simply describing, but must analyse the point and point the way to fighting back. We must struggle with ourselves and other oppressed and exploited people and against the ruling class and their lackeys. When we talk of a Revolutionary Gay Liberation Front, we are talking of a GLF which will concern itself with making a revolution for ALL the people – a non-white-male-dominated revolution which will liberate people, not just gay people or working class people but PEOPLE. This means uniting with all progressive people to fight the monster called capitalism. This will be a critical, non quantitative relationship (i.e. not you do one thing for us and we'll do one thing for you, but a sharing of effort in the struggle). It will be a critical relationship because we only learn to change the brainwashing this society gives us by criticism and self-criticism. We must unite with other countries who are making their revolution and are now on the road to socialism, on this same basis: this includes countries such as Cuba, in spite, or rather because, of its oppression of gay people and women.

[8] We must not take an uncritical position and ignore the crimes and stupidities directed at us. However, in spite of some important failings that especially concern us, we feel that the Cuban revolution is a source of hope to all oppressed people. To appreciate what it has accomplished one only has to compare conditions in Cuba ten years after the revolution with conditions in other Latin American countries where disease, illiteracy, high mortality rates and malnutrition are rampant and people live without hope. A 'gay nationalist' attitude in Cuba would have done nothing to improve the lot of Cuban gays – or straights.

[9] Marx and Engels put forward the slogan 'Workers and

Oppressed People of the World unite . . . you have nothing to lose but your chains.' This is one of the slogans we must take up as our own and start to apply to move towards the Revolutionary GLF. We must cease considering the individual sexist as our enemy regardless of his class position; we must strive and struggle against the system which maintains sexism as a way of dividing the masses and of reinforcing the values of private property. For in this society, women and gay people are considered to be the property of their partner and indeed of the men in society itself – to be raped and murdered by the system whenever it wants – a society where workers are considered to be the property of the factory owner to be hired and fired at whim, and where schoolchildren are the property of the ruling class, which decides what they should be trained for.

[10] We must unite with black people, women, workers, children, anyone who is struggling for freedom, and we must not reject them if they are scared of us at first – they have 2,000 years of brainwashing to overcome too. As a sister said in *Come Together* No.8: 'And now they are more frightened than ever because they can't turn and say to any white man that at least there's a black man to kick around, because the black man won't let him. They can't say to any man, at least you can be king to your woman, because women won't let him. And they cannot say, what has been the most corrosive thing to say to any "straight", at least you're not "queer" because WE won't let them. When they can't use sexism and racism then force is the only thing they can use . . . And we must go on getting stronger, go on fighting because we have no choice but to fight for our liberation. And as our critique of the system must be total, so must our weapons be.'

[11] We have got a revolution to make, but revolutions are not made by creating ghettoes of freedom in our minds, they are made by and for ALL the people – let us develop a critique

> of the way in which society inflicts itself on all the people, let us try and discover the best way to smash this decadent Capitalist/ Imperialist system, let's apply that – unite theory and practice, unite with all oppressed people and start to create a society where we can breathe as free people.
>
> ALL POWER TO ALL THE PEOPLE – REVOLUTION TILL VICTORY.[5]

The following attempts to answer the article point by point.

(1) Elsmore's set-up is that members haven't analyzed their position, while he has.

The organising principle of GLF was the shared experience of suffering imposed on us by sexism. Racism is the corollary of sexism, both stem from the fear of the 'other'. No one joined GLF because of economic or class issues as proved by the rejection of clause V of the Principles.

(2) This shows how out of touch Elsmore was because everyone who took part in the protests against the FoL was aware of its sinister fascist overtones. The probable reason for him not joining the demo in Methodist Central Hall is that it was organized by the counter-culture in GLF.

(3) Our presence on the anti-IRB march was doing exactly what Elsmore suggests GLF should have been doing: uniting with the protesters on a critical basis. His quote from a paragraph of 'GLF Against the Bill' in *Come Together* 5 reads in full:

> We were not only there because as a liberation front we aim to help fight all forms of oppression, but also because many, in fact, most of the people on the demo were real male chauvinist themselves and therefore our enemy. We were there to *confront* the male chauvinism of working people. We felt that if we could get people to let go of their male privilege they will have no further interest in this oppressive system,

> and will therefore fight harder against it. So our presence was really important, because we are starting to work alongside women, black people, and now those sections of youth and the working class who see the importance of *our* demands as well as their own, to break the old society which puts us all down and to build a new one on the basis of all our needs. Bill. [Bill Halstead].

This position also answers the accusations in paragraphs 6, 8 and 9.

(4) Here again Elsmore is out of touch. The controversy in California had already been thought through some time before, and the conclusion was: gay nationalism is twice as bad as straight nationalism. GLF already supported Prescott and Purdie's position of being wrongly accused, but had to carefully separate that from support for the AB, otherwise the argument could be that we support Prescott and Purdie, therefore we must support the AB.

(5) Elsmore presents us with two abbreviated misquotations from Engels: he goes on to suggest that there may be other class antagonisms, and proposes we should unite with unknown folk and tilt at their oppressions, but doesn't say why we should be diverted away from our own suffering, except by appealing to a sense of injustice over the theft of property and means of production that divided society into the haves and have-nots.

We already had a sense of injustice about our own position, why put it aside as gays before us on the left had done and got nowhere for it? A struggle to recover property and tools does not alter, and never has altered the oppression of women and homosexuals: it is simply a fight between two sets of men otherwise united in their overall power.

But just to give his readers a headache, Elsmore conflates his two mangled statements of Engels, throws in sexism, creates a double bind, and a tautology with plausible logic: 'The first class antagonism cannot be solved without also solving the second, and vice versa. Thus it is useless to discuss class struggle in isolation from the struggle against sexism, as do most Marxists, and equally useless to discuss sexism in isolation from class struggle.' A conclusion I think, which attempts to prohibit debate on sexism and maintain straight left orthodoxy.

Damn the headache: at the risk of being called a terrorist, I recommend the trenchant blade of Saint-Just, and with his maxim tempered in the French revolution cleave the sense of injustice and the double bind: 'We do not fight for the revolution on behalf of other people. We fight for the revolution for ourselves, and only incidentally for others.'

Engels in *Origin* and Wilhelm Reich in his *Sex-Pol Essays* based their work on pioneering ethnographer Lewis Henry Morgan (1818-1881) whose study of the Iroquois (the Seneca adopted him) and the Trobriand of Melanesia unravelled the sexually freer matriarchal societies' gens kinship groups and their evolutionary descent from savagery – group marriage, through barbarism – paired marriage, to civilization – monogamy.

Reich, who interrogated Morgan's text with his own Marxist and psychoanalytical disciplines found that during savagery the prohibition of incest was the first impulse towards sexual restriction. And in the following development of barbarism, that primitive communism lacking development resulted in social organizations determined by sexuality being intruded upon by the suppression of genital freedom. 'It first becomes apparent in the prohibition against sexual intercourse within the clan, i.e. the group of all maternally cosanguineous relatives. Considered from the period of its conception, this process of sexual suppression is older than the class conflict between male and female; it is this process that first led to class antagonism.'[6]

Engels: 'Pastoral tribes separated themselves from the general mass of the barbarians: the first great social division of labour. [The improved economy and conquered tribes] brought slavery in its wake. Out of the social division of labour arose the first great division of society into the classes of exploiters and exploited, masters and slaves.'[7]

The other statement of Engels that Elmore employs without quoting the first sentence, presumably because it involves sex, reads in full: 'The first division of labour is that between man and woman for child breeding.[8] And today I can add: the first class antagonism which appears in history coincides with the development of the antagonism between man and woman in monogamous marriage, and the first class oppression with that of the female sex by the male.'[9] That is male superiority: sexual class, a divided society, sexism.

(For us who don't labour in that particular garden we can expect for our disruptive lives the full force of heterosexual antagonism. For our freer sexuality we can expect schemes that severely restrict our access to productive labour and its rewards. I consider that sexism, racism, heterophobia and misogyny are stratagems of heterosexualism that fortify the fiction of male superiority, seeking to restrict our lives with threats of patriarchal violence that bolster a fictitious morality reproduced in every generation through state institutions and familial organization that permeate the individual.)

Heterosexualism, the patriarchal politics of male supremacy over women, children and property is the result of the sexual suppression in monogamy that creates gender antagonism, exploitation and class creation. Taking Reich's finding that sexual repression is older than the conflict between male and female and has led to the oppression of women (and homosexuals) by men, I think the queens and women were correct all along, that attacking sexism is to attack the root causes of class: attacking class alone leaves the sexist in place.

(6) GLF was made up of black and white gay men and women, a few bisexuals and transsexuals, so it was already involved with other oppressed people. Its social class composition was the

upper-middle, the academic, professional and lower middle class; the petit-bourgeoisie, the working class majority, the lumpenproletariat and the unemployed. There were occasional visits by aristocrats. It's very possible that the sexual revolution is the first revolution to involve the lumpenproletariat: it certainly involved sex workers.

To fight class chauvinism within GLF on anything but an individual basis would have divided and destroyed the movement. It would have been the excuse for a putsch.

The star of the cancelled GLF Benefit Concert at the Seymour Hall was David Bowie, whose manager decided it wouldn't look good for his boss's career if he was seen to be supporting Gay Liberation. Bowie then denounced gay lib as 'aggressive'. Lyndsay Levy arranged the gig as she knew Bowie in Edinburgh when he was a dancer in her friend Lindsey Kemp's company.

(8) 'Since its beginning, the Cuban revolutionary movement, first in a veiled way, later without scruples or justifications, has pursued homosexuals with methods that go from the common ways of physical aggression to the attempt at psychic and moral disintegration of such individuals ...'[10] Cuban gay men and women had been rounded up and placed in concentration camps where they were brutalized and used as slave labour. The news of what happened to gays in Cuba came in a letter from Cubans living there, which was published in *Gay Flames* and reprinted in *Come Together* 8 in August – two months before Elsmore wrote his piece. 'This situation, because of the international scandal that it provoked, was eliminated as an appendix of the obligatory military service, but have kept farms of prisoners who are exclusively homosexual.'[11] The Cuban revolution is held up by Elsmore as a source of hope to *all* oppressed people, while at the same time the plight of our gay Cuban brothers and sisters is to be sacrificed for the sake of his hard-left beliefs.

(9) 'We must cease considering the individual sexist as our enemy regardless of his class.' 'We must stop struggling against

him, and instead struggle against the system he is in charge of.' As I suggest in (5) above, attacking the system leaves the sexist in place. Bill Halstead wrote that 'we went to confront the workers with their own sexism ... if we could get people to let go of their male privilege they will have no further interest in this oppressive system, and will therefore fight harder against it.' It is as though Elsmore sees the system and those who support it as somehow separate. His argument underlines *the* major difference between Gay Lib and the dogma of straight left-wing thinking. We know from instinct as sexually oppressed individuals that the personal is political. The position of both the left and the right is to separate the personal from the political, which by the uncoupling separates the sexist from the system and makes capitalism appear to be an inevitable and separate entity from people, and the inevitable and only way to organize society. This ideological agreement between left and right hides the real separation of capitalism's autonomous system of economic production, which has developed its own morality and internal logic that in a divided society constantly increases the wealth of the rich and causes the ruination of everything else. It is the concretization of the eighteenth century view that God put the rich on earth to enjoy their wealth, and the poor to work for nothing and pay for everything.

(10) I am intrigued by what Elsmore quoted and what he didn't quote in this paragraph from the article titled 'We're Getting Stronger' in *Come Together* 8.:'And we must go on getting stronger, go on fighting, *"not through an imposed revolutionary discipline not through a macho hang-up about straights,"* but because we have no choice but to fight for our liberation. And as our critique of the system must be total, so must our weapons be. "*We must learn to fight with songs, dances, theatres, films, to fight on the streets and then melt away when they come to attack somewhere else. We must master every weapon we deem useful and dig using. We must fight together. I cannot win but we can and nothing will stop us.*

ARMED LOVE."' [sic]. Why did Elsmore need to quote from this article at all? It is signed by Angela in *Come Together* 8, the Youth Group edition put together by Tony Reynolds, then living at Agitprop. This was the first edition of the paper produced outside Media Workshop control. There were no women in the youth group at the time according to Alaric Sumner, so Angela is a mystery figure. Elsmore also fails to introduce her by name, but as a sister, yet her name is published, which in itself is unusual for articles in *Come Together.* The quotation does not advance any argument, but is simply a rallying call to fight, with that word used twice and 'weapons' once. The fight theme continues to an ending that would be totally unacceptable to Media Workshop for this article and is shrewdly omitted. When I re-read 'Towards a Revolutionary GLF' for the first time in 40 years I immediately recognized the quotation, and I remembered how it ended, but Elsmore's paragraph ending was different. The words 'ARMED LOVE' weren't there. I had to go back to *Come Together* 8 to make sure my memory was correct. So thinking about how that paragraph does end: 'And as our critique of the system must be total, so must our weapons be.' I noted the emphasis on total, and weapons, and how that could be intriguing to someone into armed interventions, curious about the implications and wanting to know more. I can see the paragraph set up as a cipher, with the last line being the key to unlocking through 'Angela's' article a covert message of armed love. An armed wing? Was Angela, Andy? Was Andy Elsmore trying to recruit for the AB, or is it that he wanted others to think he was?

Alerted by Sarah Grimes, Mary McIntosh debated Elsmore's paper with Elizabeth Wilson, Angie Weir and Tony Halliday. They particularly noted the assistance of Aubrey Walter, David Fernbach, and Phil Powell in rewriting the article. Wilson and Halliday then decided to go to the next Media Workshop meeting as anyone was entitled to do, to oppose or promote issues they felt strongly about.

Tony Halliday: I and others went along to a meeting of the collective at Mick Belsten's place about it. It wasn't a very good article, but it became a *casus belli* over the control of *Come Together* – people in the collective were starting to control what went in and what didn't, particularly Aubrey and Phil Powell. Mick himself wasn't hardline on it. Elizabeth was with me and we sat and argued till dawn. Sarah Grimes and I were the only ones who stayed to the end. We were attacked for just turning up to the one meeting, but Sarah was a regular member of the collective and was on our side. What I felt was happening was that one group with rather Maoist notions was attempting to impose an identity on GLF, to purify the movement.[12]

Elizabeth Wilson: Tony Halliday and I had to go off to this meeting where there was this tremendous row about this article and *Come Together* and we had to go to this meeting in Barnes with that nice man Mick Belsten. I think that Aubrey and David transposed Marxism and Leninism to sexual politics. So my memory of this meeting: it was previously – the Maoist line was – you must not only spread the word to the working class, the proletariat – you must be in the proletariat – you must be with them. So they simply transposed that to the gay scene. So it was a bit elitist to be in with Gay Lib – so you would be in with all the straight-gays in *The Coleherne*, and somehow try to get the message to them. So that meant in a bizarre way that they were opposed to the avant-gardism of Gay Lib or feminism. It's a very contorted sort of position really. But that's how it seemed – that somehow the target audience was the men in *The Coleherne* – the last people who were going to be interested.[13]

Aubrey Walter and David Fernbach with their student New Left background were not gay bar people. They saw *The Coleherne* as full of gritty working class bikers, when the majority of the leather queen patrons were opera-loving, home-owning divas, all sporting crash helmets but few owning bikes.

I wonder if Elsmore's article was a bit of a shock to Fernbach and Walter, that it put into words their own secret plans. Their analysis and criticism of the movement as it now stood, their conclusions on the need to expand, and the direction that should take couldn't be far apart. Whatever the political differences between them, all three were organized around class politics and fighting capitalism.

As we have seen, it was Engels who located capitalism, the means of production, and its consequent class oppression within the family structure. By organising the dispossessed masses to fight their class oppression, the left hoped to topple capitalism, despite a bloody history that saw one set of thugs being replaced by another, and capitalism itself moved from groups of individuals to the state in so-called 'communist' countries, through all of which the family remained completely unchanged.

Despite the fact that the general meeting had voted down clause V of the Demands showing that gays did not join the movement to organize around economic class issues, Fernbach, Powell, Walter, and Elsmore as members of the organized left were so rigidly faithful to their political training, and so hidebound in their political thinking that they could not let go of class issues and fully embrace the fight against sexism that GLF had discovered to be at the root of our oppression. That was their hubris. Attacking sexism for all four had to be a slippery slope that led from the oppression of gay men to the oppression of all women, and consequently involved an alliance with feminism which they were perfectly well aware of but could not face up to. Sexism, they could see, had given the women and queens something new to think about, a foundation for questioning straight left-wing dogma, yet all they were prepared to give in relation to women was a theoretical acknowledgement that an alliance was needed. The refusal to go further must have been to do with their desire to subject the movement to Maoist ideology and lead it in a new direction, in other words it had to do with a power they wished to maintain and protect rather than question or think about, anymore than they would want their new working class recruits from the ghetto to think about such things: consent was all that the Maoists would require of them in the swerve away from confronting their own misogyny.

The way to reshape GLF that Fernbach and Walter envisaged was also spelt out by Elsmore: using the class issue as a tool to purify the movement and purge it by pitting the working class members against the intellectuals. That is all the intellectuals except themselves, thinking that their purged rump would appeal to the ghetto, and that they were continuing their 'scientific' search for a revolutionary sexual politics. But such changes based on ideology cannot be scientific or scientifically validated without first discovering a revolutionary tactic and developing a revolutionary practice that becomes a revolutionary theory against which changes could be measured.

'The project of transcending the economy and mastering history must grasp and incorporate the science of society, but it cannot itself be a scientific project. The revolutionary movement remains bourgeois insofar as it thinks it can master current history by means of scientific knowledge.'[14]

Perhaps Elsmore's profile on the left influenced Fernbach and Walter to assist with the rewriting of the article. From a Maoist point of view Elsmore was just another tool; rewrites wouldn't do the pair any harm, they would be the good guys to many other men in the collective, and the article would reveal where opposition lay to their own plans. The women of course were not fooled by any of this since discovering at the first reading that they would be purged.

Angie Weir: Aubrey and David eschewed alliances and the importance of that. At the end of the day they thought men could do it. Men. A reconstructed man could be in the forefront or spearhead of the revolution. So women became a problem really. Anyway Aubrey and David's idea was, I mean there was a lot of good things in it; you had the sort of leaders of the men's revolution, leaders of the women's revolution, leaders of the socialist revolution or working class, and somehow the leaders would all come together and make everything alright.[15]

The problem for Fernbach and Walter was how to deal with the women. The fierce rows within the media collective over the way sexism was treated in the article would erupt again at the next meeting. They knew they could not stand up to the women's arguments or to the call for further rewrites that could water-down the arguments. They knew their position was a betrayal of what the women believed in and worked for, just as they knew it would be a betrayal of the organic development of the movement, and a downgrading of the *Manifesto* and the way forward that it outlines. Their solution was a red herring that would both counter the socialist women's objections and distance themselves in the eyes of most men in Media Workshop from Elsmore's ideas. Fernbach and Walter redefined their Maoist ideology by incorporating another ideology they were beginning to explore, but later renounced, called Radical Feminism, in which gender is more important than class, which allowed them to criticize the article they helped rewrite – for its overloading of the class issue.

Mary McIntosh: My memory is that we thought the collective were being undemocratic and high-handed. One of us was on it and was completely over-ruled and we then sent some more people to the meeting. The collective had no basis beyond those who got together to do the paper, so there was no special status, and turning down an article was something

> that hadn't been done before. We thought there was a lot wrong with the article, it needed rewriting, you wouldn't necessarily agree with it but this amounted to censorship. And there was a meeting at our house where we heard what had been going on and planned what to do next, but we were outmanoeuvred. That was the first time that David and Aubrey and people started calling us male-identified and saying we had no right to speak on behalf of women, which I didn't particularly want to do. I didn't have that kind of attitude, but it really developed our sense of being women.[16]

The final answer to Fernbach and Walter's dilemma with the women was to denounce the Marxist socialist women as male-identified lesbians who had no right to speak on behalf of other women. They were no longer the right kind of gay women to talk about sexism because male-identified lesbians must be as sexist as men, if not more so. The pair moved the goal posts before the second meeting of Media Workshop; they could now justify their betrayal of the women to themselves, argue against the women with their new Maoist radical feminist terms, and completely disregard what the women said in return.

The misogynist crudity of labelling the Marxist Socialist women like McIntosh, whose contribution to the Manifesto had been crucially important, as male-identified lesbians, looks to me like the opening gambit to discredit her in the eyes of the younger women, and the first ideological salvo of Maoist inspired Radical Feminism aimed at splitting the women's group in two as a prelude to driving them to separate from the men. The Maoists were preparing to fuck it all up, but put nothing in writing at this time about their plans for a purge of women and queens, however three months later this was made clear in their article 'Gay Activism and Gay Liberation: a message to gay brothers,' reproduced in Chapter 15.

David Fernbach and Aubrey Walter were followers of Mao

Tse-Tung, and Phil Powell who had successfully organized the Notting Hill Pub demonstrations was a Trotskyite. An educated working class lecturer with a wife and two year old daughter, they lived near Fernbach and Walter in another large West Hampstead mansion flat Michael James called Martini Mansions. Powell, new to the collective, and busy ingratiating himself with Fernbach and Walter, who remembered him from their time in the anti-Vietnam war movement, observed their Maoist manoeuvres that set Elsmore up as their front-man.

The debate at the second meeting in Barnes over the revised article went on for nearly twelve hours. While Brackx, Wilson, Grimes, Belsten, and Halliday were against censorship, some of the other members of the collective were for banning the article, or failing that, wished to take the battle to the General Meeting so the decision could be made there.

Bob Mellors, who always maintained an independent position with a modest, earnest and considerate manner, produced his own reply to Elsmore's article.

> I would like to support two important points from the article which shouldn't be lost in a general criticism of it. Then I want to put forward an alternative proposal for a revolutionary GLF.
>
> 1) We have not been sufficiently critical of our gay sisters and brothers in GLF, in other homosexual organisations, or in California. I think we should oppose separatist moves on the part of gay people to establish a new gay ghetto. This does not recognize the different oppressions of other people and it is not an effective way of achieving gay liberation.
>
> Unity, criticism, unity
>
> But on the other hand we should be glad whenever gay people act against our oppression. GLF, groups like the Minorities Research Group, CHE, the Scottish Minorities Group and American gay groups are all a response to the

oppression we feel. These movements arise because we, as gay men and women, can no longer tolerate the situation as it is. We should seek unity with all gay people and at the same time criticise what we think are wrong actions, but we should do this with a desire for unity.

2) We are a predominantly middle class organisation and we have failed to take into account the different needs and attitudes of our working class sisters and brothers. Also the men in GLF are male-chauvinist, and generally the organisation is suited to the articulate and highly-educated. Some people will feel put down by this kind of paper debate. We should think about all these problems.

As things stand at the moment I think the pressure on All Saints Hall means the first thing we must do is to encourage local GLFs which should be organised so that all of us can express ourselves and take part, and no gay sisters or brothers will be excluded when they agree with gay liberation. This exclusiveness is unintentional but we must take it seriously. It would be good if Wednesday night discussions were in small groups whenever possible.

I support the call for a revolutionary GLF, but I think we should work for this in a very different way.

'Serve Gay People.

We should build up a mass support among gay people. We should talk to all our gay sisters and brothers about what they and we think and feel about our oppression. We all know the double-standards and the secretive existences of homosexual people. Few of us have left this entirely behind. We know life can be comfortable in the closet but we should be able to tell people why we think coming out will help our situation. We haven't got all the answers but we know that gay people coming together is a good thing.

Lesbians and homosexual men are not only oppressed as homosexuals but also as women, as blacks, as workers, as freaks, as old people, as transvestites and in other ways. Obviously we must relate to these oppressions. We must oppose male-chauvinism, racism, capitalist exploitation, the commercialized cult of youth and 'beauty' and all kinds of ignorant prejudice.

But what brings us together is our homosexuality. If a black sister or brother feels more oppressed as a black than as a homosexual, she or he will want to work mainly with Black Liberation, unless she or he feels that Gay Liberation may be more successful at the present time.

Similarly a gay worker may feel more oppressed by his work situation and he will want to do something about that. But she or he may feel that the chances for success in the foreseeable future are greater for Gay Liberation than for a socialist economic revolution.

But it would be unfair of gay people who feel *more* oppressed as blacks, as workers or in any other way, and are *less* concerned about their homosexuality to try and impose their primary interest on GLF, just because GLF is a more vibrant and growing organisation.

Why are we oppressed?

Last week's article is quite right when it says we have no answer to the question 'Why are we oppressed? Why are homosexuals oppressed in almost all societies in the world?' The article gives an inadequate answer in a quote from Engels and gives the idea of a divide and rule. The manifesto is a basis for discussion on this and we should use it.

We can see that there almost has to be a tie up between sexual oppression and the economic system since sex and making a living are both so basic parts of human life. We can see that the way the family is organized is very convenient for the economic system. We can see the use of sex in advertising. But all this is little more than a suspicion; we are not sure exactly what the connection is.

What this means in political terms is that we do not really know whether a sexual revolution must necessarily go hand in hand with an economic revolution. We can see that gay liberation is not possible within existing society, that there is no place for homosexual people in society as it stands, but we do not know how radical the change we want as gay people has to be.

These are issues we have been thinking about. The manifesto is a starting point. We must continue the discussion. The writers of last week's article should give us a more detailed explanation of their own theory. I think for either side to pretend to have all the answers is false.

Revolution

I agree that we should see ourselves as part of a wider revolutionary struggle, but if you look around at how much workers, women and blacks are doing for the revolution they seem to be in much the same position as we are. There are small so-called revolutionary socialist groups who have theories about the forthcoming socialist revolution, but their lack of effect suggests that either their theories are wrong or that they are adopting the wrong tactics in the present situation.

I think if we try and impose on GLF this ineffective kind of theory, which does not relate directly to the oppression of gay women and men, we will lose a lot of support among gay people *for no very good reason*. I think the correct tactic at this time is to build up mass support for Gay Liberation among homosexual men and women. We should criticise each other and develop our political theory by learning from each other.

I don't think this means we should not support other oppressed groups in an active way. But I think we should put more thought and consideration into this support.

Finally I should like to comment on the Media Workshop, some of whose objections to last week's article seem valid, some of which do not. I am glad to see that they have now

> decided that *Come Together* should be an expression of the feelings for liberation of all lesbians and homosexuals men, whether they are in GLF or not. This fits the political strategy I think we should adopt. I think we all have a duty to help Media Workshop in this aim through criticism of *Come Together.* I think there should be a meeting of the Media Workshop a week or so after each issue where *Come Together* will be criticized by as broad a range of gay people as possible. This would be with the intention of making *Come Together* an effective expression of gay anger and gay pride. There should also be opportunities to criticize the activities of other groups in GLF.
>
> I do not think my ideas are more or less 'political' than last weeks article. I think they are more revolutionary in the present situation in Britain. Bob
>
> Serve Gay People! Unity, criticism, unity.[17]

I don't remember the debate at the general meeting beyond being asked to take the two papers away and study them. I think many didn't really understand Elsmore's article but saw the jargon, the assumptions, the double-bind, the divide and rule, and took instinctively against it. Bob Mellors' broad, calm, thoughtful review, inviting everyone to be more self-critical and to think about the direction we wanted to take the movement in was just so much more understandable, readable and jargon free, with choices members could more easily identify with. The following week, when it came time to vote, the majority decided that the article should not be published. Media Workshop continued with *Come Together* 10 which was in the pipeline, after which the established method of producing it began to change as changes in the movement occurred.

The attempt by the old left like Elsmore, the New Left Maoists and the Trotskyites to take over and change the direction of GLF failed when exposed to the light of the General Meeting. They retreated to their ideological bases, analyzed the opposition and reshaped their plans for the next opportunity.

One of the main tenets of coming out was being visible in one's own community, so it followed that local GLFs would be established, as noted in the organizational suggestions of Fernbach and Walter attached to the Principles and in Bob Mellors' critique above, proposing the formation of local groups in London. Mellors went ahead and founded Camden GLF on 25 November with a meeting at Forresters Hall, Highgate Road, NW5.

Aubrey Walter comments that he saw the formation of local groups as an antidote to the progressively fractious character of the all-London meetings where there was an initial opposition to establishing these groups, perceived as dividing the Front into powerless blocs difficult to unify for co-operative action. Some felt the local groups would allow the straight-gays a place to hide from feminist criticism of their male-chauvinist position. Walter saw the development as responding to the real needs of GLF members who could no longer identify with the meetings at All Saints. He felt the more intimate setting of local groups were more constructive and released unexpressed enthusiasm for many new projects, such as his Camden group's coffee stall for cruisers on the Hampstead Heath trolling ground. Walter states: 'The local groups became the focus for different types of activity. Notting Hill was the centre for those into radical drag, while Camden became the focus for a soft-male image and for the Marxist feminists.'[18]

Walter's description of the difference between the radical drag queens of Notting Hill and the Marxist in Camden was to claim that the Marxist men were feminists with the attribute of a soft-male image. This could be read as a criticism of style, but when the Marxists are bourgeois and the radical queens working class then it is ideological; with the term soft and feminist implying lack of soft, non-feminist – obscuring and disguising class antagonism.

David Fernbach was a New Left believer in the discredited robotic Althusserian Marxist theories that totally failed the students and workers of France in 1968. If the use of such ideas had forced Fernbach into a downgrading of sexism to bring about a men only movement that GLF rejected, wasn't it time to overthrow those theories? Unfortunately, received revolutionary ideas come from and are filtered through institutions whose primary concern is the institution's own established and continuous survival.

> Without revolutionary theory, there can be no revolutionary movement. We said it till we were sick of it, hoping in this way to set our minds at ease. It is time now we learnt the lesson that the Cultural Revolution and the ideological revolt of the students [in 1968 Paris] have taught us. Divorced from revolutionary practice, all revolutionary theory is transformed into its opposite.[19]

In other words Marxism becomes the philosophy of order.

The metamorphosis of gay men into drag queens in 1971 was a mainly, though not exclusively working class phenomenon that can be seen as responding to and challenging the structured and orthodox beliefs of the bourgeois Marxist ideologists. This oppositional tendency also appeared in the Women's group at this time, between the Marxist socialist women who were mainly middle class and some of the younger working class sisters starting to explore Radical Feminism.

The ideological battles that erupted over 'Towards a Revolutionary Gay Liberation Front' brought to the surface the underlying class divisions. It made the women realize there was no place for them in the movement, and although divided by class and a newly emerging ideology, they continued working together and moving forward towards feminism. For the queens came the realization that they were more than just friends, but an identifiable group sharing common ideas of anarchic gender role playing that initiated a new political dialogue with each other. Whilst the Maoists and Marxists had shifted their position somewhat by exploring radical feminism, and Aubrey Walter, Richard Dipple and some other Marxists had started to adopt a more feminine, more androgynous look in Camden GLF, it proved too exhausting for them to keep up an alien appearance and to view actions through the lens of gender, and they later renounced that position and returned to the comfort of class politics and the reclining chair. Again it was a twisted position for them to have adopted, calling themselves feminists, given that they were working towards an all male GLF. It left them with two choices: self criticism as suggested by Bob Mellors, or to found a Gay Marxist Group and explore more ideology. They chose the latter.

When David Fernbach abandoned radical feminism he cleverly sowed confusion by naming us radical feminists. We objected, reasoning that only women could be feminists, and refused to call ourselves by that name. His thinking of us as feminists because we wore drag suggested to me that his Maoist Freudian slip was showing. But the joke was on us: the name was a gift to the straight-gays: they had absolutely no idea what it meant, but, radical feminist sounded so good it just stereotyped us for them. And that's how we became labelled the radical femmes, or as we called ourselves to reject the imposition – the radical queens.

Whilst all the frenzied activity was going on behind the scenes in Media Workshop, a friend of Angie Weir's, Roz Delmar in Women's Liberation wrote to Mary McIntosh:

> Mary, Here is copy of letter written to GLF. It's in the Office Collective file and we might act on it later:
>
> Dear Sisters and Brothers at Gay Lib, At the NWCC Nottingham meeting last Sat. – a women's lib conference was

set for October 15th in Skegness (Lincolnshire) – there are official accommodation arrangements for 500 – but many more are expected. Just bring a sleeping bag I guess and friends!

It's a drag but so few women from Workshops were there – a motion was passed to allow men. By the Maoists and Socialist Women (consciousness-raising has been denounced as a false channel for hostility against capitalism!) mainly.

Well, so I thought why not have Gay Lib. Come and say – do whatever you want! Perhaps gather all the Super-Male lefties into a Workshop on Male Chauvinism. Something really revolutionary in an active way – not just rhetoric. I talked this over with members of the Nottingham group and you can say we asked you. Friday night it all begins.

Write: Barbara Yates . . . Roslyn Smith . . . or anyone you know in W.L.! [20]

The National Women's Liberation Conference first met at Ruskin College, Oxford in February 1970. Some 300 women were expected – 600 delegates turned up. In October the conference met again at Ruskin College and formed the Women's National Co-ordinating Committee (WNCC) and formulated a series of demands into what was called the four campaigns: equal pay and opportunities; equal education and training; 24-hour nurseries; free contraception and abortion on demand.

The function of the WNCC was to act as a clearing house and disseminator of information between local groups, but like all such loosely based groups it began to coalesce, justify its role as important and assume an authority over the network. It then became clear that two groups of Maoists, the Union of Women's Liberation, and the Women's Liberation Front had representation on the WNCC out of all proportion to their membership in local groups, and that they probably viewed the women in the movement as potential recruits to their own ideologies.

The meetings of the WNCC turned into frigid, mechanical affairs, lacking any sisterly warmth. Efficiently kettled, it was impossible for the women to discuss the substance of differences between them, and became a regimented fight over instilling ideals rather than any consideration of their content. It was a frustrating and disillusioning reminder of time spent in the male left, many new members were appalled and some never attended again. The bureaucracy, meanwhile, consolidated and employed those male tactics of steamrollering their own proposals through, and crushing all others. The result was that the more libertarian women, unable to bear the in-fighting, absented themselves from the group organising the Skegness conference, leaving the bureaucracy to programme the event to its own advantage.

Angie Weir had attended the Oxford conference and through her WL group knew how things were unfolding. With their new-found, year-old sense of confidence in their position, the GLF Women's Group decided to go to Skegness and talk to the women there, to find some kind of sisterhood, and over a weekend of close contact to reveal their own.[21]

> *Sarah Grimes*: A minibus went up with GLF women and the Grosvenor Avenue women. There'd been some sort of strategy worked out, obviously, among some of the women, the Grosvenor Avenue women and Angela and the others who knew how the women's movement had been developing before Skegness.[22]

Arriving in Skegness in their white minibus the women were surprised to find themselves at a National Union of Mineworkers Holiday Camp. At reception they discovered they would be sharing all the camp's public amenities with attendees to two other conferences taking place there, the IS, and the Derbyshire Miners' Delegates. But the shock that awaited them was discovering they had to share the allocated sleeping accommodation they found themselves in, not just with women, but with a group of straight men who had come there to 'support' 'their' women. Even at a women's conference they couldn't get away from men! They returned to reception and were allocated another space.

> *Elizabeth Wilson*: Skegness was a miners' holiday camp really, that's what it was, so in the end we all deployed to a room with our sleeping bags, and somehow we Gay Lib women were put with the Maoists. It was a church hall and there was a dais at the end with this red curtain across, and they had created this sort of *cordon sanitaire.* So we woke in the morning and we went to look behind and they were already sitting up in their sleeping bags reading the thoughts of Mao from their Little Red books. They were extraordinary – like a caricature.[23]

Bureaucratic indifference and the need for centralized control and conformity through obedience to hierarchy had the conference opening on the Saturday morning with academic papers being read from the platform, after which the passive ranks were to politely discuss them in smaller groups. The programme started with:

> Morning Session: The Causes of the Oppression of Women.
>
> 9 – 10 am Plenary Session – introduction of papers. (1) 'Causes of the oppression of Women', by Margaret Coulson, Lancaster Socialist Women's Group. (2) 'On the oppression of Women and their Liberation: The role of the Women's Movement', by Maysal Brar, Union of Women for Liberation. (3) 'The Oppression of Women in the 1970's', by Bristol Groups. 10 – 12pm Seminars – On the Causes of the Oppression of Women. Lunch 12 – 1 pm. Afternoon Session: Role, Structure, and Function of Women's Liberation Movement. 1 – 2pm Plenary Session – introduction of papers.

(1) 'Organisation: Or How Does the Tail Get To Wag the Dog', by Oonagh Lahr, Little Newport Group WLW. (2) 'The Future of Women's Liberation Movement in Britain', by Watford Group Members. (3) 'The Roots of Women's Oppression and the Road to Liberation', by Women's Liberation Front, N7. 2 – 4 pm Seminars – On the Role, Structure, and Function of Women's Liberation Movement. Supper 4 – 6 pm. Evening Session 6 – 9 pm Plenary Session – Report back from Seminars, and general discussion of issues raised in day's papers and seminars.[24]

In the first session, the crudely rationalistic terms of economic powers and wants put forward by academic bourgeois women and men talking about the lives of working class women completely ignored women's psychological conditioning and the male dominated culture of society, and concentrated entirely on the material plane. For all the women listening who had come to talk to each other this was unbearably alienating.

Mary McIntosh: The first day there were the Maoists, including men, trying to take over. They were all arguing over process and the control of the movement and whether men should be involved. Their argument was that you had to have a properly elected committee, and they were it and so forth. This Maoist line was being put out – as soon as the lesbians came out, we were told we were a bourgeois deviation and that we would disappear under socialism.[25]

Janet Dixon: On the Saturday morning we shuffled into the camp's concert hall for a 'plenary session'. As I took my seat it dawned on me. Amongst the couple of hundred or so there, were some twenty or thirty men. Not only that, on the stage was a long table, and yes you've guessed it, among the dignitaries were several men. We sat through some very boring speeches which attempted to make the thoughts of Mao, Marx and Lenin exciting and accessible to a bunch of dumb women, and then broke for coffee. In the camp canteen I looked for the woman who had encouraged me to come to what, by the minute, I was beginning to feel was a god-forsaken hole. I wanted to know why she thought I would be the least bit interested in all that drivel I had just had to sit through. It turned out she was just as fed up as me, and we were not the only ones.[26]

Angie Weir: It was non-stop agitation at the Skegness conference and there was a great deal of dissatisfaction being voiced throughout the morning. We were sat in these workshops discussing socialist texts and people were absolutely pissed off, so after lunch we just decided that we would appeal to the conference to split up and reorganize itself.[27]

Sarah Grimes: I was the one who got up on the platform! What happened in the first session was very much dictated from the platform; pseudo-Marxist papers being read out, and there was a great deal of regulation. There was a terrific sense of alienation amongst many of the women, a reaction against the leadership, and I guess what the Maoist women were positing was part of an economic analysis. Men were allowed in and were on the platform. So in the break there was a little caucusing going on with the GLF women and a few other groups, about what we should do, how to deal with this … we knew we had to go up and stop it, and I think I was just chosen as someone with a new face, who could go up to the platform and get the microphone, because they had control of it, and were deciding who to give it to. They wouldn't be suspicious of me. So I went up and said, 'I think we should all go outside and discuss things in small groups, I don't think

> this is the way it should be; we should be talking about our lives', and they said, 'You can't do this', but we did and people just moved out. It is what they wanted.[28]

> *Wilson*: Sarah Grimes was a very pivotal person in that, she just sort of in her very quiet way, just went up on to the platform and took the microphone.
>
> *Weir*: And me! It was Sarah and me!
>
> *Wilson*: Yes but you'd expect it of you, whereas you wouldn't of Sarah.
>
> *Weir*: Exactly. Anyway, basically, Sarah and I went up, and they had all this whole programme of studying Mao's laws and all the rest of it, on the Saturday morning, and she spoke first, and then I said, 'We don't want this. Here we are, gay women, and we don't want this,' and we urged all the conference to break into small groups and leave the Maoists and to come with us, and they did.[29]

Two thirds of the conference spontaneously rose up, walked out of the hall and formed into small groups outside where they began informal discussions, particularly with the GLF women. The atmosphere instantly changed. Some of the women had been left a little nervous, and alarmed at the violent strength of feeling that came with the creation of this new situation, but now many others were finding their voice and the freedom to play their part.

> *Grimes*: It all got a lot more clear after that. It was discussion about women's experience, talking from the heart about the basic situation of, for instance, women with children. It was still the economic situation but more related to people's lives. And of course it was at this point the GLF women were able to raise the point of lesbianism. I think we were a bit cocky about being the sexual vanguard, and there were tensions with other women feeling threatened, as if they were afraid we might be

> saying that lesbianism is the only way, which we weren't saying. So then people started coming up with their own deep personal feelings and angst.[30]

When the conference re-united for the early evening session GLF tried to get the issue of lesbianism on the agenda. Up till then there was little in the way of personal hostilities, but suddenly they had to fight a barrage of filibustering.

When a GLF sister had the microphone, the chair ignored the point and moved on to something else. They were accused of being 'red herrings' or having 'private problems'. By creating a false polarization of politics on one hand and sexuality on the other the women were dismissed as a gang of individualists with no contribution to offer. GLF was described as a subversive political organization that had come to the conference to deliberately disrupt and destroy women's liberation. The bureaucrats' arguments were blatantly contradictory, with absurd descriptions of facts so mendacious, that a return barrage of jeers from all over the hall only ended when it was finally agreed that the subject of lesbianism was recognized as one important to women's liberation, and put on the agenda of Sunday's discussions.

The press who were attending the conference had earlier told the GLF women that the Derbyshire Miners' delegates were having a strip show that night. Some of the women felt they were being set-up, but what could they do. To ignore it would be to betray the sisters, and to do something about it would have the strippers thinking it was being directed against them. Yet it was the perfect metaphor for why they were there, and some thought there was no choice but to trash it. So the women acted with mixed feelings and the outcome was confusion all round. When the strippers appeared on stage so did the gay women dancing a conga line and chanting as they crossed, breaking up the strippers who told them to get off the stage. Some miners yelled and booed, and some of the men from the women's conference who were there for 'their' 'women' got up on stage and started pushing, punching, and hair pulling to get the gay sisters off. The miners to their credit then joined in by freaking at the men for the way they were treating the women.

Being nothing new for a Saturday night out, the women undaunted, brushed themselves down and sauntered off to the IS Ball. The IS was heavily male in composition, there were few 'chicks' to dance with, and the men found all the women declined their offers and were off dancing with each other in groups. Group dancing then broke out everywhere, and it wasn't long before the IS men also began dancing together.[31]

On the Sunday morning the GLF women set up their book stall in the entrance hall, as did a group from IS.

> *Weir*: It ended up that we were absolutely flooded with miners, and some of them were so, mmm … they wanted to talk to us and we had interesting discussions, and they didn't want to go to the IS stall, so the IS people hung around the outskirts of the miners, trying to grab their sleeve and saying, 'Can I interest you in the proletarian revolution?'[32]

At the conference two groups were formed to discuss 'sexism and homosexuality', and those groups grew so large that both were divided into two. It was a wonderful tribute to the sisters of GLF that all the women there had been thinking about the subject and wanted to talk about it. Some women talked about radical feminist ideas of relationships with men being impossible in this society with its gender role conditioning. Others knew all that but didn't see it as applying to themselves, their line being, 'Yes I know, but mine is different, he really understands.' Others again did not see the issue confronting women in terms of men versus women, so they couldn't see lesbianism as the solution to women's oppression. The GLF women had no single agreed-upon line to put to their sisters, but sat with them equally, joining in the discussions, listening, extending and exchanging ideas.[33]

McIntosh: It was a very important meeting for the women's liberation movement; it was the first of the big conferences ... And of the big interest in lesbianism. There was a lot of interest in it at the time in the women's movement. Lots of them played with lesbian relationships in the seventies. We didn't want to be anti-straight though, we weren't separatists. Our motivation for being gay was not a feminist motivation – we just were – and then we came to feminism. 'Any woman can be a lesbian', became a popular view in the women's movement, but I remember Sheila Rowbotham about that time, talking about trying to come to terms with the fact that she loved her man but was nevertheless a feminist. That was the sort of thing that you couldn't talk about by the mid-seventies in a feminist meeting. But we were very supportive of that and I remember saying, 'We mustn't be anti-heterosexual – those women's bed is the front line of battle with men, and we must admire them for that struggle in their private lives that we've escaped.' We definitely were supportive of straight women at Skegness. We weren't trying to win them over, but we wanted to be able to talk about our sexuality and lives. [34]

Grimes: Then it ended with a plenary session which was basically just trying to cobble together some organisation. It had no structure ... Some women from Bristol took it on until the next conference and that's how the structure arose which worked quite well for several years, of groups taking on co-ordination between one conference and the next.[35]

Wilson: After Skegness we came back to GLF and got this very uninterested reception to what had happened, which was very interesting you know, because people should have been interested really.[36]

Dixon: As the seventies wore on the numbers of lesbians in the WLM increased dramatically, the rumbles of discontent turned into roars. Lesbians put their weight behind issues such as child care, abortion, race, battered wives and rape. In return we wanted the skeleton of sexuality wrenched from the closet and flesh put on its bones. The WLM had begun to come of age. We had stopped trailing around after the men in the left, contorting ourselves in the hope of receiving some grudging crumbs of approval. We had our own campaigns and set of demands, and what's more, amongst them was a woman's right to define her own sexuality.[37]

GETTY IMAGES

GLF Street Theatre performs outside Bow Street Magistrates Court as 4 members of Women's Lib are put on trial for disrupting the Miss World Contest at the Albert Hall. *Left:L-R;* Tarsus Sutton, Marion Prince, Marshall Weekes, Jane Winter and Paul Theobald. *Right: L-R;* the author and Neon Edsel.

RON REID CAMERAPRESS

RON REID CAMERAPRESS

First appearance of GLF with the Trades Union and organized left on the anti-Industrial Relations Bill march, 21 February 1971. *Top: L-R;* Paul Theobald and Bill Pearce. *Below: L-R;* Mary McIntosh, Tony Halliday and Tony Reynolds holding the banner.

COME TOGETHER WOMEN'S ISSUE 7.

Annie Brackx

Barbara Klecki

Mary McIntosh

Elizabeth Wilson

LESBIAN COME TOGETHER 11.

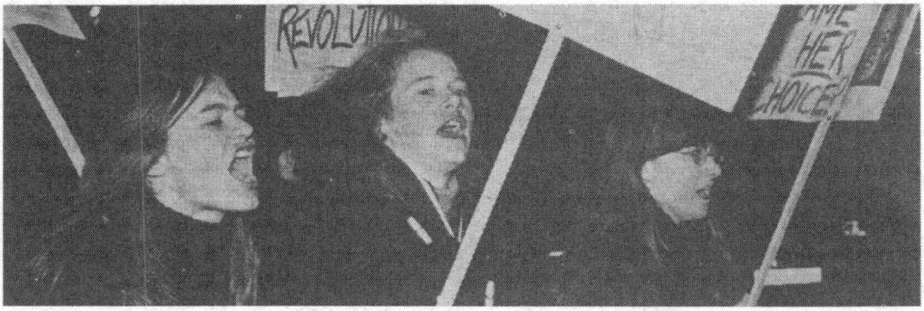

Gay Women's Liberation demonstrating outside Holloway Prison

JOHN CHESTERMAN/HCA

HOWARD LLEWELLYN

Above: L-R; Bill Halstead and Aubrey Walter at the National Think-In at Leeds University. Ready to drive to Edinburgh the next day, *Right: L-R;* Janet Phillips, Andrew Lumsden, Richard Dipple, Tony Halliday, Bette Bourne, Mick Belsten.

Below: L-R; The author, Andrew Lumsden, Janet Phillips, John Chesterman in sun glasses, *centre* back to camera Tony Renolds.

HOWARD LLEWELLYN

JOHN CHESTERMAN/HCA

Andrew Lumsden speaking at the Traverse Trials, *Traverse Theatre*, Edinburgh, 20 June 1971.

INDEX OF POSSIBILITIES

John Chesterman

REX LAY

GIOVANNI RODELLA

Above; Nicholas Bramble as the Spirit of Porn in the demonstrations against the FoL in Trafalgar Square. *Left;* Mario Mieli the founder of FUORI! at the first Festival of Cineteatro, Palma, 1977.

HOWARD LLEWELLYN

HOWARD LLEWELLYN

Gay Day in Hyde Park before the rally in Trafalgar Square protesting the Age of Consent law. *Above:* Bobby holding up his placard stands next to Malcolm Bissett.

HOWARD LLEWELLYN

JOHN CHESTERMAN/HCA/9

Top: Gay in Hyde Park with *Right;* John Chesterman. *Below:* The march leaves Hyde Park headed by the GLF Youth Group with *Left;* Malcolm Bissett reading one of the pamphlets produced for the occasion.

JOHN CHESTERMAN/HCA/9A

Top: L-R; Rosie and friend in Hyde Park.

JOHN CHESTERMAN/HCA/9B

Above: Carla holding her lover Rosie's hand addresses the crowd in Trafalgar Square. Tim Bolingbroke looks out from behind the GLF banner.

HOWARD LLEWELLYN

28 August 1971. The first ever Lesbian & Gay demo in Trafalgar Square organized by the GLF Youth Group protesting the Age of Consent clause in the Sexual Offences Act.

HOWARD LLEWELLYN

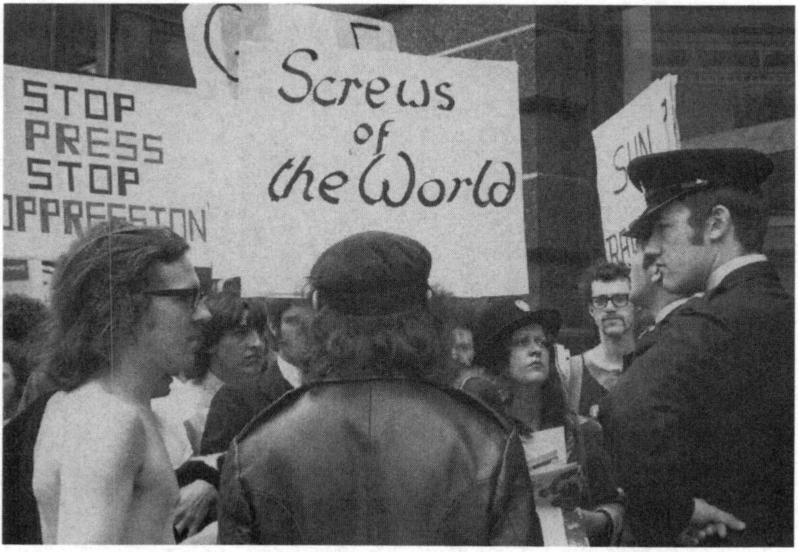

HOWARD LLEWELLYN

GLF demonstration against Fleet Street in general and the *Daily Mirror* in particular. *Below: Left;* Michael Mason and *Right;* October.

GLF protest the Festival of Light rally in Trafalgar Square.

Above: L-R; Michael Reading, Nicholas Bramble, Rachel Pollack and Michael James. *Below: L-R;* the author, Peter Reed, violin, Mary McIntosh, Claudia, Jenny and Frankie Green. Tim Bolingbroke the nun blesses Bette Bourne and John Church.

Text: *Left:* in the doorway of Foyles bookshop Barbara Klecki following Reuben's method, aborts Lyndsay Levi with a wire coat hanger and releases kilos of Calves liver from between her legs. *Right:* All Saints Hall GLF General Meeting with *Back: second left;* Roger Carr, *Left: 2nd row;* Tony Halliday, Mary McIntosh and *centre front;* Bill Halstead.

Queens Pride March. *Top:L-R: back;* Nicholas Bramble, Aubrey Walter, Tony Reynolds, the author, Tim Bolingbroke, John Church and Bette Bourne. *Front: L-R;* Michael James and Mick Belsten. *Below: L-R;* Mike Rhodes, John Church, Cloud Downey, Michael James and Alaric Sumner.

Top: Stephen Crowther wears the best frock in the commune; bias cut pale green pan velvet. *Below:* The Alternative Miss World Contest 1971 held outside the Albert Hall. *L-R:* Frank O'Looney, Miss Laid, her name too, Terry Madely the winner with a flower in his mouth and Peter Flannery, wardrobe mistress.

Top:Right; Bruce Burchill of the Notting Hill Squatters Group wrestles with a landlord heavy trying to evict the radical queens from their squat in Colville Terrace. *Above:* The Champion 5 outside Marylebone Magistrates Court the morning after their arrest. *L-R:* Richard Chappell, Douglas MacDougall, Bette Bourne, Peter Reed and Andrew Lumsden.

RON REID CAMERAPRESS

The commune at 7A Colville Houses. *Clockwise from top:* Lewis Rabkin, Bette Bourne, Mick Belsten, a visitor, Michael James, John Church, the author, Tim Bolingbroke, Stephen Crowther, Nigel Kemp and *top left;* Julian Hows who wasn't available for photography that day.

LUNCH MAGAZINE/HCA

L-R; Bob Mellors and the author on the communes' stall at 305 Portobello Road.

RON REID CAMERAPRESS

Richard Chappell

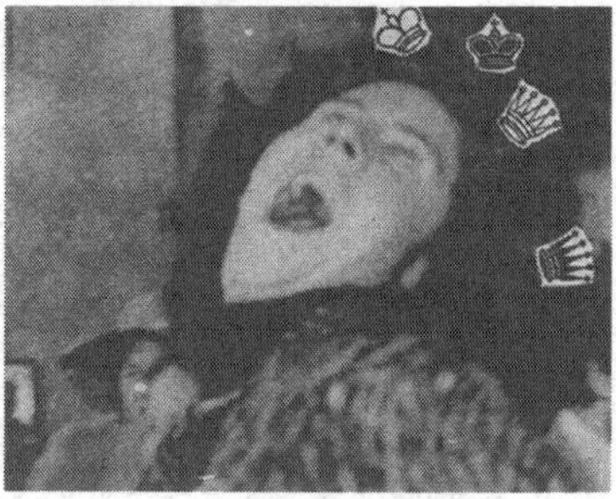

Steve Bradbury

BY KIND PERMISSION OF
IT INTERNATIONAL TIMES

Top: Tim Bollingbroke in the communes make-up room at Colville Houses. *Above:* Julian Hows in his role as a representative of the National Union of School Students.

RON REID CAMERAPRESS

A knees up in the commune at 7A photographed for the back page of *Come Together* 15 GLF Notting Hill issue. *Clockwise from top:* Richard L. John Church, a visitor, Lewis Rabkin, Stephen Crowther, Bette Bourne, Nigel Kemp, the author, Mick Belsten, Tim Bolingbroke and Michael James.

Chapter 9

A British Army Hero

> A Government with a standing army will soon find an excuse to pick a fight.
> Leo Tolstoy, *Government is Violence.*

At a time when the British left, on the whole, really didn't want to know about Ireland, and had all sorts of 'good reasons' not to support the struggle against the occupying British army and the State, a man called George Lennox, dressed in a khaki greatcoat and dark glasses came by invitation to the last Wednesday meeting in October to talk about the government's introduction of Internment without Trial in Northern Ireland and to urge us to join the Anti-Internment march the following Sunday. Lennox explained that people in the province arrested and not released or charged within 48 hours were to be jailed indefinitely, particularly those with a known history of political resistance. When he finished speaking he was assured that we planned to be on the march, then just before sitting down he was reminded of our rule that all new speakers at the general meeting must declare their sexuality. Lennox replied, 'I'm gay,' which surprised most of the meeting, myself included, and then added, 'I was told I'd be given a crash-pad for the night, so I hope that's alright.' Michael James and I had come to the meeting knowing we were top of the crash-pad providers list, what we hadn't reckoned on was a big heavy man like him turning up.

There was nothing for it, after the meeting we went over, introduced ourselves, and took him to the pub, hoping he'd meet someone and get off with them, but it wasn't to be, we had to take him home. The next morning he refused to leave. Fait accompli; our instincts had been right from the moment we'd clapped eyes on him. He'd thought: 'A couple of queens, I'm well in here.'

> George had been put into an orphanage age two-and-a-half when his parents split up. [At 14] 'I decided to fuck off. I knew my father existed somewhere near Glasgow, and I managed to find his address. I fucked off from him after six months and I came down to London for a few days. I got taken back. Then I got presented to my mother whom I hadn't seen before. From there it was another sort of fuck up. We had completely different worlds.'[1]

At fifteen Lennox joined the army and spent two-and-a-half years as a boy soldier before taking a short-hand and advanced clerical course. He was posted to Germany and then in 1964 to Aden, where his job as a teleprinter was to examine content and classify messages, which he did from an office in Fort Morbut, HQ Middle-East Command. In the next compound was Ras Morbut where there was a corporals' club that newly promoted Lennox used. Also in the Ras Morbut compound was the guardroom for the area, and twenty yards away from that a building known as the Initial Interrogation Centre, which was used for Adeni political prisoners. His other duty was patrolling and guarding the perimeter of Ras Morbut, which included the Interrogation Centre. At various times when he was on guard duty, army intelligence officers would come over to the guardroom and use the telephone to speak to HQ. From what the soldiers on guard duty overheard, they were able to form a good idea of what was going on in the Interrogation Centre, on top of which, almost every night after suspects were taken in, the corporals in their club could hear screaming and shouting, like somebody being badly hurt, coming from the building. The state of affairs was just accepted, 'We'd have a laugh and joke about it. There's another cunt getting done in.' One time Lennox just happened to glance into the Interrogation Centre compound and saw an Adeni detainee taken from the building into the compound where a bunch of soldiers beat him until he passed out. They then revived him and beat him again until he passed out a second time.

In March 1966 Lennox was posted back to Germany to take charge of the Statistical and Records Department at BAOR HQ in Rheindhalen. In October he read in *The Sunday Times* a report by Amnesty International on the torture of Adeni civilians by the British Army.[2] The Amnesty report was rubbished the following Sunday by *The Sunday Times* Aden correspondent, Peter Mansfield and the paper's editorial concurred.[3]

Lennox began to think about what he'd seen and heard in Aden and what *The Sunday Times* was trying to do. He hadn't known anything about Amnesty, but had heard the name in Aden when their request, and one from the Red Cross and the UN to hold investigations, were turned down by the British High Commission. Looking at what the two sides were saying, he thought it would only be right to tell the newspaper what he had witnessed. He wrote to *The Sunday Times* hoping to correct their bias by providing information the paper had no access to, and hoping also to redress the reputation of Amnesty International, whose allegations were being examined by the Bowen Commission set up by the government.

> Lennox: Purely in a naive moral kind of way, this is how I was thinking in 1966, with my Scottish Presbyterian sort of background, where you have right and wrong, black and white, rewards and punishment kind of background. That's how I used to react at all levels. I saw it as a wrong, and I wrote and expected them to publish my letter.[4]

Later he received a note from the Bonn correspondent of *The Sunday Times*, Anthony Terry, in which he referred to 'the particular problem you have,' and his wish to meet and talk about it. He met the correspondent and a woman introduced as Mrs. Terry, and related his story. Terry sent his report directly to the War Office.

Months later in January 1967, a uniformed sergeant major from the Special Investigation Branch (SIB) apprehended Lennox and questioned him, claiming he was investigating on behalf of the Bowen Commission. The sergeant then left him alone in the interrogation room for a few hours with piles of papers and photographs in front of him in which Lennox discovered statements from other soldiers in Aden, some of whom he remembered, claiming they knew nothing, and had neither seen nor heard anything amiss in the Ras Morbut compound. When the SIB sergeant returned, Lennox told him he must be an idiot and to fuck off.

In April, he was playing in the inter-corps Rugby Festival in Paderborn. He was in the final and coming off the pitch at the end of the match when an officer he didn't recognize came up to him and said, 'Corporal, do you mind coming with me.' He was taken to a car containing three other officers and driven to Guttersloh airport, right up to a small twin-engine plane, and escorted aboard. The aircraft landed at Northolt, the military aerodrome in North West London which Lennox recognized from previous visits. A car was waiting, and the party were driven to a house somewhere in North London where he was locked up.

Three days later he was taken by car to another, larger house. He was held in a room with no toilet and denied the use of one. Meals became irregular; he was left there for days before being questioned about his connection to Amnesty. That particular evening his dinner was two poisoned potatoes that gave him diarrhoea. The next night, still suffering attacks, feeling nauseous and exhausted, he began to breakdown into self-doubt, confusion, conflict and remorse. The following day he was taken to an office and told they had evidence of his involvement in all sorts of plots. After hours of interrogation he was marched to another room, similar to the first, and locked up again. During the night he woke up feeling frozen. Within minutes he was hot and sweating – then just as quickly frozen again. Outside it was pouring with rain. There was thunder and lightning, it was dark – then suddenly light and just as suddenly dark again. He lost all track of time, and tried reckoning it out from knowing he could hold his piss for maybe fifteen hours. He became disorientated, withdrawn, and beginning to wonder who he was. He started talking to himself, talking to the wall, talking to the chair, talking to the desk. Once he saw a man emerge from the wall and speak to him. Then he found himself in that office again, ready to tell them anything.

It didn't help, Lennox was sent back to the same room. Years later he learnt he'd been given LSD, because all the shapes in the room had begun to dissolve, distort and ripple. He saw things in the corners of the room – voices climbed into his ears. Again he found himself in the office, and now they were accusing him of involvement with subversive organizations and anarchist groups. What they did to him after that Lennox can't remember.

Eventually he was moved into a proper room with a toilet and shower. Meals started coming regularly. Altogether he reckoned he was there for six weeks. Then one morning he was taken down stairs, given a uniform and told – '"There you are, you're a soldier again."'[5]

He was put in a car and sent to the Cambridge Military Hospital, Aldershot, and placed in a ward for the emotionally disturbed. Heavily sedated and completely withdrawn he was examined by a least three psychiatrists who told him nothing. He found he couldn't see out of his right eye and remembers complaining. He was taken to St. Thomas' Hospital for an eye test. He met a psychiatrist there he later saw on TV who said to him 'There's nothing wrong with your eye George, but tell me: you do want to get out of the army, don't you?' Lennox was confused and said no, he enjoyed it. He can't remember how long he was at Aldershot, but one day he was told he could go on leave. He went to his mother's in Scotland. Two months later, out of the blue, he received his discharge papers that claimed he'd failed to meet medical standards. Enclosed with the papers was £112 and a little book saying he was discharged with exemplary conduct.

On 17 January 1972 Lennox told James and I that the story of his life in the army was being published in *7 Days*, and asked us if we would help him by street-selling copies of the newspaper. The next evening we went with him to the newspaper office and met some of the staff and reporters over a cup of tea, before loading up with newspapers and going to Earls Court to sell them outside the tube station. When James and I finished selling our copies we decided to go to *The Boltons* for a drink. Lennox who still had papers to sell said he would join us later. He didn't show, and he didn't come home that night.

Lennox, still selling papers, had been picked up by the police who just happened to be carrying a warrant for his arrest on them for 'non-restitution of stolen property'. He was taken to Earls Court Police station and kept there without charge until the following afternoon, when he was transferred to Gerald Row Police Station. Later that night he was charged with holding-up the Bureaux d'Change at Victoria Station. The next day at Bow Street police objected to bail, arguing that Lennox lived in a 'commune'. *7 Days* reported:

> Police also objected to bail on the grounds that at the time of the alleged offence Lennox was supposed to have been carrying an automatic pistol.
>
> Several national newspapers have expressed interest in the case of George Lennox, but no reports have yet appeared.
>
> Repeatedly, during the week, we contacted the Ministry of Defence and asked army spokesman there to confirm or deny

> the allegations Lennox had made about army methods. They told us that the article was being studied, but we are still waiting for a statement.[6]

It was several more weeks before Lennox was released on bail.

Chapter 10

Court Circular

> Like most gay people, I know myself to be part of a minority feared, disliked and persecuted by the majority and this gives my life a complexity and an extra dimension unknown to straights.
>
> Dennis Altman, *Homosexual.*

On Remembrance Sunday a delegation of some 15 members organized by John Chesterman attended the wreath laying ceremony in Whitehall. Each wore a badge designed by him that displayed a pink triangle. The group included Sue Winter, Andrew Lumsden, and Michael James.

> As they waited they were approached by the Thought Police who told them they could not lay the wreath at the Cenotaph 'because it was too political.' And this when every other organization – religious, civilian and military – was wearing every kind of palaeo-fascist insignia and all but goose stomping with the nationalist pride of it all. So Gay Lib removed their badge and then marched down Whitehall and laid their wreath in an orderly fashion alongside those of other minority groups not represented in the main ceremony. They stood back and paid their respects to the unmourned dead.[1]

The wreath of pink carnations was in the form of a triangle representing the badge worn on the uniform of gay prisoners in the Nazi death camps. To the wreath was attached a card with lines taken from Chesterman's poetic GLF Demands, with the last line changed. 'In the names of the tens of / Thousands, / who wore the badge of / Homosexuality in the gas chambers / and concentration camps, who / Have no children to remember and / Whom your histories forget! / *We remember. / The Gay Liberation Front.*' It was the first public commemoration of the holocaust of queens and dykes hunted down in every town, city, prison and concentration camp between the North Sea and the Urals, in which over one million of us were liquidated.

'Within minutes two flat-hatted, black "bus conductors" went over to the wreath and ripped off its copper-plate label. They were subsequently found to be working for the Department of the Environment [DoE] which is responsible for the event and is apparently answerable to no-one but itself.'[2]

Another card was made and pinned on, and that too was torn off and substituted by one from the DoE stating, 'Honoured remembrance on behalf of HMS *Hull*.' The next day GLF demanded an explanation from the DoE about its right to act as a censor at the wreath laying. They refused to comment. Afterwards, GLF issued a press release which ended:

> In view of recent press reports of threats by militant groups to disrupt the Service of Remembrance, we should like to put on record that whilst we shall continue our militant campaign for Homosexual Rights, our action today is a serious and sincere token of remembrance for the many men and women who suffered and died for no other reason than their sexual preferences.

CHE, who had been present at the planning stage following on from the Leeds Think-In promised to attend the commemoration but failed to show up. An article headed 'Cenotaph Ceremony' had appeared in the CHE magazine *Lunch,* claiming they would be present at the remembrance, and included this tortuous coded sentence: 'Let it be made clear that this is to be a "distinctly dignified" assembly, one that no person with the real interests of the homophile community at heart would deny this very pious act of remembrance would give less than the fullest support, and many more would feel it their duty to attend the wreath laying.'[3]

Among the hectic schedule of meetings and demos in October, Street Theatre had also been holding rehearsal for *The Alternative Miss World Contest*, having been invited by Women's Lib to join their demonstration outside The Albert Hall on 6 November. New to the group was Terry Madely, a friend of Michael James's, another was Bette Bourne who immediately began insisting on rehearsals for the revamped version of the show played at Bow Street. Bourne was to play the compère Dirty Dick, Madely was Miss Used, I was Miss Understood, and to my shame I can't remember the name of Miss Laid whose flat we rehearsed in.

When we arrived on site, coaches from all over the country were disgorging Mecca Bingo Prize Winners, two thousand alone from the Midlands. Chauffeur driven Rolls Royces set down Grand Metropolitan Hotel and Mecca shareholders, while protesters chanted, 'Down with Mecca Pimps,' and, 'How dare you Judge Women.'

Women's Lib Street Theatre performed their *Flashing Nipples Show*. Wearing body stockings, a light on each breast and one on the crotch, they lined up in two rows to flank a pathway the audience were forced to walk along to reach the main entrance. 'Outrageous,' shrieked one grand dame in furs, 'You should all be out working.'

Chesterman, who had printed a flyer for the event, also found money from somewhere to erect bleachers against the wall of the building, and to one side he'd set a little marquee, not much bigger than a sentry box in which we could change from bathing suits to formal evening wear. It was another freezing cold night in drag as we huddled together trying to keep warm and not fall out of the tent and ruin the surprise. Dirty Dick with a loud-hailer called us out and quizzed us on our hopes and wishes. We strutted our stuff, goose-pimples and all, and the audience were invited to judge the winner. Madely as Miss Used won the competition and was presented with a giant silver phallus.

Afterwards, with the contest starting inside the Hall, we all went to the Royal College of Art next door and watched Women's Lib films until it was time to demonstrate again as the audience started leaving.

Once outside, we blocked the roads around the hall where the Rolls Royces slowly reappeared, determined to part the crowd and push us back. One woman attempting to stop a Roller was seized by a policeman shouting, 'You can't hit Rolls Royces,' but she was pulled back into the crowd when the chauffeur got out brandishing a starting handle. The police then formed two ranks to allow the important guests to reach their limousines, but the rest of the audience was held inside for a while in the hope that we would disperse. We didn't, and eventually the audience exited in a fury. One man lashed out. A lady wielding a handbag hit a woman. Others fainted at the sight of us. A huge fat Texan male continuously told women that what they needed in the bedroom was a rooster like himself. Casualties littered the pavement, starkly lit by the big 'sun-ray lamps' from Chesterman's video camera. A lady complaining she didn't understand the point of the demo was pushed by the police into a crowd of us crying, 'But I work for Mecca.' Chanting protesters stood outside the many doors of the hall, running away when the police approached to take up new positions outside other exits.

The buses for the contestants arrived and we rushed in front of them and started dancing, which drove the police mad and had them yelling abuse as they forced us away so the coaches could get to the back door, just opposite the solid ranks guarding the BBC television van. The subdued contestants climbed aboard their coaches, and one or two waved as their coaches set off, edging forward behind our group of dancers.

Peter Tatchell: As soon as the signal was given, the main body of protesters moved to surround the bus. The contestants had

> to wait for police reinforcements to arrive to drag us out of the way and make a corridor to let them pass. [The police charged, we fled and the coaches sped off]. One group did try to break the television cables which relayed the event to outside broadcast units, but because of the previous year's disruption when the BBC van had been blown up, there were a lot of plainclothes police officers and people were quickly pounced on.[4]

The place was also crawling with Special Branch looking for any likely bombers who might have returned to celebrate. As the last of the audience were finally leaving, a white Rolls Royce sped away carrying Eric Morley, managing director of Mecca, and his guest, the winner, Miss Brazil.

James, with his FoL trial at Bow Street just four days away didn't feel he could risk being apprehended, so he'd been on emergency duty manning the phone in the office instead. I rang to tell him the demo was over – he could lock up and come home.

After that the only people left were the demonstrators and the police. We demonstrators reached out to each other and joined hands all the way round the Albert Hall. There were enough of us to encircle it in a double ring, and away we danced in opposite directions until the police had gone.

The GLF Court Circular for November was filled with the longest list of appearances that had ever been seen for any other month. The Newssheet for 3 November announced: 'Gerrilah Theatre. Seats provided free by the Lord Chancellor. Artistes wardrobes and hairstyles courtesy of GLF. Pigs supplies by Commissioner of Metropolitan Pigs. Audience participation required from you.'[5] The Chepstow Four appeared on the 10 October and were remanded on bail until 14 January. Douglas McDougall, Michael James, and Michael Reading, Carla Toney plus the eight from Women's Lib Street Theatre appeared at Bow Street on 10 November. Paul Theobald, Martin Rowlands and two non-GLF men appeared at the Guildhall on the 18th. Paul Theobald (again), Chris Blaby, Tim Bolingbrook and myself in one court, and Nicholas Bramble in another, all at Marlborough Street on the 22nd. John Church, Malcolm Bissett, Neville Smith and Les Tebbs at Wells Street on the 29th.

I was acting as Michael James's MacKenzie for his trial at Bow Street and feeling anxious about my role I broke into a run for the stop when I saw our bus coming. 'Never run for a bus Girl, especially when you're going to Court' – said James. James was wearing big floppy trousers in pale green, a pale yellow wrap-over dress, showing off his necklaces, and a long gold velour maxi-coat, with an Indian scarf wound around his head. I needn't have worried; we arrived at Bow Street in plenty of time. There we found Michael Reading in a striped T-shirt under his fur coat, and Douglas MacDougall in platform heels, a long skirt with a broderie anglaise blouse and a dark blue velvet coat with a red fox fur around his shoulders. His hennaed hair, pale skin and the red fox fur was a beacon in a vestibule filled with black uniforms, court officials and seedy lawyers.

Michael Reading, who was barely twenty and one of the nuns arrested on the plinth in Trafalgar Square, was the first to be called. He was charged with behaviour likely to cause a breach of the peace, his arresting officer claiming 'He took a cucumber from his right hand to his left hand and lowered it to his private parts and made masturbatory gestures at the same time jumping up and down shouting, "Fuck, Fuck, Fuck."' Reading denied the cucumber story and told the court that dressing as a nun was using humour and parody to show that there were many people who disagreed with the Festival of Light's view of life.'[6] He was soon returned to the lobby having been found guilty, fined £10 and for £50 bound over to keep the peace for a year.

Michael James was the next to be called. We entered the court and seeing the usher indicating the dock, stepped up into it and sat down. James then began asking for me to be recognized as his

MacKenzie friend, when he was interrupted by the court officer shouting, 'Gentlemen remove their hats!' 'I'm not a gentleman and this is not a hat,' said James. 'Take off the hat,' ordered the magistrate. 'Why?' asked James. 'Take off the hat.' 'Why?' 'Take off the hat!' 'I can't.' 'Why not?' 'Because it matches my dress.' The magistrate leant forward, 'Take that thing off your head.' 'Excuse me but this is not a hat, this is a scarf, part of my dress, and I'm here to be tried on a charge. What I wear is entirely up to me, it's not up to you. You don't buy my clothes. You have no say over what I wear!' 'If you don't do as I say, you will be charged with contempt of court.' 'I'm not in contempt of court; I'm in contempt of you.' 'Take them out,' said the magistrate, 'and don't bring him back until the hat is removed.' We were grabbed by the arms, pulled out of the dock, marched out of court and pushed violently into a small utility room. We both spun round from the opposite wall as the officers came in saying, 'Right, off with that hat.' James drew himself up, 'It's none of your business what I'm wearing.' 'You heard what the magistrate said,' one threatened as he approached. James yelled, 'You just try and touch me again – dear. Lay one finger on me, and I'll have you for assault. Believe me!' The pig tried to reach James, who moved behind me and dodged from side to side, bellowing over my shoulder so loudly everyone in court must have heard, 'I'm warning you, I'll do you for assault.' The pig backed off, and I was instantly convinced James knew something about the law that I didn't. But it's more likely that Lily calculated it was getting ridiculous, and bringing James back into court with his hat still on might give him the pleasure of seeing James sentenced for contempt.

Returning to the hearing, the magistrate could only splutter, 'I see you choose to remain contemptuous of this court.' 'No I'm not contemptuous, but as I've said already, you don't buy my clothes and you've no right to tell me what to wear.' The resigned beak decided 'Let's get on with it, shall we?' The arresting officer's lips moved as fast as a priest's at a cheap funeral, '... and James was chanting, "Jesus loves us all. Even a Gay. So fuck one to-day."' 'Not me, dear,' James responded, 'I'm sure I could do better than that if I put my mind to it.' 'You are not here to boost your ego,' said the magistrate, 'keep to what is relevant.' 'Relevant? It sounds to me like that chant was made up in the police canteen, and he's accusing me of chanting it.'

Standing in the dock, James was so near the bench he was within handshaking distance of the magistrate. 'Tell me', said the magistrate, 'what happened.' James, happy to oblige, explained why the demonstration had come about, and when asked about his role in it said, 'I chose to be an authority figure, and decided to come as a wicked schoolmarm, wearing a black dress with a white collar, a severe wig with a bun at the back, and I carried a cane.' 'Did you', enquired the magistrate, 'wear button boots?' 'The ones with little buttons down the front?' asked James, instantly alive to the nuanced question of a possible fetishist, 'Yes I did your honour, black ones.' 'Case ... Dismissed,' was the fevered reply.[7] As we left the courtroom Douglas MacDougall was sailing in, 'Go girl, you show 'em,' said a triumphant James as we passed. MacDougall did his best and took his time, but ended with a £5 fine and a one year conditional discharge.[8]

Two weeks later at Marlborough Street it was role reversal time with James as my MacKenzie, and me the accused. I dressed as I was at the time of arrest as the Alternative Mary Whitehouse, in matching blue patterned skirt and jacket, heels, her trademark upswept glasses and a wig. Paul Theobald, Chris Blaby and Tim Bolingbroke were with me in the dock.

Blaby, who was dressed as a nun on the demo, was accused of shouting obscene remarks by his arresting officer who claimed that the people in the crowd were upset by his behaviour. We were quite some distance away from the crowd and shouting any kind of slogan was far from our minds. Blaby strongly suggested the officer was mistaken, because he wasn't there to insult anybody, and hadn't shouted anything at all. Yes he was dressed in a nun's costume hired for the occasion, as we had been invited to attend the Festival in the same clothes we had worn at an earlier event. In any case the outfit was not complete and he couldn't have been mistaken for a real nun because he had a couple of day's growth of beard.

The prosecuting solicitor Mr C S Porteous, cross-examining Blaby, revealed the line the court was going to take: 'You know this was a Christian gathering and there were people there with sincere views who were trying to say that what goes on in a permissive society is wrong. Were you not there only to ridicule that?' Blaby: 'I was there to show that the permissive society isn't so bad.'[9]

Theobald's arresting officer described him as wearing make-up, a toy helmet, a gas mask and carrying a toy gun, and then made the claim that Theobald, was making a pumping action with a banner, and this annoyed Festival supporters, and arguments broke out in the crowd, especially among the younger people present. The magistrate, Mr Edward Robey (son of George Robey the famous music hall star) suggested that no one could have been insulted by the wearing of a comedy policeman uniform, which prompted the officer to agree.

When it came time to cross-examine my police accuser, I started to make a point about the police lying in wait for us by asking if the police had been given instructions to arrest us before they had seen us. 'Completely irrelevant,' said the magistrate, 'do you have any more questions?' I put the same question to the policeman again. 'You don't have to answer that,' the bench instructed. 'Why not,' I interjected, and asked the question again. 'Will you please pay attention to what I say and stop interrupting me.' 'I'll stop interrupting you when you stop interrupting me.' 'Take this man down!' I was pulled out of the dock and marched off to a large empty holding tank behind the courtroom, where I sat on a bench thinking, 'you stupid queen, you've fucked this one up.'

Bolingbroke's constable swore that Bolingbroke was dressed as a nun wearing a sash with the words 'Lesbos '71' on it, and that he started to struggle. Cross examined by Bolingbroke, the accusing officer said that 'because of the obscene shouts and the dress and the attitudes of the group he feared a breach of the peace as people attending the Festival seemed to be disgusted by their behaviour. At the time Cliff Richards was singing his opening number.'[10] Bolingbroke told the court that basically we were a street theatre group. We had nothing whatever to do with other groups who were present, and the shouts referred to in evidence had not come from us. We had been invited by Mr Goodwin of the FoL, who was anxious that people of different views should come along. 'We went to express our views and we decided to dress up because we felt it suited the spirit of the occasion.'

> Cross-examined by Mr Porteous, Bolingbroke said he had not given any great consideration to what was written on the sash he wore. It was part of the general theatrical thing and the object was not to ridicule.
>
> The magistrate: 'Would not Catholics – more possibly than others – take the inscription on your sash as meaning that nuns are a lot of lesbians. Wasn't that the impression you wanted to give?
>
> Bolingbroke: 'I don't think so, no. I don't think it would cause offence at all. What's wrong with lesbians?'[11]

I was in the cells long enough to feel the chill before I was taken back into court and stood in the dock once more. A witness for the defence was then called, The Rev. Roy Leonard Smith. Who's he, we quizzed each other as the priest came in, a Roman Catholic priest – he was made to tell the court. He had seen two people dressed in nun's type clothing.

> He did not hear them shout or do anything offensive. The police seized the two dressed as nuns and then a scuffle broke out as they sought to bundle them and others into a police van.
>
> Cross-examined by Mr Porteous he agreed the two men were clearly not nuns although dressed as nuns and that there were a lot of people at the demonstration, sincere Christian people, who had respect for nuns but in his opinion the fact that they were dressed as nuns did not necessarily imply that they were ridiculing nuns. He did not notice the sash marked 'Lesbos '71'. Asked by the magistrate what he would have thought if he had seen the sash he replied: 'I should have thought it odd.'
>
> Mr Robey said that if people chose to wear fancy dress at a big gathering it did not of itself mean that they were insulting. He did not think that the charges against Feather and Theobald had been made out and they would be dismissed. In view of the nature of the Festival, however, he thought that those dressed as nuns were in a different category. At such a gathering as the Festival of Light many Christian people, particularly if they were Catholic, might take great offence at the costume worn by Blaby and Bollingbroke. Of course the police had to do something about it. He was satisfied that that behaviour at that place at that time was likely to cause a breach of the peace and he found the charges against the two men proven.[12]

Blaby and Bolingbroke were fined £5 each with £5 costs, and now had a criminal record.

For Nicholas Bramble, the ordeal was not yet over. His trial was adjourned because his arresting officer had not turned up. At the subsequent hearing in the New Year they found the officer's notes had been 'mislaid'. The case was quietly dropped.

On 1 November, Army Tank HQ at Everton Street was bombed by the AB, and on the 6th Lloyds Bank in Amsterdam, the

Italian Consulate in Basle, and the British Embassies in Rome and Barcelona were all attacked in support of the Stoke Newington Six. The establishment was in a spin because the AB bombing campaign continued despite the arrest of the alleged conspirators. The police were again all over left-wing groups like a virulent rash re-checking their files and the whereabouts of suspects. On 9 November five policemen and one policewoman raided the office of WLW with an explosives warrant, but were more interested in searching for address books. The use of an explosives warrant on this occasion was another instance of 'dirty tricks'; a cynical use of the compliant media to reinforce the idea in the mind of the public that there was a link between the AB and Women's Liberation, and to spread more terror generally.

The cross-referencing of address books and intelligence from covert surveillance eventually pinpointed a member of GLF and a stalwart of its Women's Group who was also active in Women's Liberation. Two days after the raid on the WLW the Bomb squad set out to arrest their suspect.

> *Angie Weir*: I was having a nap after work ... There was a knock at the door and I sort of heard this knock and Elizabeth or Tony actually shouted, 'There's somebody come to see you,' so I got up and wandered down, half undressed and met Inspector Long charging up the stairs with several members of the Special Branch and dogs and god knows what. And they searched the house and I thought, we all thought, it was just another search but then they said, 'One other thing – you're coming with us,' and I was carted off to Albany Street. Then I was taken to Tottenham Court Road and then to Holloway. I was very pleased to go to Holloway because it was very tiring being questioned in the police stations, it was extraordinarily uncomfortable and the food, such as you get, is so disgusting it's unbelievable. And when I got to

Holloway, the reception wing was the old wing in which they held the suffragettes when they were on hunger strike, so I thought that was rather good.[13]

Elizabeth Wilson: I suppose that was the end of my relationship with GLF in a way. I don't know how much I had in common with people around the trial but there wasn't any alternative but to be involved in that ... I think they [the police] were disgusting because they never treated us as badly as they did Grosvenor Avenue because ours was all a nice middle class home and they could relate to that, they were always quite polite and I can remember them going through some photographs and one of them was a girlfriend of mine and they were sniggering over that and saying, oh, she's a good looker, isn't she? But that was the extent of it really. They never took up the carpets, which is a standard thing, whereas Grosvenor Avenue just got turned over time and time again, they just thought they were the scum of the earth ... Agitprop got done over time and time again, I don't think I've got much to grumble about compared with what happened to other people, let alone what happened to Irish people and so on, it was all fairly benign.[14]

Angie Weir was charged with conspiracy to cause explosions and remanded in custody. On 18 December they arrested her friend Kate McLean at Grosvenor Avenue who was remanded on the same charge, and the two found themselves part of the group arrested at Amhurst Road, which now became known as the Stoke Newington Eight. (SN8).

Chapter 11

Trials and Tribulations

> A people who have suffered so much for so long at the hands of a racist society must draw the line somewhere.
> Huey P Newton.[1]

The Old Bailey Trial of Ian Purdie and Jake Prescott opened on 10 November under Judge Melford Stevenson, who was one of the few remaining judges to still carry his black, death sentence hanging cap into court. Purdie's defence was conducted by Mr Schindler QC, while Prescott's counsel Mr Duncan QC was a venerable and deferential 76 years old, who had accepted the case only ten days before the trial commenced.

'The older QCs appointed were interested only in conducting a straight legal defence, and proved unwilling to tackle the political questions underpinning the whole trial. They rarely made any objections – not even to the constant presence in court of Habershon, which was illegal as one of the main prosecution witnesses.'[2]

The state had earlier failed in an attempt to try Prescott and Purdie alongside the Stoke Newington Six, so the Crown devised a legal formula to link the two firmly together.

> On the first day, Ian and Jake's defence counsels accepted, without dissent, an amendment to the charge of conspiracy to include the names of the Stoke Newington Six. This meant that the prosecution was able to cite at length, and at every juncture, details of all 27 'outrages' even though Ian and Jake were only alleged to have conspired for a few months, in 'some' of the incidents. This should have been challenged then and throughout the trial, not only for the sake of Ian and Jake, but also in the interests of the Six who were not present.[3]

For two of the 27 separate attacks going back to 20 August 1967 two others had already been convicted. Not that the jury were informed of that fact.

The only new piece of evidence which came to light during the trial was when Prescott was being questioned by his counsel about the handwriting on three of the envelopes containing the AB communiqués concerning the Carr bombing, which he admitted was his own. The three envelopes were posted from Barnet on the night of 12 January 1971 to *The Times, Guardian* and *Mirror*. '"Where and who with?" The question was rapped out. "No comment," said Jake. No, he would not name the people concerned, he had made enquiries and they were not prepared to come forward. He said he was told the envelopes were for another purpose but he was not prepared to name names.'[4]

He had not disguised his handwriting unlike all other AB communications had. His defending QC clearly defined the nature of proof required when he said: 'Associating with a conspirator is not enough. Even knowing a conspirator's views is not enough. There must be proof of an actual agreement to commit the crime charged.'[5]

Purdie chose not to be put in the witness box. 'In Purdie's case the evidence was solely his political beliefs and the people he knew. Shindler, Purdie's defence counsel, rested his case on the fact that there was no case to answer.'[6]

Apart from Prescott's admission of writing addresses on three envelopes, the prosecution's evidence relied entirely on the stories of two convicted offenders, with whom Prescott shared a cell for a few nights in Brixton prison whilst on remand for stolen cheques. According to Habershon, 'Mr A' and 'Mr B' claimed that Prescott had confessed to them that he was the bomber.

> In his final summing up, Judge Melford Stevenson started detailing the case against Prescott. He made the first reference to a common theme in his remarks: 'His defence as it has been

developed in this case, has involved the most grave accusations … to the effect that Chief Sup. Habershon himself was a party to a most wicked conspiracy involving Habershon and "Mr A" and "Mr B" to place false evidence against Prescott.' If they found that Prescott had taken part in the two bombings (that is if they believed Habershon, 'Mr A' and 'Mr B') 'does it leave any real doubt of any kind – if you are satisfied of those facts – that Prescott was a party to that conspiracy?'[7]

Stevenson spent a whole day presenting the case against Prescott, and a damning thirty-five minutes against Purdie. The jury retired at 2:21pm … At 7 pm the Judge called the jury back into the court and asked what was holding them up. They were in doubt, they said, over Count 3 against Prescott (the Carr bombing) … 'What possible doubt could there be?' Stevenson said. 'Either they believed "Mr A" and "Mr B" and Chief Superintendent Habershon, or the alibis.' The jury foreman replied that they had considered a third alternative. 'They must,' said Stevenson, 'reach a verdict.' So at 7:10 they retired again … At 7:46 they returned to declare Ian Purdie not guilty of conspiracy, and Jake Prescott acquitted on the two bombing charges, but guilty of conspiracy.

Prescott pleaded guilty to each of the cheque charges. Judge Stevenson handed down the sentence, leaving no doubt what he thought of the jury's verdict: 'Fortunately for you, the jury acquitted you of two counts …' Fifteen years for conspiracy and 5 years (concurrent) for the cheque offences.[8]

Twice married, Judge Melford Stevenson's home in Winchelsea was called 'The Truncheons'. On his visits to the Garrick, the West-End club, he was usually accompanied by beautiful young men, so Alan Bray once told me. Melford Stevenson was also the judge in the trial of the Kray twins, Ronnie for the murder of George Cornell and Reggie for the murder of Jack 'the hat'

McVitie. Ronnie Kray was gay, and as is often the case with identical twins, if one is gay the other one is too. Ronnie and Reggie were well known on the gay scene for their lusting after young men, and for throwing lavish parties at their place in Walthamstow, famously attended by Lord Boothby, a bisexual Conservative (who as an MP began in 1954 to campaign for homosexual law reform) and notoriously gay Labour MP Tom Driberg, who between them provided establishment protection for the twins' criminal empire.

George Cornell who was part of the South London Richardson gang, bitter rivals of the Krays, in a queenie spat and hissie fit called Ronnie a 'fat poof'. War was declared. A Kray friend, Richard Hart was murdered, and Ronnie was out for revenge. Cornell out of sheer macho effrontery, decided to anta gonize Ronnie by visiting the *Blind Beggar,* a pub deep inside Kray territory. A tip-off led Ronnie to his enemy. George Cornell found himself looking down the barrel of Ronnie's luger. His last words were, 'Look who's here.' Others claim he added, 'You fucking poof.'

At the Kray twins' trial some lawyers felt Melford Stevenson could have suggested that provocation might have been a motive for Ronnie pulling the trigger, but he chose to make no such direction. Life imprisonment then was understood to be a minimum ten to twelve year term that must be served before permission could be granted to apply for parole. The twins were each sentenced to life imprisonment for a minimum of thirty years before parole could be applied for. An example of the cruelty inflicted on homosexuals by the sycophantic hetero-sexual closet queen's need to emphasise his heterosexual pose and loyalty to the orthodoxy. 'When Stevenson stood as Conservative candidate for Maldon in the 1945 general election he opened his campaign by declaring that in the interests of a clean fight, he would make no allusions to the "alleged homosexuality" of his opponent, Tom Driberg who heavily defeated him.'[9] Such patriarchal heterosexual closet queens are, I'm beginning to think, the chief blackmailers and persecutors of gay men, the ones who control the levers of heterophobia.

At the time of Prescott and Purdie's appearance in one court at the Old Bailey, another court there was hearing the case of the Mangrove Nine, whose trial was to last 11 weeks. Connected to GLF in the spirit of solidarity with other revolutionary people, their defence fund was supported with money collected at GLF General Meetings.

When GLF came to Notting Hill there was already a two-and-a-half year history of police harassment, raids and arrests at a restaurant in All Saints Road called the Mangrove. When Frank Critchlow opened the restaurant to sell Caribbean food, he did not realize that when his place became a centre for the West Indian community, it would also become a focus for the policing of that community.

With increasing police raids, aided by a right-wing council that rescinded Critchlow's late-night food license – not because anything was found to be amiss, but simply because the restaurant had been raided – an Action Committee for the defence of the Mangrove was formed with the Black Panther Movement, and a protest march organized for 9 August 1970 designed to pass Notting Hill, Notting Dale and Harrow Road Police Stations. The demonstrators carried placards and shouted slogans like, 'Hands off Black People.' 'Stop Pig Police Brutality Now.' 'Say it Loud, I'm Black and I'm Proud.' 'What We'll Fight For, and What We'll Die For – Black Power.' 'Black Power – People's Power.'[10] From the moment the march left All Saints Road, the police were out in force, on foot and in coaches, and as more black men and women joined the march, the police became visibly angry at the support the protest was receiving, and called up reinforcements. In Portnall Road, after two hours of orderly and peaceful demonstration by what was now 500 brothers and sisters, the police decided to break things up and waded into the crowd with truncheons drawn, clubbing indiscriminately.

At the committal hearing at Marylebone Magistrates court on 29 December 1970 one of the nine was sent to trial for attempted murder of the policeman who arrested him. All were accused of incitement to fighting and causing affray, and some individually for assault on police. As the committal proceedings drew to a close, the prosecution, on orders from the Director of Public Prosecutions, attempted to drop the incitement to affray charge and instead substitute incitement to riot. The magistrate refused the prosecution demand, telling them, 'The necessary stamp of truth has not been achieved.'[11]

On 5 July 1971, the attempted murder charge was dropped. The defence lawyers accepted the change, and only then discovered that the riot charge had been re-imposed despite the magistrate's decision at committal, and the new Bill of Indictment was signed by Mr. Justice Melford Stevenson.

The trial began on 4 October. The case came before Judge Edward Clark and the jury was composed of ten white people, eight men, two women, and two black men. Radford Howe and Althea Lacointe defended themselves, as did Rhodan Gordon after dismissing his barrister.

> Addressing the Jury at the end of the trial Ian MacDonald, defence counsel for Barbara Beese, demanded that all nine be acquitted. 'I applied for an all-black jury at the request of the defendants and it was based on the Magna Carta. Unless you are aware of the experience of the black community in dealing with the police, it will be easy to go along with the prosecution case. The defence haven't been allowed to bring any evidence on this experience of black people and you would have been told to ignore it – but how can you decide whether these people are guilty or not unless you understand this experience.'
>
> 'For the prosecution to prove the riot charge, it is essential

to prove violent intent and the prosecution must appeal to what is called your white nationalism, your inbred racialism. The prosecution is playing on a stereotype image white people are meant to have of black people. We are brought up to think that just under the skin they are still savages. The prosecution is based on this kind of approach, and this could not take place, unless, senior officers at Notting Hill and at the Dept. of Public Prosecutions, who are the people who decide what charges there should be, had this stereotype view of black people.

'After ten weeks, no-one in this court has heard clear evidence as to how the Portnall Road trouble started. I suggest that there were police officers in Portnall Road who were out of control. It has been said that truncheons were drawn to fend off bottles and stones, but try it, try to fend off bottles and stones with a truncheon. You are asked to believe the most absurd rubbish I have heard, truncheons are not for defence – they are used for attack, to hit people, to break up a demonstration. At one stage the judge said he would cancel the bail of the next person to laugh in the dock, but this is not Russia, yet I believe we have been subjected to naked judicial tyranny.'[12]

Rhodan Gordon summing up in his own case turned to the judge and said:

'I don't want a suspended sentence. You can give me four years or three years instead.' The judge, who lives in Notting Hill, knows as well as anybody that black people on suspended sentences do not remain long out of prison – and that this was the very real and pertinent point that brother Rhodan was making in his statement from the dock.[13]

The jury found all defendants not guilty of riot and those

charged with grevious bodily harm also not guilty. Barbara Beese, Radford Howe, Rothwell Kentish, Godfrey Millet, and Frank Critchlow were found not guilty on all charges. Anthony Innis, Rupert Boyce, and Althea Lecointe were given suspended sentences for actual bodily harm or affray. Rhodan Gordon was found guilty of affray, and given a 15 month suspended sentence to run for two years.

The next morning 17 December 1971, in the street outside his home in Portobello Road, and in front of a number of witnesses, Gordan, who was a community worker, 'was first insulted and then viciously attacked, prior to being arrested by PC's Saunders and Pugh of Notting Hill for alleged obstruction and assault.'[14] Gordan was assaulted again at the police station, in an attack which also involved the station sergeant, Sgt. French,[15] after which he 'was invited by Superintendent Matthews to sit down around a table and discuss the deterioration of police-community relations in the area.'[16]

The *Evening News* reported: 'What has been called the "Mangrove" trial over incidents at Notting Hill has ended, and despite suggestions that a mainly white jury would be prejudiced, the most serious charge was dismissed – and five of the nine defendants were completely cleared. Perhaps coloured citizens will think a little better of our jury system after that.'[17]

In an interview Radford Howe said, 'Since the case I have thrown my lot with the Black Panther movement,' and concluded: 'What I know is that we black people will continue to struggle against the state.'[18]

For another 30 years or so, police regularly arrested Frank Critchlow on trumped up charges. The last one carried a bail condition which prevented him from going within a mile of his restaurant, and the case took so long to come to court that with mounting rent arrears he lost his business. But the police had become just too clever, and too careless. In order to cover up the details of that arrest they had to part with a load of money. Frank

Critchlow personified the black struggle in Notting Hill, and was a much loved leader of his community.

The first GLF commune to be established was in North London, and one of its more active members was nineteen year old Ted Walker-Brown:

> The Bounds Green commune came together in 1971, it was the first time I got to speak to Warren and David Fernbach. I went up to Warren because I was so impressed by him and he and David Fernbach were speaking together and they mentioned a suggestion about a commune and pointed out some people who were interested in it. And I spoke to them and we started the commune together ... Noel and I started going round together and I was afraid it would be a problem to have somebody under age in the commune.
>
> We had a rota for doing the dishes and cleaning but we ended up cooking almost in couples, which became an issue because Noel and I got a lot of hassle from people for being a couple. They were very critical of us for having a nuclear family set-up but we didn't care, we just wanted to be together and that was that. We didn't feel apologetic about it. I didn't believe freedom meant not having anything but communal relationships.
>
> We shared clothes and there was a lot of debate about the men having to wear whatever was available including women's clothes. If you didn't, you were hanging onto your male image and so forth. So there was a lot of cross-dressing but not drag, not full drag. We just put on a blouse or a skirt because it was around and occasionally we'd go out in public in it, but in those days unisex was becoming more fashionable and with the hippie thing of wearing flowing robes, a skirt didn't seem to be like a skirt as such. We had weekly meetings about problems, mostly they were about sorting out the bills

and who hadn't done their washing up and cleaning. The sharing ethic was very strong. People would move in with their suitcases and after a while they'd stop worrying about particular items and what was whose. It even got down to toothbrushes and I put my foot down at that point. I said, 'My toothbrush is mine and I'm not having twelve other people into it.'

The commune lasted for two years. We pooled our money and some were working and others signing on. Noel worked most of the time in a really straight job in architecture and it was a running joke because everybody else would be dressing in whatever they were dressing in and Noel would be popping off to work in his suit, looking exactly like everybody else on the street. Actually it had a certain amount of repercussions in his job, where you were expected to bring people home and he couldn't. Because he would have lost his job straight away, if they saw twelve guys and three women and this communal bedroom. We had several low key parties, they seemed low key to us because we were used to having about twelve people around playing loud music all the rest of the time, dropping acid, because in those days acid was considered to be mind-expanding rather than just a silly game.

We had a very nebulous political concept. First of all it was simply trying to break down the norms of society and not living like a nuclear family ... People had their own philosophies but we weren't collectively Marxist or anything like that. So we did sit around for a couple of meetings trying to talk about what were the roles of women, what were the roles of men. I tried to initiate a discussion about race but as I was the only black present and it didn't work very well. It was just me lecturing everybody, and everybody being very liberal and so on, they would say yes to whatever I said and it didn't get anywhere. On the occasions that we did meet with particularly the Colville queens, we felt quite intimidated but admiring of them because they did seem to analyse everything. They would wear make-up, for example, and think of it as a political act, disrupting, and the people who wore make-up in our house wore make-up because it was pretty and they didn't give a damn about whether anybody was changing the world or changing sex roles and so forth.

In the commune Noel and I became a couple pretty soon. Everybody had either relationships with other people in the commune or a steady girlfriend or boyfriends and it wasn't an issue. Most of the men in our group were fairly conventional in that sense and Danielle, who was the only woman by that time, had a steady girlfriend. She never dressed like what would be considered to by dykey and we all looked quite hippie, but not a bunch of queens in make-up. Except for Blossom.

We didn't have a television, deliberately. Partly because we felt that we'd all wind up watching it and be brainwashed. I think that was our only political act, not to be dominated by TV programmes which emotionally hit us. A lot of us had problems with our families and were running away, to be blunt, from family problems. We didn't bother much with newspapers, we read *IT*, *Oz* and the radical papers and we went to demonstrations which were fun, not for political reasons. We went along to the big GLF meetings. All of us flipped through the [functional] groups but none of us got involved with them for any considerable length of time. [19]

Mark Roberts: I got a space with the Bounds Green Commune until about a year later when it broke up and we moved to Muswell Hill. Bounds Green was a ground floor flat, fairly roomy, or it would have been roomy for a couple, say, but we had fourteen people there. We had to stack the landlord's furniture up against the walls to make some space. The bedroom was the biggest room and a sea of divan beds and mattresses. The living area was the kitchen with a bathroom tacked on the back, and then two very small rooms, one of which was a walk through from the kitchen to the bedroom, so no private space at all. I used to find it very comforting to go to sleep in there, in a room with other sleeping bodies. It was painted a dark colour and the curtains were drawn, the light was only very dim, it was very relaxing, very comforting hearing people breathing, you weren't alone. We all put a fiver a week in the kitty, which in those days was enough for the rent, food and power. Most people were actually working, I was claiming unemployment benefit at the time but I could still afford to live that way and pay my share which was good. In a way it was a little odd, I mean the vast majority of people there were holding down full-time jobs, so it wasn't really a right on commune, most people were in couple relationships. We were quite international as well with exiles, people from Franco's Spain and Americans, and Danielle who was French. Blossom was the only drag queen. When the commune broke up it was Blossom who looked after me.'[20]

For seven months the expectation of a paperback edition of Reuben's book had been threatening us. Another, so-called, highly respected publisher, Pan Books, gained the contract to profit from the doctor's immoral views by considering them as ethical, scientific, psychiatric facts. There was much anger expressed at the emergency meeting of Counter-Psychiatry, Action Group and Street Theatre, held a few days after the paperback edition came out. There was also a heightened confidence that came from a successful summer of protests. This time there would be no initial exchange of letters between us and the publisher, nor anymore leafleting of bookshops: this time the target would be the books themselves.

Lyndsay Levy, the Tynesider who had been involved in

theatre in Edinburgh joined GLF in the spring and became friends with James, Bramble and I when she joined Street Theatre. Her idea for the protest against the book was to re-enact Reuben's method of abortion. The demonstration on 30 October began in front of the doorway of Foyle's bookshop, with Lyndsay Levy screaming in pain as Barbara Klecki armed with a coat hanger, poked about under Levy's skirt until she released from between her legs pounds of bloody calves liver. Then as managers and sales assistants rushed out of the other doors to see what was happening, we all pushed past them, tipping over the display stands and throwing Reuben's books onto the floor. We then went down the Charing Cross Road trashing the other bookshops stocking his work.

Another method of attacking the book, one favoured by Nettie Pollard, was to surreptitiously tear the corners of the cover and crease the pages. The Action Group had also produced two stickers, one stated: 'Warning. This book does not represent the majority of Medical & Psychiatric Opinion,' and the other: 'This book is Poison. Everything you Always Wanted to Know About Sex by "Doctor" David Reuben is Inaccurate Hysterical and Dangerous.' With gum on the reverse they were ready to be stuck on the book's cover. John Chesterman had the clever idea of designing a postcard which read: 'Pan Books, 33, Tothill Street, S.W.1. In view of certain criticisms of Dr. David Reuben's book, "Everything you Always Wanted to Know About Sex", Pan Books Ltd., undertake to refund in full the retail price and postage if you are not fully satisfied, and if you give your reasons. Please fill in this form and return it together with the book to the above address.' Using these means the campaign continued for many months.

The moral anger against Pan Books took another turn in December after they failed to answer letters asking them to receive a delegation from GLF to discuss matters. Ralph Vernon-Hunt, the managing director described as 'a loveable old publisher who stands to make a mint of money out of libels on nice people', was more hard-nosed and called the police for help when demonstrators entered his offices. Meeting at St. James's Park Tube, the protesters, including many from the transsexual group, came along with a fifteen foot cucumber made of chicken wire and papier mâché which was used to parody one of Reuben's homosexual fantasies, ceremoniously bumming each member of the group at the side of the road during the march to Pan Books' offices. Entering the foyer, Peter Tatchell upended two sacks full of dead light bulbs all over the floor while others dumped carrots, cucumbers and wire coat-hangers.

Peter Tatchell recalls: 'When the police arrived their reaction was a mixture of belligerence and amusement. They knew what we were doing was illegal but they didn't quite know how to handle a fifteen-foot cucumber. So to speak.' [21]

Chapter 12

Transvestites and Transsexuals

Androgyny is not an easy binding of this or that aspect of masculine or feminine behaviour. It is a definite contradiction of counterposing drives. An escape from androgyny is what we, as a species, are aiming for. That is what our sexual deviations are all about.

Bob Mellors. *We Are All Androgynous Yellow.*[1]

Two Americans joined GLF sometime after the move to Notting Hill. Edith and Rachel Pollack were both in their early thirties and soon became recognized as an odd couple, with their stylish, carefully chosen second-hand clothes which looked good on Edith who was an average size woman, and softened the image of Rachel who was well over six foot tall, and built like a rugby player. They saw themselves as a lesbian couple, which I found difficult to accept; Rachel was not a man on sex hormone treatment and Edith who was a retiring type, made them appear to my eyes as a heterosexual couple.

Earlier in the summer Bobbi came into the movement. He was about twenty, cherubic, foxy, creamy-pink, a dark haired mop-top, pre-op tranny, with large well developed breasts and a unisex style of dress. He said he loved women and declared he was a lesbian. Bobbi earned his money by turning tricks on Park Lane. He lived right on the edge and I was fascinated to know how he managed to avoid the punters' discovery of his genitals. He obviously realized I didn't know very much, and played along by demonstrating his technique, which seemed to me in the use he made of his hands, to be completely implausible. Only years later did I discover that there are a host of men out there who love pre-op trannies – chicks with dicks – only to lose all interest in them after the operation. Towards the end of Gay Lib, Bobbi became good friends with Bob Mellors, who was then beginning to formulate a system of masculine and feminine gender combinations. Later Bobbi went through a crisis and had his breasts removed, then acquired them a second time through implants.

Claudia was also about twenty. I'm aware of again describing physical characteristics over personality, but appearance and the ability 'to pass' is a major concern in transsexualtiy and transvestism. He had shoulder length dark blonde hair, a thin pale face with a crooked nose, a slim body, and his sexual object was men. He was not very well educated and had been living in a local council hostel before joining Gay Lib and moving into the GLF house in Penge. Claudia was an early member of GLF whom I got to know better in late-1973 when I was living at Bethnal Rouge. My strongest impression of his life then was the amount of time he spent finding hormone pills on the black market in his struggle to convince Dr. Randall, the consultant at Charing Cross Hospital in charge of sex change operations in the UK, that he fulfilled Randall's criteria of living and working for two years as a women in order to qualify for the transsexual programme. Getting a job in an economic depression was impossible, and an outrageous class-based demand to make on someone with little self-confidence like Claudia, so it became an increasingly frustrating and depressing preoccupation for him.

> *Nettie Pollard*: 'There was lots of discussion on whether pre-operative transsexuals should be able to go to the Women's Group. They were never banned and some did go. The main thing is that virtually everybody who was transsexual in GLF was male-to-female. In later GLF there was a transsexual group and some came then, but at the early meetings there weren't. Claudia was the first one, quite mad but in a queeny way. Then there was Bobbi who tended not to wear skirts and

dresses. She was wearing silver boots and black trousers and going to the women's group, and I thought I wonder if Bobbi thinks that he/she is wearing women's clothes. In a way he didn't look any different in male clothes.'[2]

'Don't call me mister you fucking beast!' is the title of an article in the January 1972 edition of *Lesbian Come Together* 11, giving an insight into the Transvestite, Transsexual and Drag Queen Group, particularly the views of Rachel and of the male transvestites who joined that function group, but, and it must be stressed, never visited or came out at the all-London meetings. The group had been in existence for several weeks before Pollack wrote this article.

> So far about forty people have called or visited. Some have come regularly, some have drifted off. Almost all have been women – people born males who live as women, or more commonly, dress as women whenever they get the chance. Transvestite men – people born female who live or dress as men (if the language confuses you it confuses us too, it's not meant to include us) have so far not come forth. We're working to break down these barriers, but for now this article will be the experience of transvestite women.
>
> How many of us are there? Nobody knows or has any real statistics, but there are 60,000 people in the UK taking sex hormones. Add to this the people who want them but the doctors won't give them, the people who want them but are afraid to ask, and all the transvestites who at the moment aren't interested in hormones. The amazing thing is, most of us think we're a tiny minority.
>
> When we're alone we tend to accept the stereotypes. By getting together we've discovered how ridiculous they really are. No one in the group has ever said, 'What horrible trick of nature has made me a woman trapped in a man's body?' We

just don't think that way. The psychiatrists who electro-shock us think we're pathetic or tragic, but even those who are very much in the closet enjoy being transvestite as long as there's some outlet.

The whole question of roles needs to be examined, and particularly what we as transvestites, transsexuals and drag queens can contribute to a new understanding of how they operate. Some of us are opposed to roles because they can limit self-discovery. We don't want to discard the male role just to take on the female role. Others think that transvestites can show people that roles can be fun, if you're free to take the ones you want and then discard them when you don't want them anymore.

A more central question is how to relate to other women. When we talk about our hopes and fantasies it becomes apparent that what we want above all is to be accepted as women, primarily by other women. But will we achieve this by looking for ways in which we share experience with regular women or by developing a unique transvestite consciousness?

Sometimes the second approach seems real militant and proud, at other times it seems a cop-out, accepting the prejudiced view that we're not women, that we're some freaky third sex (or fourth or fifth?). Possibly we can find some light by considering the situation of black women and gay women, who develop black pride and gay pride, but still explore their feelings as women. Think how much more inspiring and beautiful the women's revolution will be when it joyously includes all women. Think of a Holloway demo with transvestite, transsexual and drag-queen women, gay women and heterosexual women, black, yellow, brown and white women, mothers, daughters, poor women, rich women, working women, housewives and career women. Certainly, whatever course we take as transvestites, transsexuals and drag queens,

> we must first destroy the trap wherein regular women set up standards by which they accept or reject us.
>
> Certainly one thing becomes more and more clear as we come together: pass or not pass, we can't let anybody tell us what we are. One sister said that after six months of psychiatric treatment she discovered that no one knew her like herself. We can't let anybody tell us we're men, when we know we're women. As Holly Woodlawn once said in New York, 'Don't call me mister, you fucking beast!'

The article was signed by, 'Roz Paula Rachel Della Edith Susan Perry Patty Christine.' Neither Bobbi nor Claudia were part of the group.

If the subject of transvestites and transsexuals is confusing, Pollack is not enlightening when it comes down to who is happy with their body and who isn't, as she appears to identify herself as a transvestite having laid claim to being a lesbian. Indeed all the categories, transvestite, transsexual and drag queen are blithely elided here, when in fact they are uniquely different. Transvestites are people of either sex who enjoy dressing in the clothes of the opposite sex. They have no wish to change sex; they are comfortable with their bodies and their sexual orientation. Whatever the need to cross-dress satisfies, the tactile experience of being enclosed and restricted by women's dress, fetishistic erethism, or, the freedom of male clothing, the gain in status or financial power, they appear to have only one thing in common, a desire to pass, and to be accepted by their partners and society. They do not require the intervention or the imprimatur of the medical establishment to feel at ease and at one with themselves. Perhaps the wearing of drag for the transvestite is the key to experiencing in a more amplified way their already conscious awareness of the opposite sex within themselves.

Drag queens are gay men, proud of their sexuality and happy with their bodies. Pollack for some reason merges two distinct kinds of people and exchanges the terms, drag queen and transvestite women. The collapsing of transsexuals, transvestites, drag queens and their differing sexualities is bewildering, and makes me wonder if he perceived his own identity as diffuse.

> *Nettie Pollard*: The problem about transsexuals was twofold. One, that transsexuality wasn't particularly well known at the time and a lot of people didn't believe it existed, and that maybe these people were gay men who weren't particularly well adjusted because of the way that straight society looked at them. And there was the problem that they wanted to join the women's group and the women's group was based on common experience and often talked about things like childhood experiences. And I felt extremely torn on the subject myself because I felt that transsexuals were perfectly valid, and didn't feel that they should be excluded, but at the same time I realised that their history wasn't entirely the same as women.[3]

As Nettie Pollard says, at first we thought transsexuals were gays with rigid black and white heterosexually polarized minds that could not perceive of any alternative to the heterosexual model, until surgery had corrected what the mind had partitioned off. But we became aware through meeting transsexuals that this was a heterosexist view based on the same polarized binary model that kept us down, and was designed to ignore, deny and obscure the trans-sexuals deep feelings for who they are as people.

> *Nettie Pollard*: Some of the women felt that these people had very male attitudes and were very patronising to women and trying to steal women's oppression while not giving up their prick power. There was a great deal of feeling of that. And certainly a lot of them weren't particularly aware from the feminist point of view, so they may have reflected male

attitudes that they'd been brought up with ...I don't think there was any time when transsexuals were utterly banned from the women's group.[4]

It was Rachel Pollack, a man whose sexual object was women, demanding to be accepted as a woman, by the women, that influenced the radical queens, as did the statement in his article above that chauvinistically proposed, 'we must first destroy the trap wherein regular women set up standards by which they accept or reject us.' We came to the opinion that you can remove the penis from the body but you cannot remove it from the mind. Or to put it another way, male to female transsexuals are nurtured as boys, and an isomorphic change doesn't alter that history. The demand from the transsexuals to be accepted as woman was a key problem for the women and the queens of GLF. Pollack's setting up of the Transvestite, Transsexual and Drag Queen Group helped to examine their situation and position. Here are his findings:

DECLARE YOUR SEX
TRANSVESTITES TRANSSEXUALS COME OUT

Transsexual and transvestite oppression, like all gay oppression, exists on two levels: one, the legal and physical dangers, and two, the mindfuck of isolation, guilt, and shame. Transvestism is against the law, no matter what age you are. A transvestite faces arrest every time he or she leaves the house. At demos the pigs always grab the people in drag first and hit them the hardest. It is no coincidence that of all the people arrested at the Festival of Light the only person facing a prison term was dressed as a cigarette girl. And think a moment what the pigs would do to a transsexual if they undressed her in the precinct house.

And still the mindfuck is worse. Transsexuals and transvestites who strive to come out have nowhere to turn, no one to meet. There are almost no drag pubs, no drag magazines. The entire bibliography on transvestism and transsexualism together can be counted on your hands with fingers left over for obscene gestures. If a transsexual or transvestite tries to be open and proud, and isn't lucky enough to have the equipment to pass on the street, she or he can expect ridicule and possible assault just for going to the grocers.

And yet – whenever we bring up the subject at a Gay Lib meeting people complain we're wasting their valuable time.

This oppression must end now.

Gay men have finally begun to recognize that they are responsible for smashing the oppression of women. It is equally the responsibility of all gay people to help transsexuals and transvestites come out. A transvestite or transsexual woman should not have to demonstrate or prove to lesbians, individually or collectively, that she's a sister. On the contrary, they must say to her, 'Come out. You belong here with us.'

In New York City the Street Transvestite Action Revolutionaries sought to join the Radicalesbians as sisters. They were denied membership on the grounds they were 'genital males'.

This oppression must end now.

Some revolutionaries, very proud of their advanced thinking, tell us we're reactionary if we identify with a particular sex, even though it's the one opposite from that of our birth certificates. Drag queens and butch lesbians are put down for supposedly clinging to stereotyped gay roles. People refuse to recognize that they are expressing a strong transvestite component in their personalities. In fact, the isolation of transvestites and transsexuals is so strong that many women who dress in men's clothes, take men's names, and think of themselves as male will be angered at anyone calling them transvestites, because they feel they shouldn't be associated with 'limp-wristed queens'.

Further, when a drag queen tries to adopt a more simple feminine style she will be put down for not being good enough as a woman. People who would consider it barbaric sexism to expect a man to prove his masculinity will demand that a drag queen prove her femininity.

We are told, 'Why do you care if you're he or she? Break down gender roles.' But just as a woman must fight sexism as a woman in order to win full expression of her male and female elements, so must transsexuals and transvestites fight oppression as themselves. The entire gender argument is a lie, as a transsexual's very existence destroys gender roles far more effectively than all the speeches put together. Many transvestites dream all their lives of passing as women. In fact, because they are not allowed to be women they spend their whole lives passing as men.

This oppression must end now.

Many gay people are confused by the separation between 'gay transvestites' and 'straight transvestites'. But this is an artificial split, imposed on us by those people who seek to isolate us and deny our identities. A transsexual or transvestite is gay because she or he is transsexual or transvestite. Some of us are into men and some of us are into women. Some of us are homosexual, some of us are heterosexual, some of us are lesbians. But we are all transsexual or transvestites and it's these identities that must be recognized and encouraged. To be gay means to break the rules of your official sex, to cross over the guidelines set up by the family, the schools, and the church. Some of us cross over by sleeping with the wrong person. Some of us dress the wrong way. Some of us do both. We are all gay.

Very few people, if any, would argue that because homosexuals and lesbians have slightly different experiences women don't belong in GLF. On the contrary, most would argue that it's GLF's responsibility to actively seek out gay women and encourage them to join. It is equally GLF's responsibility to encourage transsexuals and transvestites. We are all fighting the same oppression. Read what David Reuben says about transvestites. And what distinctions does a skinhead make?

No we are all fighting the same guilt. The words, 'queer, bull' we all have to shrug them off.

Most important we are all breaching the same barriers, the same rules: a man is this, a woman is that, and don't you dare cross over.

'ALL OPPRESSION MUST END NOW!
DECLARE YOUR SEX.
TRANSSEXUALS TRANVESTITES COME OUT' [5]

Rachel Pollack tells us that it is GLF's responsibility to encourage transsexuals and transvestites to join our revolution, however the way we saw it was to encourage transsexuals and transvestites to make their own revolution. Pollack and the Transvestite and Transsexual group state that gay men 'are responsible for smashing the oppression of women'. The radical queens would deny that as emphatically as their sisters and many left brothers, and would say it suggests the view that women can't do it by themselves. The radical queens saw their role in supporting women as one of showing solidarity. Then we have Pollack telling women they must say to the transsexual, 'Come out. You are one of us', when the women had decided otherwise. It appears that the only role transsexuals are going to allow lesbians and gay men to play is that of handmaidens to the transsexuals' own coming out. And while the answer the New York Radicalesbians gave to transsexuals wishing to join their group was expressed as genital difference, the women in London GLF were much more thoughtful in saying that transsexuals and transvestites were not women, by reason of their different history. The reply did not rest on genitalia, but on the gender-role differences their histories make.

The historic and social constructs that shapes our lives from the moment we are born, with boys being treated in a different way to girls breeds through heterosexualism a belief in male superiority. Becoming an isomorph of the opposite sex does not change that history, as Rachel's view of women and their role, as expressed above, would in its male chauvinism seem to confirm. Collapsing the fundamental differences of imposed gender roles, sexual history and sexual orientation brings nothing but confusion and atomized identities. Transsexuals and transvestites are not gay. Male transsexuals who transform themselves are not women, and female transsexuals transformed are not men; they are 'gynamorphs' and 'andromorphs'. I think the difficulty is the shedding of masculinity, not its 'more playful' attainment by the andromorph. For gynamorphs however, the similarities between who they feel they are, and their realignment, between their ideal of being a woman and the isomorphic physical reality seems only to confuse their situation. The demand of male-to-female transsexuals to be treated as women by women is from a feminist point of view, 'gynamorphism'. Gynamorphism denies women's history. Gynamorphism denies women the feelings, experiences and needs of their own bodies. Why do gynamorphs demand that women validate their sex change, especially as women are not in a position to do so? And does the demand come from both gynamorphs whose sexual object is men and gynamorphs whose sexual object is women? Or is the problem one of class antagonism with gynamorphs discovering that their social status is below that of women, on a par with sex workers – the lumpen – and that their demand is really for equality with women?

Rachel Pollack is right on two important things: transsexuality makes nonsense of binary gender roles, and transvestites and transsexuals must fight their oppression for themselves.

Pride in who they are can be gained no other way. Only by finding their own place can they undermine sexual categorization and help release gender roles from genitalia.

In May 1972 there was a National Think-In at Birmingham University. During the first session of the day the discussion had naturally been about coming out. Aubrey Walter giving his rap on the difficulties of coming out in the provinces pointedly addressed us while telling the meeting how it would be almost impossible to come out in drag in the provinces. A voice from the back of the hall interrupted: 'I don't agree with that'. We turned round to see a man in drag standing up, who was over six feet tall. 'My name's Julia. I'm a transsexual. I've been living and working as a woman around here for well over a year by now. I work in a garage down the road. I'm a petrol pump attendant.' In *Come Together* 14 produced by Birmingham GLF that summer, Julia B. wrote:

Coming Out as a Transsexual

> I have, in the last twelve months, 'come out' as a transsexual and I can truly say that I have never been happier. Further and ultimate happiness for me lies somewhere in the far distant future, but it is a goal to aim for.
>
> At the time of my coming out I had never heard of GLF or its aims and ambitions, so my coming out was possibly much more of a personal ideology than for our brothers and sisters who have attended a number of GLF meetings and been helped by them to obtain true happiness.
>
> Unlike most other brothers and sisters, my coming out was prompted by police action, after being taken to court for 'conduct likely to cause a breach of the peace' (not 'piece'). After this experience I retreated even further into my shell and was so disillusioned by the publicity I received that I attempted one of the age-old methods to finish it all. Happily I am glad to say I failed, otherwise I would not have found the

happiness I now have.

After a few months of living as a hermit I contacted the Samaritans, and after a few meetings with them I was able to talk about myself, my aims and ambitions, and finally reached a complete understanding with myself.

Once I had admitted my true inner self to others I felt great relief (this I take to be one of the main aims of GLF), and thereupon decided to be myself all the time and live life as it suited me and not the way I had been committed to live since coming out of the womb.

Prior to this, my marriage (to a woman) had broken up and my wife was seeking a divorce, together with the custody of the children because of my attitude to life, namely brought about because of my jealousy of her femininity and her ability to become pregnant and know true happiness within straight society.

Once I had decided to come out I did so. The last time I wore male clothing was the day after I had made my decision, when I was so apprehensive that I had to go to the local paper shop to buy cigarettes at 6.30 in the morning (ugh! what a time to go out). Since then I only wear female clothing and now I wonder how I ever wore such constricting clothing as trousers and male clothing in general, as there is not so much scope within that framework to express your individuality fully.

Since coming out I have been ostracised completely by my former friends and neighbours, I have been harassed on many occasions by the police, but now that they have spoken to me on a number of occasions and they seem to realise that if we are to get along together their attitude must change, as I most certainly will never return to their ideas of straight society.

I live in a small town (20,000), just north of Birmingham, and consequently I am known to a great many people who knew me 'before'. I imagine, by the way they laugh, sneer,

> and jeer at me that they are embarrassed by me, but I have not yet found out if this is because they will not admit their own inhibitions to themselves.
>
> Since joining GLF and getting one of their badges, I feel happier again as I realise the numbers of gay people in GLF and outside it (unhappily at the moment) understand and accept me as a person, and not a pair of trousers or a dummy in a shop window wearing whatever clothes society in general dictates that I should be attired in at any given moment. Wearing the GLF badge is like a shield to me and it feels as if it is protecting me, although now that I have accepted and revel in my femininity, I now have to be liberated again as in many ways I have accepted the suffering of women and lack of liberty afforded to them by male-orientated society. For instance, I feel wrong in smoking in the street or going into a pub on my own, but I don't suppose I can hope for complete miracles to happen in such a short time and will have to work hard at my accepted role in life.

Beyond learning outward social conformity, it would be nice to think that Julia B could go even further by learning about women's history, and the history of the Feminist struggle. Such learning would help all pre- and post-operative gynamorphs who wish to be treated as women, and if they sincerely wish to have the respect of the sex they identify with, then wanting to learn that history would seem essential. What is certain is that transsexuals, just like homosexuals, challenge the immoral and undemocratic, offend the moral and the aesthetic standards of the hegemony, and will be part of the new.

Each to their own: Julia B began to organize the transsexuals and transvestites around Birmingham.

As mentioned, Bob Mellors was a close friend of Bobbi, and through that friendship Mellors became fascinated with the subject of transsexuality. In looking for ways to illustrate the confusing and conflicting sensibilities of masculinity and femininity, Mellors used the system of Yin and Yang; the broken line of Yin (- -) representing the feminine and the unbroken line of Yang (–) the masculine.

With these he formed a trigram, the upper line signifying gender, the second and third lines below representing the male and female sides, with the marginally stronger drive in the middle row and the marginally less strong in the bottom row. The trigram can then be read upwards as the two sexual drives aligning or conflicting with each other and with the subject's gender. He uses the gay vernacular of Butch and Bitch, Superbutch, Superbitch, Unbutch and Unbitch to describe some of the resulting combinations of congruities and antagonisms. These also demonstrate the meaninglessness of the terms heterosexual and homosexual, attraction to difference and attraction to sameness.

As a big movie fan Mellors knew that cinema and popular entertainment are nothing if not reflections of the interior lives and aspirations of all segments of the population. Under the cinematic heading 'Coming Attractions' he analyzes a selection of films:

> Bitch to Bitch: '*her* femininity to *her* femininity – Don Siegel's *The Beguiled. His* femininity to *his* femininity – Richard Burton & Rex Harrison in *The Staircase. His* femininity to *her* femininity, and, *her* femininity to *his* femininity – Woody Allan & Diane Keaton in *Annie Hall* – Elizabeth Taylor and Richard Burton in *Who's Afraid of Virginia Woolf* – St Francis and St Clare in *Brother Sun, Sister Moon.* (As bitching femmes none of those would accord with the Pope's description of heterosexual relationships.)
>
> Bitch to Butch and Butch to Bitch. Normal husband-wife relationships: *her* femininity to *his* masculinity, and, *his* masculinity to *her* femininity – *Love Story – First Love, etc. etc.*

Queer husband-wife relationships: *his* femininity to *his* masculinity – *Laurel & Hardy, Morecambe & Wise,* Barlow & Watt in *Z Cars. Her* masculinity to *her* femininity – *The Killing of Sister George.* Inverse husband-wife relationships: *his* femininity to *her* masculinity, and, *her* masculinity to *his* femininity – see any *Carry On* film.

Butch to Butch: *his* masculinity to *his* masculinity – Clint Eastwood & Jeff Bridges in *Thunderbolt & Lightfoot* – Paul Newman & Robert Redford in *Butch Cassidy & The Sundance Kid. Her* masculinity to *her* masculinity – *Lesbians Ignite! Her* masculinity to *his* masculinity, and, *his* masculinity to *her* masculinity – Clint Eastwood & Sandra Locke in *The Gauntlet,* and, Faye Dunnaway & Warren Beatty in *Bonnie & Clyde.*[6]

We have seen that we gays are not alone in our preoccupations with butch and bitch. We are not the only people with odd-packets-odd-contents relationships. The fact is that each and every member of our species, Homo Sapiens, is to a greater or a lesser degree androgynous. We are all, each and every one of us, partly masculine and partly feminine. It is precisely because we are all to some extent androgynous that the odd-packets-odd-contents relationships are the ones that so often strike a chord and entertain.[7]

For some people, however, these androgynous tensions are quite formidable and may never be brought under effective control. Like perpetual adolescents these people are continually at odds with themselves, torn this way and that. Trying one thing then another, stumbling from disaster to excitement to disaster. These are the people who find themselves in odd-packets-odd-relationships. Such people, while trying to resolve their own inner tensions, explore new ways of behaving, and it is in this way that new ideas and new modes of behaviour are brought into the world. This is how the people who are more highly androgynous, whom we can

> accurately call sex-deviants, become the breakers of new ground, the spearhead of evolution.[8]

Mario Mieli, a radical queen, member of GLF and renowned Marxist thinker who returned to Italy to found FUORI! in 1971, developed out of his wide reading an idea he termed trans-sexuality, which he defined as:

> The infantile polymorphous and undifferentiated erotic disposition, which society suppresses and which, in adult life, every human being carries within him either in a latent state, or else confined in the depths of the unconscious under the yoke of repression. Trans-sexuality seems to me the best word for expressing, at one and the same time, both the plurality of the erotic tendencies and the original and deep hermaphrodism of every individual.[9]
>
> In general, we call transsexuals those adults who consciously live out their own hermaphrodism, and who recognize in themselves, in their body and mind, the presence of the 'opposite' sex ... Society induces these manifest transsexuals to feel monosexual and to conceal their real hemaphrodism. To tell the truth, however, this is exactly how society behaves with all of us. In fact we are all, deep down, transsexuals, we have all been trans-sexual infants, and we have been forced to identify with a specific monosexual role, masculine or feminine ... In any case, in those people who recognize themselves as transsexuals today, we can see the trans-sexuality (bisexuality) that is latent in everyone. Their particular condition has brought them more or less close to an awareness, potentially a revolutionary one, of the fact that every human being, embryologically bisexual, maintains for his or her whole life, both in the biological and psychological aspects, the presence of the other sex. I believe that the resolution of the present separate and antithetical categories

of sexuality will be trans-sexual, and that trans-sexuality discloses the synthesis, one and many, of the expressions of a liberated Eros.[10]

Chapter 13

Party Games and a Serious Proposal

> If we want to find our place in the world there is only one place to look. That is on the biggest stage of all – that of the evolution of the species.
> Bob Mellors. *Homosexuality, Androgyny and Evolution.*

One of the continuing complaints members attributed to the lack of organization in the movement was the high turnover of new members at the general meeting. Others were beginning to question the role of the meeting itself, now that there was a move towards forming local groups in London. The 15 October 1971 Think-In had failed to come up with any ideas to improve the situation at All Saints Hall, but it did initiate a weekly Diary or Newssheet, put together by the Office collective, giving contact details for each function group and local GLF, along with notices of actions being planned. The role of the Think-In itself was also being questioned, and the one arranged for the LSE on the 18 December was called especially to look at all these problems again. Richard Dipple was beginning to be irritated with this process.

> It shouldn't be necessary for us to have to talk about new members. After all, when does one stop being 'new'? Once a person's face has become recognisable as 'having been here before' it is very easy to assume that he or she does not feel 'new' anymore and therefore we don't need to make the effort to communicate. But we are all new to lots of people every day. If we can experience ourselves and each other more we will find it easier to relate to new people, because our energy will be going out to reach others rather than being directed

onto the 'problem' of 'new members' or the 'problem' of 'the Wednesday meeting'.

We split up into small groups in the morning and the feeling in our group was that we didn't want to talk about the 'problems facing GLF' (In other words we were pissed off with the same boring 'topics for discussion'.) We held hands, touched toes, felt feet and we started talking – to each other and about each other. It was interesting that although we had not imposed our feelings on the other group in the room in any way, their general reaction as they left for lunch was one of ridicule and slight annoyance that we weren't being serious enough. As we were now the only group in the room we spread out more. We rearranged the chairs, created a tube-train in the middle of the room and were served Russian tea as we stepped over dead bodies, bit train inspectors, got caught in sliding doors, and even managed to walk through solid walls.

The initial general reaction of the other groups when they returned was that we could carry on our childish games while they carried on the 'think-in' in other rooms. However, we objected and the meeting was reconvened to listen to reports from the groups. The lack of understanding which many people in the other groups expressed about what we had been doing showed that what had been happening was inside each of us. That one cannot describe this experience; one can only describe how it came about. So the fact that I no longer have a hang-up about my feet and that my warts are going to drop off soon are not as irrelevant as they may seem. Our group 'non-report' was as much a report as the others were, one which expressly stated that really they 'hadn't arrived anywhere'.

However, the attitude prevailed that 'the think-in must go on' so we put away our tube train and someone chalked up a suitable agenda of topics for discussion and we once again split up into small groups. Sadly, we dispensed with 'idle chatter' and discussed – wait for it – yes, you've guessed, 'new members' and, surprise surprise, 'the Wednesday meeting'. We dutifully presented our decisions and conclusions to the others and we listened to the others present their decisions and conclusions to us and we all went home.[1]

Dissatisfaction with communications was being felt in other areas too. Sometime in the late summer or early autumn, I remember walking along a street in Bayswater with Andrew Lumsden, who surprised me by asking what I thought about the idea of having a national gay newspaper. I told him I thought we already had one in *Come Together*. Each new group that emerged in the country was sent copies of the latest editions – didn't that make it a national paper? If the movement was to grow and develop then so would the paper, surely – what would be the point of having a separate one?

Andrew Lumsden, as a journalist at *The Times* saw it differently. He'd been in touch with major newspapers trying to get them to publish just a simple piece about gay liberation. He was a friend of the editor of the *Daily Mirror* who wasn't in the least prejudiced, so he was shocked when this friend refused to publish anything about GLF, claiming it was a London thing. His own paper *The Times* also refused. Eventually the *Spectator* published his article, and through that he met Jill Tweedie of the *Guardian,* who then visited GLF at Lumsden's invitation to witness a Wednesday meeting and later wrote several pieces on the movement. He also approached television, receiving a lot of support from Julian Pettifer at *Panorama,* where a short interview with Barbara Klecki, Lumsden, and Warren Haig was made and eventually broadcast after several mysterious delays.

Lumsden: I was so angry that the principal Labour Party supporting paper and the principal top paper both refused in the space of a fortnight to carry a description of what the GLF

> was in the simplest terms, just that it existed and a little information … it seemed to me that there was only one thing to do and that was to have a newspaper of our own.[2]

Lumsden spoke of his frustrations with other members, listened to their reactions and then in the late autumn put his ideas in front of the general meeting.

> *Lumsden*: Denis [Lemon] was the only person who immediately said, 'I am desperate to do this idea.' I mean others said, 'That's interesting, I'd like to come along to have a talk.' But I think it caught Denis just at exactly the moment when everything else was running into the sand, and he loved the idea of it somehow. He came up immediately after the meeting. I was standing up against some pillar and saying, 'I think the time has come to have a newspaper.'
>
> Aubrey and David didn't want it: I don't mean they would destroy such a proposition, but they didn't want it because they wanted the campaigning writing, whereas I said explicitly that I thought that this should be a paper giving information, distributed nationally. It was the moment when things were splitting in all directions, so people were constantly coming from Edinburgh and Glasgow or Middlesbrough, turning up and saying we never seem to quite know what's going on.[3]

Denis Lemon was in a very good position. He already had a team at his bidding in the Action Group, Martin Corbett and David Seligman among them. They had all been subservient to Chesterman in the FoL Campaign, and to both Chesterman and Powell in the Police and Pub Landlord demonstrations. This proposal was a whole lot bigger – they could be in control – it could be a career.

On the same day as the National Think-in at the LSE, an alliance of men from the Action Group and others not active within any of the GLF function groups had already arranged another event for the 18 December. Alan Wakeman a businessman who had tried to promote the band of a straight couple he was managing as the official house band of GLF decided to throw a party to celebrate the support given by the local people in Notting Hill to the presence of GLF on a Wednesday night. Since that support came from the regulars in the pubs whose landlords we had been forced to fight, this was not to be a knees-up in one of the locals with his folk group *The Solid British Hat Band* giving a free gig, but a Christmas Party for deprived children in the neighbourhood 'who wouldn't get a party otherwise.'[4] At a general meeting Wakeman passed his hat round for the idea, which met with 'much nodding and approval', but not with official approval from either the meeting or the Co-ordinating Group.

> *Wakeman*: It came back to me with £55 in it, which is not bad going twenty-four years ago. Afterwards about six or seven people came to me, including Graham Chapman of Monty Python. One of the others was Warren Haig. Jim Anderson of *Oz* was one and we had our meetings in the house where he lived with Germaine Greer at that time, near the church hall. She was to be seen coming and going and I was impressed by the company I was keeping. Jim Anderson was notorious at that stage because of the *Oz* Trial, and I was a fan of Germaine Greer.
>
> I volunteered to do the invitations. Graham Chapman said he'd do the conjurer, someone else, possibly David Seligman, [Denis Lemon] said he'd organise a theatre troupe [No Blame Street Theatre] to come and do a little play and they were what led to trouble with the press. At the time I was part of a band called the *Solid British Hat Band* and they sang folk songs at the party. We gave away 200 invitations because that's what

> we could cater for, someone did food with party staples like jelly and we went on having meetings once a week relentlessly until the party happened, and it was pretty chaotic.[5]

The invitation to the party was issued in the name of the brothers and sisters of GLF which was untrue, they had no approval, and no women worked with this straight-gay group. Although the party was organized by journalists and wannabe-journalists, their failure to arrange any security resulted in two male strangers, one with a camera, wandering around, chatting to children, and taking photographs of them as they ran riot.

> 'And Now Kiddies ... Let's Jeer at the Police' ... 'It's the "Gay Brigade's" idea of a party piece for children.' The Christmas party sketch that took a swipe at the police went down rather well with the organisers, the Gay Liberation Front, who want a better deal for homosexuals. If you're sitting comfortably, try to visualise the scene … Actor dressed as policeman pretends to cosh with his 'truncheon' various people, including (a) a hippie; (b) an alcoholic woman tramp; (c) a drunken Irishman, (Members of those well-known 'persecuted' minorities, you know). Policeman then gets a couple of custard pies in his face (laughter) and someone asks: 'What's blue, smells, and has flat feet?' Answer from the cast: 'A dead copper' (more laughter). Now then, here's the real punch-line: This sniggering tableau was staged at a CHILDRENS PARTY. Was this quite the sort of party piece for children? Was anti-police propaganda really the thing for the young? [6]

Alan Wakeman's story is that the day after the party everyone in the GLF office was in tears because the *People* had outed 20 year old Bob Stevens. Stevens had turned up at the office a week or so earlier having been thrown out by his parents when they discovered his sexuality. For some reason the office procedure for his situation was ignored. The youth should have been accommodated by someone on the crash pad list, but wasn't, nor was he sent to the Youth group which is where he belonged. Instead he was indulged and became in Wakeman's words 'a *de facto* member of the office collective' breaking the rule that new members couldn't join the collective for three months. The *People* journalist, who talked to Denis Lemon and the Vicar of All Saints, could have been working undercover, tricking them into talking and Stevens into declaring, 'Actually I'm bi-sexual so I get the best of both worlds,'[7] but why the tears when Bob Steven's family would discover he'd landed on his feet, and their neighbours realised what rotten bigoted parents he had.

> Wakeman: But even that bad thing had a positive outcome which was totally unexpected, which was that the phone started ringing and by about midday on the Sunday of the *People* article, people were ringing saying 'I think it's really great what you did, throwing a party for kids, I just wanted you to know,' and others were saying 'How can I join the GLF, I read about you in the *People*,' and in the end the number of phone calls that were from people who'd ignored what it said and simply picked up that this existed outweighed the number ringing to abuse us.[8]

Fortunately the only other paper to pick up on the story was *The Kensington Post*, which was reasonably factual in reporting the comments of an unknown GLF spokesman called Stuart, followed a week later with a denouncement of GLF by the Notting Hill Community Trust, which was answered the following week in the letters page by an unknown Denis Lumsden of GLF.

The potential damage to the movement by the actions of these do-gooders could have been disastrous, but for the fact that public awareness directed by media attention was concentrated at that time more on homosexuality than paedophilia. But they had skated on thin ice. Members of the Paedophile Information Exchange had been active in GLF urging us to support their repellent demand for an end to age restrictions in sexual relationships with children.

While most activists that weekend in December 1971 were still trying to build up the movement, the straight-gays were beginning to breakaway and deliberately undermine it. The 19 to 26 January newsletter announced: 'the Action Group has died of advanced rigor mortis.'[9] The men supporting Lemon would no longer be spending their time campaigning for GLF. Their loyalty now was to each other and their plan to establish an independent newspaper, and I remember feeling they no longer supported the movement. But rather than leaving they concentrated on the boy's toys: the money, the office, the meagre assets of GLF. Among their supporters were Tony Salvis, GLF Secretary, and the Treasurer, Michel Peled-Plaschtes, a French antique dealer. The members of the former Action Group now began a long-term presence in the office, overseen by Corbett and Seligman, aided and abetted by David Max McLellan who worked for Housmans the office landlord, and I believe kept a watching brief on office activities for the straight left.

Chapter 14

The Parting of the Ways

> What is a lesbian? A lesbian is the rage of all women condensed to the point of explosion . . . Lesbian is the word, the label, the condition that holds women in line . . . Lesbian is a label invented by the Man to throw at women who dares to be his equal, who dares to challenge his prerogatives, who dare to assert the primacy of her own needs. *Women Identified Women,* March Hoffman. Rita Mae Brown. Ellen Bedoz. Lois Hart. Cynthia Funk.
> Radicalesbians, New York, 1970.

Pat Arrowsmith was an organizer for the Direct Action Committee against Nuclear War, the Committee of 100, a co-founder of CND, and served 11 prison sentences for her political activities. She was also a reporter on *Peace News* whose offices were above Housmans' bookshop and could often be seen working in the basement, where back copies of the newspapers were stored on rows of dexion shelving you had to pass between to reach the GLF office in a tiny room at the back. In 1971 Arrowsmith was also assistant editor at Amnesty International. She submitted her article on life in Holloway Prison to Media Workshop who included it in *Come Together 7, The Women's Issue* under the title of 'The Straight Gay World of Holloway.' Her original manuscript title reads:

> **The Gay World of Holloway**
>
> As a lesbian, I found it quite liberating to be imprisoned in Holloway. For here, on some wings, it was, if not actually 'queer' to be 'normal', then at least perfectly normal to be 'queer'. It was in many ways a refreshing change from the

straight world outside. For the first time, I found it acceptable, indeed advantageous, to be homosexual. As soon as fellow-prisoners realised you were a lesbian, you were likely to be popular and sought after – that is, if you appeared to be butch. This unwonted popularity could in fact occasionally prove something of an embarrassment: you could not strike up a platonic friendship with anyone without it being construed as an affair.

Attitudes to lesbianism varied somewhat from wing to wing. It was the accepted way of life on the wing where I spent my last sentence – an open, 'therapeutic' wing for relatively long-term old lags. Here, the screws usually turned a blind eye to what went on. Couples made no attempt to hide their feelings for each other, but openly embraced and walked about arm in arm. Women could, if they wished, spend a fair amount of time alone together in pairs (or more) in their cells with the doors pulled to. It was unwise to march straight into someone else's cell if the door was not open – most people were tactful enough to knock first.

I remember an incident in which two women were caught 'having if off' together one Saturday afternoon, when, according to the rules, they should either have been in the Television Room or locked up singly in their own cells. They were punished – but for breaking this minor rule, not for making love.

This quite permissive attitude on the part of the authorities was, probably, due to the fact that a number of them were undoubtedly lesbians themselves – as residential staff at most single-sex establishments frequently are. Some lesbian prisoners were apt to boast that actual screws had propositioned them, even offered them bribes for their favours. This may or may not occasionally have been true. The prison rules do not in fact mention homosexuality as such, but merely forbid 'indecent behaviour'.

Lesbian relationships were the norm also on the 'Borstal Recall' Wing. I worked in the garden with many of the inmates of this block. They openly discussed among themselves and with their officer all that went on. But on the 'Star' Wing for first offenders (where, albeit a recidivist, I once spent most of six months because I was a 'civil' prisoner) official attitudes were somewhat different – perhaps because the women here were considered redeemable and as yet uncorrupted. Here, cell doors could not be pulled to, and no less than three women at a time were supposed to be in a cell. Among the prisoners themselves on this wing, attitudes towards homosexuality were, on the whole, not quite so casually accepting as elsewhere in the prison.

Despite this openness about and acceptance of lesbian relationships on the recidivists' wings, I was amused on one occasion by the general reticence at one of our large 'group counselling' sessions. A girl was in trouble over having escaped from the wing one evening and got into another wing where her girl-friend was living. For some time, the group discussed this incident purely in terms of the ethics of the girl having got the screw in charge into trouble by managing to escape. No one seemed able to bring themselves to mention the crucial matter: the lesbian relationship. This may have been because, on this particular occasion, the whole wing was assembled together, plus the Wing Governor. Eventually I stated that we were really discussing the rights and wrongs of homosexuality. Afterwards, one or two people marvelled at my temerity.

There is a considerable amount of artificiality about Holloway lesbianism. Some of it smacked of false, school-girl-like 'pashes' (not that all school-girl pashes are false of course) – a way, probably, of relieving the tedium of prison life. People would break rules by writing notes to each other, sometimes even when they were on the same wing, able to meet and talk openly anyway. And it was not unusual for a woman to 'turn', or pretend to have 'turned' simply because she was in Holloway, where being butch could be quite rewarding: your girl-friend was apt to keep you in fags; people chased you with offers of small gifts bought with their meagre earnings. Even accepting that most people are more or less bisexual, still it seemed reasonable to conclude that many of the Holloway butch-chasers were simply women who outside were quite straight (often mothers with families – as indeed some of the butch types themselves were) but, while inside, were merely trying to make the best of a bad job and find themselves a mock cock.

This led to another kind of artificiality: many Holloway lesbians were appallingly straight. Whether transvestite, partially transvestite, or not, it was customary for the butch types to attempt to appear in every way as masculine as possible, strapping back their busts, contriving false penises with sanitary towels, only (if what they said was true) making love – never receiving it. All this was more difficult in years gone by when you could not wear your own clothes in Holloway. The only hope then for a butch to appear totally masculine was for her to get one of the prison jobs (gardening or painting) that entailed wearing a shirt and dungarees. Otherwise, she had to do the best she could in her regulation cotton frock – roll up her cardigan sleeves to expose tattooed forearms, roll her stockings down to look like knee-socks (this was actually against the rules), cultivate pseudo-side-boards to embellish her eton crop. Now, however, it is possible for the undiscerning visitor to Holloway to wonder whether she has made a mistake and is actually in the Scrubs. For women prisoners can wear their own clothes these days, including, if they wish, masculine gear. So butch types (phony and genuine) can wear drag (bar belts and ties) and really go around looking like straight husbands – on open wings, their fem partners may even offer to do their washing and ironing for them.

The problem now for butch and semi-transsexual lesbians is that, to appear both 'with-it' and male, you should not have close cropped hair. Yet the moment the most masculine looking female face is framed in longish hair, it inevitably ceases to look quite so male. A very butch, more or less transvestite woman on my wing started to conform with fashion and let her hair grow down her neck. At once she looked somewhat more feminine. Foolishly, I suggested she cut her hair short again. She was unable, however, to accept that anything could ever make her remotely resemble her own sex – I nearly got punched for my advice. There is no doubt that gay women can have a sense of freedom in Holloway that as yet they can never or seldom experience outside. On the other hand, homosexual roles there tended to be rigid and conventional, conducive to the male chauvinism that Women's Lib and Gay Lib so firmly oppose. I have written this article in the past tense as my last prison sentence ended two years ago. Fashions and attitudes in Holloway may have changed for the better since then.

In mid-January 1972 there were two protests on the same day outside Holloway prison, one by Women's Liberation who were insisting that no woman should be jailed, and that the £500,000 spent on psychiatric facilities at the 'new progressive Holloway' was a con trick, where punishment was being disguised as treatment. The other protest by Radical Alternatives to Prison (RAP) was against the jailing of Pauline Jones, 23, who suffered a miscarriage, lost her baby and was then deserted by her boyfriend. She took a baby from outside a shop in Harlow, Essex, and kept the infant for five weeks. She had been sentenced to three years in jail in October, reduced to 21 months in December, and since imprisonment had developed Meniere's disease.

Nettie Pollard: 'I went to the Pauline Jones demonstration at Holloway ... I'd stayed the previous night at Faraday Road after the Women's group meeting, and we went along as a group.'[1]

Mary McIntosh: I don't remember how much it was GLF and how much the women's movement, but I remember crowds gathering to shout at the back of the old prison. We were shouting to and fro with women at the windows of their cells. It was about conditions, they were being banged up for 23 out of 24 hours and there were a huge amount of drugs being prescribed. Pat Arrowsmith's book had come out, so every dyke felt they had something in common about it.[2]

In the afternoon scuffles broke out between the demonstrators and the police, and Parkhurst Road was blocked for a while when protesters sat down across the traffic lanes. Four demonstrators were arrested.[3]

Julia L: I got arrested outside Holloway prison. We'd gone along and were standing there. Barbara picked up a stone, there were a lot of gay women there and she started throwing it. I took it away from her and I said – I'll never forget, 'Don't throw those, we're not here to be violent,' and this bugger behind me grabbed my hand with the stone in it and said, 'I'm busting you for having an offensive weapon.' I said, 'But hang on, you've just heard me tell her to put it down.' He said, 'I know,' and laughed, 'but it's in your hands, isn't it?' It was an Inspector in plain clothes. You know how you don't know how you're going to react to things? Well, I grabbed this lamp post, wound myself round it and screamed to the women across the road, 'I'm being busted!' whereupon a tidal wave came running across Holloway Road and all hell let loose.

As soon as they got one hand off the lamp post I got my leg

round it. I struggled; I lost a shoe and my bag. They got me to the police van and you know how a cat is when it doesn't want to go? I was like that. And as they got me in one side, the other people they'd arrested ran out the front door of it. Anyway, they bundled me in there and I said, 'Where's my shoe, where's my handbag?' and I tried to get out but they bundled me back in. Then the doors opened and someone else was chucked in, I can't remember who, and away we went. So we got to the police station and there were people from RAP there, somebody from an old theatre group I used to be in who was older and middle class, and a middle class woman who was going out with a working class man. A black guy was arrested too, and an Indian bloke had been pushed through a window and they had him up for GBH. I was in a cell with another white girl and the police put a black woman in with us and I'll never forget, the policeman said, 'I'm sorry girls, I've got to lock the door now.'[4]

Mary McIntosh: The Holloway prison thing led to a very long-running trial where I was a MacKenzie. It was at Old Street, where there was a stipendiary magistrate and he remanded it from Saturday to Saturday over what seemed like a very long period. He would come in his tweeds because it was Saturday and he was going off to his country seat as stipendiaries will. He sat there in his tweeds and clearly enjoyed the whole thing. We did this elaborate questioning, very respectful. Every question was done by consultation between the MacKenzies and the accused. We took notes of the answers and suggested questions and ways of formulating a point as a question. But we had a Mackenzie for each of the accused and there were five or six of them. We had a bench, we weren't in the dock. People with cool heads got chosen as Mackenzies, like me, though I wasn't combative enough. Some of them were brilliant. And of course you were always liable to more arrests at the demonstrations outside the court, so they piled up, one on top of another. It was one of our theatres, the courtroom.[5]

Julia L: We had a group trial with Mackenzies because that was politically right on. I told my school and the headmaster was marvellous, he said, 'Never mind.' So every Saturday I went off to this court. I had this spell from Lyndsay and you had to stare at the magistrate and sprinkle it on the floor and concentrate on being found not guilty, and it always worked. So I was staring at this red-faced chap, and as it all went on – the first person to be let off was the white middle class man (I went in a skirt and twin-set and crucifix. I told them I was a teacher). The white middle class girl was cautioned – her boyfriend was fined heavily. The black bloke was held over for owing maintenance, and the Indian bloke was sent off to the High Court … My case was dismissed after five weeks.[6]

The evening of the day of protests and arrests culminated with a RAP meeting at Conway Hall,

which was not what its organisers had hoped it would be: a liberal gathering salving its comfortable agonised conscience by listening to a few selected souls expounding on Pauline Jones as one of the 'poor, disturbed' women in Holloway we all 'pity', and who need to be moved into 'A stable family home' which could 'help' them. Death to the liberals; anger, far more than conscience, was aroused when the two WLW women who had come along as speaker-saboteurs opened the meeting by attacking liberalism in all its manifestations, and pointed out that we *all* move from one prison to another: home, school, factory. They went on to analyse in more detail the politics of being a woman prisoner – briefly: women are jailed for having no money. They steal from supermarkets to

> provide food and clothes for their kids; they prostitute themselves (and are jailed for *being* supported by men); they break the rules of a National Assistance scheme designed to keep families out of subsistence level. Motherhood is gloried only when there's a pay packet to support it; unmarried mothers are jailed for *not* being supported by men. The total loading of the entire legal system (male middle class judges, juries, barristers etc.,) against women was paralleled with the position of blacks (cf the Mangrove trial), a point emphasised by the brother speaking for the Black Workers Unity League.
>
> The women's urging that we cease to see ourselves solely as victims was completely disregarded by Lord Soper, who, as former chaplain to Holloway, discoursed on the workings of women and pregnancy (the awe and mystery therein) – and therefore the need to put Pauline (specifically) into special care, etc. The liberals present refused the validity of recognising that we are *all* 'disturbed' women, and that the new Holloway with its totally psychiatric units will be about 'curing' political prisoners in larger numbers than ever before. Some of them left early, in disgust at what they termed our 'violence'; they didn't want to know about the gay sister beaten up on the demonstration, about the violence done to us in our heads in the prisons we *all* live in *all* the time.'[7]

So far we have mainly heard the voices of educated socialist gay women whose activism had transformed them into Marxist feminist lesbians. Theirs was a triple perspective coming from an involvement in the history and practice of three struggles, the Left, Gay Lib and the Women's Movement, each with its own styles, analyzes and alignments. Women like Mary McIntosh, Elizabeth Wilson, Angie Wier and Sarah Grimes were Marxist socialists before the advent of GLF. There were also a number of other women active in GLF and the Women's Group from working class backgrounds, some of whom had no previous experience of politics. And although the differences between the two groups of women were substantial, they continued together as sisters when it came down to women's issues like the one at Holloway.

> *Carla Toney*: It's been a very different kettle of fish for the middle class women and the working class women ... I don't question their commitment and it wasn't any unkindness on their part – it's English society and its divisions ... but they became the spokeswomen – not the working class women. I remember an early meeting of the Women's Group at my flat ... Max and Libby were there and Mary and Elizabeth. They were talking about the difficulties of coming out in their profession and Max said, 'Me and Libby don't have any trouble coming out in our profession,' and Elizabeth said, 'What's your profession?' and Max replied, 'Industrial cleaners.' You could have heard a pin drop. The gay liberation movement, unlike the women's liberation movement at that time, was not solidly middle class. Of course a lot of people were, but there was everyone from Lady Rose to Max and Libby. The mixture was much greater and in that sense it was far more exciting – all these different perspectives, there were black people in gay liberation but not much in women's liberation at that time.[8]

> *Elizabeth Wilson*: I think that people like Carla – with Americans, however left-wing they feel they are, that generation, they were tremendously anti-Communist. That was the mindset ... I felt there really was a blind spot; Communism was just evil and Carla got into that ...[9] The essential debate which spilled over into everything was in the *Come Together* collective. There was this ongoing ideological debate between Marxism and radical feminism, and Carla was very influenced by David and Aubrey, so there were disagreements within the

women's group and disagreements in GLF as a whole, which rather exacerbated the tensions between the men and the women.[10]

Toney: We'd all gone over to Elizabeth's house and they explained how we should be more committed politically, and the issue of Rachel came up, and while the meeting was focused on Rachel it was also a working class rebellion against indoctrination by the middle class – we walked out. It split on class lines over whether Rachel could join the group – the middle class women didn't want her to join but the working class women were tired of being lectured. At one meeting I was tired of hearing about Marx, and I said, 'Marx, who's Marx, the only Marx I've ever heard of is Groucho.' We kept getting these lectures and the issue over Rachel was also a spit in their eye.[11]

Julia L: I heard about these short life houses ... I was put on a list, which was short because nobody knew about it. There was the Festival of Light and all the theatre groups in London got involved. I was sent by my group, which was mixed, and not gay, to meet the women's theatre group at what turned out to be Angie Weir's house ... I went down into the basement of this house and looked around and went 'Oh!' I ended up sitting next to Caroline Thompson and her girlfriend Lorna and we were chatting, and they said they hadn't got anywhere to live so I said, 'I've got some space, come and live in my house.' [at Faraday Road, Notting Hill] So this gay couple moved in.

Caroline and Lorna moved into the house and I met their friends and one thing led to another. The politics started and the men were slowly forced out of the house – straight men in this house! It was silly really and very stressed. Other women moved in and poor old Alan was the last to go, a friend of mine ... and then gay men moved in. That was okay: Richard Dipple. Aubrey used to visit and various other people. At that point it was gay fellowship, we are one, we are united. There's that dreadful article about where we share socks and T-shirts and all the rest of it. And meanwhile I was the only person who was working in the house, the only one who ever did, and I continued to work the whole time I was in the house. How I ever did it I don't know, because we were stoned out of our heads at night. I'd be home an hour and I'd be smashed.[12]

Janet Dixon: The squat we lived in was falling down, but like Patience and Sara, we tackled our problems with a pioneering spirit. We saw it as an opportunity to demystify the male worlds of plumbing, electricity and carpentry. We read and experimented until we could stride into builders' suppliers ask for one-way cistern inlet valves, 1.5^{mm} triplecore insulated, or three-inch steel angle brackets, just as though we had been born knowing all about it, like men! [13]

Julia L: It was all one big happy family and lots of gay politics and sharing and men and women coming round. The doorbell would go, October would walk in – in her school uniform straight from school. Everybody was welcome, we had women's meetings there, gay men's meetings, you name it. Slowly the word spread and so many people stayed, all over the place. And we had the ghost ... people would be in the darkroom and their cigarette would be thrown on the floor. It was eerie.

So more and more people would come round, Rachel and Edie. There was Rachel, six foot three in a tight red dress with shoulders like a lumberjack, huge Adam's apple, thick pebble glasses and, 'Hi, I'm Rachel.' Oh, okay. Everybody was welcome. Then there was Bobbi who we thought was a woman, turned out to be a man who'd had breasts implanted

> and then he had them cut off. It was all terribly matter of fact and if there was anybody weird in the neighbourhood, gay, transsexual, whatever, they were down our house. More and more people.[14]

The house became the focal point for the GLF women's group, particularly the working class women who began moving in and identifying themselves as radical feminist lesbians. Radical feminism had developed out of the second wave of the Women's Movement in America in 1968. Radical feminism is not radical in the sense of a position in the field of the Left, but radical in that it assigns to gender, and, gender alone, the most radical division of human experience, and one that is relatively unchanging.[15]

One woman who represents the level of political awareness of the young women in Faraday Road was Janet Dixon, who had spent time in the straight left, but had not become fully engaged politically because of its machismo, the consequence being that when she joined the women's movement, as she said at the time, neither she nor her sisters understood socialism: 'we saw socialism as yet another squabbling position in male politics.'[16] Radical feminism, however, developed by women for women, in an American society where race not class is the issue, held out the tantalising prospect of an uncomplicated 'pure' feminism women could fully commit to; indeed it demanded exactly that.[17]

For Carla Toney, with her working class American background, radical feminism was tailor-made, and as Wilson says, Toney was very influenced by Fernbach and Walter during their radical feminist phase. With an ideology focused on gender, class issues are occluded, which only strengthened Toney's home-bred opposition to communism, socialism, Marxism and the practice of her mainly middle class, socialist sisters. Toney's adoption of radical feminism was a spit in the eye of the older women, to use her phrase, with the salience of generational aspiration buttressing her choice. Radical politics arising out of women's experience was an irresistible attraction to young lesbians lacking a political education. It was new, it was exciting, it was twentieth century; it was open to being built on. From Janet Dixon's writing – living in a commune and discovering radical feminism was like discovering the Holy Grail.

Like his Maoists friends, Richard Dipple had taken up radical feminism, so his move from David Fernbach's flat to the Faraday Road commune can be seen as his love and admiration for his women friends, and a sincere desire to share their experience. But I cannot help thinking of the advantage to Fernbach's 'scientific' political studies that he now had a direct connection to the heart of the women's commune, and his need to divide the women as a means to splitting them from the movement in order to avoid the accusation of misogyny when plotting his all male GLF. I also remember at the time of the freak-out over Andy Elsmore's article that Bill Halstead, who was living in Mary McIntosh's house along with Elizabeth Wilson, Angie Weir and Tony Halliday with whom he was having an affair, was ordered by Fernbach to move out, and come live with him, Walter, and Dipple. Twenty year old Halstead had done as he was told. Was Dipple equally obedient?

Unfortunately, radical feminism without the gravitational pull of class, based solely on gender led immediately to separatism from straight men, then straight women, then gay men, and eventually from other lesbians, with a totalising ideology that saw no difference between gay men and heterosexual men, lumping them both together. However, these were the early days, described by Janet Dixon as graduated separatism, before radical feminism was taken up in a hard-line separatist way, as the introduction to *Lesbian Come Together* 11 produced at Faraday Road shows.

> The sisters have as far as possible, tried to publish in this issue, all the articles that were submitted. We have not edited or censored anything. This is not simply an act of blatant

Sisterhood, but a conscious attempt by us not to ape the values of heterosexual society. As a consequence many viewpoints are expressed, polarisations, conflict and arguments appear. This is good. For too long the Sisters, whilst they have rejected heterosexual men and their values still feel it safe to lean on the gay brothers, instead of realising that WE have much to teach them. An attitude like 'Obviously what went in previous *Come Togethers* must have been OK' is felt by many. Most sisters and brothers have great difficulty in writing anything at all, but to find once they have that it has been rejected, on whatever grounds, must be painful. 'Repetitive, poor literary content, just plain bad, not enough space,' all these things have been said. Surely as a movement of radical feminists we must necessarily reject not only the standards of morality imposed on us by white male chauvinists, but also their cultural ones.

FUCK THE FAMILY

Our Collective is made up of six people, Jenny, Lorna, Richard, Julia, Barbara, and myself Carolyn. When we first moved into the house I don't think any of us imagined what would develop. We intended to live closely of course, but as we all soon realised this was not enough. After about a week we decided to share all our clothes; these were moved into one big cupboard. We pooled our money for food, Tampax, toilet rolls and cat food. Around about the same time a women's awareness group was started. It met at the house. Although the group was important itself, what was much more significant was that after each session, which usually lasted all night, women would stay for days talking and talking, in a way they had never been able before. Soon the actual awareness groups became defunct, but this didn't matter because the women had learnt to relate openly and honestly toward each other. This may sound arrogant or too easy. In fact it wasn't. Tears, traumas, temper, all became the order of the day. Long nights were spent talking, crying, confessing, barriers came down with painful crashes. Egos took an incredible battering; usually just as we thought we had reached a point where honesty reigned, someone would say something to show us how wrong we had been. Because it was not always possible, (for us in the collective) to be in one room all the time, we decided that if two or more of us got together and talked then anything said should be repeated to whoever was missing. This helped us to fight couples and factions.

In practical terms some beautiful things started to happen. It was fabulous to see Richard walking around in Lorna's cardigan; Jenny in Richard's underpants; and Julia in my shoes. Soon it was possible not to feel that a particular article belonged to anyone. We rearranged the rooms. We evolved a room to study in, a room to listen to sounds in, a room to talk and eat in, a room to sleep in. The next problem we had to overcome, and to a certain extent we still have to, is that of work share. Whilst people were still adjusting to their entirely new emotional life style, work in the house had to go on. Once we evolve a smooth running work share system, it will be possible for all the housework to get done without anyone noticing. This may sound as though we want rota's etc. This is not so, but we have to eat and sleep in comfort and cleanliness. It will never be possible for any collective to function efficiently if the people in it are constantly battling with a dirty, untidy home environment.

Perhaps the two most rewarding things that have happened to us are firstly, that we have virtually done away with the concept of monogamy, and secondly we now feel that we are living our politics. Surely one of the primary aims of Gay Lib is the destruction of the nuclear family. Plenty of people in the movement nod and twitch their agreement of this, but still escape to their cosy couples, their flats and get no closer to its destruction, but rather aid its perpetuation. We in the collective don't want to force our lifestyle on anyone, surely many different lifestyles are valid, but to live, eat, sleep collectively is hard. Seen as a microcosm it is seen in isolation; but when the day comes when it is possible for us to relate honestly, a completely fluid social structure will emerge. With a few of our friends it is already happening. They come to the house and at once feel part of us; in fact this is necessary if the collective is not to stagnate. Our attitudes toward the opposite sex have radically changed. Even Jenny, as an ex S.C.U.M.ite now enjoys cuddling Richard in bed, and loves without hang ups many of the brothers who come to the house.

Ultimately many things could happen to us, some already have. Our collective strength enabled Jenny and I to talk with Warren at Tottenham Tech, Lorna came out at College, Julia has reassessed her attitude toward teaching, Barbara has started planning her film, and Richard and I chaired a Wednesday meeting. An outward movement is what we are striving for. Couples in bed-sits will always be vulnerable to society's hostility in a way that a collective will not.

One of the best things we have yet got together is our completely spontaneous "tube and cinema" street theatre. Six homosexuals kissing and groping and attacking strangers in tubes; talking loudly about Lesbians in cinema foyers may seem juvenile, but to embarrass people sexually is a good political tool.

A WOMAN WHO IS TOTALLY INDEPENDENT OF MEN, WHO OBTAINS LOVE, SEX AND SELF-ESTEEM FROM OTHER WOMEM IS A TERRIBLE THREAT TO MALE SUPREMACY. SHE DOESN'T NEED THEM AND THEREFORE THEY HAVE LESS POWER OVER HER. MARTHA SHELLY 1969

A reprint from The US & Everyman paper of 7 September 1971 appeared on page 9. It spells out the Radical Feminist position:

Why I Cannot Work In The Gay Movement

Part of the oppression of society is the labelling of me as 'gay' or 'homosexual.' I am neither. I am a human being and am normally capable of loving other human beings, and relating physically to them as a part of this love. If men and women did not play roles, and if sexism were destroyed, there would be no such concepts as 'homosexuality' or 'heterosexuality'. The term would not be 'bisexuality' either, because 'bi' implies two, and implies relating to men one way and to women another. We would all relate on the pure human level, and sexual expression should be a part of this relationship. As soon as I was able to throw off my stereotypes of women and men, as soon as I was no longer mystified by men nor sought after them to complete my being, and as soon as I was able to see that love between two women was as complete as any love could be, then I was labelled a Lesbian. I am merely a woman who has seen past much of my role oppression. And the fact that I choose not to relate to men should not seem unusual. No man I have ever met is not sexist and I don't want to waste my time with relationships with men in order to 'help them overcome their sexism.' Let them do it on their own.

But heterosexuality is the societal norm of oppressed woman forming an oppressive relationship with her oppressor, and women usually reject heterosexuality for different reasons than men do. Lesbians in the feminist movement often have just totally rejected the games and sexism of heterosexual relationships, and recognised their wholeness in ability to give and receive with women. Gay men, on the other hand, have rejected women. From working with gay men in the Los Angeles Gay Liberation Front I began to see that gay men have the same stereotypes as straight men.

Their attitudes towards women are the same. All men are merely faced with the choice of either relating to women (being straight) or not relating to women (being gay). None of the GLF men could see past their stereotypes.

I reject any concepts that lumps us together. Society may oppress us equally for our rejection of heterosexuality and label us both gay, but we as women are learning to reject concepts put upon us by society. Gay men oppress us as much as straight men. If all men were gay, they would still oppress us in society. We (all women) would still be the typists and the shit-workers. Gay men, as well as straight men must challenge male chauvinism, which Webster's defines as 'blind and unreasonable attachment to a false cause' (masculinity).

I do not identify with gay men because I refuse to allow society to say I am anything other than a woman. If you must label me, call me a lesbian. The origin of the word is Greek and from the beautiful love between women on the Isle of Lesbos. They were women who found they could completely love other women.

I also refuse to identify with oppressors (gay men) as part of my struggle for my freedom to be human and form roleless relations with other humans. Perhaps gay men will learn someday. There is an 'effeminist' movement in Berkeley that may or may not be the beginning. I'm not going to hold my breath. If I ever feel we are working for the same goal – not 'sexual freedom' but the liberation of human beings from societal role-chains, then I'll work with gay men and call them sister.

But right now, although they too are oppressed, I identify no more with them than with other oppressed men (ie third world men, poor men, high school men, etc.) I want them to be free, but where their heads are at now, their freedom would be at my expense.

A BROTHER'S VIEW

I think we are looking for positive results, while we brothers are the negative force which is preventing anything from being achieved. I think we are being selfish for looking at the sisters as though they were fish in a bowl. We are crippling their efforts because of our 'wanting to learn' attitudes. We are repressing them by putting them in the same situation that they are trying to break away from. We are behaving like little boys, pulling our mommy's apron off, moreover mommy does not wish to exist.

We must take it, that the sisters do not need us. They need themselves to strengthen their own ideas. They need to express from themselves for themselves, and not for us. They don't need to go around telling the brothers how it feels to be women. They need time and the only encouragement that we can give them is to leave them alone, so that they can get on with it.

The inevitable split between the sisters and brothers is again selfish on our part. We should not be waiting to learn from such a painful thing happening. We should already see that things within GLF are unsettled and should realise that by sticking two groups (sisters and brothers) together now when our problems are so extremely different that things are never going to come together because of the bitterness which exists from pulling each other back. We have progressed, but for some time now we have been standing still. We have been trying to close the door that does not fit the space which is provided in the wall.

I think the sisters should break gently now, while still being GLF (as much as men). We should give rather than the sisters should ask for what already exists as theirs. The sisters should have their half of *Come Together* to use for themselves. Written by sisters for sisters. They should have their own office because they benefit little from the existing one.

> I think that only under these circumstances will GLF be really fruitful, and only then will brothers be able to learn from sisters. The sisters then will not be hindered, (by us, even though most of us mean well). [Richard Dipple].

The women of GLF, as we see, had become divided by both class and ideology. In addition, the older socialist sisters were suffering from the wrongful arrest of Angie Weir, incarcerated in Holloway on alleged AB involvement, whose defence work now took up most of their time. And in the movement as a whole, the women were divided from the men who would not learn, grow, adapt or change their thinking, their behaviour and their arrogance towards women. Men who resolutely refused to acknowledge their own chauvinism and secretly relished their male privilege. For the women there was also the tide of straight-gay visitors sweeping through the meetings week on week, who combined to grind down their ethos of sympathy, understanding and patience until there was nothing left but the silt of futility.

> *Angie Weir*: As the women's movement developed, more and more lesbians became involved, and eventually the lesbians in GLF decided to work within the women's movement and also more straight women became lesbians . . . [In GLF] there was all sorts of chauvinism. I remember very clearly the night before I was arrested, chairing a meeting with Denis Lemon who [later] did *Gay News*, and he was actually very new; he'd just come along and not been very involved before, and every time there was a difficult bit of the meeting I remember him saying [to me] 'Look, just stand back and I'll deal with this,' so those sort of attitudes were quite prevalent.[18]

> *Aubrey Walter*: Some of the men made it intolerable for the women the way that they behaved. People like Tony Salvis

opposed moves by pro-feminist men to get the men to look at their chauvinism.[19]

Four women from the Faraday commune, putting into words the feelings of many women in the movement, added their names to a notice declaring that they'd had enough and wanted to do something about the situation. They booked a space and put an announcement in *Lesbian Come Together.*

An Open Letter to all Sisters

The Gay sisters are holding a women's think-in on Saturday 29th January, at All Saints Church Hall, Powis Square.

We would like to see discussed at the think-in the relationship of the Gay Women's group of GLF to the London Women's Liberation Workshops, and also to GLF itself where many sisters feel oppressed by the sexism and male chauvinism within the movement.

Several sisters are now feeling the necessity to establish a separate Gay-women's group (along the line of radicalesbians – New York) that will be relatively autonomous of the heavily male-dominated GLF, and would like to discuss this along with the possibility of establishing a separate office/centre for Gay sisters and the production of a non-censored or edited radical feminist/lesbian newspaper.

It is hoped that by taking these steps that the Gay-sisters will be able to work far more closely, as a group, with the rest of the Women's Liberation Movement, to overthrow the rampant sexism which oppresses all women, whilst also not neglecting the struggle against our specific oppression as gay women.

The participation of all sisters at the women's think-in with ideas and opinions on how to unite 'bent' and 'straight' sisters, or on any other topics wanting to be discussed would be greatly appreciated as a sign of mutual sisterhood and solidarity.

Every woman is our sister! Much love, Frankie, Carolyn, Lorna & Jenny.

The Women's Think-In started off in an odd and unexpected way.

> *Nettie Pollard*: We had a women's think-in at All Saints Hall on a Saturday and there was a lot of discussion as to whether Rachel, who I think was the only transsexual there, should be allowed in, with people saying, 'Really, I'm not having that man in here,' and 'This man's trying to take over women's space.' I remember he had on purple corduroy jeans with tights and women's shoes, some sort of blouse, and this was raging on in the hall, and then suddenly this drunken man who'd seen people coming in started lurching around in the hall and saying, 'What's that man doing here?' And the women at that point said, 'That's not a man, that's a woman, now get out.' I thought that was a nice bit of solidarity for the women to say we think we'll have our differences to ourselves, but if a straight man comes in we're not taking it from him.[20]

The following Wednesday's all-London meeting proceeded as usual, with some understanding that the women wanted the second half for themselves. The usual new members meeting was called, and then the announcements started. One was a call for GLF to support demonstrations against the atrocities committed by British troops in Derry on what was known as Bloody Sunday, 30 January 1972, when 27 civil rights protesters had been shot and 13 young men and teenagers killed outright. We were reminded that if it could happen in Northern Ireland it could happen in London with us in the firing line. Another announcement aimed to remind and encourage people to attend the up-coming think-in at Lancaster University. Discussions then turned to the structure of the Wednesday meetings and the ending of the steering group whose role it was agreed would be taken over by a different functional or local group each week, who should present themselves, their work, and their ideas for a session of constructive criticism, a sort of perpetual think-in. In line with that, it was also agreed that except for emergencies there would be no more announcements or business discussions at the meetings as these would now be published in the weekly newsletter. As the break approached, rumours about the absence of women began to circulate.

I must have been caught up in some discussion during the break because I remember only just managing to pick up a cup of tea when Michael James came down the kitchen passage to tell me the second half was starting. We came back into the hall and I saw all the women had arrived and were assembled on one side, most of them sitting, and the rest stood behind them. A few men were sitting amongst the sisters, but the majority stood either side and in front, completing a circle. Among the women sat Bobbi, Rachel and Allahn McRae, who soon realized he was in the wrong place and then found he couldn't move, riveted with fascination as events unfolded. The straight-gays of the Action Group were by the stage, and opposite them were Tony Salvis and Michel Peled-Plaschtes the treasurer. We stood with Bette Bourne, Mick Belsten, Douglas MacDougal, and two new queens Richard Chappell and Cloud Downey. Roger Carr, Nicholas Bramble and Youth Group members like Tony Reynolds, Alaric Sumner and Malcolm Bissett stood facing us with the women. Aubrey Walter and David Fernbach, Richard Dipple, Bill Halstead and the other Marxists were grouped near us.

Carla Toney was saying that sexism had pissed-off a lot of women to the point where it was felt that working with gay men was often as oppressive as working with straight men. Some women had come to feel that there was no more reason to identify with gay men than with other oppressed men – that is they'd come out in solidarity with them, as they would with black, or working class brothers. Other women said it was time to strengthen their own position and fight their own battles. As both women and lesbians they felt doubly-oppressed and had come to realize that they had their own struggle and ideas to work out.

> We cannot continue beating our heads against the wall of the brothers' male-chauvinism, or the dissatisfaction with our own untogetherness, and the un-radical nature of GLF politics generally. We need to work more closely with the Women's Liberation movement, to work with and for women, to provide for all sisters a viable alternative to the exploitative 'straight' gay ghetto scene into which we have been pushed, and to work from a strong position with all those involved in the struggle for a radical transformation of society.[21]

The meeting listened in respectful silence as the women explained their desire to have their own space, hopefully an office, towards which they would like half the GLF funds to help finance their needs. Instantly the straight-gays in the hall were in uproar. It was as though a great spotlight had suddenly lit up, throwing everyone's features into sharp contrast as the straight-gay faces which had begun expressing satisfaction at the news that the women were leaving, now registered that they were demanding half of 'their' money. Open mouthed, incredulous, livid, then as their meanness seized on the flaw in the demand – the discrepancy in numbers between the men and the women and their scheming demand for half the money – calculated cynicism, contempt, self-righteousness, unction, hatred, all these thoughts and feelings brightly lit, flashed across their faces as they cunningly began to spurn the women's claim. Between the men an intuited division became starkly visible: the Marxists and radical queens on one side glared at the exposed enemy. Warren

Haig, Jim Anderson, Denis Lemon, Martin Corbett, Michael Mason, Max McLellan, David Seligman, Alan Wakeman, Peled-Plaschtes and Salvis headed the straight-gays in the bureaucratic numbers park, saying women should get a proportion – we must be fair to the sisters – a percentage of the money equal to their membership. Some proposed the women be given all the money. Others said that if the woman were walking out, they shouldn't be paid anything. Salvis sought clarification several times; there was £520 in the bank account, money the former Action Group secretly needed for their newspaper plans. The Marxists coolly observed. The queens' were sickened. Andrew Lumsden, Bob Mellors and Tony Halliday looked appalled at the straight-gays' misogyny and stubborn, infantile, reactionary suggestions. Sarah Grimes, infuriated by one brother's remark stormed out only to find herself alone and had to hang around in the street smoking furiously while waiting for her sisters to exit. Some men hoped the women would change their minds. Dennis Greenwood recalls Bobbi declaring he was leaving with the sisters. Then it dawned on the straight-gays that paying the women to go would be the easiest way to get rid of them. Their rage vanished, and the women's demand was put to the vote. The slow tally of raised hands finally agreed the women should have half the funds. Once that was clear, most of the women walked out. Salvis was ordered to record, and treasurer Peled-Plaschtes was instructed: 'To give the women who have left £260 in total and that this payment is to take priority over all others.'[22]

> *Nettie Pollard*: That night I was there, I went with all the other women to a pub near All Saints Hall and the women got quite emotional and were saying things like, the men didn't care about them, all they cared about was cottaging and cruising. It was the radical feminist type women rather than the socialist feminist type women. It was Faraday Road and the women who hung about with them. There were quite a lot of women

there, about forty or fifty, but obviously they had come in strength in order to walk out. And then we went in and it was the ordinary part of the meeting, and then one of the women got up and said why the women were going to leave.

It was at that point that I was a bit shocked because I could see relief on some of the men's faces. The ones who were saying things like, 'The women ought to be given all of the money,' I just thought, you know, it's a way of getting rid of us, isn't it, so they can just be on their own. Several men were saying from the audience, 'Give them the money, we loathsome men should … pay them to go away.' I was a lot more impressed by the men who were very upset about it and wanted us to stay but perhaps respected the decision. Some of the men did try and remonstrate with us. Eventually it was agreed that the women should be given half the money and they all went out and about two or three of us were left in there. I had mixed feelings because I really thought that I ought to walk out with everyone and I had also felt that I wanted to stay because it was clear that women were still welcome.[23]

Janet Dixon: On leaving GLF in 1972 I didn't realise that I was now a separatist: those of us who were didn't use the word. We called ourselves proudly the extremists, the vanguard, but it wasn't until we read the American CLIT papers in 1973 that we knew we had a name.[24] The decision, inspired by pure separatism, was graduated separatism. Not all of the women who took that decision were separatist by any means, but the fact that we had rejected men was not a gesture of feminism alone. After all, feminism alone does not exclude men. Some of the men in GLF had called themselves feminist, as had the Maoist men at Skegness. Graduated separatism on the other hand draws a line beyond which men cannot go.[25]

Within a fortnight of the women's walkout reactions to that event by the straight-gays can be seen in two special attachments to the weekly diary for 23 February 1972. Ralph Stephenson writing one report was a new member who had set himself up as GLF Audio News. This was not a function group and had no endorsement from the Co-ordinating Committee, and although he seemed sincere in his effort, it shows how anyone could now come into the movement and do their own thing with complete indifference to the thoughts and feelings of others.

Stephenson was in the office on Sunday when the Finance Group met, and was asked to record a phone call between Peled-Plaschtes the Treasurer, who had not turned up for a meeting with Micky Burbidge of Counter-Psychiatry, who wanted to know where the money was for his group. Burbidge was already into the conversation before Stephenson could advise Peled-Plaschtes that he was being recorded. Stephenson adds that there came a point where he could no longer rely on getting a clear recording, so rather than risk inaccuracies he switched off. Burbidge finished the conversation about five minutes later and left. The Finance group then asked Hans, a member of the Office collective to type a transcript of the tape onto a stencil, in the course of which Salvis arrived, discovered what was going on and told Stephenson he disapproved of the idea. Salvis then left the office. Stephenson discussed matters with Hans, and although both had misgivings Hans continued cutting the stencil. Salvis returned, probably after speaking to the treasurer on Housemans' phone, and persuaded the two that they were wrong to continue, so they tore up the stencil and erased the recording before writing up the story for the diary.[26]

The other attached page in the newssheet announced that when the Co-ordinating Committee met on 22 February it was faced with a crisis situation. The treasurer Peled-Plasches had failed to turn up for Finance group meetings, refused to sign any cheques, and had then resigned. There followed six propositions to get around the problem and a voting slip at the bottom of the page for a simple Yes or No to the proposals, plus three spaces to name nominees for the election of a new Treasurer at the next general meeting.

There is no record of what happened at the next all-London Meeting but Peled-Plasches must have claimed he was ill and categorically denied he had resigned, all of which the meeting must have accepted as he continued to be the treasurer. But the Finance Group plan to record the phone conversations between Burbidge and Peled-Plaschtes, and cut a stencil to print it out, indicates they wanted to publicize the treasurer's intransigence as being the source of the financial crisis.

Lisa Power wrote with reference to the women being granted half the GLF funds:

> No clearer indication of the attitude of the majority of men remaining in the organisation can be given than the fact that this money was never handed over because the treasurer, Michel, was adamantly opposed to it, and that this never became an issue for the group as a whole and was a surprise to many who were told of it twenty-five years later.[27]

Chapter 15

Knitting for Victory

> Men get laid, but women get screwed.
> Quentin Crisp

The Women's Gay Liberation Front started meeting at *The Three Wheatsheaves* in Islington, but only the radical feminist women were happy about the split.

> *Elizabeth Wilson*: There was a lot of tokenism about women really, and that was all a bit spurious in a way. Some of the men were very supportive but there was a level of hostility underlying it all in the case of some men – not all by any means. I think in the end they (David and Aubrey) made this totally disingenuous argument. The feminist line was that women should meet separately, that women should not meet within GLF but separately, period. That was their radical feminist line ... some men were on the side of the women. I don't have any quarrel with Bette Bourne or Stuart, they were a bit more clued up, but I think David and Aubrey mobilised a latent misogyny, a kind of rank and file and it was all very plausible. As far as I'm concerned it would be wrong to say that we got fed up and decided to go. I feel we were pushed out and manipulated into going. I didn't feel like we had a choice.[1]

A GLF National Think-In had been arranged for 18 February at Lancaster University. We queens didn't go as it was arranged by the 'bisexual' outrider of the IS, Don Milligan, seeking to push his gritty northern macho ideology which denied the contribution of lesbians and queens in gay liberation, and we thought it was going to be like the Leeds Think-In, a mostly male assembly. This was not the case according to Lisa Power: 'Many women in other groups around the country wanted to discuss the London walk-out.'[2] I imagine those women would have been told by Fernbach and Walter that the split was caused by straight-gay misogyny, a failure to pursue economic class politics and that the separate development they and the women found in radical feminism was the way to further the struggle. Copies of an article they'd written had been brought to Lancaster ready for distribution. It claimed to be based on 'ideas ... developed out of discussions between several brothers in London GLF, and written up for the Lancaster Think-In.'

Gay Activism and Gay Liberation: a message to gay brothers

As opposed to gay activism, gay liberation starts from the recognition that male supremacy and the gender-role system has to be rooted out; that gay men can't be liberated except in the context of a radical transformation of the relationship between males and females in general – we thus support completely the women's liberation movement, as being in our own vital interest. Gay liberation rejects the privileges that straight society offers us as males, in the interest of something much more important – the free development of our gay selves. Gay liberation is not particularly interested in legal reforms, or even in acceptance by the straight world as a legitimate minority. Gay liberation sees the very existence of 'gay' and 'straight' people as the symptom of something very wrong. We don't think we can be liberated until men and women in general relate to each other as people on all levels. Although we don't want to relate sexually to women – we are struggling for our gay identity, to be the people we are – and heterosexuality is inevitable oppression in a male supremacist society – we do love women as our sisters and want to learn from their experience and knowledge, whereas gay activists seem content to reject women as something outside their concern. Finally, gay liberation does not see the only problem in our society as the sexual one. We see ourselves as part of a broader liberation movement, and we see our aims as going together with an economic and political revolution. In fact we see all aspects of liberation as intimately bound up together; the thrusting straight man is part of the general problem, the receptivity of women and gay males is part of the general solution.

Two questions have come up in London GLF recently that have brought into the open the conflict between gay activism and gay liberation within our own movement. The first is organisation. Some people are always saying that we should have more organisation – more money, more committees, more efficiency. But this formal organisation is only efficient for a particular type of activity – lobbying Parliament, writing letters to the press, etc. Gay liberationists think our energies should be primarily directed internally, into consciousness-raising, communes and a new lifestyle, and externally, into expressive activities like street theatre that show people what we're into, into community work (day care centres for kids, etc.) together with women's liberation, etc. Informal and non-hierarchical organisation isn't just better in itself – it's more suited to the forms of activity that we think are important.

The second question is that raised by the London gay women leaving GLF to form a separate organisation. It is significant that those men who are closest to the women were most happy to see this development; they understood how the women needed to be independent from the men, and not waste their energies rebutting the men's chauvinism. But now that the women have left, the question of which path we men are to take looms larger. There is a greater danger that the gay movement will get onto a gay activist course, with all that this involves. I believe that the great majority of men in the gay

> movement can be won to the ideas of radical feminism, but over the next few months the more conscious males will have to work hard to keep London GLF a genuine gay *Liberation* front.[3]

When the above article was handed out at the next all-London meeting it drew a sharp response from Mary McIntosh, Nettie Pollard, Paul Bunting and Jeffrey Weeks, dismayed that the split was treated as absolute and final, as much as the new ideology it proposed.

> **RADICAL FEMINISM AND THE GAY MOVEMENT**
>
> We welcome David and Aubrey's message to gay brothers as a useful contribution to starting a debate on a strategy for GLF. The criticism of certain types of reformism which they call gay activism are often valid and we are in full agreement with them. However, there are two issues on which we strongly disagree:
>
> 1. *False polarisation:* The authors suggest that gay activism and 'gay liberation' (as they define them) are the only possible strategies for a gay movement. Gay liberation is then assumed to be the same as radical feminism. This we dispute. While it is true that gay reformism, which ignores the gender-role system, is totally inadequate, radical feminism is not the only valid alternative. Radical feminists are only a minority of the organised women's movement in this country, including the gay women's movement.
>
> There are many who believe that the solution to the oppression of women and gay people cannot be achieved only through a direct attack on male supremacy. Feminism has been essential in pointing out the need for a separate women's organisation capable of challenging received notions of the feminine role and of making a positive contribution to the revolutionary movement. What is needed is a fuller

analysis of the relation between gender oppression and other forms of economic, political, social and ideological oppression. But it is not enough to make a facile equation of all oppressed groups with our own oppression, as the authors seem to do. Total liberation will only be achieved by overthrowing the dominating structures of society, including sexism. Street theatre and new lifestyles have a valuable function but cannot change society on their own.

2. *Women:* Who are 'THE women' with whom the authors claim to be so close? Is it not an aspect of this same sexist culture for *MEN* TO THUS DEFINE THE POSITION OF WOMEN? Women do not want to have their views formed for them by men, however sympathetic. If gay men wish to align themselves with the women's movement they must relate to real women – in all their variety – and not to their fantasies of what women are. The authors write that 'the receptivity of women and gay males is part of the general solution.' But why should women be necessarily limited to their old receptive (equals passive?) role? It is vital for men to break away from the 'thrusting', aggressive image of male superiority.

We make these points to open up the discussion of the important issue of strategy. We hope that many others will take part in this debate and help to develop a greater sense of common direction and solidarity in Gay Liberation.

LOVE AND STRUGGLE [4]

The Marxist socialists' hoped for debate never took place. The Maoists had worked the fissures in the movement into unbridgeable divides and would now stand back to observe what happened next. As they predicted, the confrontation between the men over the future direction of GLF was directly between the straight-gays and the radical queens. It was either a struggle against sexism supporting the GLF Manifesto or a reformist fight against injustice: the politics to cure a sick society or the disappearance of some of the symptoms of the sickness, but not the underlying disease. And the initiative had already been seized by the straight-gay activists, whose secession at that moment was deliberately undercover. Meantime the Maoists concentrated on Camden GLF, secure in the knowledge that when the two factions had torn the front apart, discipline would be restored by them and the outriders from the IS.

It was during this period that Bette Bourne stopped being butch … looking. Out went Che Guevara – in came Lucille Ball.

> *Bette*: I remember the first night I went to the meeting in a dress. It was scarlet, 1930's and cut on the cross, a marvellous frock I found on the market. I put it on with a beautiful Victorian cape and walked over to the meeting; I was living close by as I still do. I turned up at the meeting and sat very quietly with my handbag. They were all talking theory and the usual scoring points off one another. Then I took out a cigarette, and just said 'Well, I don't hear the women saying much, or the queens,' and there was a terrible silence. And I went on and I said, 'I've been sitting here listening to all this stuff and it doesn't seem very real to me.' And I suddenly felt very relaxed and started enjoying being in drag. They started to call us rad femmes. It got thrown at us one night in an argument – 'You radical feminist queens!' – But we didn't take the label … it was something from outside. We would never use words like that. We would say, 'Get a frock on dear,' whenever they started ranting. We all approached it from a very basic level of what we saw. We just went with our instincts. It was very strong, wearing a dress and all that, so I just carried on doing it. Eventually we could be heard.[5]

As more of the queens who identified with feminism began to find their voice, and not only defend their position but attack that of the straight-gays, so more of them got into drag for the first time to attend the general meeting. John Church appeared in drag, as did Mark Roberts, Cloud Downey, Richard Chappel and Douglas MacDougall. Alaric Sumner from the GLF Youth group started to experiment with his 'look', as did Vincent Meehan and Tim Bolingbroke from Camden GLF. Allahn McRae and Chris Stockdale, both dress designers, wore their own creations.

Warren Haig was the most difficult straight-gay opponent that the radical queens had to deal with. There was no one else in GLF who could match his talent for oratory, and his connections to the libertarian left with his work at Compendium Books – the underground press, his membership of the White Panthers, and his seen it, done it, experience of sixties activism in North America. But brilliant as he was at capturing a meeting, thinking on his feet and fishing out a metaphor, his ideas on liberationist themes entailed a programme of civil liberty targets with media involvement that hadn't changed from day one. Haig never troubled to join any function group. He lived only for the General Meeting and media opportunities where he appeared as a beatific hippie guru wise in the ways of liberation. His straight-gay followers would patronize us for our ideas on sexism, or grow angry and say that our appearance gave gay people a bad name, that we were a heterosexual's worst nightmare, which we happily recognized anyway, and so what?

With a crash-course in a new skill, we now spent our time at the general meetings furiously knitting as we listened to the straight-gay speeches, tutt-tutting and loudly commenting on every chauvinist remark and sexist utterance. One week we were Madame Defarge, another week, after watching an ice skating competition on TV, I made up score cards like the ones used by the judges, and we all sat in a row down one side of All Saints hall, holding up the cards and awarding points for the sexist speeches. After that demonstration we were called 'The thought police'. The all-London meetings now rocked backwards and forwards with an accumulation of suppressed antagonism that enveloped everyone who attended. For a few weeks the meetings became electric, enlightening and extreme. Our theatrics and pointed commentary: 'You've got to have deconstruction, darling, before you can have a new femme reconstruction,' was not in any way unwarranted. The straight-gays refusal to acknowledge their heterosexist attitudes was so complete they had become joyless swaggering parodies. The grotesque was succinctly revealed when Warren Haig, stung by our criticism of his machismo, leapt to his feet and proclaimed: 'I'll fuck anything, man, woman or dog!'

'My Only Office is The Park' appeared in Camden's own Newssheet dated 2nd March:

> Street Theatre was criticised last week for being narrowly dictatorial at the previous meeting for creating an atmosphere in which 'freedom of speech' which some brothers thought they were defending is not as free as they would have us believe. Its freedom works only for those who are into the whole system of aggressive, linear and rational argument and who are accustomed to dominate meetings. One brother's comparison with the House of Commons was a good one. There is a limit to the sort of problems you can solve by 'democratic discussion'.
>
> Surely GLF is committed to finding other ways of talking with itself and to outsiders and we should be grateful to Street Theatre for trying to laugh us out of our mimicry of straight ways of talking and feeling.[6]

The ascendancy of the radical queens at this time also alarmed the liberal-minded, those saints who always claim they are on the middle path and so can't help but label their opponents extremists. Micky Burbidge who was devoted to the Counter-Psychiatry group and later founded Icebreakers, a group dedicated to supporting isolated closet queens and encouraging them to accept their sexuality and come out, accused me of being a zealot because I'd proposed to him and the rest of the meeting that the way to change the world was for men to wear frocks. Such accusations of alienation show how much anger had been generated in many men by the emergence of a minority who had decided to drape a few yards of cloth in a different manner. Being the focus of the majority's antagonism perhaps prevented us from realising the power we had, but we were always capable of countering their arguments with our own, and if necessary, employing the violence of their language to do so.

In an interview for *Lunch,* the magazine of CHE interviewed Jill Tweedy the *Guardian* journalist, who said:

> JT: One of the things I admire about GLF, for instance, is the almost constant unremitting pressure they apply to people. One of the great problems about Women's Lib is that people get faint hearted because they think, 'Oh Christ, we've seen it all before. We CAN'T appear again and break up this or that meeting.' Whereas GLF go on and on and on.
>
> CHE: Don't you think their earnestness and intensity gets boring after a time?
>
> JT: Yes, but also it's one of the things you learn in any minority group. You've got to go *through* people's boredom and irritation, arouse their anger, partly because you become a presence then in their lives, and partly because it's very good for YOU to be aggressive. If you're in a minority you tend to be very frightened of aggression (although a few who are strong characters anyway may feel more aggressive); the majority are timid and frightened of arousing aggression in others.[7]

Aubrey Walter: 'The radical queen communards from Notting Hill would sweep into meetings and demand that people get into drag and make-up, haranguing anyone whom they considered too much of a "man."'[8]

That of course is completely true. We were dreadful. We had found a voice based on the equality men find in drag, and this, with a growing sense of solidarity between us had become our anarchic revolutionary tactic. The only excuse for men wearing drag is to be always, absolutely apocalyptic. What is not true of Walter's view is that 'Many men were also terrorized into bizarre and unproductive forms of drag.'[9] It's true we were Camp terrorists, and very fierce, but you can't get a man who is kicking and screaming into a pair of tights or unproductive drag, whatever that would be, anymore than you can make a horse drink or turn a straight man gay at the sight of two men doing it.

Jeffrey Weeks with his sociological and psychiatric background claimed a deeper analysis of the politics of drag and the influence of the counterculture:

> Within this general framework there was a loose political tendency which called itself 'radical feminism' or, later, 'radical queenery' or 'faggotry'. This extended the logic of early arguments, such as those of Martha Shelley and Steve Danski, which saw the primary contradiction in society as one between men and women: hence it was 'maleness' that had to be wiped out. 'Male homosexuality could be the first attempt at the non-assertion of cultural manhood'... The bible of this grouping was Shulamith Firestone's *The Dialectic of Sex* (1970), which located the true dialectic of history in conflict between the sexes and looked forward to women being liberated from childbirth. The logic of the position was for gay men to subordinate themselves entirely to women's struggles, to 'relinquish all power' to women, to give them a veto in the movement, and for men to give up their 'male privileges'. One way of doing this was to embrace political drag, to dress in women's clothing without, as in the traditional drag scene, aping female glamour. So you would see hairy men walking arm-in-arm

> down the street in pretty dresses and with rich make-up: the aim was not so much to pretend to be a woman as to reject being a man and so invite personal abuse. This had its interesting personal effect, but as a political gesture was almost entirely useless.[10]

The Dialectic of Sex was just one of many books on feminism held on our bookshelves. So yes I must admit, we were guilty of possessing a copy of her work, but not guilty of being her followers. Shulamith Firestone's ideas are based largely on the science of ectogenesis, with extra-uterine devices growing babies, relieving women from childbearing. Walter, who lauds ectogenesis in the introduction to his *Come Together* anthology is the only aficionado of growing babies in bottles that I have ever met. Nor did we think maleness was the problem that needed to be wiped out, but heterosexual male superiority. But how apposite of Weeks to call the peg needed to hang his theory of the radical queens on – the Bible – so he could tell his readership all about who he thought we were and what he thought we were thinking, like the absurdist notion that we would just roll over and give women a veto on our position. That said, it comes as a great relief for me to learn that our real reason for dressing in drag was to invite personal abuse, and I'm ashamed to admit that such a thought had never crossed my mind.

Chapter 16

Gay News

> The difference between tolerance and acceptance is very considerable, for tolerance is a gift extended by the superior to the inferior.
>
> Dennis Altman

After *Come Together* 10 had been published in November 1971 without Elsmore's article, a divided Media Workshop continued to meet at Mick Belsten's place in Barnes attended by Annie Brackx and Sarah Grimes, but the other members of the collective who'd argued against their feminist politics with their pseudo-radical feminism remained antagonistic and kept away. The lesbians of the Faraday Road commune were producing issue N°·11, scheduled for January, so there was a period of waiting on new developments. Since the breakthrough into Women's Liberation, the women's group was the exciting centre of an expanding feminist consciousness and became the main focus of Brackx and Grimes' activities. Belsten, realising the three of them had been isolated by their opponents, decided in early December to hand back the organising of the group to Fernbach and Walter, so before Christmas Media Workshop meetings moved back to their home in West End Lane.

In early January 1972 Media Workshop moved to Martini Mansions, the home of Phil Powell, remaining there until the end of February before moving back to West End Lane, with the last recorded meeting there being the 6 March according to the weekly announcements in the Newssheets.

It must have been during the last week of February shortly after the Lancaster Think-In that Fernbach and Walter learnt that the next issue of *Come Together,* N°·12, was being produced by the

Office collective rather than Media Workshop. The news proved even more startling when they discovered that the Co-ordinating Committee didn't know anything about the production either. A Think-In was immediately called for 11 March at the LSE so the movement could debate this surprising development.

Denis Lemon's colleagues in the Office Collective, Martin Corbett and David Seligman, were already planning to bring out the first issue of *Gay News* in May. Their ignorance of how to produce a newspaper, and their arrogance and disinterest in the feelings of the rest of the movement, gives grounds for the idea that they could practise and gain experience by publishing their own edition of *Come Together* using the socialist finance of GLF to float their private enterprise. The newssheet put together by the Office Collective never once mentioned that they were producing *Come Together* 12. The venture into newsprint was a commercial conspiracy to defraud and malign.

Meanwhile the *Gay News* collective, as it described itself, decided it was time to reveal their existence to GLF. Notice was given in the Newssheet for 1 March:

> Maybe you've heard about *Gay News*, maybe you haven't. *Gay News* is intended to be a new national fortnightly newspaper for all gay people, hopefully coming out in May. It is NOT a GLF movement newspaper, but it seems to us the newspaper collective, that we have sisters and brothers in GLF who would be interested in knowing what kind of paper we are trying to get together, how we are going about it, where we are in relation to the paper. We've hired the back room at *The Three Wheatsheaves* for an informal discussion about *Gay News*. It's important that we hear and discuss together your opinions, suggestions and criticisms.[1]

The Newssheet for the 15 March came with an attached page giving details of the Think-In at the LSE.

> No votes were taken at the Think-In, but the following seemed to be generally agreed: (1) The Wednesday meetings at All Saints Hall should now become a purely social gathering where members from the various local and functional groups can meet each other and new members. (2) In any centrally arranged advertisements for London GLF all the local groups, their meeting places and times, should be listed. The Wednesday meeting should not be emphasised. New members should be encouraged to go to local groups. (3) The Co-ordinating Committee should take on the functions of the old Finance Group [...]. (4) The Office Collective should be made up of representatives of local groups.[2]

But a vote at the Think-In *had* been taken. The vote had been in favour of stopping publication and a refusal to finance issue 12 of *Come Together.* These inconvenient facts were not mentioned in the Diary. The deliberate omission ultimately being the responsibility of Tony Salvis, who in his role as Secretary attended the Think-In. For all those suspicious of his behaviour and that of Seligman, Corbett, and McLellan, the censorship shows how arrogant and mendacious they had become at manipulating information and events in support of the *Gay News* business endeavour.

> *Martin Corbett*: I was very involved in *Come Together* 12. It wasn't a pilot for *Gay News,* though lots of people said it was at the time. There weren't any rules about *Come Together,* anybody could do it. Media Workshop, that was Mick Belsten's gang. It hadn't come out for a long time and we had the materials so we just got it together. I didn't understand the etiquette of it all, we put people's names in if they'd worked on it because that's what I thought you were supposed to do when you were publishing something.[3]

One of the articles published in the Corbett-Seligman unauthorized edition was Rex Lay's pornographic story, 'Shirley Temple Knows'. This had been submitted to Media Workshop for *Come Together* 8, but not published because the collective felt that with the guilty verdicts and sentencing of the *Oz* magazine editors for publishing obscene articles, they could draw down obscenity charges on themselves and more generally on GLF. Lay's manuscript had been put back in the Media Workshop folder. Lisa Power commenting on the high literary merit of Lay's writing added: 'Martin Corbett, in his usual practical manner says that it was included simply because it was sitting in the *Come Together* file and nobody realized it was controversial.'[4] But the Media Workshop folder wasn't just lying around in Caledonian Road. The folder contained other articles submitted and rejected on various grounds, content or quality, which was censorship in itself, and an act that might avoid embarrassing both the writers and Media Workshop if the folder had been lodged at the GLF office, with its few drawers in a second-hand desk and no security. The folder was kept within the Media Workshop collective and taken from one meeting place to the next as locations changed. Neither Belsten, Fernbach or Walter, would have given the folder to anyone outside the collective, so I think it safe to assume it was Phil Powell, in charge of the folder for January and February, who presented Lay's story, probably to Andy Elsmore who was abbeting the straight-gay wannabe journalists. It was Elsmore's article that had engineered the collapse of the old Media Workshop collective, and who was now with Powell in control of *Come Together*, which must have been his objective all along. Maybe they planned the whole thing from the word go. Maybe Elsmore was a Trotskyite too – we shall never know – but both of them had become the beneficiaries of his writing. Both were working class men, Powell the 'bisexual' college lecturer, Elsmore the not so well educated gay revolutionary, with joint roots in the traditional macho left and the

Grosvenor Square anti-war protests.

When Fernbach and Walter passed Media Workshop over to Powell they obviously thought it was in the safe hands of a brother, while they focused on their new local group in Camden, the production of its newsletter and their writings for the Gay Marxist Group. Then the women's walk-out occurred quickly followed by the Lancaster Think-In, which had them writing 'Gay Activism and Gay Liberation: a message to gay brothers', and in the aftermath of that the criticism of their radical feminist position by Mary McIntosh and the other Marxists. Having chosen to establish their new ideology with the IS first, they discovered too late that Elsmore and Powell were not hanging around, but had become their nemesis by gaining control of 'their' newspaper.

New Year 1972 began with Elsmore and Powell representing a new purged Media Workshop filled with Denis Lemon supporters. The trade-off was that the straight-gays would learn how to put a newspaper together and write what they could, and for Elsmore and Powell the opportunity to write campaigning articles designed to agitate the ghetto along traditional left lines. The other innovation in this issue is signed articles, as Corbett emphasizes above. With Elsmore and Powell in control, the introduction of named writers obviously wasn't the politesse of thieves but adopted for a reason. The deal, I've come to believe, included the right to use the names of others in the Office Collective for the articles Elsmore and Powell wrote, allowing them to remain in the shadows as their stooges played the newspaper game. Only when the group was criticized after publication by other members of Gay Lib did Elsmore surface in the role of defender.

The front page of *Come Together* 12 carries three articles. The first entitled:

GLF SLAM POLICE

The Advise [sic] Forum at LSE on Community Relations. Friday 10-3-72. The representatives and invited speakers from Woman's[sic] Lib., The Claimants Union and Gay Liberation Front decided that they wanted no part of a forum at which a Police Chief Inspector would also speak. Proceedings began with the following statement on behalf of GLF.

We regard the presence of a police representative on this platform as an insult to the Gay Liberation Front, and to all gay men whose lives are lived in fear of the police force of this country. It is also an insult to gay women who have been harrassed, [sic] attacked and brutalised by the police. The police represent the most fascist elements in our society and by their constant abuse of the very laws they are supposed to enforce, by their lies, destortion [sic] and brutality, by their reactionary lobby to elect repressive and reactionary changes in law and their determined opposition to law reform, we thus here have a shift towards fascism. Gay Liberation opposies [sic] the cause for law and order, believing that all authoritarians are sexually repressed, and therefore constitute a grave danger to society, in their destructive attitudes to human relationships, by conditioning human beings to the church, the schools, the police, the military, and their devotion to the state machine. They are effectively war mongers and gay people recognise the police as our enemy in their war against us. Since our organisation started we have suffered systematic attacks, not only in London but wherever we've organised in the provinces. Police are still, daily and nightly, with official blessing, practising entrapment techniques in London and the provinces, in bars, parks and lavatories. We are threatened and abused by the one fact that we are open about our sexuality. We are gay, we are proud to be gay and we are angry. You are here today to discuss freedom. Please remember that none of us are free until we are all free.

The pig in question was Chief Inspector David Williams of Islington. After statements from Women's Lib and the Claimants Union, vocally opposed by the honkies and liberals present, most of our brothers and sisters walked out along with several people who wanted to know more and held an alternative forum next door. Williams finally got to say his piece.

'I'm not a police spokesman, I don't have a brief as to what I should say – I came here hoping to listen, and this is basically what *my job is*. I've not come to apologise for my colleagues. It's my job to talk to people, to talk to minorities.'

He said a great deal more in the same vein, freely interupted [sic] by two remaining brothers who also split after he'd finished, and the parting shot came from a GLF brother: 'I'm walking out of this meeting that Chief Inspector Williams is at, in respect to the memory of Stephen McCarthy.'

(Stephen McCarthy died in Upper Street police station one hour after his arrest in February 1971). [Signed] Ralph.

A notice on page 10 informs: '*Come Together* came together with the help of the following people: Martin, layout; David, general assistance; Tim and Tony, typing; Alberto, advice; Ralph, information; Simon, typing; Simon, criticism; Lyn, typing and coffee; Toni and Nikki, art work; Alan, badges. Dahling Dahling Reproduction. N.C.C.L Project Group, Sidney Levy, photography; Nigel Heading, *Time Out, INK,* Her Majesty's Stationery Office,and twenty contributors.'

I do wonder who Ralph could be. The crude language is completely unlike that of Ralph Stephenson's writings, and without wishing to over–egg my argument, more like the work of Elsmore. 'Ralph' would have been involved in left-wing politics for a while to remember the death of Stephen McCarthy, which the left at the time claimed was another case of suspicious death in police custody.

(Stephen McCarthy was a 19 year old from Islington who absconded from Borstal. He was spotted on the run near home, and during his arrest two officers held an arm each and rammed him into the concrete post of a bus stop. Back in custody he was moved from Dover to Brook Hospital Greenwich for a brain operation. He died of pneumonia in Wormwood Scrubs on 25 January 1971. The inquest jury returned a verdict of death by natural causes, adding a rider that McCarthy should have been given more medical attention whilst in prison.) 'Ralph' was repeating left-wing misinformation.[5]

The second article on the front page is headed "Suspended", below which is a photograph of a long haired youth named Rupert Harries outside Bow Street Court. 'Charged with persistently importuning for an immoral purpose at the gentlemens' convienience [sic] at Victoria Station [he] was given a three year suspended sentence at Bow Street court on Friday March 10.'

The third article is headed, *"Union Tavern"* – Billy Hays, son of the licencee [...] has had a summons taken out against him for assault after he punched a brother from GLF in the mouth outside the pub on Monday 6 March 1972.'

On an inside page Peter Waldschmidt who was new to GLF and later became a journalist at *Gay News* wrote up the straight-gay agenda he wanted installed.

> Democracy and the Wednesday Meeting.
> The accusations and couter-accusations [sic] at the GLF Wednesday meeting has shown that the nature of the meetings is wrong. WE all agree that the Wed. meetings should decide on policies and actions of GLF, but how in heaven's name can any sensible decision be taken in that chaos?
>
> The so-called democratic decisions are taken in a very hostile manner. We are supposed to love our brothers and sisters but there is only hostility and anger.

In a democratic community disagreement is a healthy sign, but this is no basis for sabotageing [sic] or preventing decisions being made.

People are getting sick and tired of hearing the same ten people speak, the same people making all the decisions, the same self-appointed spokesmen who claim to represent GLF. That isn't democracy at all. It's the same fucking bureaucracy which our society gives us.

Let's end this fucking oppression NOW.

Democracy is ruled by consensus and consent.

For God's sake, let's have a democratically elected committee which democratically makes decisions, before GLF destroys itself in the death throes of anarchy. Those who oppose sensible leadership are the supporters of anarchy and chaos. Those who support anarchy are anti-democratic.

The committee's function will be to represent ALL views in GLF – something that's just not on at the Wed meeting.

The solution is as follows: 1) enlarge the co-ordinating committee 2) enable the co-ordinating committee to formulate policy 3) allow the co-ordinating committee to arrange discussions 4) no discussions at the Wed meetings which have not been presented to the c.committee unless a vote at the meeting is taken to do otherwise. 5) major policy decisions to be ratified by the W.meeting. 6) the move to vote on a major decision at a Wed. meeting should itself be voted upon. 7) all reports to be given to the chairman. 8) more voting at Wed. meeting.

By this means people with particular grievances can report to their representative on the co-ordinating committee who will in turn (if democratically decided upon) will get it discussed on Wed, instead of it being shoved out by ego-trippers. The Wed meeting can then rule out anything which is not on the agenda.

Transfer power away from the ego-trippers to YOUR

representatives. Then we can start DOING things.

Let's try this as an experiment for three months. Love, Peter

Mick Belsten succeeded in demanding a balanced view on the subject.

Parliamentarianism and Anti-Disestablishmentarianism or Freedom, Hot Air, You and Me.

Trying to get to grips with the accompanying attack on GLF is like trying to wrestle with an octopus. The contradictions, glib assumptions, naïve desire for the law and order which it encompasses are so confusing that one is hard put to know where to begin to grapple with these half-baked views of how a liberation movement should conduct itself.

The very notion that some kind of consensus view can be arrived at to form a dogma to be imposed on the rest of us who dissent from that view, defeats the whole purpose of a Gay Liberation Front.

Such a system already exists in society, it is called Parliament, and we are assured that the consensus view of society is that homosexuality is bad, the Family is the loveliest thing known to Man, Mothers are for Mother's Day, Fathers and teachers must be *Obeyed*, a women's place is in the home, blacks make good cricketers, boxers and pop singers, lesbians make good lorry-drivers in wartime, and pansies are very sensitive, artistic people with filthy habits.

Incidentally we do not all agree that the Wednesday meetings should decide on policy. The Wed meetings are open meetings which are widely advertised in many sections of the press, etc., and anyone can walk in from the street and participate. But to suppose that our 'policy' should be decided by some late-night cruisers who have never given the problems we discuss any thought or discussion is patently absurd.

The most democratic way in which decisions can be taken

are after thorough discussion, time for thought and argument, with a willingness to listen to the criticisms of others, so that everyone who participates in the decision making process has been able to air their views, and if necessary adjust those views in the light of others peoples' suggestions.

Clearly this can only be done by getting away from marathon, phony "debates" in a large assembly. This requires separating out into groups small enough (6-8 say) to allow everyone to express him/her self on each topic. Then to meet together in a more enlightened state, to arrive at a coherent and considered view of the situation.

Fortunately a structure is rapidly and organically evolving for this kind of democracy, to replace the sham which exists and to forestall the hideous, impersonal machinery of bureaucracy proposed by Peter Waldshmidt which merely imitates the authoritarian rule of the dying culture which calls itself Government.

The local groups in London are beginning to make their own decisions, and have begun to find it valuable to go into small groups within their meetings to discuss thoroughly all the issues involved. This was brought about by the reluctance and resistance put up by people at the Wed meeting to this kind of examination of issues.

Nothing will kill GLF quicker than the stale, boring, deadly, stifling autocracy which is proposed here in terms which remind me of George Orwell's famous 'double-think' in 1984.

Long live anarchy! All power to all of the people! Mick.

There is another long piece entitled "Homosexuals and Revolution" by one Nicole, who tells us she had been in GLF for a couple of months. She makes no mention of feminism nor reference to the new Women's Gay Liberation Front, but immediately launches into yet another analysis of straight society and the gay position in terms of economic class analogies. It would have been with some relief that male readers turned to Rex Lay's penny in the slot spyhole, down on all fours, cock and bum, cottageing spectacular. There was amusement too in Rachel Pollack's "The Twilight World of the Heterosexual", where all the things that are said about homosexuals become the attributes of the heterosexuals, as in Valerie Solanas' *SCUM Manifesto*.

Chiming with the wannabe journalist's entrepreneurial spirit, Alan Wakeman took it upon himself to redesign the GLF badge.

> Lots of people have been asking what the symbol of the new badge means. Well of course a symbol can mean anything one wants it to mean. But here is a little background to how the new symbol happened: it is based on the symbol for the planet Jupiter. Our original symbol, although most people didn't realise it was based on the symbol for the planets Mars and Venus. Now, in Astrological terms, the attributes of these planets can be summed up by giving the adjectives derived from them. Mars gives martial, Venus venereal, and Jupiter jovial. Did we really want a symbol that made us out to be militaristic, aggressive and concerned with sex? The dictionary definition for jovial is merry, convivial, gay. This seems good enough. But in fact it goes deeper than this. If you are into Astrology you'll know that Jupiter is one of the most powerful and mysterious of planets and is concerned with a higher plane of life. So is GLF. As if to confirm the right-ness of Jupiter for us, the symbol lent itself easily to conversion to the GLF initials – look and you'll see.[6]

Finally we come to the statements from *Gay News*.

> On March 7th members of GLF went to talk to the collective that's trying to get together a national fortnightly newspaper to be called *Gay News*. It is not intended to be a GLF

newspaper so though the collective has about eight GLF members in it, it's also got a sister from CHE in Manchester, and Ian Dunn, who started up the Scottish gay's movement, Scottish Minorities Group. The newspaper collective, which has an office anyone can write to at 19, London St, W2 (address anything to *Gay News*), described the kind of paper it's trying to get out.

It is intended to come out in early May, priced 10p, will have several pages of news about what gays are doing (or what's been done to us), features, a strip cartoon, pix, ads personal and classified, and information about what's being done in the fortnight ahead by gay movements, Women's Lib., Children's Rights, whatever's appropriate to gay/sexual revolution. The idea is that by carrying information at present available nowhere else, and maybe looking into things that no other medium is going to spend time on it'll give us all better information on which to plan or form our views.

GLF members who went to the discussion on March 7th (another was suggested, & will be held on a date yet to be fixed, maybe three weeks from the first) were worried about the radicalism of the paper, since it's meant to be open to all sorts of gays' or others' views, wouldn't it be liberal, evasive, unpolitical? the individuals from the collective answered (this compresses a long discussion) that the act of bringing out a paper called *Gay News* is itself political, since it will be on bookstalls etc; it will want to carry personal ads, at present the subject of a House of Lords case involving *International Times (IT)*. The features will go in depth into the behaviour of institutions etc. that affect us as gays – the Samaritans, prisons, churches etc.

Sisters in the GLF women's group also talked with the Gay News collective, in February, and the same questions about radicalism were raised then. The paper is intended to be non-aligned ... but draws its inspiration, in the search for news and in the intentions behind the features, from the thinking behind Women's Lib., GLF etc: an end to gender roles, an end to sexism, and an end to sexual exploitation and oppression. Some sisters in the Underground Press and elsewhere are planning to bring out a sisters' movement paper to be called *Spare Rib*, also in early May, and this could well be the most useful paper for all of us, gay males or whatever, to read. For all that, *Gay News* is being planned by sisters and brothers to be of interest to men and women equally, as would be expected.

A few technicalities: aiming to get on bookstalls, bookshops, etc, through as much of the country as possible, we worked out that a first print order of 10,000 was the right one to go for in early May. This number will involve a cost of about £400 an issue, making no allowance for paying anyone who joins the collective, or writes, except bus fares etc. We have costs in setting up a company, Gay News Ltd, and paying for an office (one room): so we're trying to raise £2,000. Part of that, we hope will be loans – we're writing to gays and straights who might help. The company, Gay News, gives them confidence their help won't be ripped off; and the company will be trying to get charitable status – meaning it either puts any profits straight back into the newspaper (improving it) or repays loans, or gives money to gay organisations. But the main part of the finance we hope, will be from advance subscriptions: we're selling these subscriptions now, and if you want to help realise this gay newspaper in May, please tell David Seligman, Suki Pitcher, Peter Reed, Denis Lemon, Sylvia Room, Andrew Lumsden or Martin Corbett, or write to us at London Street.

The collective is open, to people as well as ideas. Please ring 437-2859 in the mornings, or just speak personally, to find times of meetings of the collective. Gay News Collective.

Also in the collective, recommended as a designer by Jim

Anderson, was Richard Adams the designer of *Oz Magazine* and of Chesterman's *The Index of Possibilities*.

So there it is, as one-sided a report on a meeting as one could expect from a straight newspaper, together with all the honeyed words capitalists use in the market place when recruiting labour with the carrot of philanthropy. Promises for the future include collective working, charitable status, financial help for struggling causes, equality – all of which were betrayed. The promise that the thinking behind GLF and Women's Lib would be the intention behind the search for news, and the patronising uber liberal recommendation that *Spare Rib* 'could well be the most useful paper for all of us, gay males or whatever, to read', coming from men with a history of ignoring women and their politics (Lumsden and Reed excepted), is incredible. Whatever indeed!

After publication of issue 12, mission accomplished, the journalists of the Office Collective drifted away and the straight-gays were no longer able to cover the staffing rota. Queens like Alaric Sumner and Cloud Downey became members. The two of them were only loosely associated with the radical queens at that time, so they were tolerated by the straight-gays because they did all the real work such as the typing, mailing, answering the phone and listening to the troubles of the runaways and rent boys while making them coffee.

The Newssheet for 5-12 April, under the banner: 'Think-In at LSE on 15 April, Saturday, Ten till Five' reads: 'The subject is a most important one considering that we have all of us just been ripped-off by the publication of the Corbett-Seligman '*Come Together*' which it is suggested you rip-off in your turn. The subject of the Think-In is '*Come Together*' and the role of Media Workshop.'[7]

The Newssheet for the following week 13-20 April responded to the suggestion of what to do with copies of *Come Together* 12 and reveals more names of those involved in its production.

> We would like to object to the assertion in last weeks newssheet that we have all been "ripped off" by David Seligman & Martin Corbett. Martin and David accepted any and all contributions which they received, and anyone who came along to help was welcome to participate. At one point there were about 20 people in the office working on *CT* 12, plus all the contributors to be taken into account. The point we wish to make (which was also the reason behind the list of names appearing at the end of the paper) is that Martin & David were not solely responsible for putting the paper together, and should not, therefore, be criticised on a purely personal level as has been the case so far. We also feel that there was no deliberate dishonesty in their approach, however debatable the policy behind their actions may be considered to be. Signed, David McLellan. Lynn Alderson. Nich Rogers. Manuel Darela. Gerald Wheakley. Lloyd Vanetta. Allan McGorrin, and Andy Elsmore.[8]

The result of the 15 April Think-In was that Camden GLF would produce the next issue of *Come Together*, the all-London general meeting was to be abolished, and the meeting in All Saints Hall would now be known as Notting Hill GLF.

The abolition of the all-London general meeting meant there would no longer be a central body large enough to exercise oversight of the office, drastically increasing that collective's power and entrenching its bureaucracy. There was hardly an issue of the Diary from this time onward that didn't carry a piece about that week's financial drama. Tony Halliday, now attending East London GLF, wrote in the Diary that the office dissipates energy to no particularly good effect, inhibited development, and its functions could be performed elsewhere.

Things were changing on the home front too. Nicholas Bramble, Michael James and I had been living with George Lennox for six months by now and were fed up with his crushing machismo. Even so, I said no to James' idea that we all escape to Bramble's house in Gorleston for the summer. Lennox was never going to leave, I could see that, but disappearing from Gay Lib, that was a wrench. James' answer to that was that we had done enough already and it was time for some of the younger ones to get it on. I saw some sense in that, so eventually I agreed.

A few days before we left, Lennox came into my bedroom with the sworn statement from the police covering his alleged crime at Victoria Station. He'd just received his copy from the solicitor in the post that morning and wanted my opinion. The police claimed that Lennox had gone up to the window of Cook's Bureau de Change, pointed a gun at the cashier and demanded money. The cashier said 'Okay, just a sec,' stepped to one side out of sight, and raised the alarm. The police then claimed that Lennox was still standing there, presumably pointing the gun at thin-air, when they arrived to arrest him. It was so badly imagined, so improbable, it made me laugh. I said to him, 'No jury's going to believe you just stood there, for what, three or four minutes at least, with a gun pointing at an empty office, believing the cashier would return with bags of money after he'd escaped with his life. It's too absurd.'

It was some time before I heard that he got three years for armed robbery, later still, that after serving his sentence he'd gone to live in Amsterdam. At his Old Bailey trial, Judge E Clark did all he could to make Lennox's claim of a political fix appear ludicrous, probing only the evidence that strengthened the prosecution case. Cook's cashier claimed the gunman had an ordinary London accent, whereas Lennox has a thick Glaswegian brogue. More tellingly, his physical description didn't match. The only other evidence was the police claim that Lennox had made a verbal confession – one that was never written down. His antecedents file was missing, and his army record had not been consulted – a standard procedure. Nor was it explained how Detective Jones decided on the 18 January, the day Lennox's story appeared in *7 Days*, that he was the suspect, and had known so precisely where to find him – two and a half months after the robbery occurred.[9]

In 1987 or 1988, when the old bar in the *Champion* was still there and the same policing, anti-gay landlord and his wife were still behind it, who should I see when I walked in one evening, but Lennox? He looked much the same, still wearing the shades he needed from the after-effects of the torture, dour of course, with a touch of 'it's alright for some' (if only he knew), but warm in his way. He was killing time between visiting his mother in Scotland and leaving for Paris the next day to meet up with his Swedish girlfriend, after which the two of them were flying back to India. They'd been here in Europe to raise more money for their work in India sinking boreholes in rural areas to provide clean water for villages, and by eliminating pools of stagnant water dispersing the malarial mosquito.

With the end of the big meetings in All Saints Hall the confrontation between the straight-gays and the radical queens was now confined to the weekly meetings of the Office Collective. The Newssheet for 24 May carried a notice that the office needed painting, 'please donate some brushes and come and help do it.' At the next meeting of the collective the queens were taken to task for their plan. 'Who were the queens to decide to paint the office? Isn't ego-tripping supposed to be a sign of male privilege?' As the countdown to the first Gay Pride Week began, an outline of the arguments that erupted over painting the office were written up and dispatched to all corners of the country.

> Well what happened: because the conflict was partly sparked off by the previous office collectives meeting, the femme men decided to try and change the offices appearance; they though it reflected the attitude of male privilege that some of the office collective maintained; they got together some paint and

on Saturday went in and painted the office in bright colours. They also reached the conclusion that it would be a good idea if they got into wearing dresses as one particular way of rejecting some of their male privileges; those who did not want to do this saw it as a rejection and complained about being 'forced to wear make-up and dresses' and that they had been 'thrown out' of the office.

These actions brought about a series of discussions on Saturday, Sunday and at the office collective meeting on Monday; while there was a lot of confusion, especially about 'labelling' people as butch and femme, about not attempting to listen to anyone else's viewpoint, about selfishness and not caring about people, and while no concrete agreements or conclusions were reached, it does seem that if people realise that they are not being rejected, and that the confusion resulted from the fact that nobody's view had been fully worked out and that we must all be open to criticism and change, then these events will be a positive benefit to GLF.[10]

Cloud Downey: It was absolutely chaotic, there was supposed to be two people on duty but they often failed to turn up, but there would be others like me who weren't on the rota [that day] but would be there. I always used to dress up for it. We made cups of tea chatted to people, there was a lot going on but it never felt like it. Anybody would come in, often with horrendous problems, and we would try to help. What kind of job we made of it I don't know. We tried to get systems going. I never really knew who the office collective were because every time you would go to a meeting there would be different people involved, and then there would be rows about who was in the collective but just didn't come to meetings.[11]

Alaric Sumner: I have a feeling it happened more than once, that we were the first and that we were working in the office

> for the evening and decided to repaint it in psychedelic colours. And that there was no trouble that night. And then we came in the next day or two and they had painted over everything that we had done, because I remember being really pissed off that all that beautiful brightness and colour had just been covered in this puke single colour which made it look exactly like a tedious office … There was intense resentment of what we were doing at the time, wearing frocks and questioning gender roles, just as we resented intensely that they wouldn't understand what we were doing. How could they possibly not take part? Because we felt that we had the true GLF theory and with retrospect I'd still say that we did; that the motive of GLF was revolutionary not reformist. That the taking of the risk of self-transformation in the street, not knowing what on earth could happen was part of it. The revolution starts with self-transformation.[12]

A few days before the first Gay Pride Week began on 23 June 1972, the first *Gay News* was finally published.

> Well here it is the first issue of *Gay News*. It is late and we are sorry about that, but we offer the first excuse and apology in the life of *Gay News* and sincerely hope it won't be the first of a long series. We talk, and always will be doing, about the *Gay News* collective. By collective we mean the people who are presently engaged in getting the paper together. There is no editor, art director, sales manager or whatever, we are all equally responsible for everything, and by the same token no one person is in any position of greater authority than any other.

The front page was taken up with a mug shot of Jimmy Savile overprinted in lurid green, while inside was a close up on Cliff Richard under the title, "Het of the Month". An example of what *Gay News* had in store for GLF appeared under the title "Come

Dancing Together".

A town hall somewhere in West London. GLF and the gay world outside come together with two groups, disco light shows, charging higher prices for drinks than most gay pubs. There are about 400 people and most of them seem to be enjoying themselves, dancing, drinking, chatting; but there are lonely isolated people, perhaps the ones who are not pretty or trendy, who sit in corners on their own.

GLF is supposed to be trying to break down this awful sexist custom where we only talk to people, dance with them, if we fancy them and want to go to bed with them. Then surely the whole point of dances run by GLF should be to start relating to the many non-GLF people who attend them, the non-politically motivated who are content to remain in their gay pub/club ghettoes, the meat markets. How can we do this? We should have group dancing; GLF literature should be available where you buy your ticket. It isn't!

Ironically, the attendance by GLF members of these dances is falling off. They are held more and more frequently and always have the same formula – disco, light show and two heavy rock groups. Not everyone digs rock music or dancing. Why not one group and a drag artist, or one group and a film.

At the last dance at Kensington Town Hall about ten people started jeering and attempting to make one of the groups leave the stage as its lead singer was gyrating in a very sexist way. They shouted, 'Sexist, sexist, get off, get off,' and finally violently mounted the stage and tried to push the group off, ignoring the majority who either saw nothing wrong and wished the group to continue, or else wanted to talk about the situation, not scream and kick; this frightened the non-GLF people who should feel relaxed while beginning to experience the true GLF ideology and it's love which still exists, though distantly. David Seligman.

The week after *Gay News* appeared, *Spare Rib*, the new magazine for women was published. It was co-founded by Rosel Boycott who had worked at *Friends* and quickly discovered there was no place for her in the underground press. By the nineties she had found her place as editor of the Tory *Daily Express*. The other founder who acted as Editor was Marsha Rowe an Australian journalist who put herself through university and worked for *Oz* in Sydney before coming to London in 1969. She worked here for the relocated *Oz* as a secretary, then for *INK*, the other Richard Neville publication, experiencing in both situations the same underground press misogyny as Boycott.

> Then, in December 1971, Marsha and two other women who had had unhappy periods in the underground press, Louise Ferrier and Michelene Wandor, decided to call a meeting for women who had had similar experiences. It was held at Rowe and Ferrier's basement flat in Notting Hill and fifty people came.
>
> 'It was like the lid had been taken off,' Rowe remembered. 'We didn't really stay on the topic of work very long. Almost immediately, it was about how you did all the shit stuff at home ... about how we supported men ... There were women who'd had to have children adopted, who'd had to have abortions ... It was all about the sexual repression in the so-called liberated sixties. But none of us had ever said any of these things to each other ... We didn't have any language to talk about what we wanted to talk about. The concepts weren't there. Sexism wasn't a concept. We just had to find a way by ... mentioning experience. This is what consciousness-raising meant. You'd start describing your experience to each other. And then you'd come to an analysis.'
>
> After the meeting, Rowe and Ferrier 'stayed up all night, thinking, "No one will ever speak to us again." That we'd crossed some terrible boundary. We were absolutely terrified,

and ecstatic at the same time. It was very strange. And, of course, everybody did speak to us again, and there was another meeting and another …' At the third gathering, Rowe recalled, 'I said, "I think we should start our own magazine."'[13]

> *Spare Rib*. A Proposed Monthly Magazine for Women.
> It's obvious … we need a magazine such as *SPARE RIB*. The need has arisen from an awareness of the limitations in existing women's magazines. ALL women are rapidly becoming frustrated with their situation which most journals either ignore, or at best mention without offering solutions. Slick and trendy treatment in magazines has only helped to increase the loneliness and isolation that so many women feel. *SPARE RIB* aims to involve people in the rapidly growing women's movement but without any bias and political stigma that clings to 'alternative women's magazines' and indeed to the Women's Liberation movement in general.[14]

On the Sunday that Downey, Sumner and friends were painting the office to cheer things up for the first ever Gay Pride Week, someone, no one can remember who, came to visit and invited them all to the party next day at 'The Place' to celebrate the publication of the first issue of *Spare Rib*.

Gay News had a formal invitation, but whatever they'd planned for their second edition was binned soon after they arrived at the party. Denis Lemon later wrote:

> The *Gay News* collective and I arrived at the party, being held at 'The Place' in North London, just before 9.30pm. The room where the party was being held was pretty crowded, and what was immediately noticeable was the lack of smiles. And the whole room, to us, had a general aura of uptightness ... I had a chat with Rosie Boycott, one of the editors of *Spare Rib*, after which the reason for the apparent bad scene became

clearer. The Radical Feminists had arrived (no one still has any idea who invited them) in a flurry of crumpled silk, grubbly [sic] cotton dresses, fur wraps, stilettos and large amounts of make-up. (One of the women present later joked with me that the make-up looked more like war-paint.) The Rad Femmes had taken exception, so it seems, to the fact that many of the women's husbands, boyfriends and male friends were also invited (the gravest sin being that *Spare Rib's* accountant was a man) and that the magazine wasn't a more extremist periodical. They were accused of selling out, and, as is obvious now, must have completely misunderstood the intentions of *Spare Rib*. Which, to me, is to communicate to as many women as possible through information, news and less rigid explanation of women's lib ideas, but without the preaching.

I have been informed by members of the Rad Femmes faction that I should not be writing this piece, as I didn't get to the party till just before 9.30pm. This I take to be an attempt at censorship; maybe they have at last realised what a grave and stupid mistake it was to create such an exhibition of themselves at the party ... at least thirty copies of *Spare Rib* had been torn up by the Rad. Femmes (they haven't got round to burning words yet), someone called someone else a 'cunt', but from which 'side' this abuse came is still unclear as I have heard so many different versions. A guy who is completely out of the game of sexual role playing was abused for being a mere bisexual; one women endured being shouted at for two hours so she could try to understand the grievances of the Rad Femmes, she was unfortunately none the wiser after her attempted indoctrination. Chris Rowley, of *Oz* infamy, thought at the time the best way of showing he had no antagonism towards gays, tried to kiss one of the dragged-up radicals, only to be bitten for his more physical attempt at communication.

After we had been at the party for just over 15 minutes the

real trouble started. This was heralded by some really frightening screaming. What exactly happened is still not clear, but someone either from the *Spare Rib* people or the Rad. Femmes, had had enough and a running fist fight started. This skirmish descended down from the party to the front door of the building, where a two sided screaming match took place. After a while *Spare Rib* people and friends began to reappear, some with cuts and grazes, others with blood running down their faces. Some people said that some of the women had had violence tableaus [sic] enacted out upon them, by members of the Rad. Femmes, but this I haven't been able to verify to my complete satisfaction. Whilst in retreat the Rad. Femmes had managed to take with them the remaining eight bottles of wine, a truly revolutionary protest.

Do the Radical Feminists represent the general direction that Gay Lib is going in? No, they don't. I have spoken to many GLF people since the event, and find that my opinions are shared by many within the movement.[15]

Cloud Downey: The *Spare Rib* affair was that we thought that *Spare Rib* was a very bourgeois organ, very conventional, run by a bunch of very bossy, poncy women. We decided to go and zap their party basically, which we did quite successfully. We were just as disruptive as we possibly could be, dancing on tables, and we all got well drunk as well. We didn't get involved in the fight. I didn't – I kept well away. I actually went out of the building when all that started happening. I've never really been able to cope with violence, I'm so frightened of being hurt myself that I tend to go away as soon as anything like that happens.[16]

Alaric Sumner: I remember walking across from the office across the King's Cross area to 'The Place' and walking in. I was told that the reason we were doing it was because they were advertising lipstick and things in this supposedly feminist magazine and therefore they were a cop-out and it was justifiable for men to go along and disrupt it. I don't remember any disruption or violence. I remember having a drink and standing around and it didn't seem to be a problem, there were people laughing and chatting and arguing excitedly, but I don't personally remember fighting or violence at all.[17]

Mark Roberts: Some famous straight hippy demonstrated his solidarity by French kissing Mick Belsten, who promptly bit him on his tongue. He was someone from some underground publication like *IT* or *Oz*.[18]

Rowley retaliated by trying to throw a punch at Belsten, only to receive one, smack on his nose. Patronising super liberal Rowley with his uncalled for sexual assault on Belsten, had entirely miscalculated.

Accompanying Lemon's piece, Doug Pollard wrote:

Last night I saw some of you at the launching of *Spare Rib*. Last night I saw you behaving like the oppressive chauvinist men you claim to despise, but in fact are yourselves. Last night I saw you deciding what other people should think, how they should behave, what they should say, and when they didn't you turned into a bunch of petulant, aggressive little children, because you couldn't get your way. It would have helped, perhaps, if, instead of screaming for attention like spoilt children, you had told someone what you had decided, what you thought, and what you felt could be done to change it, if it needed changing. It might have helped if you had shown some concern for others, no matter how blind, especially as you were in the company of people who, for the most part, were either gay themselves, or at the very least, not unsympathetic. But as usual the opportunities to create more, to build love, to understand each other, were wasted in favour of violent destruction.

I thought GLF was about love, about people, about life, about freedom, above all, about liberation. Pardon me, I was wrong. I recognise the straight gay ghettos for what they are – something where there would otherwise be nothing, frightened, confined. But I seek to break that confinement, where we can all be what we are and what we wish to be, without oppressing others. You have looked in the ghetto, in fact, you inhabit it more frequently than most other self-styled liberated gays, but you are there in the role of warders. You have come to the conclusion that, if people will not come out of the ghetto, you will build a fence of hate and bitterness about it so that they may rot in a prison of their own creation. Where you will go from there I do not know – perhaps to a final solution of the straight-gay problem, but I will not come with you.

Are you any the less men telling women what to do because you're dressed in frocks? Or are the dresses just the sheeps clothing from the safety of which you can utter your aggression, your chauvinism? How do you know what anyone else wants? Who are you to tell anyone else what they need? Who gave you this wisdom, insight, righteousness? The answer is no-one, because you have none of these things. A Stalin is no less a Stalin because he looks like a moustachioed Mae West. A fuhrer is still a fuhrer in a frock. You do not care for people, because they are neither perfect nor perfectible. You care only for principles, which can be purified. You also reserve to yourselves the right to decide those principles, and to change them at will. Neatly removes everyone but yourselves, doesn't it? You won't fight the society and the prejudices which, whilst you may claim they do not oppress you, oppress and are real to many, many people, gay and straight. It's much more fun fighting the people who were you friends and your lovers, far easier to hurt those who have tried to be open, honest and free with you, than to attack people you never meet, never talk to, and, in the case of straight people, never have any need to relate to.

Can you not see that the words, actions, and manner you employ to achieve whatever you want to achieve, is nothing more than masculine aggression run riot. Can you not see that the only end you have so far turned them to is a cold and loveless destruction of all who refuse to side with you? You are not new, you form no part of any alternative, because you use fear as your weapon, and repression as your tool. You will not frighten people into being liberated, but by the way you behave it is clear that that is what you are trying to do. And in refusing to see these things in yourself you are perpetuating dishonesty and deceit. You are sincere towards others but you lie to yourselves.

And from where came this hatred of straight people, and I say again, PEOPLE … ? Neither you nor I nor anyone else are any better than anyone else. We each have our skills and talents, unless the repression of society has twisted us so far as to render us useless. You didn't chose to be gay, and most of you couldn't chose to be straight – do you think straights are in any way different, except that it's a little bit easier for them? Do you think that the majority of straight men enjoy being dependable fathers, husbands, lovers? We are all oppressed and all brothers in our oppression, no matter how blind to the fact or how obstructive, no matter how frustrating and hurtful it is to see those who ought to be on your side placing themselves on the other, when there isn't even a need for fences.

And on top of this, you have created nothing, Nothing, that is, that is of any use to anyone but your pure little selves in the company of other pure little selves, and even then only within

> your head. What help have you been to the greater body of people who are trapped within the system, whether materially or mentally? What attempts have you made to reach them? How have you tried to understand and communicate? What have you given to someone who may want only a gay club to go to unmolested, and be free of interference and insult? I'll tell you … more insult, and from the only group of people – other gays – to whom he can relate. Where have you made any changes except in your ghetto of ideology and pink-sequins? How does that show others the way forward? How does that prove to someone that he or she is oppressed, if all you do is compound the oppression?
>
> Fascism in a frock has come to GLF. A lie masquerading as a truth, an oppression playing at liberation. Your selfishness and your arrogance are not what GLF is for. GLF no longer exists in any meaningful way whatsoever. You go your way, and those of us who still can love, and know the meaning of the word, will go ours …'[19]

Lemon was right on one thing, the queens did assume *Spare Rib* would be more radical than it was, more in line with *Shrew* published by WLW. But despite those expectations, there is some truth in the radical queens' criticism of its commercialism: it was set up as a limited company with shareholders, just like *Gay News,* and the people involved appeared similarly conventional. However, as things turned out, *Spare Rib* went on to become a collective enterprise, and in terms of mainstream publications for women, *Spare Rib's* content became more radical as time went on. The *Gay News* collective however, some months down the line, caved in to a major wobbly by Lemon who as the prime mover had been keeping up a constant criticism of their work. Having destroyed everyone's confidence and made them feel dependent on him, he manufactured a drama and then emotionally blackmailed them all by walking out and swearing he would never return. Guided perhaps by his chartered accountant sugar-daddy, the fiasco was only resolved by giving in to Lemon's demand for the title and authority of editor, and with it the allocation to him of shares in the company *Gay News* Ltd., which opened the way to his outright ownership of the paper.[20]

There was no reluctance or embarrassment on the part of the radical queens to visit the *Gay News* office just a few days later to describe an extraordinary demonstration they'd been involved in during Gay Pride Week. It was during the telling of their latest adventure that the queens discovered what *Gay News* planned to write about the *Spare Rib* party, which prompted the queens' objection that *Gay News* could not write about events before 9.30 p.m. on that evening because they were not there, which Lemon interpreted as an attempt at censorship. Indeed six months later, in the editorial of *Gay News* 12 entitled 'Your Paper and Gay Lib', they were still flogging the story of that visit to their office.

In the letters column of *Gay News* 4, Leeds GLF reacting to the *Spare Rib* affair and the laughable notion that the radical queens were trying to take over not only GLF but *Gay News* as well, wrote: 'If the London Rad. Femmes are attempting such a takeover they can be assured of our undying opposition. We might add that the behaviour displayed to the sisters working on *Spare Rib* shows a monstrous lack of solidarity.'

Birmingham GLF, however, were not so convinced:

> It does not help any to put down the Radical Feminists in precisely the terms that validate their anger. Your correspondent Simon Manson as well as featured writer Doug Pollard and rather more obliquely Denis Lemon all got at the Radical Feminists because they wore frocks, put on garish make-up and were generally a bit of a sight. That is precisely the language of male chauvinism that the Radical Feminists object to and are put down by. Of course the Radical Feminists don't look 'normal'; of course they are going to affront all

those who cling to rigid definitions of the sex role with their appearance. It is very important indeed to see that this is an absolutely crucial aspect of gay politics. It is not a question of tolerating the Radical Feminists, but of realising two crucial things – one, that we must learn from them, their difficulties and, in fact, remarkable successes in thinking through and acting out what it means to overthrow sex roles; and two, we must see that the affront they are to straight society is a political action in which we are all implicated and from which in the last analysis we shall all benefit.

Postscript [21]

Some thirty inches from my nose
The frontier of my Person goes
And all the untilled air between
Is private *pagus* or demesne.
Stranger, unless with bedroom eyes
I beckon you to fraternise,
Beware of rudely crossing it:
I have no gun, but I can spit.

W H Auden

Chapter 17

Gay Pride and Gay Prejudice

> Let's scream our tits off,
> Let's be silly and shrill.
> Let's throw our falsies -
> Over the hill.
> Bloolips, *Teenage Trash,* lyrics by John Taylor.

The first celebration of Gay Pride in the UK began in London on Friday 23 June 1972 with a dance at Fulham Town Hall, and culminated on International Gay Pride Day, Saturday 1 July with a Carnival Parade from Trafalgar Square to Speakers Corner for a Gay Day in Hyde Park.[1] The week's activities were organized by the GLF Youth & Education Group.

The main event on Tuesday was to join the picket outside the US Embassy protesting against the American war in Vietnam and their bombing of the neutral countries of Cambodia and Laos. Each week a different trade union hosted the demonstration. In Gay Pride week it was the turn of the boilermakers. The combined queenery of Brixton and Notting Hill GLF formed the Oscar Wilde demo and decided to give the Boilermakers a hand.

> *Michael James*: We were allocated a time slot with the Boilermakers Union to picket the American Embassy as part of Troops Out Of Vietnam ... we decided to put our best frocks on for the Boilermakers so we got there all glammed up and there was nothing going on. We stood around for a while and people joined us. We heard some music from Grosvenor Square itself so we went over to investigate. In the middle of Grosvenor Square there's this memorial, I think to American soldiers who've died in both world wars, with very broad

shallow steps and in front of that a huge paved area.

This American school orchestra was standing on these steps and playing. All the office workers and people were standing around the edge of the huge paved area. They were playing show tunes and bits and pieces, so Bette and I decided to have a waltz, or a quickstep or something, so we stepped into the dance floor area and danced around and were joined by other people and then we got the typists up for a dance and they loved it. They thought it was all part and parcel of the orchestra, with balloons and everything. Then the orchestra packed up in a fit of pique. They couldn't deal with it. That left us all high, so we decided to go down to Piccadilly to talk with the rent boys. So the march happened quite spontaneously.

There were between twenty-five and thirty of us, all the local queens living in and around Notting Hill and Colville Terrace. We were the only ones that had turned up. It was the general GLF turn on the picket line, but it was the queens that had turned up. I think we'd decided that we wanted to do it with the Boilermakers; actually, we wanted to meet them – obvious wasn't it? We freaked them out so much, they were invisible, dear. So then we all set off from Grosvenor Square, down through Bond Street, down Piccadilly, in all our finery and laughing and cavorting. We went down into the Underground with a couple of the boys standing there. Some more boys came from nowhere and were all standing round, they loved all this and the police appeared.[2]

Cloud Downey: The thing in Piccadilly Circus, we were all in drag and it was a really humiliating thing to do to people, we actually went into the toilets and shouted about them being closet queens and all these frightened men ran out, because we were there in our cancan petticoats and stilettos, singing and doing the cancan. And encouraging people really loudly to leave the cottages and come out onto the streets. It's not the kind of thing I remember with pleasure, though at the time it seemed like enormous fun. It wouldn't be necessary now, anyway. We were always making statements, you see, we were doing what we felt was right for us and we believed in total outrageousness – the more you threatened the order of things, the more successful it was going to be.[3]

James: So we all fled out of the Lower Regent Street end exit, hotly pursued by these two policemen. There was a big gang of us with rent boys now in tow, so we'd grown and also picked up other queens along Piccadilly, ambling around out for an afternoon or whatever. We fled down the steps and turned left sharply into the ICA, [Institute of Contemporary Arts] as if we'd disappeared off the face of the earth in seconds – the police were some yards behind us and by the time they'd got to the bottom of the steps we were nowhere in sight. The funny thing was the ICA had an exhibition of revolutionary posters and as Stuart pointed out that we *were* the revolution, happening there and then.

So we had a cup of coffee and waited about three quarters of an hour and then we wandered out again and no one was around, so we went through the arch to cross over to Nelson's Column. A couple of people got up and of course there were tourists, it was a photo opportunity and we were sitting there posing and laughing and giggling.

The police came over and said, 'Where were we going?' and we said, 'We're going to Hyde Park.' They said, 'Which way were we going to Hyde Park?' We said, 'Probably up Charing Cross Road and down Oxford Street' and they said 'Okay, we'll escort you.' So we had this amazing impromptu march. It was a few days before Pride … so off we marched … it all fizzled out in Hyde Park.[4]

The day was a triumph for Street Theatre spontaneity; a situationist comedy with every encounter turned to advantage with style and wit. Escaping one set of cops, then having another lot clear a path for our progress to the park turned the demonstration into our own Queens Pride March. The good vibes and Phun we had went to our heads, and a few of us decided that what had happened to us was real news and really important, and the world should know about it, so we stopped off at Paddington on our way home to tell the story to *Gay News*. We jammed our way into Lemon's office, sat on the floor and told our tale. It was while answering questions about our afternoon out that we learnt Lemon's opinion of what he thought had happened at the *Spare Rib* party. Having entered his pokey little office in high good humour we left in disgust.

Simon L Manson, a correspondent for the paper having witnessed our parade wrote a 'letter' inciting queer bashers, published in *Gay News* 2, but printed separately on page 5; not in the 'Your Letters' columns on page 9:

> I saw a mob of grotesque, raddled and over-painted nellies carrying placards and banners proclaiming 'Gay is Angry' as they ambled towards Marble Arch, whooping, jeering, calling out slogans and four-letter words etc., I couldn't help but feel utterly disgusted by their behaviour.
>
> What I wonder, do such people hope to achieve? Were they in anyway sensible they would realise that flaunting themselves through the streets of the capital will only shower further disgrace on all gays and incite more and more youths to go 'queerbashing'.
>
> If the object of *Gay News* is to campaign on behalf of exhibitionists such as these then your battle is completely lost, and you should toss in the towel right away. No self respecting gay would want to concern himself with these drop-outs. They are a menace, not only to gays, but to the

whole of man/woman kind.[5]

I recall very little of the first Gay Pride March. Where I stayed in London is a mystery, crashing around in Notting Hill I imagine. I remember sometime during that weekend meeting Julian Hows at Bette Bourne's flat and being overwhelmed by his youth, his beautiful green eyes, his radical experiences and teenage certainties. I remember arriving at the assembly point of the march near Temple Station, behind the Embankment, and seeing, with some annoyance Michael Mason, who was wearing a straw boater and creased linen jacket selling the first edition of *Gay News* on our parade.

As Tony Reynolds and the Youth Group had organized the Gay Pride March, he would most likely have been the first speaker on the plinth to address us, but I can't remember any of the events there. I recall going up Charing Cross Road where the whistle blowing and chanting changed to booing as we marched past Foyles bookshop, before turning into Oxford Street, where I'm sure we got up the noses of the shoppers and tourists all the way to Marble Arch and into Hyde Park. I do remember that we were very heavily policed up to that point, but that they left us with smaller numbers as we spread out on the grass. We played all the usual games which included a mass kiss-in with some serious snogging, just so people could see us doing it and to deliberately upset the police. Of course not everybody was able to exhibit deep tongue probing, but there were lots of hugs and kisses and giggling going on as well.

Lisa Power says there had been talk of how few members of CHE came on the march, but I don't think we expected any beyond the usual suspects as they were terrified of being openly gay in public, and especially of being identified with such a provocative motley throng. If *Gay News* appealed to anyone, its readership were the members of CHE, the more closeted gay men Simon L. Manson was pitching his story to, who were seized with panic at the sight of anything obvious. A Gay Pride March and public celebration of homosexuality was not for them in 1972, but with the demise of GLF, something they would later take over (like the wreath laying ceremony in Whitehall) once they were sure they had control and would not be embarrassed by people who they feared might dress or act 'inappropriately'.

In the late 1980s The Party in the Park, where money and status was involved was much more to the taste of CHE membership. That event could always have been free in London if just ten per cent of the profits on the rip-off, price-top-up of drinks in the ghetto bars had been donated to the event, but for their fawning attitude to the mafia. Instead, the West End group of club and pub owners were allowed to treat Pride as just another profit making opportunity. By then CHE members were running Pride as a closed shop, ultimately leading in the 90s to obscenities such as VIP Champagne Tents and rip-off Pride Arts Festivals where large funds set aside for the first time to pay gay artists just disappeared, leaving great holes in the accounts that were never explained by the treasurer or the Chair who decamped to San Francisco. The mainly straight musicians playing on the main stage were paid sizeable fees termed expenses; the LGBT artists performing there, particularly in the cabaret tent, did so for free with their expenses treated as a donation.

In 1986 Bloolips topped a one-night fund raising bill at the Shaw Theatre. The show involved six performers and one technician, took two weeks of solid rehearsals to put together, and raised £2,000. This sum was given to the Pride Committee, who paid that amount to Sandy Shaw to cover her expenses for appearing on the main stage. Time spent rehearsing had cost the artists £3,000. In 1978 Bloolips was banned from appearing at Gay Pride because their non-sexist, jargon free comedy *The Ugly Duckling*, in which swans came out on top, was deemed 'too political'. The censorship proved London's loss, however, it allowed Bloolips to accept a Dutch COC invitation to perform on their stage in Vondel Park for Amsterdam Pride, a gig that led to tours of Holland, Belgium, Germany, Italy, Scandinavia, the USA and Canada.

But then the first Gay Pride in London commenced in disarray. John Chesterman's Gay *International News* published from his 'fervently painted red revolutionary office', with a little help from Angus Shields' artwork and Geoff Marsh's typesetting skills, surveyed the first celebration:

> Gay Pride Week in London brought about an uneasy alliance between factions which have been in open conflict recently. The 'radical feminists' in glittering gender-fuck drag, glared defiance at the 'straight' gays as they marched beside them through London, on Saturday 1st July, or danced beside them the night before at Fulham Town Hall. At Hyde Park, after the 1,500 strong march, they separated into groups to engage the straight tourists and sight-sears in their own forms of confrontation and dialogue. The lesbians, too, for the first time since their break with the main organisation were marching with the GLF in splendid face paint and under the banner of the Women's Gay Liberation Front.
>
> The 'radical feminists', based mainly on the Camden GLF (see last *GIN*). Have been applying increasing pressure on the rest of the organisation to abandon what they regard as their conformist 'liberal' attitude in favour of a real attempt to explore the possibilities of an alternative sexuality. They believe in the release of the femininity suppressed within all men, and accept the inevitable confrontation with the straight world, and, more painfully, the movement itself. During Gay Pride Week, for instance they had travelled the London Underground trains in full drag offering the passengers refreshments and conversation. Reactions to the 'tube hostesses' was reported to be of surprise and interest.

The real internal confrontations had started two weeks earlier, when the GLF offices were taken over by them. Notice boards and other 'bureaucratic symbols' were stripped out and the wall decorated in runny rainbows of spray paint and graffiti. The group which had previously been running the office were abruptly ejected, and the 'feminists' took over. Shortly after this, they appeared at the smart opening party for the new women's magazine *Spare Rib*, and, in front of the 'underground establishment' accused the editors of triviality and commercialisation. Attempts were made to throw them out, tempers were lost, loud (and sexist) insults were shouted, glasses were broken and one of the women from *Spare Rib* was assaulted. The following day, when the hysteria had calmed, it was predictably revived by the national press dramatising the incident and quoting the editor of the new *Gay News*, who described them as 'the Charles Mansons of GLF.'[6] There were angry protests at the *Gay News* offices, which were later dismissed by the staff as 'rather boring, really.'

The situation is yet to be resolved. On one side is the feeling that the aggression and 'extremes' of the 'feminists' endangers the efforts to bring something more than just a fragment of the homosexual population into the movement, and build up its strength. On the other side is the conviction that the compromise involved is not only unnecessary but is reinforcing the ghetto situation by encouraging complacent sexual role-playing and avoiding the main issues. Although both sides believe in the concept of homosexuals 'coming out', it is clearly on quite different terms. They are both taking up intransigent attitudes, and both are claiming that the others are sabotaging the ideals of the Gay Liberation Front.[7]

Within a matter of days the radical queens went from ejecting volunteers from the office and 'offering violence tableaux' at the *Spare Rib* party to assaulting a woman member of staff. Such are the Chinese whispers on the gay media grapevine: shoddy investigation endlessly repeated because it's in print, and in this case Chesterman confusing the radical queens with the radical feminist men.

> *Jeffrey Weeks*: The increasing isolation of GLF from the gay community in mid 1972 led to an increasing tone of hysterical heresy-hunting, as the 'radical queens', by this time the dominant elements, lashed out at any reformist tendencies, attacking for instance, the founders of *Spare Rib* for selling out the feminist cause, and physically attacking members of the GLF office collective and sellers of *Gay News*.[8]
>
> The climax for me was the Gay Pride demo in '72 when there was a real tension between the radical fairies and the others who regarded themselves as revolutionaries. I had really fallen out with people like Bette Bourne and Stuart Feather and it was the worst sort of sectarianism. It cured me for life of sectarianism because it was like a religious divide. It wasn't just different nuances in a movement, it was like different groups with different access to the truth.
>
> But for me the crunch point was that Gay Pride March …There were lots of rows preceding it and there were lots of arguments on the march itself between those who were in radical drag and those who weren't. There were also rows between the radfems and the *Gay News* people. It was all very unhappy and gave people like myself a sense that the heart had gone out of it. There was no longer a Gay Liberation Front, gay liberation was becoming much more dispersed … which was the logic of the time but we resisted it.[9]

From such an authority these criticisms have a serious ring, until one remembers that the Marxists were just another sectarian group within GLF who were in their own exclusivity, isolated within the Front. But shoddy investigation and analysis has an agenda as mentioned earlier, when the critics are the elite and their objects are the led, it becomes class-based antagonism: borrowing straight-gay hysteria to vilify opponents.

If we radical queens had become the dominant element in GLF at this time, it didn't feel like it. What with the Marxist needing to keep faith with the straight left and its emphasis on direct attacks on Capitalism and class politics by discrediting our position of attacking gender roles and sexism, and the straight gays needing to vilify us with one-sided, distorted stories broadcast all over the country in order to sell their newspapers and carve out a community of readers they would protect from the horrors of drag queens feminists, we felt more like the victims. Moreover the visible gay community in 1972 was simply the membership of GLF.

Of all the times and places, it was the Gay Pride Grand Ball at Fulham Town Hall where Michael James and I met with some trouble, and on his part a momentary loss of temper, that Jeffrey Weeks seized on as another opportunity to condemn radical queenery. What we went through was just another hassle, until we were accused of beliefs so insulting it became a memory that neither of us will ever forget.

We were coming out of the ballroom in our disco drag as David Seligman, looking distraught, came up the marble staircase from the street. I don't think either of us had ever exchanged more than a couple of words with him before, but we immediately went up to him and asked him what was wrong. He told us he had been attacked by skinheads in the street who wanted to get in to the dance. Our indignation aroused; James and I went down to the door to investigate and found a lad of sixteen or seventeen with cropped hair and boots who was quickly joined by a gang of about eight others, none of them aged more than twenty. They were surprised at the sight of us, but we played it very casual and relaxed and said, 'Hi, how you doing, what's happening?' Apparently they'd all been in the fish and chip shop over the road and decided that one of the guys in the queue was a poofter and started taunting him by asking to see his willy. In the end the guy got annoyed and did just that, before getting out of the shop and running back into the Town Hall with them chasing after him. As we tried to get the story straight, two policemen sidled up and stood behind the gang. Once we got the picture, I said 'Well, what did you expect when you kept demanding to see his cock? Why were you offended? Wasn't it big enough?' We had them all laughing, including the filth, and all their anxiety forgotten, when suddenly from behind us Tony Salvis, Martin Corbett and Max McLellan appeared shouting 'All right, we'll deal with this. Off you go, you two', and immediately all our work was undone by their aggressive, macho stupidity.

James and I went back upstairs annoyed by the posturing straight-gay brutishness, and seeing Seligman near where we left him said 'What was all that about? They weren't after you – it was someone in the fish shop they were after. Why did you say they'd tried to attack you? Why lie about it?' His reply was to accuse us of being anti-Semitic. I shall never forget that moment; we were completely gobsmacked, my mind in a whirl thinking of all my Jewish boyfriends and totally unable to reply because I knew what that would sound like. James replied by pulling the copies of *Gay News* from Seligman's hands and tossing them into the air whilst stalking off to the bar. I followed as Seligman scrabbled along the floor picking up the papers.

In *Gay News* 3 Doug Pollard wrote:

> Increasing Violence Against Gays: *What are We Going* To Do About It?
>
> Gay Lib hold regular dances in London, and most of them nowadays are at Fulham Town Hall. They are openly advertised and open to all – and this combination of factors has led to trouble which may mean the end of dances at Fulham.

One guy in drag standing at the entrance to the hall when some of these kids come by and start to make fun of him. 'You a fellah? Show us your cock then!' So, entering into the spirit of things, he does. They then try to start a fight – because he flashed his cock in front of 'their' girls (jealous, perhaps?).

The following week there are groups of little 'toughs' hanging round outside the hall. With the previous week's incidents in mind, someone calls the police to move them away. A squad car, complete with uniformed inspector, arrives and shoos them away. They then park discreetly nearby. Three guys leave for the station, and as they cross the road, the gang reappears. Two run, one of them decided to make a stand; he received one severely blacked eye, and a cut needing four stitches just under the other. One of the gang has a sleeve torn from his coat, another, a lapel. At this late stage, the same squad car reappears, and the gang hastily departs. The police display their usual zeal in pursuing the formalities, but do not purse the gang. 'They are about to leave when the opportunity for the clearest description possible arises – the gang reappears. They are pointed out to the police, who question them, but let them go … 'They say they just got off the bus.' – in spite of their clearly damaged clothing. The police then leave, and our friend goes to hospital to have his face stitched.

In order to make sure the coast is clear, someone takes a walk to make sure the gang has gone. They haven't gone very far – they are apparently laughing and joking with the policemen. In anger he shouts out – to the effect that 'these pigs are supposed to protect people, and here they are having a laugh with the ones who caused all the trouble.' In a flash he is surrounded by policemen, and arrested for insulting behaviour and breach of the peace – surrounded by so many policemen that they can't all fit into the squad car, and some of them are detailed to hoof it back to the station.

The *South London Press* reported:

Trouble outside 'gay' dance.

Trouble outside Fulham town hall where a Gay Liberation Front dance had been held, which ended in the arrest of a youth, was described to the West London magistrates.

Anthony Reynolds (21), a cleaner of Martindale Road., Balham, was found guilty and fined £5 for threatening behaviour.

The public gallery was filled with men some wearing 'drag' and with their faces heavily painted. An envelope containing the fine was passed by one of the men to Reynolds as he left the dock after conviction.

Sgt. Merphyn Sault said that he saw a group of men at the town hall entrance some of whom were in long evening dresses and wearing make-up. On the other side of the road was a large group of youths who were being moved along by police. Heavy traffic was at a standstill.

Sgt. Sault added that he saw Reynolds, dressed in trousers, shirt and leather tasselled waistcoat and wearing eye make-up, move to the edge of the pavement. He shouted at the youths on the opposite side of the road, 'You — —- b— — —s'. His right arm was raised and his fist was clenched.

Reynolds, wearing a three-quarter-length white cardigan bearing a blue floral design and with his eyes heavily made up said that at a previous dance youths had been out for a bit of fun – queer bashing. The dance was organised by the Gay Liberation Front. 'They came to the door and we went out to try to talk to them. A member of the Gay Liberation Front who had left the dance was beaten up and had to have four stitches,' he said. 'The police were called and he was asked who did it. He could not see them in the vicinity. One of them got off a bus. The boy was pointed out to them, but no action was taken which obviously made us very annoyed. When I came out I

> saw police officers laughing and joking with the boys who had beaten up somebody from the dance. Naturally I was annoyed. I shouted words to the effect 'Look there's one of them. He is laughing and joking with them – British justice.'
>
> Reynolds said he did not use the expression 'You ———- b———s.'
>
> After Reynolds called three witnesses who gave corroborative evidence the magistrate found the charge proved.[10]

But if for Jeffrey Weeks that first Gay Pride Week spelt the dispersal of gay liberation, it was only for some. For the Marxists and Maoists it was the bitter end because their ideology had left them nowhere to go, but for others still developing their tactics, much remained to be discovered.

In the early summer of 1972 a house share was arranged by Cloud Downey and the others he was working with in the Office Collective. The house they rented was in Athlone Road, Brixton, a few minute's walk from the local school, Tulse Hill Comprehensive. It wasn't long before their house became a focus for the students, particularly one of its senior pupils, but also the neighbours in the surrounding houses, the school authorities, the *South London Press* and the police.

> *Cloud Downey*: A bunch of us were working in the GLF office and that's how we knew each other basically. There was Alaric, there was Ken Grant, Paul Sewell who was a Canadian guy – there were several of us – Nigel Kemp. We were active in GLF and a lot of us were having difficulty living where we were – expensive accommodation, trouble with landlords – and we thought why don't we try and get a place together, not with the idea of it being a full commune, but we were just going to share a house. We went to a number of accommodation agencies; most of them we got a bad reaction from because we turned up in full-fig with our feathers and gowns and jewels

and make-up, and most of them slammed the door in our faces, but eventually we found one which purported to be an alternative letting agency and they were a bit taken aback, but they did give us a few places to go and see. The only one that was at all possible was Athlone Road, Brixton. For affordability and size it was fine and we took it. So we paid a deposit and it was a monthly rental and it was going to be shared by the five of us. And it was great from then on really ... It was never intended to be a full commune, and then everything developed from there. It was very organic you know, people came over and stopped, then they moved in, and then we were putting extra mattresses on the floor and we realised that the five of us was ten, and then there were twelve of us.

Everybody got to know about us and it was a constant party, there were always people staying over, people popping in any time, helped us with things, helped us set the place up and in the early days it was wonderful before the trouble started. It was absolutely wonderful. Great! We thought we'd cracked it: we had a lovely big garden, people could stay over, we had a cooking rota, everything was going well. We used to drop acid every Saturday night. Every night was a party.

We were also a focus for organising demos and zaps and all the things we were doing in those days. We became a kind of political hub for all activities. People used to come round and have meetings to set up demos, and it wasn't just us, it was other left groups; the local women's group might come round, just to borrow the place for a meeting. It wasn't just our home, we actually had one room which was set aside for meetings, and people could use that and we just used to ask them for a small donation for the upkeep of the house.

Then Julian appeared; he was a schoolboy and he moved in with us. There was no sense of us persuading Julian – he came and asked us 'Can I please come and live with you, 'cos I feel safe here.' Because he was having a hard time in school and from his parents and from everybody. We said 'Of course you can, why not?' We didn't realise there'd be any comeback at all; he was just another unhappy guy that we could welcome into our presence, but it became a terrible scandal because he was under age and the school knew us, and the school knew he was living with us; everybody knew.[11]

Julian Hows: I'd been one of the leaders of a National Union of School Students demo. The NUSS was run by this cute politico. I had him. He was so bound up in really bad class politics and he wasn't very out. We closed down the school for a day and went on this march he'd organised. The night before the march, I'd been round to his flat ... [for sex] and then on the march I'd gone up and he ignored me. I was very upset and hurt. The South London section of the march only got as far as County Hall, I was carrying a copy of *Lord Dismiss Us* by Simon Raven and wearing John Lennon glasses, a 'Free Angela Davis' badge and a GLF badge I'd picked up. I got pushed up from the crowd to speak on the platform and I encouraged them to sit in at ILEA [Inner London Educational Authority] in County Hall and got arrested by DI John Bateman for causing affray or something. They'd arrested me on a private road, so I refused to recognise their arrest and wouldn't tell them my name for six hours. So my mother had had acres of trouble with me.[12]

The other group who organized the strike of over 4,000 school children was the Schools Action Union who rallied around six demands: no school uniform, no canning, no detentions, schools not prisons, no victimization, rules to be decided by the whole school.

Downey: We went to the school play. They were doing this play and Julian told us about it and encouraged us to come and to dress up as much as we liked. So we went along and put on the most extraordinary things we could find. We were done up like opera singers, huge dresses and tiaras and furs and long gloves, dripping jewellery and one of the men who went was dressed as Princess Margaret. We walked in and the place was in uproar. They stopped the play eventually and asked us to leave because of the uproar. People were yelling at us and throwing things at us. I was very glad to get away. Actually, it was very nasty, there were only four of us against all these South London mums and dads and the kids themselves could be really heavy. So after that I had nothing more to do with anything about the school. I didn't enjoy it at all, and if I had my time over I would never do it now. But at the time I was all for it and thought it was a great idea.[13]

We hadn't technically done anything illegal but we caused an awful lot of upset. I mean the neighbours actually had guns, they had pellet rifles and they were shooting at us. We were labelled perverts, paedophiles. The usual. Real hostility. The Brixton papers every day were full of lurid and mostly untrue stories about us having wild sex parties and drug orgies which was true to a degree, but nothing like the extent that ... we were just having a good time – and the fact that our clothesline was full of women's underwear – which it never was; it might have had the odd frock hanging off or a pair of tights. We never had women's underwear, there were all these exaggerations making us look like we were those filthy awful perverts ... And then it escalated and they started breaking windows. We had to barricade the house; we were piling furniture up against the windows, and wardrobes against the front door to stop people coming in.[14]

Alaric Sumner: I remember that the first occasions when the kids from the school came round, they were the younger kids and they came in to see the clothes and the make-up and whatever and just to find out who we were, to talk to us. I remember on one occasion they were trying to decide which of us was the most good-looking – all very relaxed. They were eight or nine year olds and it was fine and we got on okay with them. But the next day their older brothers came round. There were about twenty fifteen to seventeen year olds. The bell rang and I answered it. Naively (I was just nineteen), I just continued what we had been doing previously … I let them in to see our clothes and talk. I took them upstairs. Since there had been no trouble with the younger kids, I didn't think of danger. Nigel was downstairs in the kitchen.

After some talk, one of them said to me, 'You don't think I'm going to hit you with this milk bottle.' I felt strangely calm and I said something like 'I think it's quite possible but it seems completely irrelevant.' Somebody else spoke and I turned, which meant that when he hit me the bottle shattered on my forehead and cut the bridge of my nose. If I hadn't turned it might have cut my eyes. And then they all ran downstairs and vanished. I walked downstairs with blood pouring from my face to find the police in the open doorway.

There were two policemen and the first thing that one said was 'What were you doing to that boy to make him hit you?' I was absolutely outraged and the other policeman apologised. He started trying to persuade me to have an identity parade at the school to find the culprit … GLF theory at the time was that you shouldn't use oppressive state mechanisms such as the police and that the kids were only playing out their oppressive conditioning and therefore punishment through the state system would be counterproductive, so I refused. When they left I went to hospital … I must have gone back that night … I remember bricks coming in through the windows and glass falling, the curtains preventing it flying across the room.[15]

Bette Bourne: I remember the day I went over to the Brixton commune when they were having trouble with the local schoolboys, and they came past the house and yelled, 'Hello girls!' and we rushed out in our frocks, ran down the street after them, frightened the shit out of them and chased them back into the school yard, yelling, 'Don't you give us any more fucking trouble.' They'd been as stroppy as they could be and it was getting out of hand. It was like something from Mars coming at them. Men in make-up and drag, was something they had no concept of at all, nor how to deal with it.[16]

Hows: Kids were going round and throwing bricks through their windows and taunting them in the street and so on. And this was all happening in breaks and lunch hours. So I thought, as the vice head of one of the houses at the school and a school prefect, this is not on. I went to the deputy head and said this was not on. They were telling me that what pupils did outside of school they had no control over, and I said, 'That's not quite true is it? Because if it was the local shop that was getting it, you'd have two teachers posted outside.' He said, 'Well, pupils below the sixth form aren't allowed outside the school gates during break,' and I said, 'Yes, but we all know it goes on and when we've had trouble before, teachers would stand outside the chip shop or the newsagents or whatever.' He said, 'This is not a commercial establishment and they ought to get the police round.' He refused to put two people on the gate leading out to their house. So there was a bit of an uptight scene.

So I went round to see Cloud and Alaric Sumner and Ken, Richard and others. I got very upset that I couldn't do anything about it but they said, that's all right because we're going to do something about it. A few days later, a whole bevy of people came down and spent the night in the house and printed leaflets to distribute in the school the next day. I told them how to get into the school and where the headmaster's study was and all that. I spent the night before this event in a room with fifteen queens sleeping on sleeping bags on the floor and was told that I had to sleep on the sofa. This was their thing, because I was obviously jail bait. They were very, very sweet and it was, 'Look, don't touch.' So I had to put up with the sight of Bette Bourne and Tim Clark fucking like bunny rabbits about three feet away, with me lying there like the virgin queen on a cut moquette sofa, because they didn't want to take advantage of me. I thought, 'fuck that, Mary!'

The next day we went into the playground and started handing out leaflets with all these demented queens. The police had arrived before that though, and I had decided, sod it, I was going to blow all these hypocritical queens that I'd had sex with – these teachers – I was going to tell the police. They came along and said, 'So sonny, what are you doing with these people then?' And I said, 'I'm one of them.' 'But aren't you a school pupil?' 'Yes I'm a school pupil as well.' 'Well, what are you doing with these homosexuals?' 'There's more homosexuals in that fucking school than there are out here.' 'What do you mean?' 'I could tell you all their names' – and I went to pull out a list of all of them because I'd written them all down and I was going to do what we'd now call outing: I thought, 'fuck that!' And Michael James grabbed the piece of paper off me and ate it, while he was smiling at the police officer. He said to me, 'That's not nice.'

So we went into the school and handed out all these leaflets and then in the best traditions of liberalism they said, 'Perhaps you'd like to discuss this with the headmaster.' The kids were going mad. They herded all these queens into the administration block and put them downstairs. Now downstairs all there was, was the caretaker and some medical rooms. Upstairs was the head's office and so on, the staff common room and so on. As a pupil you weren't allowed to walk up those stairs without being invited. I heard one of the school-keepers, who I'd knocked off once or twice at a cottage in Brixton, announce very loudly, I think so we could hear, 'So you want me to call the police?' I couldn't believe what they were doing, I told them but everybody didn't quite want to believe me, they thought I was just being an overexcited, hyperactive child.

So I walked out and found the headmaster and told him he was disgusting and that he ought to be ashamed of himself and that he was a bastard and various other things – that he was calling the police to these people and not actually going to talk to them at all, was he? We had a furious stand-up row witnessed by lots of people and then of course the police arrived and escorted everybody off the premises.[17]

The leaflet the radical queens handed out in the school yard stated:

WE ARE GAY AND PROUD OF IT AND WE ARE STAYING

We are gay men living in Athlone Road.

We do, and dress, and have sex, and are what we want to be, which is nice for us and doesn't affect you.

Anyone who has met us knows, we are into talking with anyone. We start no trouble, no arguments. We just are.

Since we moved in, we've had shouts, bricks, two of us have been hit with bottles, most of the windows and the doors have been broken in.

We've also had a lot of support. We know a lot of you are on our side.

WE ARE NOT BEING DRIVEN OUT BY A FEW CONFUSED UP-TIGHT PEOPLE TRYING TO LOOK BIG.

We are here and we're staying. We are not taking no more shit.

We've had enough. From now on, any trouble, and we'll answer back – like yesterday and like today.

We're not going to use the school, or the police. We don't believe in them any more than you do.

We'll do it ourselves – and there are a lot of us. We have a lot of friends. Today there are dozens, next time there'll be hundreds. We believe in talking, in friendship, in understanding each other, and we'll talk to anyone anywhere – on your grounds or ours.

But we won't talk to those who attack us. We will attack back.

And there are a large number of us.

We are very strong,

Because we love each other.[18]

The story of the playground leafleting was the lead item in the twice weekly *South London Press*, which included the text of the leaflet except for the line, 'We are here and we're staying. We are not taking no more shit.' The next edition of the newspaper made the invasion the subject of their editorial:

> The un-gay intervention at Tulse Hill comprehensive school last week by a thirty-strong band of Gay Liberationists is hardly likely to attract much public sympathy for the Gay Liberation Movement or, for that matter, improve tolerance for those homosexuals in this country who strive to lead quiet, unassuming lives despite the strain of always knowing that they are exposed to physical and mental risks not shared by heterosexuals.
>
> The Gay Liberationists live in a commune near the school and flaunt, rather than disguise the fact that they are not as other men. They dress either extravagantly or as transvestites, many wear heavy women's make-up, and the washing hanging on the line at the back of the house where they live makes no pretence at being other than predominantly women's underwear.

It is hardly surprising that they quickly found themselves the target of attack and abuse from the schoolboys, who are not given to much soul-searching in seeking out victims of prejudices largely inherited from their parents.

A head-on clash looks likely. There have been enough attacks on Clapham Common, and other areas where homosexuals congregate, to know that this kind of violence is appalling, and it is understandable that the prospective victims are now showing signs of counter-attacking.

But if the boys of Tulse Hill are to be persuaded to learn how to be civilised, it would help if the Gay Liberationists would conduct themselves a little less provocatively.

It might help, too, if the Gay Liberationists made it clear that they are only seeking sexual and social toleration and are not pursuing a political line with schoolboys.

The Gay Liberation Front has a fringe interest in the New Left Trotskyist revolutionaries and the fact that their leaflet tells the boys, 'We're not going to use the school or the police, we don't believe in them any more than you do,' seems to indicate that they favour pupil power.[19]

Downey: It became that bad we were frightened of going to sleep. That's when we decided we've got to move out of here. People had actually been injured, people had been shot in the leg; a couple were attacked with broken bottles. We could have been killed. I don't think people realised how desperate the situation was, and then suddenly it dawned on us; we've got to get out. It was mainly Ken and I who decided that. We said, 'We're going. You can do what you like, but we're not staying here; we're frightened,' and of course once we'd made the decision everyone came with us.[20]

Hows: I was expelled for being a corrupting influence upon the younger pupils; that was the official phraseology in a letter to

> my mother. I begged him to rescind his decision not to give me a reference for any school that had pupils in it under the age of sixteen, because with the A levels I was doing, I needed a school and not a tech. So that was the end of my education, though in some ways it was really the beginning.[21]

The trial of the Stoke Newington 8 commenced at the Old Bailey on 30 May 1972. Jim Greenfield, John Barker, Anna Mendleson, and Hillary Creek of 359 Amhurst Road were charged with possession of arms, ammunition and explosives, attempted explosions and conspiracy to cause explosions, Christopher Bott, Stuart Christie, Kate McLean and Angela Weir with conspiracy to cause explosions, and for Christie possession of detonators. '"This is not a political trial", said Mr Justice James,'[22] before questioning potential jurors on their political allegiance.

John Barker, Anna Mendleson, and Hillary Creek defended themselves. The others were represented by counsel.

> The most significant area of questioning covered the details of what happened to the four, [living at Amhurst Road] during the raid. The police witnesses stated, and the defence agreed, that as soon as they came in through the front door they arrested Jim and Anna and whisked them off to Albany Police Station. In their cross-examination of the police officers, John and Hillary put to them that they were both taken out of the flat for several minutes for no apparent reason – only to be returned and to be confronted with the arms and explosives. Both accused the police of planting the 'evidence' while they were outside.
>
> The police insisted that John and Hillary were not taken out of the flat until after the guns and explosives were found, though they agreed that they were taken out of the flat for several minutes and then taken back upstairs. Police claimed 'they had forgotten' the sequence of events 'and could only

> remember it by reference to officer Gillam's notebook.' D.C. Doyle told the court in cross-examination that he, Gillam and Davis sat down in the kitchen and 'decided'(!) what had happened in the raid. Doyle insisted that his 'tongue had slipped' and that they had only sat around and 'discussed it'. These officers agreed that despite many, many raids between the arrest of Jake Prescott in February and this raid in August, they gathered no concrete 'evidence' until this raid, and then they got everything they wanted.
>
> A fingerprint officer D.I. Godfrey was called and asked if there was any explanation for why there were *no* fingerprints on the guns and explosives, could only come up with the reason that that the 'atmosphere was rather greasy'.

Much of the police evidence has changed – and new evidence has 'emerged' since committal [at Lambeth magistrates in January]. When it became obvious that if what they were saying about the position of the arms and explosives was true, then they would have seen it as soon as they stepped in the main room of the flat (they said originally that they hadn't seen it until ten minutes after entering the flat), they suddenly introduced some clothes, which they explained, had kept the gelignite hidden for the initial ten minutes that they were searching the flat.

Another police officer – D.S. Hopgood – admitted after lengthy cross-examination that they had actually altered his notebook recording the position of the detonators in the flat after committal, when it became clear to him that he had made 'a mistake' ('it was a mistake, sir, a perfectly innocent mistake', he insisted, over and over again) about the original position of the detonators.[23]

Major Yallop, the prosecution explosives expert from Woolwich Arsenal, had his evidence on the types of bomb materials used in the associated set of 27 explosions the accused were allegedly responsible for torn to shreds by the defence explosives expert Col. Sands. Reluctant though he was to go against a fellow officer and the Crown's contentions, he stuck to scientific methodology and exposed Yallop's facts as mere opinion. As did Anna Mendleson who cross-examined Yallop after he commented that it was 'extremely fortunate that no one was killed or seriously injured in any of the explosions.'

> Mendleson: Would you say that it was in fact a miracle that no one was killed or injured?
>
> Yallop: Yes, I would say that it was a miracle.
>
> Mendleson: Mr. Yallop, could you tell the court, what is the statistical probability for there to exist an associated set of 27 miracles?
>
> Yallop: Ah ... em ... no, I don't think I could.[24]

Michael Mansfield summing up for Angela Weir laid bare the fact that three handwriting experts had said different things about the same pieces of prosecution evidence. Seven witnesses, all virtually unchallenged, had stated that on 19 August 1971, the day she was accused of travelling to France to purchase explosives, she had attended a GLF demonstration in London. If Commander Bond had been convinced that Weir was the girl in the photograph on the travel document, why had he waited for two raids in which nothing was found, and three months to go by before charging her? If Bond had been sure, why hadn't the card been fingerprinted?

In his summing up Judge James completely ignored the Crown's total reliance on the foot high piles of documents stacked on the prosecutor's desk covering the groups' research into housing conditions and the squatting movement and used as political evidence against them, and repeated his statement made at commencement: '"This is not a political trial. Political trials are trials of people for their political beliefs which happen to be contrary to those in government. We do not have them in this country."'[25] The trial ended on 6 December having become the longest in British legal history.

> The verdict returned by the jury after two and a half days represented a compromise and a shoddy one at that. How it worked out we don't know; but we have heard information that on the Tuesday morning when they returned to court to ask James a question about the supposed find of arms, ammunition and explosives at Amhurst Road they were split 7 – 5 for conviction. Indeed at eleven on Wednesday morning the jury foreman simply said 'No' when James asked him if the jury could make their minds up about anything.
>
> But at 5.15 in the afternoon they did. It was a majority decision on the charges of the first four, but this was coupled with a plea for leniency. The foreman said that it was a majority verdict on all decisions except counts 2 and 3 (attempted explosions) where they had been unanimous in acquittal.
>
> At sentencing James said that because of the plea, he had cut 5 years off the total he was going to give. He then made 10 years for conspiracy the all round sentence on Jim Greenfield, John Barker, Anna Mendleson and Hillary Creek, and reduced Jake Prescott's sentence from 15 years to 10.[26]

Chris Bott, Stuart Christie, Kate McLean and Angela Weir were acquitted.

Rather than prosecuting Commander Bond and Chief Superintendant Habershon for their wicked conspiracies of planting detonators on Christie, and conspiring to arrange the false evidence of Mr 'A' and Mr 'B' against Prescott, both were promoted.

> *Cloud Downey*: When we decided to leave Tulse Hill, we went up to Bette's to stay and with other people around the Gate.

> And we realised that there was this big empty house opposite [42, Colville Terrace] that nobody seemed to know much about, a grand house with a flat roof and balconies. It had been bought by the Notting Hill Housing Trust who were going to convert it into flats for people on the waiting list, but they didn't have the money so it was just standing there for a long time. Tim Bolingbroke lived next door and Rex Lay and Gabrielle, so we went in. No gas, no electric, no water, but we managed. That was one of the happiest periods of my life in there. It was a much more bohemian neighbourhood. We had a few problems on the streets getting yelled at by drunks and kids but nobody threatened our home there.[27]

The commune occupied the ground and first floor at 42, and was made up of Nigel Kemp, Louis Rabkin, Alaric Sumner, Tim Bolingbroke, and Julien Hows, who were joined by Mick Belsten, John Church, Stephen Crowther and Nicholas Bramble. Bette Bourne was living in his flat opposite and visited us every day. Cloud and his lover Ken decided they wanted to be a monogamous couple, and with the commune's permission withdrew to live separately in the converted attics on the fourth floor. The second floor was occupied by Joyce Maving, an older woman and Cliff her younger lover, who had been living on the streets as a couple, rather than accept being split up by social services as a first condition for receiving assistance.

> *Julien Hows*: I left home, packed my bags and disappeared off to Colville Terrace in which most of the Brixton Queens had ended up. That was opposite where Bette lived and two doors from that was David Hockney's lover who used to invite us to tea and send up food parcels.[28]

> *Stephen Crowther*: I met Rex who was at St. Martin's and he introduced me to Bette who lived across the road, and I ended

up staying on Bette's sofa and sharing Bette's room there for a while before moving in with the commune when number 42 was occupied.

I remember being absolutely besotted with everybody and their lifestyle and I just loved the anarchic romance of it. It was just people all over the whole neighbourhood. There were people up and down the road that I used to know or was on nodding terms with. Peter Schlesinger lived down the road. Manolo Blahnic was down the road. I remember this one night I went out with Mick Belsten and Hugh Twissle, and we cemented an engraved copper plate to the middle of this big plate glass window of this estate agents in Westbourne Grove. It said 'Eat The Rich' engraved on it, and it was this cement which… it was only a small plate but it meant the whole window would have had to be removed to get rid of it. And I painted 'Eat The Rich' down the side of a Black Rolls Royce parked outside a house... I just thought it was wonderful and so exciting, and I hadn't… I didn't think of the consequences of what I was doing, I just had a big crush on Hugh and it was like – just going out and having kicks and being really naughty.[29]

Alaric Sumner: The commune – it was stressful. Talk about PC! The moral insistence upon revolutionary codes of behaviour was very interestingly extreme. It was fighting in a very fearsome and unstructured but dogmatic way to be free. There was certainly a lot of 'you ought to wear dresses, you ought to deconstruct your masculinity – and if you don't, you're an enemy of the revolution.' I find it very difficult to pin down exactly what my position was to that, because when I look back to it I seem to have floated around in relation to it all, taking sides by my actions but not inside. Obviously I was interested in the deconstruction of gender, obviously I was interested in the actions we were doing, but I certainly always

> felt that there was something oppressive about the way it was sometimes being done. And again, some of the drug stuff was quite insistent, that you ought to take it because this was the way to achieve understanding … Not everybody took acid when I was around, that was apparently later, but I remember the only time I took acid was a half tab. I can't say I was bullied into taking it, but there was a certain amount of pressure. I think encouraged is the word.[30]

Sumner only stayed in the commune at 42 for a couple of weeks before finding himself a bed-sit.

Aubrey Walter and Richard Dipple brought out an article in the Camden GLF newsletter called 'The Frock Brigade' in which they renounced their experiment of wearing drag and denounced the radical queens' demand for men to wear drag as a 'tyranny'.It was a parting shot I think, as the Maoists withdrew to Camden. Tim Bolingbroke who had first come out in Camden GLF and had become a member of the Gay Marxist Group before moving on to join the radical queens and experiencing life in the Brixton commune answered their article with one of his own:

> It was really nice to see at the end of Aubrey and Richard's article last week the statement that 'the real issue in GLF is whether or not gay men are prepared to sacrifice their very real male privileges'. I totally agree with that and I know that nearly all the other gay men I know who, like me, are into dresses and make-up would agree with this also; I consequently feel that it was a pity that the inference one draws from the rest of the article is that the gay men into dresses and make-up are not interested in this fundamental aspect of gay liberation.
>
> Certainly, drag is no new phenomenon in GLF; last year a few people were wearing dresses, but were attacked so vociferously for this that they have left the movement and are now

doing their own thing. The difference between then and now is that in the interval there has been a realisation by many men in GLF that no progress could be made on any front without a real rejection of their male privilege. This has led to a new aspect in this struggle and that is the solidarity between the men involved in experimenting with dresses and make-up, and I feel that it is this solidarity that has alarmed many people in the movement, for at last a more coherent and concerted attack was being made on these very male privileges that few of the men in GLF were prepared to relinquish.

I think it is naïve and damaging for Aubrey and Richard to assume that the men into dresses and make-up are only doing it to cultivate their image, and I would agree with them that if the change is only as deep as the make-up then it doesn't really achieve anything. The point I am making is that if they or indeed anyone else had visited 42 Colville Terrace or any of the other houses in the area then they would see that very real changes are taking place in the heads of the men who are living there. The commune at 42 is, I feel, the most concrete and sincere attempt yet made by anyone in GLF to change their lifestyles, standards and attitudes. There they do get into the 'shit work' and it is over this very point that some of the most vociferous arguments have taken place there recently. There some gay men are at last attempting to explore their relationships and work and live as a collective unit, and I feel that the problems they are encountering are an indication of the real advances that are being made. If at the Court of the Sun King they exchanged clothes every day, then that comparison is fine, but to my knowledge they didn't, nor did they all sleep, eat and live in three rooms, squatting in an empty house. What is being attempted here is the construction of a solidarity, and a brotherhood, that will know no bounds. They are trying to break down all the barriers between people and rebuild new relationships.

> I would agree that getting into drag is not enough, and I would agree that some people who are into drag do not change themselves, and indeed do not realise the many implications that it holds, but I feel that at last there are a number of people who are making a real attempt, and in a situation of greater awareness because of the love and real brotherhood that exists amongst them, to reject their male privileges. And I feel that the confrontation that has happened in GLF because of this new-found solidarity can only produce benefits in terms of real advances in our ideas, since the issue is out in the open, and real analysis and thinking is now being done. The situation is now more open and honest than it has been for a long time, and the more openness that exists the less room for misunderstandings, and the more room for creating changes in ourselves. I think that we must continue confronting people in as honest a way as possible, because to avoid confrontation is to be liberal and to be liberal is to be dishonest.[31]

At the end of the season in Yarmouth, Michael James and I returned to London hoping to join the commune at 42, but first we had to find somewhere to live whilst they considered our application. Luckily there was an empty room in the house two doors along, where Rex Lay, Gabrielle Castillo and some other gay men lived. Everyone in the commune was delighted to see us, but underlying feelings of frustration, exasperation and resentment broke through with news of another confrontation with the landlord of the *Champion*, and the arrest of Bette Bourne, Richard Chappell, Douglas MacDougall, Andrew Lumsden and Peter Reed.

Two days earlier on the Friday evening, a group of women, including Nettie Pollard and her girlfriend Gaby, had all met up when visiting the commune and decided to go out for a drink. But it wasn't just a drink, they'd decided to go to the *Champion*, and that made it a demonstration simply because of its anti-GLF policy, maintained since the protests the year before. The outcome was also predetermined by the action of Pollard's friend, who on the way from the commune to the pub in Bayswater, went into a phone box and gave a message to a radio station that there were two hundred angry drag queens going to demonstrate at the pub.

In *Gay News* 7 there is a short Stop Press item headed, 'Fracas At Gay Pub', which covers the arrests at the *Champion* that night:

> The drag gays are charged with a number of offences including one of obstructing the footpath, two of obstructing the police and two of threatening behaviour. But they say the threatening behaviour was not just one-sided. *Gay News* was told: 'What was really terrifying was not just the fact that the police pulled our hair, which you can expect. But also, as well as getting all the "Yes, ducky," "No ducky" remarks the arresting officer pulled Doug's hair in the police van and said: "We'll get you later."'

The *Gay News* Stop Press item concludes with the promise of a full report in the next issue, but the only person they interviewed and the only story published was the landlord's.

> Drag gays arrested at Notting Hill Gate's Champion pub are wrong to accuse the manager of bullying his customers, he told *Gay News*.
>
> Terry Mahon, who's managed the pub for a year said: 'One reason why I don't like the drag lads drinking in the pub is because it upsets the rest of my customers. My regular customers just don't want the drag people in the pub. And it's my job to give the customer what he wants.'
>
> The licensee of any pub has the right to refuse permission to serve anyone who he doesn't want to serve. So Mr Mahon's alright there.

He told *Gay News*: 'I've got nothing against gay people. In fact I've made some good friends among them. That's why I want to stay on longer than the brewery normally lets its managers stay at a pub.

'This pub just isn't the sort of place where drag is welcomed by the customers. When I first moved in I suggested we should have one drag night a week – a night when all the customers wore drag. And the customers were so indignant I dropped the idea right away.'

Mr. Mahon's answer came after accusations that he bullied his customers from some of the 20 drag gays who were refused service in the pub – as reported in *GN* 7.

In a scuffle at the pub following this incident five of the gays were arrested for obstructing the footpath, using threatening words and using threatening behaviour. They were held by the police from 10.30pm until about 2 am, when after being stripped, searched and questioned they were released. They appeared the next day – a Saturday – at Marylebone magistrates court and were remanded on bail until October 24.

They charge the police with insulting them, pulling their hair and refusing to allow them to use the telephone.

Mr. Mahon told his side of the story to *Gay News*: 'I told them I wasn't going to serve them, then they sat down and I asked them to move out. So I called the police. I don't think these GLF lads who come realise my customers don't want them around. If I served them regularly I'd lose half my customers. The other night, after they had been thrown out by the police, when I came back I had about a dozen drinks bought for me and people walked up and shook me by the hand.'

'They say I bully my customers, but how can one man bully 300 people at the same time? It's ridiculous.'[32]

Andrew Lumsden: They called the police – *The Champion!* It was an unbelievable disgrace, this was about three years after

> Stonewall and here's a gay pub calling the police to throw out drag. We refused to go, so the police had to drag us out. My lover was Peter Reed and I saw what I thought was Peter being manhandled by some copper and I remember trying to tackle the copper, who punched me in the face. And they hauled us all off to the police station and the next day I went off to see a doctor to get a record of any abrasions on the face. I asked him if he'd write it all down in super medical language with technical descriptions, so it sounded absolutely terrifying. In fact it was just a slight graze and a bruise, nothing much. So when we appeared in court I could read out this terrifying medical statement as to what had happened.'[33]

At the meeting in the commune to deal with our application to join, James and I agreed to put all our income into the kitty, and could then take out whatever we needed without question. All our possessions would likewise belong to the commune whether it was clothes, records or stereo systems. There was a rota for shopping and cooking, which everybody liked because it meant that we only had to deal with those chores every other week. Cooking for ten or so people was a bit daunting at first but it didn't take long to get used to the new quantities. We had to familiarize ourselves with the gas, water and electricity supply, the building and its fabric, and rules such as never leaving the place empty, and never letting anyone into the house that you didn't know. We attended the local Family Squatting Association and the NHSG who could rally numbers of people to defend houses under attack from bailiffs and landlords. As Notting Hill Housing Trust (NHHT) were the owners of the house that we were squatting, we made our faces known to the Trust Tenants' Association (TTA) set up to fight the Trusts' policy of evicting existing tenants from newly purchased properties rather than rehousing them, and we went along to the NHPA which met once a week as a forum for discussing the problems in the community.

Visitors to 42 usually started arriving mid-afternoon, the most outstanding one for me at this time was an early afternoon visit from Neon Edsel, who I'd performed with at the Miss Trial Competition in Bow Street. I had first seen Edsel at a general meeting at the LSE before I met him in Street Theatre. He had a pink dyed punk haircut and wore a black mohair sweater and skinny black jeans. His spiky fifties style radically opposed the hippie fashion of the time. Edsel was held in high regard by people who knew him because he had a stall in Kensington Market back in 1968, selling bondage outfits and clothes made of plastic, long before Punk, and collected and sold Beatles memorabilia at least two years before they broke up. In early GLF Edsel fell in love with Aubrey Walter, and although I have the impression he wrote the following at that time, it was actually published in *Camden Come Together* 13.

> We are the contorted face of all of you and you were our good quiet uncle tom brothers.
>
> In being queens, unmistakably, we have always been the everyday confrontation with the gender role. We gave up our personal humanity for Reality based on Plastic; Gucchi and Revlon. Our comedy was a total refusal to control our souls, wherever they may hide now. We died for that truth.
>
> But you homosexual man, and woman, you are the spitting image of the Man – male and female – who put us all down. When I hear you speak of your dear parents, I am angry. You refuse to reject their controls honestly, deny them obedience, passively confront their goddamn decaying fantasy world. Strike your fucking parents; they and theirs, you and your trashy sensibility are my oppressors, and that contrived lifestyle pushes us all back into a dark corner. The way-it-is is based comfortably on our every Yessir, our ever letting the control myth pass without speaking up.
>
> Every lying silence is a vicious and selfish act.

> If you are not part of the solution, you are part of the problem. You are an uncle tom and a pig, and you have nothing real to lose, except our disgust of you.
>
> You must kill the old society within yourself and your own life, or it will take you with it in its endless grey cage. You are a free agent, and slavery exists only in your head. You and only you perpetrate our past and make our present.[34]

Neon Edsel appeared at the commune wearing sandals and a white sheet. He was bearded and his hair was hennaed. No longer Neon Edsel, he had reverted to his real name of Geoffrey G. He wouldn't sit on our chenille covered mattresses but sat cross legged on the floor. He presented us with fruit and nuts as we gathered round to chat, and then proceeded to tell us that what we were doing was wrong. Squatting, he told us, was theft, and accordingly a sin.

Edsel's reincarnation as a Buddhist messenger became apparent when Karma swiftly followed his sermon. A letter arrived from the NHHT asking us to leave. They told us workmen would be arriving on 2 October and required an empty building. We immediately got in touch with the NHPA, the NHSG and the TTA asking for help, and then began collecting materials for barricading the building. We put a board across the front room window with the message: 'We are 12 Gay Men and One Big Happy Family'. We had decided we wanted to stay together and looked to the housing trust to re-house us in a similar building.

We wrote immediately to NHHT giving our history, our housing problems in Brixton, and our plans for working in the community, highlighting the fact that we are told to integrate and then told we didn't qualify for housing. We reminded them about Joyce Maving and her boyfriend Cliff who became exhausted from living life on the streets, and we demanded to be housed together because we considered ourselves to be one family. The letter concludes:

We demand a meeting with all the representatives of the Trust. We want a firm policy statement on gay people and unmarried couples. We are a family. We hear much about the plight of broken families but we are surrounded on all sides by attempts to break our family.

We will not move unless we are guaranteed a house.

COPIES OF THIS LETTER ARE BEING CIRCULATED TO THE PEOPLE'S ASSOCIATION, THE LOCAL AND NATIONAL PRESS AND THE TRUST TENANTS' ASSOCIATION. [35]

The siege lasted three weeks. On the morning of the eviction the lovely men from the NHSG and TTA began arriving at 7.30 a.m. to be met with bacon sandwiches and cups of tea. Newspapers were brought in and we all settled down to wait. At about ten o'clock, two officials from the Housing Trust and two of its workmen arrived and started hammering on the front door and hollering 'open up'. We all assembled behind the door where mattresses and planks were ready to make a barricade, and then with big smiles on our faces opened the door to our visitors. They took a step back, whether in surprise or to launch forward wasn't clear, because there were so many people in the hall it never happened. The Housing Trust representative raised his voice and declared he had a Court Order allowing him to take possession of the property. We demanded to see it, but he hadn't got one, and we knew it because it could take up to nine months to obtain one from the Crown Court, not to mention the expense, and without it they knew they couldn't get us out. He blustered and said they would be back at eleven; he was giving us an hour to remove our possessions.

Mick Belsten, Tim Bolingbroke and Lewis Rabkin then went to the Housing Trust office to complain about what had happened and to see if there was any response to our letter and the setting up of an emergency housing committee meeting to look at our case. They were assured there would be no eviction that day. But while they were talking to the housing trust, their officials and the workmen returned and made a surprise attack on the front door, smashing the glass which flew down the hall. Our defenders went out and grappled with the intruders, forcing them back down the front steps onto the pavement. The workmen then tried to get in through the basement as the police arrived to watch, but could only get so far inside before meeting a concrete barrier that resisted their attack. Finally frustrated in their efforts, they smashed the water main, which was in any case part of their policy of rendering empty houses uninhabitable. One defender complained to the police about being injured by flying glass and had the workmen warned they could be prosecuted for assault, and that was that. By midday it was all over, police, officials and workmen withdrew, we were still in possession of our home, but we were left with a major problem of what to do about water.

Joyce Maving and Cliff were bitterly disappointed by the housing trust action and decided to make their own protest. Armed with placards they went down to the Town Hall and chained themselves to the railings outside.

> For over a year the couple have been looking around Notting Hill – part of one of the country's richest boroughs – for a home. But the soaring rents were beyond their reach. After Mrs. Maving had resorted to a hostel run by nuns and her husband to derelict houses, they sought help from social service officials, who referred them to the non-profit making Notting Hill Housing Trust.
>
> 'But,' said Mr. Maving, 'we had already contacted the trust and they said there was nothing they could do because we do not have any children.' The couple now face another stretch of homelessness after being evicted from an empty house owned by the trust. That was the last straw, so they chained themselves up … 'because we have had enough, and we won't

take it anymore.'[36]

John Chesterman wrote the following in *Gay International News:*

> Mattresses wall to wall. Rock music tapes. Hammering. Nailing. Bolting. Warning sirens being wired. Poster and sequins. Conferences, discussion, post-mortems. Relays of food from the kitchen. Laughter. Every so often the ritual of unlocking, unbolting, unshoring the front door for a visitor. Torches and spanners in the flooded basement, trying to repair the water supply pipes smashed by the landlords' heavies. Wires trailing across the floor. High heels picking their way delicately between the sprawling limbs. Talk and laughter. Action high and the sudden intense feeling of being together. Or maybe it's not so sudden. Maybe it only seems that way to an outsider walking in on a family that has been together for a long time.
>
> From October 2nd, and for many days after, the GLF commune in Notting Hill Gate, London, was under virtual siege. The group of a dozen or more had been 'squatting' in a home owned by the Notting Hill Housing Trust, who had given them notice to quit because the house was due to be demolished. Oblivious of the fact that the gay 'family' would be homeless, and using every trick to get them out, they eventually resorted to violent action. Council workmen claiming to have legal documents (which they did not) tried to force the front door. The commune was prepared. For days they had been sending out leaflets and copies of their defiant letter to the NHHT. The People's Association, a local community group, came to help. Doors were barricaded, broken windows had timber panels put over them, friends crowded the rooms. The attack was repulsed and after days of nervous tension and discussion with the 'authorities' they moved. With heads held high and in their own sweet time.[37]

Chapter 18

Radical Drag Queens at Home

> There are no limits to creativity. There is no end to subversion. Raul Vaneigem. *The Revolution of Everyday Life,* p.266.

Repairing the broken water main at Nº 42 was beyond us, so we all fanned out in the neighbourhood to look for another empty house to squat. Squatting an empty building was not illegal; the criminal offence was breaking and entering, so it was necessary to find some other way of getting in, like finding an open window, which made it a civil offence under the *Forcible Entry Act* of 1381.

> *Julian Hows*: Mick Belsten and I found the film studio, out on one of our little trolls looking for somewhere else to live. It was at the end of Colville Houses, a cul-de-sac, and it was like the Secret Garden because at the end of the cul-de-sac was this long fence with ivy growing over it, it looked like the back gardens of Westbourne Park Road. But there was a gate underneath all the ivy and if you pushed at it you could walk in.[1]

The gate opened into a courtyard of crazy paving spattered with moss, and where the paving was missing, little beds of straggling grasses. The front of the two storey facade of plain red brick with its inset gable end was set back some ten feet from the terrace end of five storey stucco fronted houses shielding its Lilliputian appearance. The wide door opened directly into a large kitchen with cupboards and counters running all the way around to a sink in front of the window. To the left was a door which led to a small electrics room, and straight ahead were double doors to the studio. Behind the studio doors was a pitch-black cavern that light exposed as vaulting some 25 feet to the apex, lifting one's spirits to unexpected heights. The hall was roughly 26 feet wide and 36 feet long with walls 18 foot high. At the far end were two free-standing walls of the same height which ran from either side to within six feet of each other, and some eight feet behind that dramatic gap was the end wall with a little door giving access to a coal bunker. To the right of the entrance a staircase ran up to a corner landing from where the flight continued above one's head to a balcony running almost as far as the left hand wall. The balcony gave access to two rooms over the kitchen, the first, which had a large internal window overlooking the studio, was the office, and the second was the dressing room with wash basin and lavatory. The walls and pitched roof were battened out and covered in chicken wire that held in place blocks of sound-proofing material covered in hessian. The floor was a herringbone parquet of grey unvarnished oak. There was no bath, but we didn't need to vote about moving in.

From a trapdoor in the office we could see outside along the corrugated roof that the centre part was laid with glass. There was an enormous 'A' frame ladder abandoned on the studio floor so we were able to get up under the roof to remove two square yards of the soundproofing and let in some light. We scoured the market for long lengths of fabric, and Michael James with his window dressing skills and a staple gun spent three days up the ladder meticulously swaging the two long walls. The space behind the two walls at the far end we turned into the wardrobe; it was made for the job. Suspended on both sides of the gap, were two long rails, one above the other, probably used for storing the studio lights and just perfect for holding clothes hangers. Dresses, high heels and tights to the left; more dresses, coats, men's wear, shoes, and stockings in tea chests to the right. We bought two smaller 'A' frame ladders to use for climbing up to the racks. The place was cold so carpets were laid with Art Deco ones on top. To the left side of the door from the kitchen we placed in an 'L' shape some old leather folding screens we found in the market, making a special place for Joyce Maving and Cliff, and along the left hand wall we put two tables, a big bookcase, and the sound system. We lined up mattresses, two below each free standing wall and another six down the right hand wall, leaving a great empty space in the middle and down the centre of the room from the kitchen to the wardrobe. Lights were strung up with Chinese globe lanterns decorated with ostrich feathers, silver lame net, diamante and sequins. The bedspreads were either satin or chenille, in pinks, golds and greens.

Nicholas Bramble decided to concentrate on his sculpture, and Cloud Downey and Ken on their relationship, so they did not move with us to 7A Colville Houses. The people who now made up the commune were Mick Belsten, Tim Bolingbroke, John Church, Stephen Crowther, Julian Hows, Nigel Kemp, Michael James, Lewis Rabkin, myself, and Bette Bourne, who decided to come and live with us, but at a price. He wouldn't give up his flat in Colville Terrace and wanted the commune to pay his rent, and in return he would give the keys to anyone who wanted, 'to go there and be on their own.' I don't know of any queen in the commune who was suddenly overtaken by the feelings of 'I want to be alone', in fact as things turned out his flat became more of an entry point into the commune. We voted to accept the 'offer', although Michael James resented Bette Bourne's sitting tenant 'propertied' status. But Bourne brought in through work more than enough money to cover the rent on his flat, and who would, if they'd obtained a similar tenancy with a Council or Housing Trust flat for life, have given it up for the unsecure, shifting, precarious situation the rest of us were in because of our activism? Our living together was an experiment for all of us based on a solidarity that we defined alternatively as love.

The first thing we did when our new home was up and running was to throw a party for the men who had come to our aid at the time of the attempted eviction at 42, one of the few times we had alcohol at 7A. The bush telegraph signalled the radical queens had a fabulous new squat. Visitors came daily to view and talk, question and organize, so much so that the 2 November GLF Diary announced: 'There will be no more meetings for the time being of Notting Hill and Kilburn GLF.' As Julian Hows said, 'What was the point of sitting in a meeting talking about gay liberation and thinking about doing things about gay liberation and planning things about gay liberation, when you could sit in Colville Houses and actually live it?'[2]

One piece of news Michael James and I learnt when we joined the commune was that Mick Belsten's long term commitment to Media Workshop had been rewarded with an agreement that Notting Hill GLF would produce issue Nº·15 of *Come Together*, which was duly published in early December 1972. Some writing had already begun and the project was the main focus of our work at 7A for the next two months. The lead article in our issue was Ramsey Blackwood's 'Why Fear', first published in issue 9 and so impressive we thought it deserved to be republished. It is a long article edited here to just a few paragraphs. Blackwood was a unique voice in GLF, a Jamaican born to poor farmers. His teacher at the local school recognising his intelligence set him on course for a place at the top school in the colony, from where he won a scholarship to Cambridge.

> Why is it that I, you, we ... they fear GLF? Why do we fear or have feared coming out of the prisons we have felt it necessary to build for our survival and to assert, without an apology, our integrity as gay people? Further, why do some gay people feel that GLF is threatening an uneasy truce which they have made with society or, rather, which society seems to have made with them? Why do they scorn self-assertion for an apologia, radicalism for respectability?
>
> These and similar questions are prompted not only by the hostility with which some gay sisters and brothers approach GLF, but also by the misgivings they have about any

movement for sexual liberation. It is as if we have lived with the present situation for so long that no other seems possible, or that the gay community has suffered from so much violence and inhumanity that it finds it difficult to summon the will to fight back. Of that community we are all a part, and we share the fear that is endemic to it. Some fear less than others, but it is no exaggeration to say that all of us have feared what we think might happen if we openly declare that we are gay and find it good. We have feared our families etc. Above all it seems that we fear being a part of any movement which openly works to destroy myths concerning homosexuality and to realise a state of affairs where there is no need to fear ourselves and others as sexual beings.

Conditioned as we are to secretiveness, evasions, lies and self-debasement – with the beliefs that we must never openly declare ourselves or make any demands on the community as human beings rather than as sick caricatures – the opposition we show to GLF is not surprising, for it has unashamedly broken the pact of secrecy to which homosexuals have been pledged. It has asked us not to dot the i's and cross the t's, but to renounce the truce altogether and to look at the price we pay in our present ways of adjusting to society. The demands the community makes on us for suppression of our sexuality have meant that many of us have been partners in our own destruction. We have been willing to sacrifice at least a part of our personal fulfilment and stability to the community in order to receive such economic and social perks as it may offer so long as we exist behind the mask. It has often meant that we exhibit an anxiety which is not necessarily a part of homosexuality but which is imposed on it by the terms of our adjustment to society. We settle for what seems the safest and sanest way of surviving and even discount the possibility that there may be alternative ways of living.

I suspect that the opposition to the political aspects of

sexual liberation has nothing to do with right – or left wing politics as such, but to the fact that we have been conditioned to be apolitical in order to survive. But sex and politics are bosom companions. In the first place, it is difficult to examine the implications of our sexual ideas while remaining unaware of the extent to which they are determined by what is considered socially and politically feasible – even such apparently simple ideas as man and woman. Secondly, sex is one of the measures we use to engage in a peculiarly political activity – the distribution of goods, services, status and economic rewards, what some theorists have called 'the authoritative allocation of values'. To the extent that what is regarded as normal is used as a standard for the distribution of justice, rights, goods and possibilities of personal fulfilment (and we should remember that gay people are still thought of as risks in certain professions), to that extent we are necessarily involved in politics. What has been the case to date is that most of us have acquiesced in the type of politics which assumes as its only acceptable basis the heterosexual way of life. This does not mean that we have opted out of politics, but in our fearful lack of protest we have become willing victims. To move from fear to wholeness, to stop being puppets and become responsible actors, necessarily calls for political involvement at both levels of actions and ideas. If it be left-wing to attack political regimes anywhere in the world which have oppressed gay people, and the ideologies that they have used, then so be it.

You or I may not feel oppressed, but to the extent that we think it necessary to hide or to apologise, implicitly or explicitly, for being gay, to that extent we are. And if, as I think, our apologies and secretiveness are based upon fear, the questions raised but certainly not exhausted here remain relevant. Why do you, do I, do we, fear GLF? Why do we fear to achieve our own liberation?

In 'Watch Out Kids: Deschooling …' Julian Hows wrote:

> Last week two of us from the commune went to a secondary school in Leicestershire to talk about Gay Liberation to a mixed group of students up to the age of 17 or so. We were in full slap bangles and baubles and beads complete with handbags and parasols. […] After a pub lunch we were shown into the redbrick Victorian house which had now been made over to the sixth form as more or less their own. (This is not a boarding school as it happens.) Then bang! We were ushered into the room itself which was jammed with young people from 15 to 17 all smiles and giggles. We were introduced and asked to say what GLF was exactly(!) I said how it started in America and how it snowballed from two brothers at the LSE through the split of the women and the gradual spread of Gay Lib throughout the country. One of the first things that had happened, by the way, was that one or two of the students arrived in make-up as well. So when we saw them we were very pleased and took it as a sort of complimentary joke … in fact I assumed that they were queens also and far out. But we learned afterwards that it had been done to send us up and that of course it hadn't worked because we didn't mind in the least. Anyhow, the atmosphere was by now warm and friendly, so we felt our way forward to the subject of the commune here in Notting Hill and inevitably on to the dreaded S-E-X.
>
> Of course we were pleased to hear that we had commanded the biggest audience in their series of 'minority group lectures' by far, and that we knew why, and that in our view 'that is as it *should* be'. Sex and our sexuality was after all the most fundamental part of our psychic life and the main point therefore of our visit. We all naturally dwelt upon these matters for most of the rest of the afternoon. The burning question of what we did in bed with each other was answered and listened to with total calm and understanding all round. I

think they realised that we were trying only to be honest, and were obviously surprised at the fact that we seemed prepared for the sort of honesty that they were clearly into, and thank god for it. This tremendous feeling of purity and unsullied zeal for some real knowledge was overwhelming.

One of the questions we asked was, were there any people in the room of over 50 students and 'teachers' *who had gay feelings for anyone* hitherto? One of the male teachers and one of the male students both said they had. I thought of this as the most important thing that happened that day and said that I thought that it was very difficult, to say the least, to 'come out' in such a large gathering and that those who hadn't for good reason been able to should think of the whole question *in particular reference to themselves* and that if such feelings had or did in future develop that they should welcome them and be open about it as far as ever possible.

This led on to talk of guilt and shame and all the rest of it … I could go on for hours as we were with them from 1.30 till 6pm so I won't. *But It Was One Of The Most Exciting, Friendly And To Me Deeply Instructive Events Of My Life.* POWER TO THE PUPIL!

Alongside Julian Hows' article was an extract from *The Dialectic of Sex* by Shulamith Firestone dealing with 'the myth of childhood'. Page 4 carried 'War-Baby Working Class Gay', Michael James' story of his childhood awareness of class and his developing sex life. Here is an extract:

As kids we had a ball, with the bomb sites as our playground in the winter and the [Plymouth] Hoe and the beach in the summer. We were a total community of children, who hadn't a care in the world and had quite friendly relations (most of the time) with the other street gangs near us. The concept of wealth gradually became apparent through our education.

We were being made aware ever so subtly of our parents' lowly status through the process of education. Not only were we made aware of it, but also made to feel ashamed of it as well. Just to take the edge off our guilt about being poor, we were encouraged to collect pennies for the 'poor black babies' who were worse off than ourselves, or so we were told. (Where were the seeds of racism being sowed?) This, together with all the stories of how things were much better before the war and food was much more plentiful, you didn't need ration books, and sweets were to be found in abundance. Slowly, slowly the seeds of discontent were beginning to take root. The beginnings of the 'divide and rule' policies of the ruling minority were beginning to manifest themselves among the gang. We were beginning to compare status with the rest of the kids, and the gang started to break into various 'class groups' with the very poor right at the bottom to be shat on by all the others.

From the age of seven right up to my going to grammar school at twelve, my sex life was very constant in its frequency and pleasure. There were at least five other boys in the gang who used to get it on with each other, either in pairs or all together. A boy called Russ and I were lovers for three years. He was the leader of the gang and was everything I was not, big, beautiful and strong. His parents owned two shops down the road, so he was in fact middle class and the leader in every sense of the word. He was two years older than me, and when he failed to get into grammar school his parents gave him hell. We were still lovers right up to the day he first saw me in my new school uniform. He saw me coming across the bomb site and attacked me with a knife. God alone knows what shit his parents had been throwing at him to freak him out so much.

'The Good Old Days' on page 5 was written by Mick Belsten, and accompanied by a photograph of Lisa Minnelli in Cabaret, astride the words 'experience NOSTALGIA divinely decadent!' Here is an edited version.

> Have you noticed how we've been having the 'good old days' shoved down our throats lately? Everyone seems to be wallowing in good old nostalgia.
>
> It's a lovely game that everyone can play, as they desperately try to top each other at the 'Do you remember …' bit.
>
> It is also the most insidious of pastimes, leading us to the fatal trap of conservatism and reaction.
>
> Does the mere fact that someone can claim to recall Douglas Byng (whatever became of ...?) not forgetting of course dear old … somehow demonstrate that 'life' was better in those far-off days?
>
> The 'aural wallpaper' that was the 'wireless' in the 1940's brain-washed millions of people into swallowing all manner of humiliations, degradations and misery allied to a total loss of freedom, in the guise of the national interest.
>
> As liberties (the few we had) were crushed, freedoms stamped on, black market fortunes made, dirty international deals done, murders and assassinations carried out, 'allies' stabbed in the back and betrayed, insular british chauvinism ran rampant, veiled in a haze of cheer-up, stiff upper lip, backs to the wall, all pull together philosophy numbing us to the oppressive rules of war.
>
> The black-out seems (in retrospect) to have symbolised a whole nation's attitude to any genuine 'enlightenment' … after all … don't you know there's a war on?
>
> I remember … damp, sweaty, smelly, cold, dripping air-raid shelters, identity cards and ration books (how long before they come back?) evacuees, refugees, prisoners of war, American bases (still with us) like occupying sentinels. And the propaganda, jesus! (I think your British Broadcasting is wonderful.)

Nasty Nazies, cuddly Russians, valiant Chinese, heroic Albanians, greasy Wops, nutty blood-thirsty Nips, big buddy Yanks. Ah! But do you remember Nice, Good, Clean, Handsome, Wholesome, Wellspoken, toothsome clipped saintly faithful brave wry world-weary fearless self-sacrificing English Men …?

Our bombs were polite, family-loving, well-bred bombs; theirs were sneaky, caddish, treacherous, uncouth and more murderous bombs. Ah yes but war's a dirty game you know.

Oh sorry.

Hollywood! What bliss it was … remember Greer Garson, Walter Pigeon, Norma Shearer, ooh and George Murphy, John Wayne, Ronald Reagan.

'Remember them? Christ, how can I forget them. I'd need a bloody lobotomy. There's no escape. Nostalgia comes oozing and blubbering at me everywhere.

But I can't forget … I can't forget shrapnel, dried-eggs, air-raid sirens, Spitfires, barrage balloons, fires, screams, blasts, search-lights, Air-raid Wardens, the Home Guard. Crushed mutinies, squatters (the homeless, bombed-out), 'direct hits', 'missing aircraft', 'Killed in action', 'missing believed dead', gloom, misery, paranoia.

Remember the FitzRoy? The Standard, Ward's Irish bar, the Union Jack Club, Jermyn Street Baths … the sailors, the guardsmen, Ivor Novello, The Dancing Years? Ivor got nicked for cottaging . . . .

Ah, The Old Vic, Donald Wolfit, Larry and Ralph, John Neville. John Gielgud GOT NICKED FOR (cottaging) Shhh . . .

Lord Montague, Marlene Dietrich, *Pal Joey*, Hermione Gangrene. Emily Williams, Aly Khan, Lady Docker, Jack Spot, Christopher Fry, Issy Bonn, Ronnie Ronalde, Peter Wildeblood, Kenneth Hulme, Diana Dors, Shirley Bassey, Larry Parnes, Tommy Steele, Hymie Zahl, Danny Carroll, *Soldiers in Skirts*. The Little Hut, Bobby's Bar, The A & B,

> Waterloo, Leicester Square, The Café de Paris, The Londoner Club, The White Bear, The Golden Lion ... OSCAR WILDE . . . NOEL COWARD . . . CHRISTOPHER ISHERWOOD . . . CABARET . . . CABARET . . . CABARET . . . Wodehouse and Pound and Eliot and Auden.

There is a theatre review for a show we ended up buying tickets for and protesting against from the stalls during the performance:

> *Hulla Baloo* – Criterion, Piccadilly. *Hulla Baloo* – Fulla Shit – contrary to *Gay News'* blind, sexist etc. type review. The show was extremely sexist, very male and *racialist.* I cannot understand how Chelsea Brown (who is coloured) performs in the same show as Jimmy Edwards, singing a song praising Enoch Powell (plus audience participation) with lines like – 'Keep England white – keep it fish and chips – no strange tints, etc. etc. etc.' Rogers & Starr continually send-up their own gayness and gay people generally. A send-up which was a put-down.
>
> *G.N.* – 'A fun evening tinged with blue humour, but nothing to really offend anybody.'
>
> *C.T.* – 'A foul evening tinged with bad humour, and lots to offend somebody.'

We reproduced the Scum Manifesto by Valerie Solanas – *SCUM: The Society for Cutting-Up Men.* We also reproduced the French article, 'FHAR Rapport Contre la Normalité', under the title 'Men'.

> You whose name stands for both the male and the human race, you who are always dreaming of power, why do you always have to use words that bring to mind domination and violence? ... Why, if you put down straight men's oppressive male chauvinism do you talk about them 'opening up their

arses' and fucking them physically and psychologically?

Of course it is necessary and right to show we all have some homosexual feelings. To do that, because you are men, do you really have to consider only men? Everywhere and always men are the only point of reference, our only valid spokesmen, the one's whose power you envy for some strange reason! The penis symbolises in turn the sceptre and the truncheon. What interest can women have in all that? None at all.

In bourgeois and patriarchal society SEX is the penis, the dagger for our sheath. Homosexuality? It's a sexual practice amongst men since we women don't have any sex – only a hole!

To get rid of prick power would mean reaching such a capacity to love that it would become impossible to go on using the penis, vagina or arse of one's partner to convince oneself of this false superiority (which hides so many fears). We, lesbians, want to speak of our love, as we are sick of seeing men flaunting their sex and nothing else. Our pleasure has nothing to do with any idea of power and oppression. We want to live, and to that we will 'rape' hearts and minds. Sex will follow naturally … and that won't be rape!

Why, since you are gay like *us*, do you concentrate on straight men? To put down their arguments? But why this need to justify yourselves. Maybe as revolutionaries you feel the need to get into dialogue with other straight revolutionaries? What about your revolutionary brothers and sisters? Sorry, but you really seem to forget them. If we come into contact with someone gay (say in the Renault factory[3]) it isn't in talking to him about the workers that we will get across to him; all the left does that to him. It's in talking about his homosexuality, for nobody does that.

Anyway, look at these other 'revolutionaries'! All are vying with each other in bureaucracy and Stalinism. If we are really revolutionaries, surely it is better to break away from this idea of revolution which prefers to play verbal games with the enemy rather than to learn from the experience of living. We need to leave behind once and for all this state of mind, *just as the revolutionary mind has left behind reformism.* Both abstractions and theories are male and reactionary. It is due to them that penis power is 'the way of the world'. Let's do away with the abstract. Since we are a movement we are a reality 'WOMEN IS PEOPLE'. Automation has totally upset the classical Marxist theory of the proletariat. Take the example of a handful of men running a paper mill (all qualified technicians and engineers) and ask yourself WHERE IS THE PROLETARIAT? It's the army of managers. It's Black Africa. It's the endless Third World. It's the mass of women.

Consequently we don't need to justify ourselves, in the way you do, for not being workers or from being cut off from the working class. On the contrary, our oppression will outlast that of the working class if we don't put across our position. And the problem for us cannot be divided, it is that of our place in the world, *and* at the same time that of our sex. It is impossible to separate the two: while you as men divide your problem. You experience social oppression sometimes – and only sometimes – but sexual repression *all the time as homosexuals.* How can you catch on to this complexity, you who are never oppressed as men? We, we are always oppressed as women. And the lessons of the past are plain, crying out to be seen. No revolution (all of them made by men) has liberated either women or homosexuals.

As for straight men who look on us – starting off together on a long journey – without understanding, let them remind themselves of this: never could what has been written here be aimed at them, as only gay men will be able to understand it.

Contrasting the French article was one by the Socialist Women Groups – 'Socialist Women and GLF' which ends as follows:

> In the Manifesto adopted by the Socialist Woman Groups at their Conference this year it was agreed that one of our aims should be: 'an end to sexual repression and exploitation ... including recognition of the rights of gay people'. We have to work out in detail the relationship between this type of oppression – that of homosexual people in particular and sexual oppression in general, the overall social and economic structure of society, and how the fight for gay liberation can relate on a practical level in the struggle to overthrow capitalism.

Scattered through the pages are poems, one by Allen Ginsberg, 'The weight of the world is love', and one by Germaine Greer, 'Words to my Gay Ally and Myself'. A short story 'A True Fairy Story' and a little piece 'The Barracks . . . or the Boudoir' by Alan Watts from 'Does It Matter, Essays on Materiality'.

Lewis Rabkin wrote about the difficulties we were all having with our 'brothers' in Gay Lib titled 'Of Queens and Men':

> I am sick and tired of going to GLF meetings, discos, dances, etc. and being seized upon and attacked as a 'radical feminist': it seems that people cannot see me as an individual, purely, it seems, because of the way I dress. Surely this in itself says a lot for prejudice in GLF. Nobody has ever explained to me what a radical feminist man is, what this term, so freely thrown about, actually means. As far as I can make out, radical feminists are women; I myself am a man. When thrown at me it is fairly obvious that the term is not exactly complimentary, and thus it is a put-down for radical feminist women, and therefore all women. Whenever I ask the men concerned what it means, they usually react with a 'don't give me any of that' and vague none-too-audible mutterings of 'fascists in frocks, telling us what to do'. I explain that I've never met the man before, and am certainly not interested in what he does, so long as his

behaviour is not oppressive to others, including myself. After all, revolution is about fighting oppression on all levels, within and without. The inevitable reply is the 'I'm-not-oppressing-you-you're-oppressing-us' routine, which continues, in reply to my startled eyebrows, with the 'we were quite happy until you started coming here wearing dresses and make-up'. 'The whole way you walk in with a group of your friends is condescending.

We *are* defensive when we walk in, just as a young Jewish boy, I used to feel defensive walking into a room where I knew the people inside, or some of them, were definitely prejudiced. And I know that when I go into a GLF meeting, nine times out of ten I'm going to get a hostile reaction. I know that at least half the people in the room think of me in terms of all the wild rumours and myths that have been spread by individual power-hungry men within GLF, their commercial gay press (or would-be commercial gay press) which is devoted to dividing and destroying GLF, a slight case of vengeance lust – we wouldn't let them get to the top in their man-games; the underground press whom we wouldn't let rule us; the straight press. And all these have played on the prejudice against feminine men that somewhere has been instilled in us all.

I suppose that I have learnt to ignore all this, learnt, for my own protection, not to let it upset me, and ignore the people who react to me in this way. It is this that frightens me; I want to talk to them to explain where I am at, but their prejudices categorise me. Can they not see that this is no way; that they are being manipulated; that the only way we can get anywhere is by listening to what each other has to say, rather than scoring a win over the next one?

On page 26 of our 27 page issue Bette Bourne wrote 'Street Theatre', which is abridged here:

Right now I'm putting up a gauze between me and my audience; the gauze being a rather unattractive thing called print. I call it a gauze because a gauze is something which hides or rather blurs whatever it is in front of, i.e. the dramatic truth. Take a young child for instance (whose perceptions are always more accurately discerning than most): he sees a man in the street wearing nail varnish. That tiny explosive fact tells all, the instant the child sees it in most cases. Quick, detailed information imparted in an amusing and stylish fashion. No elaborate plot … very little rehearsal … has nerve/will travel … involves audience … No Gauze.

If you walk gaily along Oxford Street in the distinguished company of three hundred other Queens being Gay and reacting to the audience around you, you will find several important things happening, you don't have to learn anything, the lines or q's are all given to you by the audience, you simply take and use them to clarify things according to your own awareness of the political situation you are in, and most of the situations we find ourselves in as out gays are intensely political: Politics being Life an' all.

The children are the ones to learn from. They know and can teach all there is to know about Street Theatre … they will tell you when it's boring, when the plot isn't getting anywhere. They can satirise the arses off any one of us. All we have to do is acknowledge their uncluttered genius. Be with them as often as possible … re-learn the natural skills we all once had … look with wonder at a child creating a whole fantasy world, utterly real at the same time … by the simple device of *being*. If the play isn't fun and by that I mean dramatic, valid, powerful, involving … even intensely tragic … a child will turn away, yawn and pull down the curtain. The main thing to remember, I think, is that acting cannot be taught. Shakespeare once let dizzy old Hamlet say, '*To be or not to be?'* It's a very simple question, isn't it?

Just a few days after the eviction attempt at 42 Colville Terrace, the *Champion 5* trial opened at Marylebone. Bette Bourne was charged with obstruction of the police in the execution of their duty, as was Richard Chappell, while the other queens from Kilburn; Douglas MacDougall was charged with obstruction of the pavement, and Andrew Lumsden and Peter Reed with threatening behavior and threatening language. I was Bette's MacKenzie; Michael James acted for Lumsden and Reed.

'On Tuesday 24 October yet another chapter of Notting Hill Pig Canteen Humour opened to a packed Gallery.'[4] In the audience was reporter Bob Sturgess for the CHE magazine *Lunch:*

> After the routine clutch of petty shoplifters, alcoholics and loiterers had made their drab appearance and been given the statutory small fines, it was visually stimulating to see the dock suddenly fill with the five accused from GLF. Richard Chappell wore an ankle length black satin dress with matching pill-box hat and net veil; Douglas MacDougall (of the same address) wore a pink polka-dot dress and green glitter around the eyes, while Peter Bourne (actor) wore, to great effect, a red patterned velvet dress. All three pleaded not guilty to the charges, but were remanded on bail till December 14 because an essential police witness was not available to give evidence. Total anti-climax was avoided by the decision to proceed with the trial of Andrew Lumsden (formerly of *The Times*, and dressed most fetchingly in the fabric equivalent of a Shirvan carpet) and his 'affair', Peter Reed. They were both quick to insist on their legal right to retain with them in the dock a friend to act as their adviser whose attire cannot yet be disclosed.[5]

One outstanding image of the trial from my seat with Bourne in the well of the court was the sight of Hows sitting in the front row of the public gallery above us. 'The court hearing began with a man in "drag" fanning soap bubbles and blowing kisses at Magistrate Mr. Kenneth Harrington.'[6] The 'dress circle' was overflowing with queens and women in drag. Groans, sniggers, loudly whispered asides and the odd burst of laughter greeted the prosecution evidence. Mr. Harrington was continuously demanding silence.

> It became patently obvious even to those of us who were not directly involved in the actual incident at *The Champion* that the whole trip was brought by the prejudice and paranoia of the sick landlord of that doleful pub. After an hour and a half of lies, mudslinging and downright distortion of the whole scene, we adjourned to the pub across the road for lunch. Fifteen assorted Glittering Queens, four sisters and various brothers descended on *The Constitution* in Bell Street.[7]

> *Nettie Pollard*: At lunchtime we went to this pub, an Irish pub, very ordinary, for a drink, and I remember someone saying, rather depressed, 'I do wonder if we'll get served.' And we went in and they went 'What a lovely colourful group you are, come in', and they were so nice to us and we thought, 'doesn't that say something? They think we're adding to the colour of the place and isn't it nice to have us', which was so different from gay pubs who didn't want us.[8]

> *Bob Sturgess*: The hearing resumed promptly at two o'clock with the public gallery bursting at the seams under its eye-catching complement of gay brothers and sisters – the *dernier chic* in a galactic riot of tulle, organza and green-painted toe nails. After the lunch-time drink-in at a friendly neighbourhood pub, spirits were high, and only the nervous tic on the Magistrate's face indicated that the party was not being enjoyed by all.
>
> The crunch came after a mere ten minutes. Despite earlier

demands for 'SILENCE', the public gallery could not resist the odd lubricious titter and, at precisely ten past two, there occurred a particularly camp piece of behaviour which caused the gay brethren (metaphorically) to throw away their corsets and abandon themselves to ripple upon ripple of 47% proof laughter.

[The air above the public gallery had suddenly filled with balloons. The police guarding the doors lunged forward to capture them but the balloons escaped their grasp. They rushed down the steps, up the steps, leapt in the air, and in a desperate attempt to confiscate just one, collided with each other and fell to the floor].

The Magistrate, still laboring under the Kafka-esqe incubus of the morning, decided to take action. He ordered everyone out of the public gallery, thereby raising, in the minds of some, grave constitutional issues concerning the inalienable right of the British public to ensure not only that justice was done, but that it was seen to be done. There was also the very real danger that to leave the Court would be to bring our country one step nearer to the secret locked-door sessions of a police state and Lord knows what else. Two seconds sufficed for the gay brothers and sisters to consider these imponderables and decide that the nation's interest would best be served by a tactical withdrawal.

After the clearing of the public gallery, Michael shouted at the magistrate: 'You old queen, how *dare* you sit in judgement on us Gays.' Somewhat daunted by this personal approach, the learned magistrate no-doubt felt that he could best retain his grip on proceedings by adjourning them.[9] [James] was then dragged out of the dock by PC D9, sustaining light injuries to his arm. PC D9 did not stop there. He grabbed a boy with a camera round his neck, opened the camera and exposed the film.[10]

[Numbers of police then emerged from the gaoler's room,

and in their well practiced manner linked arms and started pushing everyone from the public gallery down the passage towards the exit].

Those who knew the next Authority-Baiting-Game-Move promptly sat down in a provocative rustling of skirts and silk under-knickers. Whereupon the police (who also knew the game) did their Big-Daddy-to-Naughty-Child-Bit and, manfully overcoming any mild nausea felt, employed the minimum of force necessary to expel screaming brood hens onto the steps outside.[11]

[James who was talking to Sturgess, showing him his injuries and explaining how he knew the magistrate was gay] – 'How can you doubt it? One can always tell ones' own,' – was tapped on the shoulder by a constable: 'Magistrate wants to see you. In there.'

History does not record the exact length of the spoon with which Michael and the magistrate handled each other at their interview, but the upshot was that Andrew stood firmly on his rights and refused to re-enter the dock unless Michael was in there with him.

The landlord of *The Champion* appeared mild enough when he first entered the witness box, but Andrew quickly laid bare his underlying truculence and made entirely credible that he had said things like: 'You're revolting, you're not men… Get out of here!… I won't serve you… I'd give anything to kick you lot in the face…' 'Or maybe,' said Andrew to the magistrate, 'it was in the behind. It was somewhere, at any rate…' Or Andrew again to the landlord: 'You're prejudiced aren't you?' 'No.' 'You've made very free with the word "drag", haven't you?' 'Drag!' asked the magistrate, looking puzzled. 'I'm given to understand that it alludes to articles of female attire, Your Worship,' intoned the prosecution. 'Do you know what "drag" is?' Andrew asked the landlord. 'Yes I do.' At this point, Andrew got Michael to stand on the dock bench, his bare knees showing prominently under what, to the layman, appeared to be a white bed-sheet. Whereupon, Andrew directed the landlord's attention to this vision in white. 'Is that drag?' 'Yes,' replied the landlord. 'Well, it's not. It's a kaftan. It's worn by male Arabs. That shows how little you know about drag, doesn't it?' 'Do we have to be dragged through all this?' asked the magistrate wearily. 'Speak up!' said Andrew, 'I can't hear you.'[11]

[Two at a time the authorities began allowing people to re-enter the public gallery. The arresting officer took the stand for his cross-examination by Lumsden].

'Officer, it's been established that Peter Reed and I are lovers and that he entered the police van of his own free will, to be with me after my arrest. He was not himself arrested until much later. Doesn't that strike you as odd that despite this he was charged with exactly the same things as I was?' 'Not really.' 'You all met together at the police station to decide what charges you could dream up to stick on him, didn't you?' 'No.' 'You said Peter Reed and I were in female dress, is that right?' 'That may be so.' 'What made you mention that? How is that relevant?' 'It may not be relevant,' said the magistrate, 'but he was asked a question, and he had to answer it.' 'I thought,' said Andrew, 'that it was for the magistrate to disallow irrelevant questions.' In that case,' said the magistrate, trying his best to affect boredom, 'I rule that it was relevant.' Reassured by this support from the bench, the constable went on: 'When the other defendant –.' 'My lover, you mean?' interrupted Andrew. 'When the other defendant attempted to regain access into the pub, I barred his way, and he was very rude to me. "You fucking big brute," he said to me.' 'You fucking big – what?' asked the magistrate. '"You fucking big brute," - Sir.' 'You said that to him, you mean?' the magistrate asked, a trifle nervously. 'No. He said that to me.' 'He said to you: "You big fucking brute?"' Can I take it that -?'

'No, Sir. The fucking came first, if you follow my meaning.' Renewed twitters from the public gallery. 'SILENCE!' said the magistrate, 'or you'll have to go.' The magistrate crossed out some lines, rewrote them and read them out to the constable: '"You fucking big brute". 'Is that right?' 'That's correct, Sir.' Andrew engaged in a long whispered discussion with Michael, which caused the Bench some mild irritation: 'If we don't get on, we'll be here all – .' 'I'm conferring with my MacKenzie lawyer.' And, finally: 'I want to call another defence witness.' In rustled yet another of Andy's friends, with a plunging V-line back that eventually came to rest at a perilous depth. 'Do you always dress like this?' asked the incredulous Worship. 'No, but we like to look nice when we go out.' More delighted titters from the public gallery. The presiding magistrate's patience had been sorely tried by the procession of defence witnesses – in drag to the last man – who had sailed into the witness box in ankle-length dresses and wide-brimmed Ascot hats to protest their contempt for established legal procedures and, incidentally, the innocence of the two Gay Lib defendants.[12]

In evidence, [Lumsden] said that he and Reed arrived at the pub to meet their friends at about 10 p.m. The landlord was creating a disturbance and he joined his friends inside.

Lumsden denied the fact that the police had asked them individually to leave. Police used unnecessary violence when they threw protestors to the ground, he said. They were determined to make arrests to justify their call-out, he claimed. He had not used the language alleged, nor threatened anybody.

Reed claimed he was outside when he saw police taking his friend to the van. He realized that he was the cause of his friend's plight through going back to the pub to warn the others. So he walked over to the police van, unescorted, he said, and climbed inside.[13]

After the summing up from both sides, it was abundantly clear that by any stretch of the imagination the pigs had failed to prove the charges conclusively. But the 'Queen Pig Beak' tripped into 'Solomon' and cut the baby in half. He dismissed the first charge [threatening language] and found the second charge proven, [threatening behaviour] trying to keep both sides happy. No Deal Duckie. Once again the courts have given the rubber stamp of approval to pig perjury. The catch word is 'if you're gay your guilty!' Andrew and Peter need the money to pay their fines. [Both were fined £5 and each bound over in the sum of £20 to keep the peace for twelve months]. Peter is a student and Andrew is unemployed. There is still another three brothers due to come up for the same bust. What chance have they got? The guilty ones of this case are the HETERO IDENTIFIED GAYS who use *The Champion*. They sold their brothers out for the price of a pint of bitter – at least Judas got thirty pieces of silver. How much longer are they going to continue to pour money into the pockets of a man who patronises and despises them? WAKE UP YOU STUPID QUEENS. DEMAND THAT *ALL* GAYS ARE SERVED. THE POWER IS IN YOUR HANDS. Do not oppress us as straight society does.[14]

Come Together 15 carried this notice penned by Bette Bourne:

I wore sequinned eye make-up, a purple wig, large drop ear-rings, and kissed another man in front of over a hundred people. Was I busted for wearing drag in a public place, for indecent behaviour, for breaching the peace? No, I was paid £20 a week, the audience contributed 50p per seat, applauded politely, and the newspapers raved about 'art'.

(On the morning of December 14 five gay brothers will re-appear at Marylebone Court, as a result of appearing at *The Champion* pub some weeks ago in a variety of eye make-ups, ear-rings, and assorted slap and drag. More than one of us may well have kissed another man in front of easily a hundred assembled there. The landlord called the kops. The audience booed us. They cheered as the kop dragged us out. Five brothers were arbitrarily arrested. Next day the newspapers raved. The cast was named, the costumes and slap were described, and the fact that sisters and brothers were viciously hauled out of court for behaving like people was too like life to be mentioned.)

I was paid, and applauded, and went home to a relaxing joint. The show closed. The theatre went dead. I feel I came back to life.[15]

The trial of Bette Bourne, Douglas MacDougall and Richard Chappell on 14 December 1972 was a much quieter affair. It was held in the smaller Court No. 2 under a different magistrate, who could be relied upon to uphold the court's dignity and not let proceedings get out of hand as they had at the previous trial. There was also a massive police presence, both outside the court and in the corridors, no doubt to help put the message across that the authorities were not going to be made to look as foolish on this occasion as they had been in October. Justice was summarily executed.

MacDougall stated that he couldn't be guilty of obstruction because that implied he was stationary, when in fact he was being walked down the street by PC Allan, and that previously the same policeman had told him to 'fuck off or I'll bust you.' The magistrate claimed MacDougall's evidence conflicted with his witness, found him guilty, and fined him £5 plus £2 costs with four weeks to pay.

Bourne and Chappell were accused of jumping up onto the back of PC Allan and of pulling his arms in an attempt to obstruct him in the execution of his duty. Bourne said he saw PC Allan dragging MacDougall into the police van by his hair, and that he went to find out the reason for his friend's arrest. Both said they were anti-violence and were not the kind to attack large policemen. The other prosecution witness, PC Wiseman claimed that both Bourne and Chappell had sought through physical means to prevent the arrest of MacDougall and that he had witnessed their behaviour closely.

Summing up, the magistrate claimed that the evidence of the two policemen had not been seriously challenged, nor had their integrity such as to cause him to doubt their evidence. In his opinion the charges were proven and he fined them £15 plus £2 costs each with six weeks to pay.

Some weeks after we settled into 7A a friend of Bette Bourne's, Mary L moved into his flat. She had her own leasehold flat in Shepherds Bush, but on her meagre single mother's allowance decided to improve her situation by sub-letting. She was a posh, well educated, handsome woman in her late thirties from Tyneside, with flaming red hair, prominent high cheek bones and green eyes. Very occasionally when she genuinely smiled she could look beautiful, but most of the time she was full of anger, flashing resentment and fierce hatreds. Dressed either in dungarees or loons she was the prototype political lesbian. Her son Richard was three and a half years old, pale, blonde, beautiful and cowed. With ten queens happy to act as cooks, cleaners and child minders to a seemingly right on woman who might be turning lesbian, it didn't take her long to decide to move out of Bourne's flat and into the commune.

Jane B. was another of Bourne's friends. Twenty one and filled with all the pretensions a working class girl from Bournemouth could possess. She would state quite baldly to anyone and everyone that she had her baby for money, for the social security benefits and a place to live. Hippie rock chick was her style: she had gone out and chosen a young musician from a local south coast band to be the father. Lorrian was thirteen months old when we met him, brown eyes framed by long black lashes, rosy cheeks, ruby lips and the most perfect translucent pink ears I've ever seen. After one of Jane's early visits to the commune I remember taking her home to the single mothers' hostel at Tranmere Lodge in the Harrow Road, with its ugly institutional interior, stale smells and noise, which made me appreciate why she'd prefer to move in with us and forego the nightmare conditions of the council hostel, even if it would have led to being given her own flat.

While Jane B. didn't care which of us looked after Lorrian as long as someone did, Mary L. used her motherhood to exercise control over us, and her radical feminist attitudes intensified that by trying to make us feel guilty for being men, a trick that Jane quickly picked up on. But all of this, of course, is hindsight. Essentially we were very happy for them to join us, childcare became central to the routine of the commune, and the presence of child and baby a source of joy.

Richard was taken each day to the Powis playgroup set up by the NHPA, which charged 5p a day to attend. It had been in existence for four years and was unfunded and ignored by the Royal Borough of Kensington & Chelsea (RBK&C) council, its social services and pre-school playgroup association because of its socialist foundation. The council's excuse for not funding the playgroup was that there was no mothers' rota for supervision; the mothers were of course working mothers with no spare time to participate. The play leader Mark Treasure's maximum earnings were £12.50 per week, and Judy Wilcox, the community worker with the NHPA spent more time fundraising and organising jumble sales than she did with the children. A few months later in February, 1973, RBK&C council gave a grant of £1,700 to their own pre-school playgroup, who in turn gave the Powis playgroup £100. Hackney at that time gave their pre-school playgroups £21,000 and Lambeth £40,000.[16]

Michael James: One day I was at home in the commune and there was just me and little Richard, and I'm lying on one of the beds right opposite the Hi-Fi and the speakers and Richard had been jumping all over me and jumping up and down on the bed, and I had some really nice flowing dress on and was feeling really relaxed and chilled-out, and then he went to the bed at the end, then he walked all the way up past the speakers and I'm just laying there stoned off my head watching him, and I suddenly… there was all that thing of him being educationally… not advanced – whatever, he couldn't speak properly and she used to shout at him… Mary, and he walked past the first speaker and suddenly his head shot round and he came back and he looked at this speaker and then he walked away again and then he came back again, and I thought 'Oh that's strange,' and then he went up to the next speaker and did the same thing again, and then he went between the two speakers and I thought 'he's been deaf all these years and he's heard these loudspeakers.' And I picked him up and wrapped him up and took him to see Judith Atkinson the doctor, and when I got in to see her – and this child: Richard was so beautiful and he would cuddle into you, and I explained the whole thing to her and I said, 'Judith, I think he's got a problem with his ears.' So Judith looked into his ears and she said, 'Yes, you're right,' and booked him for the next morning to have his ears syringed. That little child walking past the speaker and suddenly like an electric shock he'd heard something…[17]

Bette Bourne: I remember going down Portobello market with Lorrian in his pram and the men on the stalls jeering. I was in drag and the women were saying, 'Leave him alone,' you know, 'he is not doing you any harm, and he's got the baby there he's looking after.' So as soon as they saw the baby in the pushchair; well it was a kind of protection in a way, because they didn't want to frighten the baby.[18]

Rex Lay had a stall on the Portobello Road under the Westway flyover on Friday's, which he wasn't using so Bourne arranged for us to take his pitch. Roger Carr and Frank O'Looney, who had become lovers, had a stall below *Frendz* offices, which they let us share on Saturdays, so we set ourselves up as dealers.

> *Stephen Crowther*: We'd get up really early and go up to Golborne Road where the dealers from out of town would come in, and you'd be able to buy those lovely long chiffon scarves with the pointed ends which were stunning, and buy loads of stuff and then take it down and sell it, open up at eight o'clock on the stall under the flyover. I remember the Pink Fairies playing off the back of a truck there one Saturday afternoon.[19]

We found frocks of all kinds from the twenties to the fifties that could be pulled out of black plastic bags on Golborne Road for 50p each, which we sold further down Portobello, if we didn't want to keep them, for £2.50 or more. We bought fur coats, hats, wigs, handbags, fox furs, shoes, art deco and fifties plastic jewellery, broaches, badges and ceramics. We returned to the commune about eight o' clock in the morning with the new purchases and collected the unsold stock packed in our collection of abandoned prams. We wrapped our feet in newspapers, tied our hair up in headscarves and left in single file wheeling our prams up Portobello, past the stallholders of the fruit and vegetable market waiting for our convoy. The women on the stalls, knowing what we were doing, treated us as market people like themselves, and would call out stuff like 'Cheer up darling, you can't have a sausage for breakfast every morning'. 'Ere, got some nice bananas for you and your friends', while some of their menfolk looked sullenly on because she was enjoying herself. Other men would be shouting 'Market! Watch yer backs!' We kept telling them 'Don't bother, darling. We like meat with our potatoes', but it never made any difference.

Chris Stockdale joined the commune in early December. He called himself Dolores:

> A stallholder, a fruit and veg man made some remark, some funny remark and handed me a huge carrot, that of course I immediately nibbled into the shape of a dick and wielded it walking down the Portobello Road to the great delight of the other stallholders and the shoppers. As for reactions, the stall-holders didn't give a damn… they were a nice bunch all in all.
>
> And then there was another time going down Portobello Road, I can't remember what I was wearing at that time, but I had a telescopic cigarette holder, but when it was open I couldn't reach the end to put a cigarette in, so I had to ask passers-by to light my cigarette. We had a good time in Portobello Road, it was all a bit provocative, but it was also good fun. A less amusing experience was being accosted by Miss Mouse [a rag trade harridan]. She was pretty determined to get the skirt I was wearing. Very determined. It was a fifties one with a print of Martini Labels that I was wearing with a black off-the-shoulder sweater and those black satin stilettos from Bally, and she came up and said, 'I love your skirt, I want it. How much did you pay for it? I want to buy it off you.' And finally for a 10 or 15p skirt I had £25 quid which was a profit that probably went back into the commune. It was as the French say – 'buttering the spinach'. She was a very determined woman was that one.[20]

Bette Bourne, John Church and I were on the stall once, each of us wearing formidable looking toque hats of the kind favoured by the old Queen Mary, when a party of rich Italians called their friends over to look at us. Cameras were raised so we demanded they buy something, but they refused, so we got into a mock rage yelling, 'What do you think we are – sex objects?' We rushed around the stall screaming 'Fuck off,' and chased them down the road shouting 'Bloody Italian bourgeoisie!' We didn't have cameras ourselves: we didn't believe in stopping time, in immobility; our concern was free flowing events not iconic frozen moments so we weren't having rich tourists photographing us for nothing.

Another good source for buying was Tuesday mornings at Maidstone market. We used to leave at 4.30 a.m. for the drive out through Lewisham and the North Downs. I remember on one of the first visits Julian Hows running up to me saying he wanted sixty pence to buy a Clarice Cliff teapot he'd found. The spout had a chip in it but it was too good to let go of, and too cheap to say no to, so we brought it home and put it on the bookcase and kept the commune's money in it. From then on Clarice referred to the kitty, as in that's what we've made, and that's the float we borrowed from Clarice. Michael James felt guilty because he bought some rum truffles for himself before putting the rest of his giro money in Clarice.

> *Julian Hows*: We were all getting money various ways. We were mainly on the dole and I, being still a youngster, had to go to the youth employment office in Shepherds Bush and register to be employed. I went down there in a frock. A very nice Grecian frock, boots from Granny Takes A Trip, red-hennaed hair, long cigarette holder and a gold lame clutch purse. I thought, well no-one's going to make me fucking work, dear. So I wandered down there, went in and nearly got mobbed by the sixteen year old Uxbridge boys. This man interviewed me and freaked out, got me to fill in a form and said I didn't ever have to come back. They gave me money over the counter and said I could just phone them in future and confirm I was still looking for work and they'd send the giro.[21]

Once *Come Together* 15 was printed we then had the job of selling the copies which involved standing around on the pavement outside the gay bars and clubs from about nine in the evening until closing time. There was also an afternoon just before Christmas when a few of us decided to go down to Piccadilly Circus and sell them under the arches. We weren't there long before we were surrounded by curious young rent boys eyeing us up and checking out the paper which they bought and started reading there and then. They were excited and intrigued at the idea of us all living together in a commune, so we spent over an hour talking to them in little groups. Gradually they drifted off until just three or four were left whom we finally invited back, which is what they were angling for anyway. So home they came to meet the rest of us, view the pad and have a meal. Afterwards one of them decided to stay. He was blonde, handsome, sturdy and fast becoming besotted with Chris Stockdale vamping around. Most of us were already in bed, and it was almost time to switch off the lights when Stockdale and his new man emerged from the wardrobe. Stockdale was wearing the best frock we had, a 30's full length backless evening dress with halter neck in pale green pan velvet cut on the bias. His new love was wearing nothing but our theatrical golden Centurion's helmet with red ostrich feathers. He swept Stockdale up into his arms, ran along the room and all the way up the stairs to the balcony, kicked open the office door and disappeared inside.

I remember on Christmas Eve lying in bed after the lights were turned off watching the drifting night time clouds through the skylight and falling asleep to the sounds of light breathing all around me in the winter darkness. We had eighty four visitors on Christmas Day. It was shift work in the kitchen and a production line in the tobacco factory.

> *Julian Hows*: Three or four of us would be sitting on the mattresses holding court for various groups or interests – look, it's automatic, my hands are automatically trying to roll joints as I talk about it! Stuart would be rolling one sort of joint, I'd

be rolling another and then Chris would decide, sod this, let's make the joint into the object, so he would make the joint a foot long, put the joint into a long roach which had pearl's draped from it, or butterfly wings in wire and paper, or diamante or ostrich feathers. It was life as performance art.[22]

On Boxing Day we closed shop, dropped acid and went to the Roundhouse in the afternoon to see Le Grand Magic Circus which thrilled us with its mixture of circus and theatre skills, its spectacular costumes, and intelligent witty content. At one point when I was peaking I thought the revolution had begun. That it was actually happening now! Afterward we came home to find Bette Bourne in the kitchen keeping an eye on Lorrian and Richard while cooking dinner.

Michael James: I've still not forgiven Bette for ruining the lamb on Boxing Day. I did all the Christmas buying; bought everything. They all went out on Christmas Eve, and I said, 'Leave me, I'll do all the cooking for Christmas Day lunch and I'll have Boxing Day off' because I wanted to go and see La Grand Magic Circus. Bette had seen it before and she said she'd do the Boxing Day dinner. For Christmas I'd done beef, turkey and pork, and a huge big thing of mashed potatoes which Mary L and Tim had spent ages... they did all the veg the two of them. Julian and Stephen did trifle. Then there was loads and loads of salads and bread, cheese and nibbles, and I know I didn't drop any acid because we were all reserving it to go to the Roundhouse on Boxing Day. And we came back from the Roundhouse and she must have put a whole fucking rosemary bush in with the lamb which made it totally inedible and I was fucking furious. I still haven't forgiven her for that.[23]

Andrew Lumsden: I loved the commune, which I wasn't part of. It was like stepping off the planet. You went into a no-daylight

> zone where there were places to sleep strewn all over the floor, posters to do with pop groups, endless sounds always on, you were always offered dope or acid. The welcome was lovely. It was unstructured to a degree that was terrifying if you had led any kind of structured life and I think there were people who came and went very quickly – in about ten minutes. None of the ordinary ways of coping seemed to be there. Somebody might be walking round without their clothes on, somebody else spending hours and hours making-up. Somebody might be making love on one or another mattress, all in this twilight. Twilight gives the wrong impression, I remember colours. There were blues and golds, yellow, all under artificial light. Candles. Somebody stole the candles from the church rather apologetically one evening when there was no alternative, and the vicar said 'That's all right' when he was told – 'If you needed them, you needed them'.[24]

Some mornings Mick Belsten, always the first up, would gently rouse me with a kiss, a lovely smile, a cup of tea, and a joint. Generally when everyone was stirring, about eight o'clock or so, Julian Hows would regularly rise up ivory-pale and sleepy, his well endowed at half-mast and pointing to the right, he marched across the room and upstairs for a pee, followed by many pairs of eyes half hidden beneath bedding and fingers. After Mick Belsten's welcome to the day I would get up to find the clothes I'd discarded at the foot of the bed had been cleared away. Style decisions that early were never my forte. I would find after climbing up and down the wardrobe ladders that what I had in mind wasn't there, and then whilst re-thinking the look for the day someone would wander in with another joint, making the indecision even worse. Breakfast could last till lunchtime. Being so many, housework and laundry duty came round roughly once a week, shopping and cooking roughly every two weeks,

Tuesdays, Fridays and Saturdays were for the stall, and Wednesdays was my day in the GLF office. Other days my only job might be to collect Richard from playschool or take Lorrian out in his pushchair. Generally we would be home in time for dinner about seven, and on Friday evening everyone was home to formally talk about any problems we had, and to unravel the knots that occur through never having lived with each other before. Saturday nights were reserved for tripping.

Michael James: I didn't do the stall often, what I used to do was make sure – I was brought up in an Irish household and you've got to eat – these dizzy queens, dear, couldn't shop to save their lives, so I made sure we had food in. I went down with whoever was around and got our evening meal together, got our Sunday lunch, and the rest of the week more or less organised itself, but as long as we had food on the weekends. Then we'd all be back by about three on a Saturday.[25]

My ex Roger Rousell, now had a flat just south of the park and we would all go over there to take baths on Saturday afternoon and early evening. And to be fair I must add that everyone was into shopping and cooking. Tim Bollingbroke was a particularly good chef among the twenty year olds with a developing interest in vegetarian recipes, and Nigel Kemp in his turn, always produced perfect cheese soufflés.

James: In between early tea and the last of us coming back from Rosie's, someone would have scored acid for us. On the odd occasion there was no acid, we were out till midnight in Bette's van knocking on dealers' doors, but we never had a Saturday without acid, we always got some eventually.[25] I never dropped acid till I'd got my make-up on.[26]

Stephen Crowther: We used to take acid on a regular basis. We only had a limited number of LP's and tapes. We used to play *Crown of Creation*. We used to take-off to *Crown of Creation*. We had *Blows Against The Empire* and there was Crosby, Stills, Nash and Young, *Hunky Dory, The Man Who Sold The World* and Lou Reed's *Transformer*. And one night I took too much acid. You and I went to go somewhere to score some acid – it was liquid and I was licking the dropper and I took a green microdot as well. I'd taken all this acid and nothing was happening, and so that's when I took the green microdot, and then it all came on and hit me, so I think you and Michael gave me a couple of Mogadons and tried to talk me down, and you held my hands one on either side of me and took me for a walk – and then I felt great – meanwhile everybody else was *not* having a good time.[27]

Bette Bourne: The great thing about the commune was of course that it denied all the straight ideas about drag. For instance: a lot of us fancied each other and a lot of us had sex together and that was something drag queens never did together previously. What we were doing was breaking down the male and female stereotypes and the sort of married couple thing.[28]I remember one of my suggestions was that we should all be naked in the commune, to get used to each other's bodies. I think I just wanted to get them all stark naked… I was constantly told off for bringing boys in – I thought this was what gay liberation was about. Mick Belsten said, 'There's not one young boy that walks through that door that doesn't end up in your bed! He was very angry, and I said, 'Well, I hope it continues.' I was very interested in sex.[29]

There was a lot of sexual tension at one point and Julian said, 'Let's have a Roman orgy,' so everyone said, 'Oh yes, Oh yes.' But Julian actually got it together, he went and got some grapes and he and Stephen made some pillars making it practical, building cardboard pillars so it all started to look

> like an ancient Roman palace and of course if you'd had enough dope or acid it did look like that. Anyway, we all started getting it on and I was getting it on with Michael, and it was all going well, and then Michael and I fell off the mattress and I was convulsed with laughter, but Michael got cross and upset that I was laughing at him. But somehow it was all childlike as well. Let's have a Roman orgy: some cliché we'd heard. We didn't know what a Roman orgy was.[30] [But] some people sat about looking disapproving – people who were less confident about their sexuality.[31]

I remember one occasion when Bette Bourne and I ended up trying to get it on. It resulted in us sitting on the mattress effetely stroking one another. It would have been more help if one of us had turned the other over and given them a massage. It was pathetic for both of us, and I don't think it right of him to think of others as disapproving: left out, abandoned, ignored, that is what was really going on. One time, after John Beeston, a friend of Nigel Kemp's from the Medburn Street commune, had joined us, he and I had drawn the 'short straws' and neither of us could move to even a simple naked embrace. It was meaningless and left us both feeling empty and sad. Idealism between the sheets was a flop.

> *Michael James*: The Roman orgy, it was theory that was not practicable. If you don't fancy someone it won't work. The only person in the commune I fancied physically was Mick and that was a fantasy thing and I knew if it came to reality, it would have never worked between the two of us. Somebody said you should be able to have sex with everybody on the planet ... you can't dear, we've got agendas and tastes however right or wrong that might be, but that's the reality – we've got them haven't we?[32]

When Tim Bolingbroke celebrated his twenty first birthday he invited his mother and sister over for dinner. Inspired by the local Caribbean cuisine he chose to cook goat for the main course. Chris Stockdale contributed by making a cake called 'Our Little House', with almonds, cherries and mixed peel, that was cut to shape with a chimney and walls of brick coloured almond paste, and a tiled roof, two windows and a door in plain marzipan. Someone had the idea of adding hashish to the ingredients. Tim Bolingbroke thought that okay; he decided that if his mother and sister chose to eat the cake it was their decision. The night before the party we all went out, leaving Stockdale and James to do the baking. We came home to find them collapsed on the floor in front of the oven. When they came round and saw us they swore they'd only licked the bowl and eaten the few crumbs left from making the construction.

Mother and daughter arrived for dinner and we did our best, as they did too, to ignore the yawning chasm that lay between us as we racked our brains to entertain each other. The goat was served and complimentary noises made. The lights went out; the cake came in, Tim Bolingbroke made a wish and blew out the candles before cutting the cake and serving his mother, his sister and the rest of us. Best behaviour prevailed for another hour or so before mother decided it was time to drive back to Ealing. We heard later that nearing home, both mother and daughter began to feel unwell, and swore they'd never eat goat again.

John Church's mother also came to visit. John looking wonderful greeted her in a beautiful white Victorian blouse and full length black skirt. His mum, already in her seventies, was still working as a waitress at the Savoy. She was a single mother who had been in service all her life, John's father being the son of one of her employers. She was tiny, sharp, and bright as a button, not by any means a stage mother, and after tea she looked at us, surveyed the room and said 'Well it's all theatre really, isn't it?'

Bette Bourne: There was a marvellous thing; Richard's fourth birthday. Tim and Julian got together and made this gigantic jelly with hundreds and thousands, and dolly mixtures and smarties, and it looked amazing. I remember it swaying slightly because it must have been two feet high. They made this circular base with plywood with wheels underneath, and they made these tiers. There were three tiers and it was like a castle, and the middle and tower was orange then green, and walls and towers in purple. And it was beginning to sway, and we were all worried in case it collapsed before Richard came in through the door, and finally Mary and Richard walked in … and his face; he walked all the way round this great big jelly which was taller than he was, and it was marvellous and everybody was so sort of moved and happy.

I mean there were times in that commune when we reached a kind of bliss. I think it gave us the energy to carry on and it was a bliss that we hadn't really encountered before. It wasn't drug induced, it was *that* kind of communal action.[33]

Chapter 19

Radical Drag Queens in the Community

> Revolutionary theory is now the enemy of revolutionary ideology, *and it knows it.*
> Guy Debord.

We were all invited to drop acid with Phil Powell at his flat in Martini Mansions one Saturday evening in January 1973. Powell had asked Mick Belsten to trip him out, and Michael James to help him come out in drag. James was thrilled to have this important politico with a wife in Women's Lib, and a daughter aged two tucked under his wing.

On our first visit, Bette Bourne for a joke packed a toy pistol in his handbag. As we entered the flat he pulled it out and pointed it at Powell saying 'Stick 'em up.' Powell exploded into a furious lecture on unacceptable behaviour towards a revolutionary gay brother. Perhaps he was nervous at the prospect of tripping with acid queens he barely knew, or maybe he believed the Marxists' nonsense about actors, but it was not a good beginning, and taking acid with strangers is not the wisest thing to do for a first timer. Still he wanted to go ahead, so we dropped our tabs. Predictably Powell's lack of trust in many of us started to give him a bad trip – just as we were all taking-off. James and Belsten had to hold and reassure him for a long time before he let go enough to relax and enjoy the experience.

After that we went over to Powell's to trip a number of times. Wife and daughter were always absent when we were there of course, as was the lodger, the mysterious dark beauty that Powell was frequently seen with and assumed to be his boyfriend. But as the weeks passed I began to find that I couldn't establish a friendly relationship with Phil Powell, it was all very uptight and wary, while he seemed to be getting on very well with everyone else. Talking through problems at one of our Friday commune meetings I voiced my impressions only to be told I was just being paranoid.

At the beginning of February Michael James told us that his mother was moving house, and he was going down to Devon to help. He followed that up by saying that he'd decided to move to Amsterdam to live, initially at the house of a woman he'd recently met at a party, who had invited him over and would help him find a job. Once everything was settled in Devon he would come back to London and stay at Phil Powell's for a fortnight while he sorted out his passport and tickets. I was very surprised by his news and questioned his withdrawal, but he'd made up his mind. Some twenty years later he explained:

> *Michael James:* Political correctness had crept in somehow, not overtly but subversively, and I felt I didn't have the freedom to wear trousers when I wanted to. I felt there were times when I didn't want to go out and be looked at by everyone in the street; I just wanted to slip out quietly. There were people who were giving us a hard time for doing that.[1]

Things had gone wrong for Michael James some weeks earlier. One Sunday morning when we were all coming down from our trip he chose to practice his spiritualism and cartomancy on John Church, persuading him he could predict his future. James arranged Church's chosen cards, consulted the book of interpretations and discovered it gave a dire reading, but rather than make something up from what he knew of Church, stupidly proceeded to assassinate his character with all the authority of the Tarot laid out before him. Church was deeply upset. The next day James decided it was he who'd been slighted and misunderstood, and attempted to win the younger queens over by justifying his behaviour while pouring scorn on Church. They were not having that and confronted him at the Friday meeting. The row ended with James shouting ''I swear to God I'd cut my tongue out first before I'd ever say anything like that', to which Church bellowed 'Then why did you?' James left the commune with virtue stubbornly intact, adamantly refusing to admit his mistakes or accept that his mother's practice of divide and rule was also his own.

Soon after James left for Amsterdam, the gossip in the commune was that Phil Powell wanted to move in with us. This was confirmed one Friday night when Mick Belsten proposed we have a formal meeting with Powell who would come over to 7A and make his application. For some reason I didn't attend that meeting, and can only think that it must have been held on an afternoon when I was working at the office. What I do remember is arriving back in the commune from wherever, and straightaway asking how the meeting had gone. I was told that Powell had come along and applied to join, but he had tried to impose a condition – and the condition was that before he moved in he wanted the commune to expel me. It seems my paranoia about Powell really was a heightened sense of awareness after all.

Years later I told that story to Tony Halliday, whose response supported something I'd always felt about Phil Powell – doubts about his gay sexuality. We both remembered Powell's young and pretty boyfriend, but the boyfriend was never seen on his own in GLF, he only ever appeared with Powell, always with their arms draped around each others' shoulders, schoolboy fashion, not touching or constantly stroking each other as lovers do. They would kiss in greeting and parting, yet neither of us could remember seeing them snogging, nor recall anyone ever saying they'd seen them in bed together.

Aubrey Walter: It wasn't just queens who got into the politics of drag. I remember one person who had been straight,

> married and had a kid. He got into radical drag from having a guilt feeling about being male and having been straight, oppressing his wife and acting like a real 'man'. He would travel around wearing bizarre clothes, like a short crimplene shift frock, run-down sling backs, wild long thin hair, fairly conventional make-up and a handbag. Whenever he went on public transport he would be mocked and laughed at, and threatened and thrown off buses. So he developed this really aggressive manner of getting on tubes and buses, glaring around and threatening the other passengers first – he would also deliver his lectures in drag. Everyone thought he was really brave.[2]

Camp cuts through artifice and exposes the false. It is a quality heterosexual closet queens hate and Powell lacked. His initial overtures to James and Belsten had been carefully placed. He knew his appeals would attract their giving natures. But he wasn't interested in James' Hollywood style glamour tips, he knew drag was not his style; he didn't like drag, he didn't enjoy it. His sincerity was the mask of deceit: Powell was preparing to undermine and discredit us, the last remaining opposition to the straight left in the movement, and if to accomplish that purge meant wearing drag, then he was man enough to make the sacrifice. Who cared if he looked like widow Twanky. Flattering James' aspirations to bring out another queen was his way to gain trust, infiltrate the commune, and destroy what remained of our authenticity after its shredding by Marxists, Maoists and the straight-gay media they embraced. Bette Bourne's instinct to pack a toy pistol in his handbag when preparing to visit the hidden menace had been weirdly portent.

Unquestioning dogmatism: deaf to new ideas, the self-righteous straight male left will betray the revolution every time. Their inability to be spontaneous: limiting possibilities at the beginning doom them from the outset. Applying old practices to the new, they are in reality preparing to make excuses for their failure. For the left in GLF, practising communism was nothing more than lip service, while liberation was actively denounced.

Liberation is not given to anyone. Liberation is something you have to fight for. When Liberation presents itself you have to grab it with both hands; you have to take it and make it your own. The ideologues, failing both opportunities, turned round and declared our communism and attempts to liberate ourselves as nothing more than utopian idealism and lifestyle politics.

> *Bette Bourne*: I remember saying a few months after being in the commune: 'I've got to do some theatre! I've got to do some theatre!' And Mick saying 'Well fucking do some!' I went to French's [Theatre Bookshop] and got twelve copies of *Lysistrata* and we had a play reading, and Joyce was a knock-out actor, she was amazing and funny. Chris Stockdale played his part like Marilyn Monroe, and that caught on and a lot of people started doing movie stars and it was really funny because it is a wonderfully funny play. But read by drag queens it was unexpectedly full of vitality, and it spoke to us because it was about – we wouldn't fuck the men unless they stopped fighting. Lysistrata, this young woman, leads this campaign. It was written over two and a half thousand years ago, so that's pretty amazing when you think about it. I mean I picked it up because it had a lot of women's parts; it's all women, there's no men in it – and it was very anti men and we were doing all that. In the commune I remember a terrific feeling of excitement and euphoria in there. We were all taking this huge fucking chance with our lives, and that's partly where the love and the energy came in.[3]

Some weeks after we moved into 7A, Nigel Kemp installed a new twenty year old boyfriend called Jamie, who'd had the money and the sense to buy himself out of the army. He was now broke, unemployed and not claiming benefit. They became an exclusive couple and over time their situation didn't change except in one particular. Sometime in February Kemp announced that he could no longer bring himself to claim unemployment benefit and had signed off. Troubled, we asked him how he planned to earn some money. He said he didn't see any necessity to do so as we had all agreed we were free to do as we wanted. Faced with that reply we had no choice but to accept his position. He added that if we ran out of funds, he would agree to sell his books on Victorian typography and donate the money to Clarice. Meanwhile he continued fulfilling his duties, though now I began to see his cheese soufflés as barely more substantial than his financial contribution. A few weeks later Mick Belsten decided to stop working in his brother's metal finishing business, and announced he too wouldn't sign on. I thought he did it to challenge and embarrass Kemp, but if he did, his tactic didn't work. I took Belsten's job over for a while, but it was a filthy operation, cleaning old lacquer off brass bedsteads and other objects. I didn't stick at it for long, and could see why Belsten didn't want to continue with it either, especially in view of Kemp's behaviour.

One day in the GLF office during this time I found in the mail a letter from Agitprop addressed to various groups with news that they were giving up their lease at 248 Bethnal Green Road, and inviting the addressees to think about taking over the shop and maisonette above it. I'd been thinking for some time that what was missing in the commune after completing our issue of *Come Together* was a project, a focus that could involve us all. I slipped the letter in my handbag and brought it home to show the others, particularly Mick Belsten, who I felt was nursing an ambition to write, and Nigel Kemp who had been in publishing, but no one was interested in the idea of running a bookshop. The next day I took the letter to the others I had in mind, Andrew Lumsden and Richard Chappell over in Kilburn, who had for a while been talking of forming a commune of their own.

Andrew Lumsden: And then I left *The Times* after all and went to Bethnal Rouge and became the sort of person Denis Lemon couldn't stand, one of the radical feminists. It was a time when everybody exchanged helpful information about what was going on and somebody said Agitprop were moving out of where they were in the East End and looking for people to take over the lease and wanted to chose who would take over. So we went and were interviewed. I remember nothing about the interview, I should imagine the way we looked was enough. Agitprop said we could have it.[4]

Lumsden and Chappell gathered their friends together and moved to Bethnal Green which became a second home for Colevillia, and Brick Lane market a new source of goods for the stall.

Chris Stockdale: One thing at the commune: the building next door was being renovated and on the building site was the most beautiful hunk. He wouldn't take that step, but he was interested, because sometimes in his break he'd come into the courtyard and have a cigarette with us. I was so subjugated by the beauty of this man, young, good looking, full of muscle, working on a building site. He was fascinated by what he saw coming and going, and he was inquisitive and you felt that he wanted to... perhaps not get up in drag, but maybe have a gay experience and maybe change his lifestyle: it wouldn't have taken much pushing. Somebody else who was more diplomatic or more persuasive might just have managed. But unfortunately I wasn't. I wasn't the one, which was very sad.[5]

Gentrification of the housing stock in North Kensington accelerated after the Labour Party 1969 Housing Act, which brought in improvement grants to raise the standard of living for tenants of rented accommodation. The properties that were improved, instead of raising the tenants' standard of living, brought with them increased rents that made them unaffordable, forcing tenants out of their improved homes. Rather than making the housing situation better, the new system served only to reduce the amount of accommodation available to people on low incomes. Between 1969 and 1973, 40 per cent of the area had been changed from low rent to high rent accommodation – three quarters by conversion to luxury flats.

When Sir Malby Crofton, the hardnosed, pugnacious, stock-broker and conservative leader of RBK&C council decided to hold the Mayor's Banquet at the Isaac Newton School on Lancaster Road, between Portobello and Ladbroke Grove, a school he planned to close, he provoked a lot of anger in Notting Hill. We joined the large NHPA demonstration outside the school on the evening of 16 March to protest the councils' support for speculative developers and his presence in the district where his policies had caused so much misery and homelessness. When the Rolls Royce's and chauffeur driven sedans drove up the road we pelted them with rotten vegetables. About forty police arrived to clear a passage so the limousines could enter the school playground, but the way was blocked. The police then turned and brutally attacked the nearest protesters, who began dodging between the vehicles that were trying to edge forward. We escaped into the Grove to watch, and as the news spread, pubs emptied and people jumped off buses to join the fight against the police. The battle went on for nearly half an hour before the road was cleared. Seven people were arrested.

In April the report commissioned from Mr. Frank Clinch the RBK&C's Director of Redevelopment was published. Clinch's recommendation to the housing problems of Notting Hill's Colville and Tavistock wards was a simple Compulsory Purchase Order (CPO) on all multi-occupied, unimproved houses. That solution was far too radical for the most right-wing Conservative council in the country, an affront to their policy of improvement grants that boosted the profits of private landlord by sixty percent.[6] Immediate attempts were made to bury the report. The council's public exhibition of the changes that the report would bring to the area, held at the North Kensington Library, carried no advertisement to illustrate the project on the outside of the library, and no one was available inside the library to explain it. Neither were there any copies of the 326 page Clinch report available to either read or purchase.

The Rev. Peter Clark of All Saints Church helped the Housing Group of the NHPA to mount their own People's Exhibition on the railings outside the church.

The council spent weeks debating whether they had the power to purchase and preserve whole terraces of housing for the low-paid inhabitants of the wards, before finally facing up to the fact that they were indeed legally empowered to buy up entire districts for rehabilitation purposes. Following on from their People's Exhibition, the NHPA held a meeting in All Saints hall attended by some 250 people. We were told the council did have the power to implement Clinch's preferred solution of purchase through CPO's, but they were still dragging their feet. The meeting produced a unanimous vote in favour of a total CPO of the area and immediate Control Orders to be put in place to prevent speculation before the CPO's came into effect. People then went to Knightsbridge and demonstrated outside the home of councillor Methuen, the town planning chairman.

On the 15 May, some six weeks after the Clinch report was published, a public meeting between the council and local residents was held at the church hall. On the stage were seven councillors, including Mr. Methuen accompanied by his wife, one Alderman and ex-mayor, and 13 officials including two assistant town clerks, the Borough solicitor, the director of planning and Mr. Clinch.

> [In the hall] there were about 300 to 400 people, representing all those who live and work in the area, including the market

> traders and small shopkeepers, and gay commune members. The evening started with an argument about the compulsory purchase orders to take away houses from private ownership. The people said they did not believe for a minute the Council was going to use them, and anyway compulsory purchase orders are not enough because they give one year to private landlords to sell the house to speculators. The answer is Control Orders, which could be applied immediately. The Council solicitors agreed that the Council has the power to get them if they want to.'[7]

The councillors claimed they wanted to know what local people thought of the Clinch report, but said they were not there to listen to demands and would only consider suggestions. As people started to air their views they were told by the councillors sitting on the stage to stand up and give their names. People responded by shouting back at the councillors, 'You stand up – for the people! Stand up! Stand up!' An Italian man stood up, a member of Lotta Continua, and made a long speech in Italian, which councillors interrupted claiming they didn't understand what he was saying, only to be challenged from the floor by people asking why they had not brought interpreters with them to an area they knew perfectly well was home to large numbers of Italian, Spanish and Portuguese refugees from fascism.

All Saint's Hall itself was scheduled for demolition, effectively leaving the whole of North Kensington without a sizeable public meeting place. Moving on from questions about the housing situation, people demanded that the empty, un-used Baptist Tabernacle be purchased for use as a community centre, with provisions for the elderly, children's playgroups and as a free school in connection with the local truancy project. In the face of increasing demands the councillors clung to their mantra that they could not make decisions about anything, that they were only able to listen to what people had to say, which they would then consider. The response was to tell the officials what the peoople had been considering for years, while nothing has changed. 'Clinch cost £150,000 and we've been telling you all this for years – for free!'

The market traders were agitated because the council wanted to do away with the fruit and vegetable market (it continues to do so to this day) because it makes the area dirty. The small shopkeepers were equally angry at the councils' plans to pull down the entire block with the Electric Cinema, to make a multi-storey car park and a vast supermarket. Sainsbury's had already put in a building application. The councillors denied it. The tradesman and stallholders said they had proof of it.

We introduced the homelessness issue by raising the case of Joyce and Cliff, who lived apart for eight years in single sex council hostels waiting to be rehoused, before finally choosing to live on the streets as a homeless couple rather than spend any more time separated. The councillors decided that they would consider their case, we said we could hardly believe them; the same promise had been made by the council a year ago and absolutely nothing had happened. Then came the case of a Spanish family, Mr & Mrs Chipolina and six children being evicted from the two rooms they lived in, and forced to move into one room at the council's homeless hostel. The councillors' attitude was that an alternative had been provided and we should all be grateful for the provision. The whole meeting rose up in disagreement and decided that the councillors would not leave the hall until some agreements were reached on all the issues that people had raised.

The doors of the hall were locked and barricaded around 10.30 p.m. and the Chipolina family sent for. People took over the stage and forced the councillors to take down all the details of the Chipolina's situation. Up until midnight the meeting tried to negotiate with the officials on all the problems within the community, but they refused to consider any of the 16 draft proposals that were drawn up. There were eventually 12 demands, each discussed one by one and adopted by everyone present.

When it was clear the councillors would not sign up to the demands it was decided to lock them in the hall overnight until some agreement was forthcoming. Nearly 200 people volunteered to remain, some of whom went home and returned with food, homemade wine, fruit, guitars, bongo drums and flutes. Everyone started dancing and later shared a supper. Afterwards small groups formed, some with councillors to discuss the areas problems. Julian Hows developed his own method. Sitting in the lap of one councillor after another he begged the man to be reasonable, promising in return a night of unbridled passion. Talk went on until just before 7.00 a.m. when the councillors were asked to move upstairs so there would be space for the playgroup which began at eight o'clock. With Mrs. Methuen behaving aggressively[8] the idea of moving the councillors upstairs was abandoned. Finally about 10.30 a.m. the police made their presence known outside the hall windows, so the barricades were removed, the doors unlocked, the councillors released, and all of us who had kept them company through the night went home to breakfast.

The previous evening, just as the meeting in All Saints Hall was starting, the Paddington Branch of the IS began holding their weekly meeting in a flat nearby. 'They noticed a lot of police about but continued with their meeting oblivious of the political event going on but a stone's throw away.'[9]

We had a run-in with our own landlord. One morning about six o'clock I woke up to find eight policemen, two workmen and Mr. Hanson, owner of the film studio, lined up across the bottom of our beds. Mick Belsten was already up, half dressed and staring intently at one of the officers he must have been exchanging words with. I looked around to see more of us wake up amazed at the scene, some plumping up their pillows in anticipation of laying there to watch events unfold. 'Get up! Get out of bed!' roared the one in charge. Not knowing what was going on, two women and eleven or so unshaven queens wearing nothing but nail varnish, some with toe-nail varnish, and a few unashamedly wearing yesterday's mascara, slowly emerged and stood around posing in languorous indifference to the glaring presence of the constabulary. 'You're trespassing on this gentleman's property. You've broken the law! You've an hour to pack up and get out, so get dressed and get on with it.' We drew ourselves up, raised our eyebrows – those of us who hadn't shaved them off crossed our arms and said, 'Oh no, no, no, no, no! We're not having any of that. We've done nothing wrong officer, we're squatting here. There's nothing illegal about squatting.' Belsten said, 'I've already told them they need a Court Order.' 'Haven't they got one?' we asked. 'Dawn raids! Coming in here at this time of the morning; ordering us out without a court order. That's breaking the law officer. Aren't you the naughty ones? If you haven't got a court order officer, then you should leave right away – you're trespassing!' We gave them barefaced cheek by turning to the owner and saying, 'Sorry, Mr. Hanson, it is Mr. Hanson isn't it?' as he tried to hide inside his cashmere Crombie, 'the place was empty and we were homeless – but now we've made a home here we'd like to stay.' Our naked appeal pricked the chief Lily into announcing: 'We'll be back in the morning with the court order and I don't want to find any of you lot here when I return'. Head up, he marshalled the raiding party and retreated. They never came back.

> Court of the Sun Queens. Colevillia.
> It is regretted that we were unable to visit Morecambe as set forth in our recent pamphlet due to disturbances caused by the piggery at the behest of the bourgeoisie last Friday. Colvillia was attacked by police and a gang of reactionary building-site clods under instructions to evict us and on no

> account fraternise or enter into friendly relations with us. Forcible entry was made but the attack repulsed after hand to hand fighting in the Grand Salon (front lounge).
>
> Local support rallied to our assistance and the mob retired to consult with solicitors but threatened to return on Saturday to carry out the eviction.
>
> Colvillia is now under siege conditions. No further attacks have materialised.
>
> Local supporters were entertained in the evening at a reception given on their behalf. The corps of Astral Queens were in attendance and selections of music were played from Noel Coward, Jefferson Airplane and Evelyn Laye.[10]

The only other trouble we had with the police was on coming home from a party one night. Bette Bourne had just driven us back in his white mini-van and parked up near the commune, knowing we were followed up the dead-end street by a police car, whilst riffling through handbags and stuffing dope down our underpants. So we waited, and this policeman came over, stuck his head through the window and sniffed the air. 'Are you wearing Patchouli oil, Sir?' Bourne said, 'Patchouli oil? Me? No Officer, I'm not.' Lily said, 'Right, get out of the van.' So one by one, six of us got out of the mini-van all in glorious fifties drag with lots of petticoats that we started shaking out – it had been a bit of a crush in the back. The policemen couldn't believe it; he took one look at us, walked back to his car and drove off.

Julia B. from Birmingham who'd kept in touch, was visiting us one time when the electricity failed. She said she'd worked as an electrician and offered to help, so we took her into the electrics room, a maze of boxes and trunking beyond our comprehension, which she figured out, and asked for a ladder. I put the ladder in place and held it there while Julia B. filled her handbag with screwdrivers, pliers and spanners and climbed up to the largest box without even kicking off her sling-backs. I looked up in some alarm, I could even see right up her skirt, as this immaculately dressed, six-foot-two transsexual, her handbag of tools over one arm, poked about with the screwdriver, undid nuts, reached up with both hands and with a sudden yank, pulled out from under the box two cables as thick as your wrist which swayed around like live snakes as she wrestled to cross them over from one hand to the other and jam them back in the box again. And it worked.

Having earned her keep so to speak, Julia B. started coming down once a month with up to half a dozen of the transsexuals and transvestites from her Birmingham group. Sometimes after dinner on a Friday night we would look up to see a file of rather ordinary straight looking men coming through the kitchen door, smiling a little nervously and following each other across that end of the studio and up the stairs to the office and make-up room. About an hour later, when we might have forgotten what had happened, the doors on the balcony opened and down came a group of women in candlewick dressing gowns and nighties ready to have a chat and a cup of tea before sorting out which beds they were going to sleep in. One or two of them later came down to stay during the week so they could visit Dr. Randall at the Charing Cross Hospital, but the main focus for them on Saturday was to get used to going out on the street dressed as women and doing a bit of shopping.

> *Stephen Crowther*: We'd host transvestites from time to time who came down from up north. It was so funny, they were lovely those guys. There was a butch lorry driver and then they'd dress up and go to the Porchester Hall Drag Ball or something. I remember one coming in and he was kind of bow legged and he was wearing white PVC boots, knee length, and a matching white PVC shoulder bag and sort of holding it so the strap was really tight, and marching round the commune.[11]

On Friday 4 May, most of us from the commune went to the National Gay Think-In at Essex University arranged by Marion Prince. Bethnal Rouge was there, and GLF groups from Camden, East and South London, Cambridge, Lancaster and Leeds, plus a group from CHE. Saturday morning's programme had two film shows; the first a Czech movie with purported lesbian content called *Daisies*, the second was *Boys in the Band*. Afterwards there were workshops on Feminism, Marxism, and Sexism, a women's workshop and one for students. A report on the Think-In for the 10 May Newssheet tells of the writer's visit to the student workshop:

> which discussed the research the National Union of Students ought to do (it has to produce a first report on gays, in November) – anyone with ideas, or interested in helping, write to NUS. We also discussed other ways we could use the NUS Gay Rights resolution – like: support for gay groups, publicity, poster campaigns, contact with Trade Unions, etc. Again, ideas and offers to NUS. The other workshops gave me a strong sense of déjà vu: I've heard it all before. But the gay Marxist paper coming soon should be interesting (Lancaster GLF are doing the first two issues, they welcome contributions).
>
> The summing up session saw some unedifying bickering concerning the relative oppression of women and men. The divisions seemed to turn as much on age as on anything else.[12]

We went to see *Boys in the Band* and then joined the sexism workshop. There we listened to a blanket condemnation of the gay characters portrayed in the movie, described as reactionary, effeminate, cruel, self-hating, and self-obsessed stereotypes of the ghetto by the leftist gay men present. They gave no acknowledgement or recognition that the earlier generation portrayed in the movie had fought their corner, suffered public humiliation, loss of jobs, loss of homes and imprisonment even for their right and determination to have a public meeting-place, even if it was in the ghetto. No acknowledgment was made for their maintaining territory that we were only too thrilled to discover for ourselves when growing up. Gay bars and clubs by their very existence radiated a sense of community and the possibility of collective endeavour that one imagined the left would celebrate as part of our hard fought for inheritance. Not a bit of it. Where else would the fight against our oppression start but in the interface between the private and public sphere, such as the *Stonewall Inn* or the *Champion*. Definitely not in the Gay Marxist Group. We began to think it was their lack of humanity that was cruel.

For the newly organized, badly instructed gay Marxist students at this Think-In, it had now become fashionable to criticize earlier generations of gays, since they themselves as a result of three years of struggle by a few thousand others were the beneficiaries of an alternative scene that supported their needs.

What we encountered at Essex University was the new gay status quo, an emerging gay establishment. It was there that the gay Marxists set in stone their views on effeminate men as 'self-hating, arrogant, homophobic gadflies' to quote the words of the Maoist Peter Tatchell when publicly queer-bashing Quentin Crisp in the *Independent* [13] on the tenth anniversary of his death. Forty years have passed since *Boys in the Band* were denounced. In my view some people – including Tatchell – still cannot accept that prominent gay men can be camp – and have serious things to say. Crisp never for one moment thought of himself as an icon of the gay community, or ever wished to be one – let alone the gay hero status some tried to thrust on him, which so piques Tatchell. If Peter Tatchell is going to condemn people for one mistake, which in Quentin Crisp's case was a truth Tatchell totally misunderstood,[14]I can't look uncritically on a gay activist who renounced gay liberation by going back into the closet in a mad pursuit of bourgeois power through the Labour Party, and then more openly made a second attempt 16 years later; although I do acknowledge that he finally appears to have accepted his humanitarian role, which I know has come at the cost of considerable physical injuries.

The puritanical gay Marxist opinions voiced at Essex later surfaced among some Marxist inspired radical feminists[15] who retrospectively accused GLF men of promoting S&M and started criticizing the 1980s generation of younger lesbians for their sexual role-playing. The Marxists among them looked to theory to justify their condemnation. There is the logical correspondence between gender and labour, but what turns you on (though it may be mediated by the spectacle) is located in the floating world beyond reason, so theory had no answer. Recognising that people often identified with their sex roles before they were conscious of them was not acceptable. The fixed sex roles of those trapped by sexual abuse as children was no excuse. Those were not the *desired* answers: they wanted to revile sexual role-playing and would fly over every humane obstacle to do so – and therein lay the answer. By considering sexual role-playing as some kind of mechanical jiggling between butch and femme a theory could be based on cybernetics. The product of an automatic machine is a function of its input which for radical feminists included desire, disgust and a moral certainty. Voila! A young generation of lesbians were puritanically denounced for sexual role playing.

Radical feminists are to be applauded for being the women most vociferously united against the degradation of their sex through prostitution and pornography. But because radical feminism has determined that there is no difference between gay men and straights, radical feminist women feel able to transpose the unequal, male dominant heterosexual model of sexual relations onto gay men's sexual relations, claiming that gay sex takes place on a similarly unequal basis. Even in the ghetto where the lowest perversity of gay oppression is the fascist criminal role-playing of master and slave, these alienating fetishized sex-roles mediated by images of the spectacle are nevertheless made by mutual consent. Gay men act out their sexual role-playing knowing it to be a fantasy.

When radical feminists can see no difference between straights and gays it follows they see no difference between straights, gays and transsexuals, except perhaps for one thing: transsexuals are a people disorganized and in a weak position who can easily be beaten up on. I can well understand the lesbian panic at the prospect of a gynamorph[16] taking up a counselling position at a women's rape centre where their history disqualifies them, and on the grounds that rape victims could suffer needless additional trauma by discovering their trust had been put into the hands of a former man. But that is not to say that a gynamorph couldn't be equally sympathetic, after all gynamorphs are just as likely to suffer rape, as well as suffering the fear of rape. And yes, there have been a couple of stupid gynamorphs making male chauvinist claims about who makes a better lesbian, but to use these rare instances as an excuse to beat up on an entire community is the rage of fundamentalism. The response by Stonewall, the campaigning body of the LGBT community, to the radical feminist protest was to banish trans people. The organization designed for reform has become irredeemably reformist: a predictable trajectory for petitioners to government who are always weakened and seduced by central power. The heterosexualist corruption of Stonewall and its bourgeois supporters shows they cannot see the contradiction at the heart of their action: sexual apartheid doesn't remind them of anything.[17]

With these sometimes malicious, sometimes stupid ideas made up by straight-gay Marxists of both sexes, and never challenged, there runs the thread of elitist complacency, conformity, and the intergenerational rivalry first seen at Essex.

No wonder that in the late 80s and early 90s the younger generation dumped their oedipal prejudice on gays, seeing them as the establishment, and defined their opposition to them by choosing to be known as Queer. It is an opposition that embraces all lesbian & gay rejects – camp queens, role-playing lesbians and trans people seeking support in a larger community. Sure, the word they chose when hurled at the older generation causes anguish, or at least makes us wince at a barely healed wound, because it's impossible to forget how it had been – and, of course, how it still remains – but queers were not excluding other queers.

Julian Hows' preoccupation with ageism and being the youngest in the commune left him feeling increasingly overshadowed by the older queens. One day he removed the door from the loo in the make-up room, claiming the lavatory door, symbol of privacy, was a bourgeois privilege. I preferred to agree with Stockdale that it was instead nature's call, but none of us did anything about it. Hows' teenage revolt then led him to demand that we install a TV. We were horrified, so he opened the coal bunker at the back of the building which was large enough for four or five people to stretch out in; furnished it with tenting and cushions, called it the Arabian Room, plugged in a TV and banned everyone over the age of 25 from entering. But we recognized that it was their time and their place and it was good for them. Now when we older queens were getting ready for bed, the younger ones moved in to their own space. Jane B. following the stash quickly joined them, and it wasn't long before Julian Hows and Jane B. began an affair.

Mary L, from whom we dreaded the accusation of being called male chauvinist pigs continued to hold us in thrall. She and her friend Jenny thankfully spent most of their time in the women's commune at Faraday Road. For over a year the women's commune had been moving towards separatism, but we were still welcome there, and they still visited us. Both Stephen

Crowther and I remember the sisters' last visit when it was decided to hold a séance, something I deplored. We were all in the main room as spirits were being called up. Suddenly there came an enormous crash from the wardrobe. When we went to look we found the big mirror lay shattered on the floor.

With money from Clarice, Jane B started dealing drugs. I thought she was selling blow, but the younger ones knew differently, and I should have known better, seeing her scabby customers. Then one day we found Clarice empty and Julian Hows gone. He was gone for five days on a holiday in Paris, and of course being so young and handsome, when he returned he was forgiven. Such was the price of freedom. At least he had a good time, though we didn't extend our hospitality to the numbers of young French men who began arriving penniless and expecting somewhere to stay.

> *Stephen Crowther*: When I left, one of the things I had difficulty with was the money thing because of my student grant, and I was having to give up my grant and everything, and I was expected to give it up, and the sharing money thing of putting it in the tea pot … I had difficulty with that I now know, I realise it caused me problems. Basically as a commitment to the commune – I mean this is how I remember it at the time, this is how I understood it at the time – was to prove that commitment, to show that commitment, I should hand over all my money and I was kind of a bit reluctant to do that. It was a term's money, and then I'd have to struggle, and then I'd have to buy equipment or stuff like that out of it, and then it would be a problem asking the commune to buy stuff for me, or maybe it was that I'd started to think of moving on by that stage anyway. So maybe I was looking for any reason to back up that decision, as it wasn't working for me anymore. I'd also started taking speed just then, and I remember staying up with Tim all night on speed in the office, just drawing, and

> that's when I felt separated a bit, and that's when I met Brent and Barry and started going round with them.[18]

By mid July of 1973 the commune was collapsing. Struggling with ageism, striving not to play mummy-daddy, older brother-sister did no good. Heroin turned our home into a waiting-room of addicts on their journey to oblivion. Like dry rot's dirty-white fingers of hairy fungus silently eating through living structure, fear drove us out. Nigel Kemp and Jamie left with his typographical investment intact. Tim Bolingbroke found a religious sect in All Saints Road running a vegetarian restaurant and went to work in their kitchen. It was rumoured that they prayed over the vegetables they were chopping. He was looking I think for a more spiritual side to sexuality having exhausted the political. I heard later that he joined the Bhagwan. Christopher Stockdale moved to Bethnal Rouge. Lewis Rabkin returned to South Africa and became active in Johannesburg. John Beeston returned to Medburn Street. Bette Bourne and John Church returned to Bourne's flat. Stephen Crowther crashed at his new friends. Mary L with Richard regained her flat. Mick Belsten joined a squat just off Portobello Road. Julian Hows, Jane B. and Lorrian squatted another house. I went to visit Michael James in Amsterdam.

Aubrey Walter in the introduction to his anthology of *Come Together* published in 1980 wrote this about the radical queens:

> The problem of how to implement the *Manifesto*'s ideas in practice was difficult. How were gay men to give up their male privilege? The radical queens thought that the way to link up with the women's movement was to eschew everything 'male'. The radical queens argued that gay men should give up their male privilege materially, for a start by giving up their privileged male jobs. They should then experience what

it was like doing traditional women's work, such as housework, child care, etc., or go on Social Security and experience a leisured poverty, and so put time and energy into changing their personalities. It was also felt necessary to show the world you were giving up being a man, and this is where drag came in – it was a visible sign of what you were into.[19]

It was clear that the feminism of the radical queens didn't extend to coping with the traditional shit-work women have been lumbered with... The 'frock brigades' love of dressing up seemed to indicate the desire to have their cake and eat it too, to experience the "glamour" some women cultivate, without the everyday oppression.[20]

We didn't eschew everything 'male' in linking up with the women's movement, but everything *heterosexual.* Drag was a statement of our homosexuality: nothing to do with housework, which we'd been doing since first leaving home. Loss of male privilege starts with putting all one's possessions and money into the commune while contributing fully to work that produces a clean and happy home. And naturally we cannot experience the everyday oppression of women, but we witness – everyday – the mindless cruelty of men.

Peter Tatchell: The radical feminist approach was that for men to don drag and live in communes was the route to gay liberation. Most of us had some sympathy with that position but felt it wasn't sufficient. It wasn't possible, in our view, for lesbians and gay people to completely withdraw from society into some sort of gay utopia ... Those who primarily focused on a civil rights agenda or were involved from a radical leftist perspective tended to be very wary or even disparaging of the alternative lifestyle strategy.[21]

Peter Tatchell joined the Action Group when he first came to GLF claiming he was not interested in abstract theoretical discussion, but wanted instead to relate ideas to action. However, when he found the Action Group was not the centre of power he joined the Maoists, where he learnt their politics by repeating their opinions as above, and following their 'abstract theoretical' line that transformed mending and making-do in a squat, and revolutonary activity in an economically depressed area, into a utopian lifestyle choice.

Sarah Grimes: 'Though the radical feminist men were talked about as being into personal liberation, they were actually quite community oriented…The actions countered the political posturing'.[22]

David Fernbach in his article 'The Rise and Fall of GLF' claims that the drag queens of the Notting Hill commune were 'idealist feminists', while the group surrounding him were the 'materialist feminists'.[23]

The idealist categorization comes from Hegel, who was the first modern philosopher to utilize the ancient Greek art of dialectical investigation. For Hegel '"The Idea" is the creator of the real world, and the real world is only the external appearance of the idea.'[24] Marx took his tutors dialectical reasoning and inverted it, declaring: 'The ideal is nothing but the material world reflected in the mind of man, and translated into forms of thought.'[25] Marx interrogated facts with facts, seeking the underlying laws governing material phenomena, the development of its general forms of motion, and their transformation through different historical periods.

The difference between the Material and the Ideal is that between change and fixity, motion and rigidity, the quick and the dead. The difference between the drag queens and the Marxists was one of class, the imposed social condition, useless for human survival, fixed by birth and inherited antagonism.

The drag queens did not spring forth fully armed, as did the

Marxists, but arrived in GLF as men of a practical nature befitting their class, raised their awareness, confronted the world anew and discovered that the best way to magnify their homosexuality was to change their gender appearance, which eventually transformed them into anarchic, communist drag queens. How did the Marxists change? We know that Fernbach added and later discarded radical feminism in his combination of ideologies, but that only shows his reliance on ideologies, fixed systems that through the passage of time can only result in ideal, i.e. false conclusions.

The metamorphosis of gay men into drag queens is I suggest a manifestation of one of the general forms of motion that comes together under stress from the bourgeoisie as the visible instinctive antithesis to their authority, organization and social relations. (The early-modern Mollies displayed the first form of that motion; the Dilly Boys of the roaring twenties another manifestation). The appearance of a new phenomenon of motion threatens ideological authority and must be challenged if the ideology is to retain its credibility. In Fernbach's case his authority has no facts to counter with, and is thrown back on class antagonism and denunciation to transfer the hidden pole of his own fixed idealism onto his opponents, while claiming the opponent's materialist position as his own.

Keith Birch was a member of the Gay Marxist Group and lived in a gay Marxist commune. 'Even though the number of people who set up communes together may have been quite small, the interest in the movement and its underlying ideology was widespread, especially amongst the young and middle class.'[26]

Keith Birch tells of how he and some friends had been attracted to the idea of living in a commune and the difficulties of finding a place to rent, but eventually they found a flat and settled in. What emerged was the usual problem of two or three individuals who did most of the talking and consequently the decision making, and the others feeling disempowered and ultimately finding the only solution to that problem was to move out and set up elsewhere, without the verbose, in another flat. On average there were twelve men living together, sometimes more sometimes less, as people left and others moved in. As they also provided a crash pad, the numbers could go up to twenty for short periods. They had only one bedroom, and although some members had developed into couples they were open. These always complicated relationships obviously created tensions, which they sometimes talked about, and sometimes avoided, finding it easier to have sex with outsiders. To solve the practical necessities of daily life:

> Every member of the commune was expected to pay an equal share towards the rent, bills and kitty for food. This was agreed after much discussion because the differences in employment and the level of each person's wages meant that for some it was easy while for others it could be a problem. However it was felt that if everyone contributed, it would not lead to feelings of dependence or ill feeling, and it would show commitment and responsibility towards the rest.[27]

These young men were Marxists, experimenting with communal living, committed to developing their communism perhaps for the one and only time in their lives when such an opportunity would arise, surrounded at that unique time by a network of supportive comrades within GLF, and yet they could not apply 'from each according to his capacity, to each according to his needs' to their own, self-created situation. It begs the question, where was their experimentation?

The failure to apply a basic principle of socialism to their situation, the clinging to equal shares, enabled the better paid 'communard' to profit by his position while continuing and over time maintaining the impoverishment of the lower paid. This has to be a recipe for creating ill feeling, not ameliorating it, and a failure on their side to exercise rectitude and divest themselves of their profit for the common good. It is a flight from responsibility on both sides. The attempt to avoid examining the feelings of dependence and ill will was a complicit failure to identify and explore the problems inherent in giving up male privileges, and a clear agreed refusal to do so.

As for the other problems in living together, Birch found 'the rota system for cleaning shopping and cooking did not last, as its formality led to inconveniences and an oppressive feeling to conform.'[28]

The commune lasted two years after which Keith Birch decided 'to research other communes, backed up by personal observations.'[29] The communes he visited were straight heterosexual communes where the women did most of the work and child care, while the men spent most of the time smoking dope 'but had more time to play with the children.'[30]

The following is Jeffrey Weeks' view of communes in GLF. He makes no attempt to differentiate between the commune in Bounds Green/Muswell Hill, the Camden/Somerstown commune, or the ones he never visited, the Brixton/Notting Hill/Bethnal Rouge radical drag queen communes. His view of communes must have come from the one Birch and his fellow Marxists formed:

> They were often unstable entities, riven by personal jealousies despite the ideologies, divided by questions of who should do the work, beset by a constant stream of visitors looking for 'crash pads', temporary stopping-off places. As a transitional phase in exploring new relationships, they were often personally liberating, and they seemed to offer in embryo an alternative to the nuclear family. But they were also utopian. If they set out to be something more than temporary ways of living together, they came up against iron laws about

> property, and how to live and work together harmoniously and uncompetitively within a hostile economic and social environment. They also conflicted severely with the emotional structuring of most members. The need for pair-bonding might well have been a result of bourgeois conditioning – but to say that did not will the need away. Nevertheless communal experiments did emphasise an important dichotomy – that between 'personal' liberation on the one hand and political action on the other. Rarely did the two meet.[31]

Our individual activism caused us to be evicted from our bed-sits and flats. The same thing happened to us collectively in Brixton. We got around the iron laws of property by squatting, by appropriation. We knew the slogan, 'Property is Theft,' without knowing of its author Pierre-Joseph Proudhon 'the father of anarchism'.

What we couldn't get around was money, and a crisis happened when middle class Nigel Kemp refused to contribute. Kemp was modest, didn't make emotional demands, and probably didn't withdraw money from Clarice for anything other than food. But his action caused dispute. Louis Blanc's dictum of social equality is: 'From each according to his capacity, to each according to his need.' I could say Kemp's input was zero and his needs were seven. He might have considered he was giving in other ways, and reckoned his input as seven, and his needs as four. Even if Kemp accepted that we were talking hard cash, there remains a discrepancy. Who can determine his capacity? Who can evaluate his needs? Who can act as judge between the commune and Kemp, or Belsten, over a difference that comes under the law of supply and demand? Blanc also proposed that Liberty, Equality, Fraternity, be reordered to Equality, Liberty, Fraternity, as though Liberty proceeded from Equality. We queens thought of fraternity as male bullshit. Proudhon thought fraternity hid a 'secret intention of robbery and despotism' and said that Blanc's mantra, 'From each ... To each ...' – 'began the wretched opposition of ideology to ideas, and aroused common sense against socialism.'[32]

Competitive personalities and harmony within the commune were sorted-out by discussion. The one time we failed to reach agreement was in struggling with the consequences of Michael James' spiritualist will to power. As for the effect of our commune on society, I can only say that when a group of blatantly obvious queens are agitating together in the local community, they challenge people's perceptions of themselves by presenting other ways of being. It opens eyes, causes people to think, widens horizons, and raises awareness.

Of the things that middle class Marxists cannot stand, the worst is perhaps aspirational members of the working class. They see the working class as so many sausages they can march forward when the time comes. An inspired working class individual is not only out of step but suggests that different individuals can, as indeed they do, develop at different rates. That is a threat to the Marxist hegemony.

The disaffected bourgeois Maoists and Marxists seeking unity through proletarian struggle follow an ideological path to revolution. If successful in raising the level of consciousness of their supporters, such a group become *the* authority in the struggle for change. When change occurs, however, the pre-revolutionary ideologies become outdated, transformed into their opposites, and if not discarded will turn the group into the authoritarian resistance to the new. That is what happened to the Maoists faced with the new situation their ideology had not foreseen: the appearance of drag queens and the criticism by the women and queens of their 'politically correct' 'feminist' position, when their own desire, based on not liking women and having no wish to form an alliance with feminism was driving them to seek an all male movement. Instead of struggling against their prejudice and abandoning their ideology and power, they added radical feminist ideology to their armament in an attempt to divide and weaken the women. The use of ideology in the new situation turned the Maoists into counter-revolutionaries against the newly emerging feminism.

Unable to devise revolutionary practices in line with their ideology, and having put the cart before the horse, all the Maoists and Marxists had left was their ideological authority to denounce the revolutionary praxis of others and prevent that practice from developing into a revolutionary theory. What the English Left had not learned from the French was that ideology is the *enemy* of revolutionary practice.

No amount of armchair cogitation can produce answers about alternative ways of doing things. The real alternatives appear only to those actively engaged in the struggle and who remain open-minded enough to adapt to the results and changing circumstances. The individuals who made up the commune that squatted in Notting Hill were there because they acknowledged, developed and invested in a shared politics, a shared love and a shared necessity. They were committed in all senses to each other, to their own liberation, to the political actions that defined who they were individually and collectively, and to the commune as a whole, which was not just interacting with the gay community, but also with the larger working class community it was surrounded by.

The pursuit of personal liberation within the commune was neither selfish nor libertarian. As Oscar Wilde said 'There is no art without beauty, no beauty without harmony, and no harmony without the individual.'

The paradox of individual liberation is that it can only be achieved through the collective, and only when that collective is part of and engaged with the larger community.

At the beginning of the book I said that coming out was an act of self-revelation. For radical queens self-revelation and the search for liberation continued throughout their activism, first as individual homosexuals, then as drag queens and finally as communards. Substitute self-revelation with self-realization and their project resonates beautifully with the radical theory of the Situationist's International, whose unitary triad for liberation is self-realization, communication and participation. What is liberation but the self-realization of the uniqueness of one's own subjectivity, which cannot be realized in isolation from others, in the world of things, but only in the commune where love is the spur to communication and participation, where we find our own urges to create, to love and to play. The queens put their will to create into their self-realization instinctively because all they had to go on was their individual selves. Their passion for love was put into communicating with each other and their desire to play became their communal participation. Within the commune, self-realization allows your lovers to see themselves in you, as you look for 'the richest part of [yourself] hidden within them.'[33] 'To love only oneself through other people, to be loved by others through the love they owe themselves ... this is what the passion of love teaches, and what the conditions of authentic communication desires.'[34] 'True love is revolutionary praxis or it is nothing.'[35]

The male left in GLF could never come up with such insights, because they never experienced life in that way. They failed to take their life and experiment with it during the period of the sexual revolution. They preferred instead to use the black art of politics, spending their time and energy labelling their opponents with their own worst qualities.

The commune of radical queens dispersed, but the women's commune at Faraday Road continued.

Julia L: The house ended up just as women. Richard moved out. Mad Lizzie, Sapphire, Lorna, Caroline, Barbara, me, Lynn, there were lots of us. We were still together as a household, we had a lounge and a huge bedroom where women could stay, everything was free love and everything else; you can use your imagination. Of course relationships started happening and splitting up and the dramas were out of this world. Everything was analysed in full ... people came from all over the country and then another women's house set up in Kilburn. You could pick up the phone and get them without having to dial a number, we were convinced that we were tapped, everyone was paranoid. You'd dial another number and still get the women's house. It was outrageous.

There were in-house arguments because people were starting to vary in their politics. I taught boys and girls, and my cat was a boy cat, much to everybody's horror. Splits started happening because we had this separatist idealism, but I couldn't live with it because (a) I liked my father, (b) I had a cat, and (c) I taught boys. I remember one day sitting in bed and the door opened and everybody piled in because of my politics; they didn't agree with them. Shouting and screaming, real mob handed but I was quite a strong personality and I wouldn't budge.

The other house went separatist too so we had this separatist clique. A friend of mine came round and brought me a Christmas tree and they wouldn't let him in, they had to open the basement door and bring it in. Some of us were having a very hard time, but we were still together. Gay men were shunned, ordinary men didn't exist. It ended up with some of us moving and one woman wanted a child and she'd worked out how to have a female child, separatist and so forth, and what happened was, of course, she had a boy child and then it all changed. That was a bit of a hoot.[36]

Janet Dixon: The first stage in the process of making men disappear was to ignore them totally. One by one the men in our mixed household left or were thrown out. We stopped going to GLF, and to mixed gay discos and on mixed demos. We sold all our male records, stopped reading the newspaper and watching the telly. When I wrote letters home I addressed them to my mother only. I sat alone in the canteen at college, I stopped drinking in pubs and chatty male bus conductors and shop assistants were met with blank stares.

At first it was men who were not allowed into the house and although this position resulted in a lot of criticism and ridicule, most feminists had some sympathy so long as we didn't seriously advocate separatism for all women. But of course this was inevitably what we did do. As a result of the huge curiosity our stance aroused we had to continuously explain and defend our politics. We had literally hundreds of almost identical conversations. These were often emotional and traumatising, and left us exhausted. We would often find out later that these conversations had been reported in a distorted way. All sorts of rumours spread about what went on in our house. We had, 'shaved our heads so as not to be sex objects, and boarded up our windows so that men in the street couldn't see in.' We also 'drowned male kittens, beat up the man who came to read the meter, and held covens where we stuck pins in male voodoo dollies.' We were easy targets for ridicule, and because we were angered and hurt by all of this, we withdrew further into ourselves, and stopped having contact with heterosexual women almost entirely.[37]

In the winter of 1975 the council evicted us from our squat and those of us who formed the nucleus of that original women's house were dispersed around the country. I felt very stuck. I was trapped by a set of dictates I had imposed on myself and others, and my aggressive public image doggedly intruded itself into my personal relationships. I was frustrated by my ghetto, sickened by my reputation, I needed a fresh start. I had to let go of separatism.

In the spring of 1976 I decided to act on a need I had felt for a very long time. I wanted a child. By June, after one attempt at conception, I was pregnant. (This, in the days before widespread artificial insemination, meant a public climb down from separatism.) My separatist friends said I was selling out, and taking on the role of mother was doing what the patriarchy had trained me for. In any case they would never sanction sex with a man for whatever reason, not to mention taking the risk of giving birth to a male child. Women who I had attacked for bringing up boy children wanted to know if it had been an immaculate conception or simply parthenogenesis, and what was I going to do with it if it were a boy? Although I did what I could to try to conceive a girl, I couldn't be sure that I had. In any event both sets of protagonists were right. My aggressive five-year ego trip along the path of separatism was over. I had to face the music, I had to face myself.

Halfway through my pregnancy, I fell asleep one afternoon and had a very powerful dream. In it I saw my child's body inside my own, but it wasn't curled up like a foetus. It wasn't a baby either, it was a child of about three, and what's more it was a boy with a shock of fair hair. When I woke up I was almost as amazed by the fair hair as I was by the sex, because both his 'father' and I are very dark. In the spring of 1977 I did indeed give birth to a boy who later grew that shock of fair hair.

Finally, I think the issue which more than any other led me to break with pure separatism was women's compassion. Women have massive amounts of love invested in fathers, lovers and sons, and many of these women despise the system their own men may be helping to sustain. Haven't women always so been torn? But to insist that women somehow amputate their love and compassion is to ask them to destroy the very thing which in my view favourably distinguishes us from men. Patriarchy has shown women that there is no such thing as peace, there are just gaps in the wars. To me, we were not offering anything different.[38]

Chapter 20

Bethnal Rouge – Curtains – The GLF Legacy

> The dialectic is not through a majority to revolution, but through revolutionary tactics to a majority.
> Rosa Luxemburg.

The all London General Meeting was born-again at the Conway Hall, Red Lion Square on 29 May 1973. The revivalists were Alan J M Bray, assisted by Brian Burt who founded the GLF Christian Group in reaction to Simon Benson forming the GLF Jewish Group back in 1971. The resurrection was attended by about 100 straight-gay men and a handful of women. The radical queens from Bethnal Rouge put up a stall, Warren Haig was there, but the left and the counterculture had moved on. By the second week around 40 members were excited and confident enough to march on Fleet Street where they raided the offices of several newspapers, dropped leaflets onto in-trays and pasted up demands in the toilets. This outburst of energy was immediately exhausted by the effort. The organizers and office clique had nothing new to offer, except the blame game against the radical femmes for their destruction of the original Front.

In July there was a report from Hendon GLF about the *Hendon Times* running a series of heterophobic articles each week on homosexual's cottaging in a local park. This rallied the straight gays to protest at Hendon on the 25 August. Some seventy members from London went to support the local group and demonstrated outside the newspaper's offices, and also outside the home of the editor. Yet again enthusiasm was spent; it was the last campaign. Being glad to be gay proved unsustainable.

The other major happening in August was Peter Tatchell

persuading the meeting to rubber stamp him as their official representative to the Young Communist League World Youth Festival in East Germany. At the Youth Rights' conference at Humbolt University in East Berlin, Tatchell's attempt to bring up the subject of revolutionary homosexuality was repeatedly prevented from reaching the eyes and ears of young communists by the combined efforts of the Party, the British delegation of Young Socialists, and the NUS delegates. Microphones were switched off, his pamphlets set on fire, his placards torn up. Tatchell's resolute determination to overcome those attacks revealed the inconsistencies of these new 'allies' in the cause of gay activism.

There was no such excitement in London. Bob Mellors, then an office volunteer, took stock of the situation and the new gay establishment. 'Unity and Brotherliness in GLF', abridged here, was his finding:

> A thing that has been bothering me a lot recently is how little I feel I have in common with some brothers in GLF. There seem to be quite a few gay brothers who I dislike quite intensely because of the way they behave and because of things they say.
>
> I find this rather depressing because I know that I come to GLF because of my sense of loneliness and because I need to meet other gay men and women. I think this must be true of most of us. The only people I feel I have something in common with are the people living in communes, although I have differences with many of them. Other than that I seem to prefer the company of gay men who shun any kind of 'political' activity and have a healthy scepticism about the whole thing and get on with what they like.
>
> I find that a 'gay' Marxist is much the same as a straight Marxist a 'gay' Christian the same as vicars I've met, the *'Gay' News* staff just as oppressive as any straight journalist and the

gay Icebreakers seem just as confused and confusing as any straight Samaritan or do-gooder.

All these kinds of straight people – Marxists, vicars, journalists, social workers, academics, and Samaritans – are the sort of people I can't stand – they all seem to be finding ways of avoiding their own problems and avoiding being honest with themselves and with us. These sorts of people are always oppressive to gay men and women. And I tend to dislike their gay counterparts as much as the straights themselves.

I am always much more conscious of my dislike for these gay do-gooders because I do feel some sense of involvement with them, so there is a feeling of betrayal when we fail to agree; we feel let down by people we expected to be our friends. We stop talking and hostility builds up.

On the other hand, if I was cast away on a desert island with the editor of the *Times* and Denis Lemon (editor of *Gay News*), I know who I'd spend my time with. I have met the Archbishop of Canterbury at a public meeting, so I know that Brian Burt is a million times nicer. If I were to meet Tariq Ali I'd probably fall in love with Phil Powell by comparison. Tony Salvis must be more loveable than Vic Feather. But until these straight pigs actually do begin to threaten my life and wellbeing in a very drastic way, or until some of us begin to change, I'm afraid I'll continue to feel that these gay brothers have more in common with my enemies than they do with me, and I'll have to try and find my real friends where I can.[1]

The next Newssheet brought a response from Tony Salvis:

Why was the last issue of the newssheet so permeated with hatred towards many gay people that I love? Why was it so sick ... sick ... sick ... Perhaps he feels a little bitter and disillusioned, because there was very little, if anything, constructive, in what he wrote. Just criticism for criticism's sake.

He pointed out how he disliked 'gay' Marxists, 'gay' Christians, and the 'Gay News' staff. Who does he like? And how patronising of him to say how lovable Denis Lemon, Brian Burt, Phil Powell, and Tony Salvis were, but still regards them as his enemies.

I bet he's never been to bed with any of the above, if not, perhaps he ought to and maybe he would find out a little more about them and they might appear a little more lovable to him, because although one can relate mentally, through words, it is not complete until one has related physically, through sex with another person, that one can begin to feel how the other person ticks.

What we need is a bit more love to wipe out the canker of hatred that seems to have developed within GLF. Then perhaps we can continue along the road to achieving the objective of all gay people (and straight people), of being free to do their own thing.[2]

Lunch magazine interviewed Bethnal Rouge in August, just after Christopher's (or call me Dolores) birthday party (where the cake was dedicated to Marilyn Monroe and there was a two minutes commemorative silence for her). There are currently 14 communards. Of the original group of eight, two remain. There are two girls, they'd like to have more. The bookshop was a real experiment. No one had any experience but after some weeks learning from Agitprop, and despite difficulties, they are glad that the shop is there. And so they have to find the money themselves to pay the rent (£170 a month) and rates (£500 a year). The shop provides a focus in social and cultural terms, and like the Oscar Wilde Memorial Bookshop in New York it is a valuable project in itself where much gay and 'alternative' literature can be seen and compared and bought.

Richard Chappell: We share everything, and make decisions

about clothes, money, the bookshop, all together.

Margaret Bannon: There were problems at first about privacy, the way people abused each others' clothes for example. But we've become more together and more sensitive.

Chappell: The last one up is the worst dressed.

Local response was mixed. Lee is the only born and bred Bethnal person there, indeed perhaps the only Londoner. He used to belong to local youth – somewhat antagonistic – started to hang out 'at The Rouge', to put on make-up and so on, then freaked out and joined them. Now when he goes into the local pub he runs the risk of getting beaten up. He was beaten up by a man who accused him of 'giving drugs to his sister'. But the real reason was that he had deserted the local scene to join the alien 'Rouge'.

Bannon: Someone tried to blow up Nicole's motor-bike. And we've had milk-bottles thrown. But it's a very varied reaction to us, like its people from the same place which is mostly the local young boys' club and the local pub *The Green Gates*, and they're either very interested in us, and come up and use the place, or else they're totally aggressive.

Chappell: It's a place to come and put on make-up before they go on to King's Cross. A lot of them are straight and into a sort of David Bowie glamour-trip. They'll come in and accept you on the level of bizarre clothes and make-up.

Stephen Bradbury: It's really nice because our local pub around the corner is run by two gay women. And a number of other local people are gay, or sympathetic. When we had trouble with the rates we went over to the solicitors just opposite, and they've been giving us free legal aid, and they wrote a letter to the Council asking for permission for us to pay monthly. Our local vicar let us have the Hall for our jumble-sale to raise money for the £64 a month for rates.

Bannon: There's this one woman who comes in, and she's having this break-up with her husband, he beats her up, and she says that we're the only people she can talk to. The only people she can communicate with.

Bradbury: There was the E2 festival for the East End and we had a stall there. It was like… incredible, all the people and the kids…

Christopher Stockdale: They had a concert at the Festival, pop, and we went and like, the kids just followed us, little kids, and we sat down to listen to the music. And we were surrounded by the huge crowd of little kids, and they were spitting at us and throwing cigarettes and toffee-apples.

Bradbury: Everything! Like, we just sat on the floor and the music began and we started to dance.

Chappell: The lead-guitarist!

Bannon: That was bizarre.

Bradbury: Like gradually we got into dancing, and into talking to people…

Bannon: Then the lead-guitarist noticed the lack of people around the stage and said over the loud-speaker, 'There's something *queer* going on over there but if you don't take any notice it'll go up in a *pouf* of smoke!' We had to write a letter about the festival to a guy at Oxford House the Christian Community Centre which helped finance the festival, and we included a paragraph about this incident, and the man we sent it to turned out to be the guy who had denounced us. And he came round and apologised. They offered us a hall and a group to hold benefit-dances!

Chappell: There's a gay discotheque locally [Tricky Dicky's at Liverpool Street] and after going there for about six weeks we were told not to go any more. They stopped us on the way out and said, 'Are you from the Commune down the road? Sorry, but too many complaints. You've got to stop coming.' There was an obvious sexual reason because they're into a very male homosexual scene, but otherwise it was difficult to see why.[6]

In September the office collective stabilized with sixteen or so members, but they couldn't shake the feeling that they were an elite and not to be trusted. The track record of many of its members was too well known to every long-term activist, but a new member Jamie Gardiner felt the need to defend the reputation of the people he worked with in the office, so he wrote: 'The structure of GLF' in which he admits that 'the Office Collective is particularly in danger of becoming what a Women's Liberation writer calls an 'informal elite' and goes on to deny that the Collective is closed. This is not true, for anyone may join.'[3]

Gordon King of the Somers Town commune disagreed with that and pointed out the change in usage of the office from a resource for all members to an exclusive domain for the office collective.

> It's happened again. The MEN have: formed a GROUP ... took over the CAPITOL (our office) – started to make rules for others than themselves ... printed PROPAGANDA on a newssheet ... took complete control of PUBLIC Property ... THE SAME OLD RITUAL ... wot next? Forms in triplicate, secretaries, candidates for parliament???? .... The office collective say "ALMOST" anyone can join. I don't want to 'join' anything, so apparently I can no longer use 'our' office ... and of course ALL the GLF mail and expressed opinion is now to be answered by the MEN from the Stone Age, men who don't use their own minds, but copy all the mistakes MEN have made since the world began. I don't want to stop them using OUR office, but I and perhaps others expect to be able to use it as well without 'joining' anything.[4]

Picking up the threads after visiting Amsterdam, reading and hearing how the office needed volunteers, and reckoning it was well over three months since my last involvement, I decided to join. What didn't occur to me at the time was that my approach to the office collective would be seen by them as the action of one of the fascists in a frock. To rejoin I had first to attend the weekly Office Collective meeting, which for some reason did not take place in the office but at the home of one of its members, so the first thing I had to do was find out the address and time. There was no published telephone number in the Newssheet for the meeting so I was forced to get in touch with the office. I rang and explained what I wanted, and why, only to be told that they couldn't give out the telephone number of their members to strangers just like that and I'd have to visit the office in person. So I went in and saw a young man in his early twenties, busy with important paper work and full of the insolence of an office environment. I made some comment about never having seen his face at Conway Hall and gathered that he'd never been there, and didn't think there was any point in going there because this was the place where all the important work was done, here in the office, the headquarters of GLF. As I suspected, when I found a vacant phone box at King's Cross that worked, the phone number I was given was wrong.

At the same time I was also applying to join Bethnal Rouge. The Rouge not only accepted me but took up my idea of moving the GLF office there because the lack of volunteers at Caledonian Road was restricting its opening hours; and it would be a way of breaking the grip on the office by *Gay News* workers and supporters like Tony Salvis and David McLellan. Bethnal Rouge had a much larger space at the back of the shop that was ideal. We made the proposal to the all London meeting, generated a discussion, but somehow didn't succeed in reaching a vote – what hadn't occurred to us was that the meeting didn't give a damn about the issue. With our plan now exposed it was either put up or shut up, so we decided to move the office by stealth the following morning.

I borrowed Bette Bourne's mini-van and Richard Chappell,

Steve Bradbury, Margaret Bannon and I arrived at King's Cross just before 8:30 a.m. as planned. What we had to do wasn't going to take more than 15 minutes, and I'd made it an early start in case we were rumbled. I knew that if anyone suspected we would make a move it would be Martin Corbett, whose instincts were sharp and who was always prepared to act on them. I parked just a bit north of Housmans in Balfe Street, gave my set of keys to the others and stayed in the van while they went off to do the deed. They returned with an armful of files and the address book, but when I checked, the office diary wasn't with them, so Richard Chappell and Steve Bradbury went back to look for it while Margaret Bannon put the files in the back of the van and climbed in. Down in the basement Chappell and Bradbury found the diary and were heading towards the stairs when they heard someone coming down. They hid behind the shelving and saw Martin Corbett walk towards the office, so as soon as he went in they ran up the stairs, followed by Corbett rushing to investigate. They both got out onto the street, Bradbury held the door shut and Chappell ran towards us waving like mad. I fired the engine and moved to pick him up, and then Bradbury made his dash because Corbett had gone back down the corridor to try and get out through the shop. The escape went like clockwork, Bradbury jumped in, the lights for Pentonville Road were green, and off we sped.

John Lindsey, of the Office Collective wrote their version of events in the next Newssheet. In a bitter three page diatribe he did make two valid points:

> [He claimed we were] getting foot and fist heavy with odd peaceful people standing around or offering oral objection... A small group of people in GLF have got themselves so liberated that they have now gone a complete circle and adopted the methods of our flat-footed brothers.
>
> Bethnal Rouge commune is in London and has plenty of

> space; it has someone there almost all the time and has gay people who are trying to make a go of a totally new lifestyle... On the other hand they are away from the centre, difficult for strangers to get to, paying a very heavy rent and rates, which makes them financially insecure, and most are emotionally so liberated that they can't communicate with most of the human race.
>
> The feeling of the collective is that there is a function to be performed at 5 Caledonian Road, and that it should be continued with: they further feel that the heavy methods used by some are contrary to the spirit and practice of GLF, damaging both to individuals and the GLF as a whole. They would like the matter discussed at the national get-together in Brighton and some guidance given on the role, if any, which other GLFs would like the office to perform, what they would like it to be called, how and by whom they would like it to be manned...[5]

The editorial of *Gay News* 34 marinated in venom for two weeks, and headed 'Radical Fascism' was another work of hysterical denunciation. My idea clearly hadn't done anybody any good, but the action had pulled the rug from under all the different interests in the bureaucracy, and the material worth it administered on behalf of the Gay Liberation Front: it forced them all to think.

By the time I moved to the Rouge in late September Chris Stockdale had left. Lee had moved to a squat in Whitechapel, and David who was American had moved on. Andrew Lumsden, who with Richard Chappell had originally taken the lease, had moved out after a couple of months because of the heavy drug use introduced by the straight machos from *The Green Gates*, and because of Chappell's indifference to the views of the other communards.

> *Christopher Stockdale*: Bethnal Rouge as a bookshop was a good idea but I'm not a shopkeeper and when it was my turn to look

after the shop I felt totally out of place. And I had this experience with a couple of books being nicked and being held responsible for not surveying correctly… it didn't make life any easier. The French from Le FHAR who visited Bethnal Rouge were in another squat but they came round a lot, they must have heard of us in Paris. I got friendly with them, had a short fling with one of them. They persuaded me, more or less, to come over just to see Paris, with the intention of spending a few days.

When I was trying to get my passport, Andrew had endorsed my request and they phoned me up – 'Eh, you can't have a journalist endorse your passport request.' I said, 'Why not? It's a journalist at *The Times* for god's sake, i'n't that enough, it's the official newspaper.' A few days later I had my passport. And the photo on it – made up like a tart. I'd had my hair dyed green so it was black on the photo. I was wearing these huge hoop earrings. I went on the coach from Victoria Coach Station down to Dover and I went through English customs, but they don't really bother when you're leaving. Anyway, I got to French passport control, 'Iz zis you in ze photo?' I said, 'Yes. I've just changed my hair colour.' Of course I'd changed my hair colour. I was a redhead when I went over to France, so I said, 'No my hair was green in that photo.' And I was wearing these enormous platform heels and of course your height is on the passport. He looked at me as though I crawled out from under a stone, but he couldn't find fault with the passport, there was nothing wrong with it, so he had to let me through.[7]

A couple of weeks after our raid on the office Richard Chappell, Stephen Bradbury, Margaret Bannon, Julian Hows and I went to the Brighton Think-In organized by the gay student society – Gaysoc, at the University of Sussex. *Gay News* 35 contains a short report claiming the discussion about the London office annoyed members from provincial cities. In fact those members were taking their first opportunity to learn about why we had made the raid. Nor did the newspaper state that there had been a vote taken at the end of the morning's discussion on our action.

Martin Corbett condemned us for the raid but made no mention of any fighting, and when questioned denied that there had been any. We then told our side of the story. After a question and answer session it became clear to us that both Leeds and Manchester GLF were persuaded by our reasons, and by a show of hands we gained approval for moving the office. It turned out that the provincial groups felt that the London office had become unhelpful towards them too.

But the action of moving the office proved futile, I was stupid not to see it would just carry on as usual, except the crisis I precipitated had caused Max McLellan and Martin Corbett to take over the stock of pamphlets, badges and manifestos and make a business for themselves as the GLF Information Service. When it became time in the 90s to reprint the *Manifesto* they cut out the section 'Aims' in 'The Way Forward', because they didn't agree with its ideas on the abolition of the family and gender roles, nor the promotion of Children's Liberation or working in alliance with Women's Liberation, nor on exploring communal living. It was their final act of revenge on an entire movement of revolutionary lesbians and gays.

In early January 1974 we were invited by Goldsmiths College Gaysoc to give a talk on our work at Bethnal Rouge, and afterwards attended their disco. I remember not wanting to go because I'd had enough of privileged reactionary students like the ones at Essex and Sussex Universities, but I was pressed to attend by the others who felt they needed the support of the whole commune. We arrived at the college in our disco drag to be met by Group 4 Total Security guards policing the place. We gave our talk to maybe thirty or so students and were in the bar afterwards buying drinks, when I heard that Richard Chappell had been attacked by the goons. I went off to find him, asking the first guard I saw what was going on. I came round on the floor with my face in a pool of blood from a head-butting. The thug was gone. I looked a real fright, and as I searched for the loo was told by one women student: 'What did you expect, coming here dressed like that.' The police then arrived so quickly it was almost as though they'd been waiting outside in readiness. I found the gents and checked myself out. When it felt safe I emerged to learn that Steve Bradbury had been arrested. I was shattered by the attack, found my coat, pulled the collar around my face and got away to the tube for Whitechapel and home. The others left for Lewisham Police station to wait for Steve Bradbury. Before his release that night the police beat him up and threw him against a glass door in the station.

I didn't need another sign to tell me this was the end of the GLF trip for me. I phoned Roger Rousell who agreed to let me stay at his place until I'd found somewhere to live. I left Bethnal Rouge in February. By the end of March they had run out of money and closed.

The other person working for *Gay News* that hadn't left the GLF Office Collective, who in my opinion consistently undermined the movement, was David Seligman, whose eyes were also firmly fixed on its ungoverned assets. *Gay News* 31 of 6 September 1973 featured an article titled 'Who needs a Gay Switchboard? ... And how it started in New Jersey.' This was followed by the announcement that invitations had been sent to specially invited groups and individuals, excluding GLF, to meet at *The Boltons* in Earls Court later that month to talk about the American idea of a Gay Switchboard to be set up in London.

By November the number of activists attending Conway Hall reduced in numbers to the point where it was no longer affordable, and the meeting moved to All Saints Hall where it quietly expired sometime in January 1974, around the same time that David Seligman's backroom dealings at *The Boltons* and *Gay*

News over the future of the GLF office was finally revealed.

> This may be the last newssheet issued. Let us try to explain why. The FINANCE REPORT explains our financial position; it also mentions the [Office Collective] meeting called on the 5 January 1974. Here is what happened. The Office collective had diminished to about six people from the beginning of December 1973, and we have become more than fed up with running it on our own.
>
> However, the crisis meeting did produce a response. Over 30 people attended the meeting on Sunday, at which it was proposed to set up a GAY SWITCHBOARD at the GLF office to be run by a collective comprising members of the various gay groups – Friend, CHE, INTERGROUP, Albany Trust etc.
>
> This proposal had previously been put to the Office by the organisers of the gay switchboard who needed premises, and approached us when they heard that the office might have to close.
>
> The Office collective basically supported the idea of the switchboard – starting at 5 Caledonian Road … with the proviso that some GLF people be on the switch board, and that we deal with internal questions which the switchboard cannot answer. For many weeks now, the office has in fact been operating only a limited service because it consisted of 10 people at the most.
>
> There were some people into GLF who felt that, with its impending closure, they would like it to continue as a GLF office only. However, the office collective explained that they did not wish to continue merely as an office collective – six months of carrying the office at a cost of £100 from their own pockets was quite enough.[8]

On the 16 February 1974 David Seligman acquired the premises and the all important telephone number that was key to the start-up of an invaluable lesbian and gay resource – a tribute to the hundred or so volunteers of the Gay Liberation Front who had kept the office going through thick and thin. The Newssheet concluded: 'GLF would still function as a mailing address and information centre, but Gay Switchboard would in fact run the office, and this would be of more benefit to all gay people.'[9]

After the revived all-London General Meeting ended in January 1974, GLF groups continued to exist for a short while in West London, Bangor, Birmingham, Blackburn, Bradford, Cardiff, Chester le Street, Coleraine N.I., Darlington, Dundee, Durham, Lancaster, Leeds GLF Office, Manchester, Newcastle, Sussex, and Warwick. Women's Gay Liberation continued into 1975. South London GLF became The Brixton Fairies who squatted houses in Railton Road and opened a gay community centre at No. 78 from which they were evicted in 1976, the year they organized London Gay Pride. The GLF Information Service continued until 1996.

GLF directly inspired the founders of Le FHAR in France and Mario Mieli who founded FUORI! in Italy. Micky Burbidge of Counter-Psychiatry established Icebreakers, and David Seligman introduced the Gay Switchboard to the UK. Aubrey Walter, David Fernbach and Richard Dipple of Media Workshop established Gay Men's Press. Bette Bourne founded the famous theatre troupe Bloolips. Angela Weir became the first head of Stonewall, while Peter Tatchell founded the other campaigning group Outrage! The Radical Feminists' separatist position became the rule for the Greenham Common Peace Camp. One of the greatest legacies of GLF when HIV/Aids emerged was the already existing networks and groups of individuals with political knowledge of the forever ongoing sexual revolution. ACT UP activists were immediately able to challenge the medical establishments' disgusting behaviour towards gays, and to everyone's benefit took over the entire ethical culture surrounding the pandemic, developing strategies for the support of those falling ill, the education of doctors and nurses, and knowledge-based interventions with drug companies' research policies.

I learnt from Bob Mellors in the early 90s that he was extremely upset at the way things had turned out, and that he regretted his role in changing gay society. He was taking too much on himself, understandably so perhaps, for he had already said he felt like the boy who'd struck the spark that set the prairie on fire.

Before GLF, gay bars and clubs were where you encountered the avant-garde, filled with men of all ages and classes mixing together, except on the drag circuit where pretend straights kept away from the queens, and in the one minority interest S & M pub where the uniform signalled apartheid. Post decriminalization, discos in all but name became the cutting edge of dance and fashion. All these venues produced dreams of togetherness and collective freedom only thwarted by the heterosexual closet queen landlords and brewery directors acting as policemen for Scotland Yard's code of permissible appearance and behaviour.

Post GLF, resistance to the sexual revolution transformed the ghetto into its opposite. Gays became camp followers, now divided by age, class and sexual inclination. Policing landlords and breweries became a mafia, owning and controlling the ghetto. They made the minority, sado-masochist masculinity of the sixties the dominant gay image idealising closet nostalgia for perverse, uniform-clad, rebel-rebel outlaws. *Gay News* first sold inside pubs and clubs, inadvertently perhaps, gave oversight of content to those closet queen club owners and brewers who used their financial strength to control, promote and protect their monopoly, whilst claiming to represent our community.

The modern ghetto is as ever a protection racket. Forty years of pushing the same stereotypes: a vampiric culture with a financial ideology rooted in heterosexualism. There's never been any criticism in the gay press of any bar or club or business entity: advertising money that gay media depends on would be cut off immediately. The porn industry's refusal to allow its stars to wear condoms resulted in at least two deaths. This could only be revealed through a public meeting at the *Purcell Rooms,* called by the *Times* journalist Tim Teemans. Responding to his criticisms the porn industry promised to regulate itself. We all know what that means.

More recently Matthew Todd, editor of *Attitude* magazine, appealed to the government through the Guardian[10] begging Cameron to sort out the mess at the Terrence Higgins Trust, which denied the crisis around crystal meth and GHB use in clubs that is leading to addiction, suicide and death in increasing numbers. Todd's naive overestimation of Tory concern is nevertheless honourably linked to the stubbornly high rate of HIV/Aids and gay youth made vulnerable to unsafe sex through low self esteem, binge drinking, and hard drug use, which he blames on heterophobia. No mention of poverty as a cause of poor self-worth, as there is no social dimension in a reactionary ghetto culture.

The successful repeal of section 28 and the reduction in the age of consent from 18 to 16 achieved in 2003 had alerted the alcohol-fuelled Lads and Ladettes to our power. Their attacks on feminism then broadened to include LGBTQ and black people – attacks acted out as parody and defended as post-modern irony (if you didn't find it funny you had no sense of humour) can been seen as having had an insidious effect on impressionable gay youth that the older generations don't seem to be aware of.

Todd has since put together a panel of experts to raise awareness of the 'drug abuse' crisis through public meetings, even posing the question: is gay culture to blame? They agree that young men are not going to stop taking drugs and fucking, that the 'mafia' isn't going to help but baulk at the only practical solution – to change the ghetto culture – because there's no money in that. Using the word 'abuser' is to employ the language of deviancy and social repression, which gay people know fuels rebellion within: 'If that's who I am, then to hell with them, that's who I'll be.' Labelling can be a self-fulfilling prophecy.

Stewart Who on Todd's panel nearly got it right – persuading drug users to form a group to talk among themselves about their experiences. Whether he knew it or not he had formed a consciousness-raising group: his mistake was to mentor the group, which collapsed I imagine because people are inhibited when authority is present. A consciousness-raising group is for members only, talking freely and honestly to the point. Faith in youth to work things out for themselves is a vital component. It was membership of awareness groups that educated the members of GLF: historic proof that C-R groups formed by activists are the first step towards social and cultural change. It's either that, or ghetto media using the 'abusers' it profits from – to keep the rest of us pure.

All authorities die disappointed. All institutions decay. Sexuality is at the core of humankind, the centre of our psyche, the organising principle of social life. Revolution is like making anything. What drives the hand to make the first mark is instinct. When you approach the barricades you don't know whether you will run away or stand and fight, but your reflex action to the situation will reveal who you truly are. That is how the new comes into being. Our revolution is unfinished; to complete it we must learn to grow it. When you join the revolution you will step from this present frozen time into historical time where you will again encounter these ideas on the politics of gender and sexuality. For the next stage we now have the knowledge that Gay Liberation and Women's Liberation continues to undermine all societies, races and creeds, challenging every individual who desires to keep humanity in chains.

Hope springs eternal! A proverb fit only to be writ large above the doors to banks and polling stations. Until the bourgeoisie accept the working class as the conscience of the economy and share their revolution with everyone there will be greed, strife, war, famine, cruelty, poverty, racism, slavery and ignorance; the bar set against the evolution of sexuality, the liberation of women and the emancipation of men's emotional nature.

The ball is rolling – all that's needed is to keep it on the right path.

Notes

Notes to Introduction

1 *The Times,* 28 July 1967.

2 Michel Foucault. *The History of Sexuality: Volume 1, An Introduction,* p.43. Originally published in French as *La Volonté du Savoir.* Copyright ©1976 by Editions Gallimard. Reprinted by permission of Georges Borchardt, Inc., for Editions Gallimard, Translated by Robert Hurley (Allen Lane 1979) Translation copyright © Random House, Inc., 1978, by kind permission of Penguin Group (UK).

3 Mary McIntosh, The Homosexual Role, *Social Problems,* Vol. 16, (Autumn 1968), Society for the Study of Social Problems. University of California Press.

Notes to Chapter 1

1 College Attacked by Gay Freaks, *Friends,* No.18, 13 November 1970, p.9.

2 Gay Liberation Guerrillas, *Time Out*, 31 October 1970, p.96.

3 Huey P. Newton, A Letter from Huey to the Revolutionary Brothers and Sisters about the Women's Liberation and Gay Liberation Movements, *The Black Panther,* California, 21 August 1970 p.5.

4 Jim Anderson, *IT* No.78, 24 April, 1970.

5 *IT* No.90, 22 October, 1970.

6 *Time Out,* No. 50, 3 October 1970, p.73.

7 *IT* Corrupts Public Morals & Outrages Decency, *IT,* No. 92, 19 November 1970, p.2.

8 Ibid.

9 Ibid.

10 Lisa Power, *No Bath but Plenty of Bubbles,* London, Cassell, 1995, p.38. By kind permission of Continuum International Publishing Group.

11 Aubrey Walter, Ed. & Intro., *Come Together: The Years of Gay Liberation 1970-1973*, London, Gay Men's Press, 1980, p.12.

12 Angie Weir in conversation.

13 *People*, 27 December 1970, p.10.

14 Bette Bourne in conversation.

15 Lisa Power, (1995), p.55.

16 Charles Marowitz, Theatre in London: The Ordeal of Isabel, A Jezebel, *The New York Times*. 27 December 1970.

17 The Importance of Participation of the Base in GLF, *Come Together* No.4.

18 See: Aubrey Walter, (1980), p.18.

19 Gay Consciousness-Raising Group, a London GLF pamphlet reprinted from *Gay Dealer,* newspaper of Philadelphia GLF. Original pamphlet produced by 'On Our Own' a collective effort by a New York Consciousness-Raising Group, New York, 1970.

Notes to Chapter 2

1 The winner was Miss Grenada. In 1970 Mecca Ltd., was negotiating with the Government of Grenada to build hotels on the island.

2 Nicholas de Jongh, Beauty O'ershadowed by the Women's Lib, *Guardian,* 21 November 1970.

3 Miss World Row: five remanded, *Guardian,* 23 December 1970.

4 WLW, *We're not Beautiful, We're not Ugly, We're Angry,* Hall Carpenter Archive (HCA) HCA/GLF/Chesterman/21.

5 Ian & Jake: "Political Views Could Be Enough," Judge,' *Time Out,* 3 December 1971, p.4.

6 *Time Out,* No. 95, p.4.

7 Police Question Women, *The Times,* 12 February 1971, p.1.

8 Carr bombing: Police still holding two men, *Evening Standard,* 12 February 1971, p.8.

9 Carr bomb: two help police raid, *Evening News,* 12 February

1971, p.1.
10 Ford Explosion, *Evening Standard*, 20 March 1971, p.11.
11 In conversation with the author.
12 *Shrew*, No. 2, p.14.
13 *IT*, No.98, 25 February 1971, p.2.
14 Angie Weir in conversation.
15 Ibid.
16 Tony Reynolds, GLF and Male Chauvinism, *Come Together* No. 3. See also, Carl Wittman, *Refugees from Amerika: A Gay Manifesto*, Committee of Concern for Homosexuals, Berkeley, republished in *Gay Flames* No. 9, Gay Flames Collective, New York.
17 Lisa Power, (1995), p.119.
18 Elizabeth Wilson, The Gateways Club and Gay Liberation, *Come Together* No. 2.
19 Lisa Power, (1995), p.120.
20 Ibid p.120-121.
21 HCA/GLF/McIntosh/7/1.
22 *IT*, No. 99, 11 March 1971.
23 Lisa Power, (1995), p.122.
24 Ibid.
25 Silver Surfer versus Imperial College Man, *Come Together*, No. 5.
26 Lisa Power (1995), p.56.
27 Ibid. p.107.
28 Bust to Show the Flag, *Come Together* No. 4.
29 Dennis Greenwood in conversation.
30 Bust to Show the Flag, Op.Cit.
31 Lisa Power, (1995), p.61.
32 Steve Mann, Gay Gig, *Frendz*, Vol 2, No.29, 30 April 1971, p18-19.
33 Oscar Wilde, *The Soul Of Man Under Socialism*.
34 Jeffrey Weeks, *Coming Out*, London, Quartet Books, 1977, Chapter 16, p.205.

35 Wilhelm Reich, *Sexual Politics,* London, Vision Press, 1951, 1961, 1969, 1972, p.29.

36 Susan Sontag, *Against Interpretation,* Notes on Camp, London, Penguin Classics, 2009, Nos. 51-52, p.290 Notes on Camp, New York, 1964. By kind permission of the Penguin Group. "Notes on Camp" from AGAINST INTERPRETATION BY Susan Sontag. Copyright © 1964, 1966, renewed 1994 by Susan Sontag. Reprinted by permission of Farrar, Strauss & Giroux, LLC.

Notes to Chapter 3

1 Homosexuality and Therapy, *Come Together* No.2.

2 *Village Voice,* 3 July 1969, p.18.

3 Martin Duberman, *Stonewall,* New York, London, Dutton, 1993, p.202.

4 *Village Voice,* 3 July 1969.

5 *Stonewall,* (Duberman) 1993.

6 Toby Marotta, *The Politics of Homosexuality,* Boston, Houghton Mifflin Co. 1981, p.24.

7 Daughters of Bilitis, Statement of Purpose, 1955.

8 John D'Emileo, *Sexual Politics, Sexual Communites: The making of a homosexual minority in the USA 1940- 1970,* University of Chicago Press, 1993, p.169.

9 Eric Marcus, *Making History: The Struggle for Gay and Lesbian Equal Rights,* 1945 –1990, New York, Harper Collins, 1992, p.221.

10 In conversation.

11 Lisa Power, (1995), p.92.

12 Ibid. p.92-93.

13 Counter-Psychiatry Group Statement. HCA/McIntosh/7/1.

14 Gore Vidal, Number One, *The New York Review of Books,* Vol.14 No.11. 4 June, 1970.

15 David Reuben, *Everything You Always Wanted to Know About Sex,* London, W.H. Allen, 1970, p.135.

16 Ibid. p.129.
17 Ibid. p.134.
18 Ibid. p.147.
19 Ibid. p.215.
20 Ibid. p.258/9.
21 Ibid. p.260.
22 Ibid. p.143.
23 *Evening Standard* 12 February 1971.
24 *The Guardian* 13 February 1971.
25 Mary McIntosh, Leaflet for Harley St. Demonstration for Counter-Psychiatry, HCA/GLF/McIntosh/7/1.

Notes to Chapter 4

1 *Frendz* No. 3 (31), 4 June 1971, p.15.
2 John Chesterman, transcript from his tape recording, HCA/GLF/Chesterman/19.
3 *INK*, No.9, 26 June 1971,Gay Power Comes Together, p. 24.
4 John Chesterman, HCA/GLF/Chesterman/19.
5 Ibid.
6 David Leigh, *The Scotsman*. 23 June 1971, Courtesy of The Scotsman Publications Ltd.
7 Lisa Power, (1995), p.123.
8 Ibid. p.124.
9 Ibid. p.125.
10 *Evening News*, 10 June 1971, p.7.
11 Elizabeth Wilson in conversation.
12 Angie Weir in conversation.
13 Robert Chessyre, *Observer*, 1 August 1971, p.3.
14 CHE Bulletin July/August 1971, HCA/CHE.
15 Robert Chessyre, (1 August 1971).
16 Burnley Confronted: The Struggle for Survival in the Provinces, *Come Together* No. 8.
17 Robert Chessyre, (1 August 1971).
18 Colin Dunne, The Permissive Society Stops Here, *Daily*

Mirror, 11 August 1971, p.11.
19 HCA/GLF/3.
20 John Norman Lloyd in conversation.
21 Lisa Power, (1995), p.110.
22 HCA/GLF/3.
23 Oscar Wilde.

Notes to Chapter 5

1 Larry Mitchell, *The Faggots & Their Friends Between Revolutions,* New York, Cadmus Books, 1977, p.19.
2 Jill Tweedy, *Guardian,* 13 December 1971, p.9.
3 Lisa Power, (1995), p.68.
4 Ibid. p.82-83.
5 *The Times,* 23 June 1971.
6 Ibid.
7 *The Times,* 24 June 1971.
8 For a full report see Tony Palmer, *The Trials of Oz,* London, Blond & Briggs, 1971.
9 Lisa Power, (1995), p.17.
10 *Time Out,* 9-15 July 1971, p.5.
11 For a near verbatim report of Mr. John Mortimer QC's Summing Up see: *Time Out* ,9-15 July 1971.
12 Alan Travis, Home Affairs Editor, Oz Trial lifted lid on porn squad bribery, *Guardian,* 13 November 1999.

Notes to Chapter 6

1 *Time Out,* 4 June 1971.
2 *Frendz,* No. 3 (31), 4 June 1971, p.11.
3 Lisa Power, (1995), p.111.
4 Grace Slick, *Blows Against the Empire,* Jefferson Airplane.
5 HCA/GLF/3, John Chesterman.
6 HCA/GLF/Grimes.
7 HCA/GLF/3.
8 Lisa Power, (1995), p.115.

9 Ibid. p.71-72.
10 Ibid. p.126.
11 Ibid. p.126-127.

Notes to Chapter 7

1 Nuremburg-on-Thames, *Frendz,* No.11, 30 September 1971, p.6.
2 Ibid.
3 Basil Gingell, Religious Affairs Correspondent, Uproar at Central Hall, *The Times,* 10 September 1971.
4 Ibid.
5 *Frendz,* No.11, (30 September 1971).
6 *Guardian.* 11 September 1971.
7 John Norman Lloyd in conversation.
8 Peter Dunn, *The Sunday Times,* 26 September 1971, p.7.
9 Gay Libs' Kissing Closed a Bar', *Guardian,* 7 August 1971, p.7.
10 HCA/GLF/Chesterman/23.
11 Ibid.
12 Ibid.
13 'Gay Folk – Flying Squad in Action', *Morning Advertiser,* 8 October 1971, p.2. (Trade paper for The Licensed Victuallers) Reprinted by permission of The Morning Advertiser Ltd © 1971.
14 GLF press statement 13 October 1971, Re: harassment of gay people in and around Notting Hill pubs, HCA/GLF/Grimes.

Notes to Chapter 8

1 'Verballed'. A police practice at the time. 'Verbals' were notes written up by the police in their notebooks *after* the interrogation of suspects, and were supposed to be a record of what had been said.
2 Lisa Power, (1995), p.189.
3 Ibid. p.189.

4 Ibid. p.189.
5 HCA/GLF/Grimes.
6 Wilhelm Reich, *Sex-Pol Essays, The Imposition of Sexual Morality* 1929-1934, London, Verso, 2012, p.228. See also Elaine Morgan, *The Descent of Woman,* London, Souvenir Press, 1972, on changes in the anatomy of the female human ape, which she proposes led to the link between sex and violence.
7 Friedrich Engels, *The Origin of the Family, Private Property, and the State,* Intro., Evelyn Reed, New York, Pathfinder Press, 1972.
8 A reference to *The German Ideology,* Karl Marx and Friedrich Engels, *Collected Works*, 1848.
9 Friedrich Engels (1884).
10 Gay Flames. Pamphlet No. 7.
11 Ibid.
12 Lisa Power, (1995), p.190.
13 Elizabeth Wilson in conversation.
14 Guy Debord, Trans., Ken Knabb, *Society of The Spectacle,* Rebel Press, London. Paris, 1967, Note 82.
15 Angie Weir in conversation.
16 Lisa Power, (1995), p.190.
17 HCA/GLF/Grimes.
18 Aubrey Walter, (1980), p.35.
19 Jacques Ranciere, 'On the Theory of Ideology – Althusser's Politics, 1969'. In: Roy Edgley & Richard Osborne, Eds., Terry Eagleton, Ed. & Intro., *Radical Philosophy Reader,* London, Verso, 1985, p.130.
20 HCA/GLF/McIntosh/7/1.
21 Based on the article, Skegness Women's Liberation, *Come Together* 10.
22 Lisa Power, (1995), p.128.
23 Elizabeth Wilson in conversation.
24 The papers of Sheila Rowbotham, The Women's Library,

LSE, 7/SHR/B/03. Across this paper in red ink is written: 'This agenda was overturned.'

25 Lisa Power, (1995), p.129.

26 Janet Dixon, Separatism: a look back at anger. In: Bob Cant & Susan Hemmings, Eds., *Radical Records,* London, Routledge, 1988, p.71.

27 Angie Weir in conversation.

28 Lisa Power, (1995), p.129.

29 Angie Weir and Elizabeth Wilson in conversation.

30 Lisa Power, (1995), p.130.

31 Skegness Women's Liberation, *Come Together* 10.

32 Angie Weir in conversation.

33 Skegness Women's Liberation, *Come Together* 10.

34 Lisa Power, (1995), p.130-131.

36 Ibid. p.132.

37 Elizabeth Wilson in conversation.

38 Janet Dixon, (1988), p.72-73.

Notes to Chapter 9

1 *7 Days,* No.12, 19 January, 1972.

2 Cal McCrystal, Amnesty accuses British Troops, *Sunday Times,* 16 October 1966.

3 Foreign Office and Amnesty clash on Torture charges, *Sunday Times,* 23 October 1966.

4 *7 Days,* 19 January 1972.

5 Ibid.

6 *7 Days,* No.13, 26 January 1972, p.3.

Notes to Chapter 10

1 *Frendz* 16, 21 November 1971.

2 Ibid.

3 *Lunch* Magazine, October 1971, HCA/Journals/45.

4 Lisa Power, (1995), p.168.

5 HCA/GLF/McIntosh/7/1 & HCA/GLF/Grimes, names and

dates in ink on back of copy of GLF Principles.

6 *Time Out,* 19 November 1971.

7 *Come Together,* 11.

8 Ibid.

9 *West London Observer,* 20 January 1972, p.16.

10 Ibid.

11 Ibid.

12 Ibid.

13 Lisa Power, (1995), p.192-193.

14 Ibid. 194-195.

Notes to Chapter 11

1 The Black Panthers *Executive Mandate No. 1,* 1967.

2 *7 Days,* 8 December 1971.

3 *Time Out,* 10 December 1971.

4 *Time Out,* 3 December 1971.

5 Ibid.

6 *Days,* 8 December 1971.

7 *Time Out,* 10 December 1971, p.4.

8 Ibid. p.5.

9 Hugh Massingberd, Ed._*The Very Best of the Daily Telegraph Books of Obituaries,* Sir Melford Stevenson, Pan Books, London, 2001, [1987] p. 31-34.

10 Statement by Black Panther Movement 15 August 1970, *IT,* No. 87, 10 – 24 September 1970.

11 *Time Out,* 17 - 23 December 1971, p.8.

12 Ibid. p.8.

13 *INK,* 7 January 1972, p.16.

14 Ibid.

15 *Time Out,* 24-30 December 1971, p.7.

16 *INK,* Op. Cit. p.16.

17 *Evening News,* 17 December 1971.

18 Judith McFadzean Ferguson, *7 Days,* 22 December 1971, p.7.

19 Lisa Power, (1995), p.211-213.

20 Mark Roberts in conversation.
21 Lisa Power, (1995), p.164.

Notes to Chapter 12

1 Bob Mellors, *We Are All Androgynous Yellow,* London, Another-Orbit Press, 1980, p.52.
2 Lisa Power(1995), p.244.
3 ibid.
4 Ibid. p.245.
5 HCA/GLF/Grimes.
6 Bob Mellors, *Homosexuality Androgyny & Evolution: Clint Eastwood Loves Jeff Bridges True!* London, Another Orbit Press, 1978.
7 Ibid. p.14.
8 Ibid. p.15.
9 Mario Mieli, Trans., David Fernbach, *Homosexuality & Liberation: elements of a gay critique,* London, Gay Men's Press, 1980, p.27-28.
10 Ibid p.28.

Notes to Chapter 13

1 Sensitivity Not Productivity. HCA/GLF/3.
2 Lisa Power, (1995), p.51.
3 Andrew Lumsden in conversation.
4 Lisa Power, (1995), p.206.
5 Ibid.
6 Ibid.
7 Ibid.
8 Ibid. p.207.
9 HCA/GLF/1.

Notes to Chapter 14

1 Lisa Power, (1995), p.133.
2 Ibid. p.133. (Pat Arrowsmith, *Somewhere Like This,* London,

W.H. Allen, 1970. Republished by Panther 1971).

3 *The Observer*, 16 January 1972, p.3.

4 Lisa Power, (1995), p.134.

5 Ibid. p.135.

6 Ibid. p.135-136.

7 Michele Roberts, *INK*, 4 February 1972, p.6.

8 Lisa Power, (1995), p.62.

9 Ibid. p.191.

10 Ibid. p.133.

11 Ibid. p.133

12 Ibid. p.233-234.

13 Janet Dixon, (1988), p.79.

14 Lisa Power, (1995), p.234-235.

15 In her book, *Love Between Women* Dr. Charlotte Wolff demonstrates there has been change over time as cultural demands have been imposed on the subjugated feminine gender.

16 Janet Dixon, (1988), p.70.

17 'Separatism is to feminism what fundamentalism is to Christianity. It is the centre, the beating heart, the essence. The dogma is of absolutes, the lifestyle is of attempted purity and the zealot is subject to continuous derision.' Janet Dixon, *Radical Records*, (1988), p.69.

18 Lisa Power, (1995), p.231.

19 Ibid. p.232.

20 Ibid. p.245.

21 Lesbian Liberation: out from under, *INK*, 25 Feb 1972, Gay News, p.5.

22 HCA/McIntosh/7/1.

23 Lisa Power, (1995), p.238-9

24 Janet Dixon, (1988), p. 77.

25 Ibid p.75.

26 The GLF Finance Crisis; A personal statement by Ralph Stephenson, GLF Audio News, HCA/GLF/2.

27 Lisa Power, (1995), p.246.

Notes to Chapter 15

1 Lisa Power, (1995), p.240.
2 Ibid. p.248.
3 HCA/GLF/McIntosh/7.
4 HCA/GLF/15.
5 Bette Bourne in conversation.
6 HCA/GLF/Beach/9.
7 *Lunch* Magazine No. 13, October 1972. HCA/Journals/45.
8 Aubrey Walter, (1980), p.35.
9 Ibid.
10 Jeffrey Weeks, (1977), p.203.

Notes to Chapter 16

1 HCA/GLF/2.
2 HCA/GLF/3.
3 Lisa Power, (1995), p.252.
4 Ibid. 253.
5 I have since discovered that *Time Out* in early 1972 featured the story of Mrs. McCarthy's campaign for an inquiry into her son's death. This news was concurrent with the production of *Come Together* 12, which gives even less excuse for stating Stephen died at Upper Street Police Station.
6 *Come Together* 12. HCA/Journals/253.
7 HCA/GLF/2.
8 HCA/GLF/3.
9 *IT,* 140, 18 October 1972, p.8.
10 GLF Newssheet, 21 June 1972. HCA/GLF/3.
11 Lisa Power, (1995), p. 254.
12 Ibid. p. 257.
13 Andy Beckett, *When the Lights Went Out: Britain in the Seventies*, London, Faber & Faber, 2009. p.223-224.
14 The papers of Sheila Rowbotham, The Women's Library,

LSE, 7/SHR/B12-14-C/1/1.

15 Denis Lemon, *Gay News* No. 2, *Spare Rib* Attacked, p.7.

16 Cloud Downey in conversation.

17 Lisa Power, (1995), p.258.

18 Mark Roberts in conversation.

19 Doug Pollard, An Open Letter To The Rad. Femmes, *Gay News* No. 2, p.8.

20 See: Gillian E Hanscombe & Andrew Lumsden, *Title Fight: The Battle for GAY NEWS*, London, Brilliance Books,1983.

21 W. H. Auden, *Thanksgiving for a Habit,* COLLECTED WORKS, Copyright © 1976, 1991, The Estate of W.H. Auden, granted by permission of The Wylie Agency (UK) Ltd., and, *Thanksgiving for a Habitat,* copyright © 1963 by W.H. Auden and renewed 1991 by The Estate of W.H. Auden, from COLLECTED POEMS OF W. H. AUDEN by W.H. Auden. Used by permission of Random House, Inc.

Notes to Chapter 17

1 GLF Newssheet 21 June 1972, HCA/GLF/McIntosh/2/.

2 Lisa Power, (1995), p.261-262.

3 Ibid. p.263.

4 Ibid. p.262-263.

5 *Gay News* No. 2, p.5.

6 *The Sunday Times*, 25 June 1972, Alan Brien's Diary.

7 John Chesterman, *Gay International News* No. 5, HCA/Journals/10.

8 Jeffrey Weeks, (1977), p.205

9 Lisa Power(1995), p.260.

10 Trouble outside 'gay' dance, *South London Press,* 11 August 1972, p.14.

11 Cloud Downey in conversation.

12 Lisa Power, (1995), p.215.

13 Ibid. p.215.

14 Cloud Downey in conversation.

15 Lisa Power, (1995), p.216-217.

16 Bette Bourne in conversation.

17 Lisa Power, (1995), 217-219.

18 HCA/Chesterman/5.

19 Opinion. Liberationist battle front. *South London Press* 11 July 1972.

20 Cloud Downey in conversation.

21 Lisa Power, (1995), p.220-221.

22 *Time Out*, 30 June – 5 July 1972, p.8.

23 *Time Out*, 8 – 14 September 1972, p.11.

24 *Time Out*, 7 – 13 July 1972, p.9.

25 *Time Out*, 8 – 14 December 1972, p.11.

26 *Time Out*, 15 – 21 December 1972, p.4.

27 Lisa Power, (1995), p.220.

28 Ibid. p. 223.

29 Stephen Crowther in conversation.

30 Lisa Power, (1995), p. 221.

31 GLF Camden Newsletter 10 August 1972, HCA/GLF/Beach/9.

32 Customers Wore Drag, *Gay News* 8, p.3.

33 Lisa Power, (1995), p.267-268.

34 *Camden Come Together* 13, p.5. HCA/Journals/253b.

35 HCA/GLF/9.

36 *Morning Star*, 21 October, 1972.

37 John Chesterman, *Gay International News* 5, p.6. HCA/Journals/10.

Notes to Chapter 18

1 Lisa Power, (1995), p.223.

2 Ibid. p.227.

3 A reference to workers involvement in the 1968 student uprising in Paris who were betrayed by the Communist Party trade union, the Confédération Générale du Travail.

4 Michael Lyneham, GLF Diary, 2 November 1972.

HCA/GLF/4.

5 Bob Sturgess, Gay Trial Phase One, *Lunch* 15. HCA/Journals/10.

6 Wild Scenes At Court As 'Gay Lib' Group Appears - Kisses blown at magistrate! *West London Observer,* 3 November 1972, p.20.

7 Michael Lyneham, (1972).

8 Lisa Power, (1995), p. 269.

9 Bob Sturgess, (*Lunch* 15).

10 *Champion* Case Erupts in Court, *Gay News* 10 p.3

11 Bob Sturgess, (*Lunch* 15).

12 Ibid.

13 Ibid.

14 Michael Lyneham, (1972).

15 Bette Bourne, *Come Together* 15, p.26. HCA/Journals/ 253B.

16 Helen Hewland, Take A Look At This Sir Malby, *West London Observer,* 23 February 1973.

17 Michael James in conversation.

18 Bette Bourne in conversation.

19 Stephen Crowther in conversation.

20 Christopher Stockdale in conversation.

21 Lisa Power, (1995), p.226.

22 Ibid. p. 227.

23 Michael James in conversation.

24 Lisa Power, (1995), p.224-225.

25 Ibid. p.225-226.

26 Ibid. p.227.

27 Stephen Crowther in convesation.

28 Bette Bourne in conversation.

29 Lisa Power, (1995), p.228.

30 Bette Bourne in conversation.

31 Lisa Power, (1995), p.228.

32 Michael James in conversation.

33 Bette Bourne in conversation.

Notes to Chapter 19

1 Lisa Power, (1995), p.275.

2 Aubrey Walter, (1980), p.23.

3 Bette Bourne in conversation.

4 Lisa Power, (1995), p.275-276.

5 Chris Stockdale in conversation.

6 *West London Observer,* 23rd Feb. 1973, The Great Speculation Scandal, p.7.

7 Notting Hill People Demand Action Against Speculators, *People's News Service,* 12 May 1973, p.9.

8 The Police and the Lock-In, *Kensington News & Post Mercury* Series, 18 May 1973, p.6.

9 Jan O'Malley, *The Politics of Community Action: A Decade of Struggle in Notting Hill,* Nottingham, The Bertrand Russell Foundation, 1977, p.135.

10 GLF Newsletter 12 April 1973. HCA/GLF/4.

11 Stephen Crowther in conversation.

12 HCA/GLF/4.

13 *Independent,* 29 December, 2009, Peter Tatchell: Quentin Crisp was no gay hero.

14 Quentin said AIDS was a fad; he meant of course, the AIDS industry. Volunteering at Body Positive I saw those post-graduates who joined the Health Sector spend all their working time searching for the next step up the career ladder. Bureaucratic time servers, they drove that charity into the ground – pure faddism. The Terrence Higgins Trust has ended up the privatised arm of government, its CEO bought off with a knighthood. Hollywood and the fashion industry – they've moved on too.

15 See: Sheila Jeffreys , *Butch and Femme: Now and then,* Published in; *Not a Passing Phase,* London, The Woman's Press, Ltd., 1989

16 See references to gynamorphy on page 334 above.

17 Since the departure from Stonewall of 3rd generation

Labour grandee Ben Summerskill, the new CEO Ruth Hunt announced in February 2015 that Stonewall would again be working with trans people.

18 In conversation.

19 Aubrey Walter, (1980), p.34.

20 Ibid. p.36.

21 Lisa Power, (1995), p. 251.

22 Lisa Power, (1995), p. 222.

23 David Fernbach, *Gay Marxist,* No.3.

24 Karl Marx, Trans. Ben Fowkes, Fwd. Ernest Mandel, *Capital,* Vol. 1, London, Penguin Books, 1976, Postface to the Second Edition, Karl Marx, p.102.

25 Ibid.

26 Keith Birch, A Commune Experiment, *Gay Left* No.2, Spring 1976, p.11-12.

27 Ibid.

28 Ibid.

29 Ibid.

30 Ibid.

31 Jeffrey Weeks, (1977), p.202.

32 Pierre-Joseph Proudhon, *General Idea of the Revolution in the Nineteenth Century,* Third Study, The Principle of Association.

33 Raul Vaneigem, *The Revolution of Everyday Life,* (1963-1965), Paris, Gallimard, 1967, p.246.

34 Ibid. p.251.

35 Ibid. p.248.

36 Lisa Power, (1995), p.235-238.

37 Janet Dixon, (1988), p.77-80.

38 Ibid. p.80-83.

Notes to Chapter 20

1 GLF Newssheet, 4 – 10 July 1973. HCA/GLF/4.

2 GLF Newssheet, 18 July 1973. HCA/GLF/4.

3 GLF Newssheet, 4 September 1973. HCA/GLF/4.
4 HCA/GLF/3.
5 GLF Newssheet, 2 October 1973. HCA/GLF/4.
6 *Lunch,* October 1973, p.18-19. HCA/Journals/10.
7 Christopher Stockdale in conversation.
8 To All Our Readers. GLF Newssheet January 1974. HCA/GLF/3
9 Ibid.
10 Matthew Todd, The Roots of Gay Shame, *Guardian,* 2 February 2013.

Bibliography

Allinder, Gary, *Gay Liberation Meets The Shrinks, Confrontation 1: San Francisco,* New York: Gay Flames, 1970.

Altman, Dennis, *Homosexual: Oppression & Liberation,* London: Allen Lane, 1974.

Auden, Wystan Hugh, *About The House,* London: Faber & Faber, 1966.

Bartlett, Neil, *Who Was That Man,* London: Serpent's Tail, 1988.

Beckett, Andy, *When The Lights Went Out: Britain in the Seventies,* London: Faber & Faber, 2009.

Bray, Alan, *Homosexuality in Renaissance England,* London: Gay Men's Press, 1982.

Cant, Bob, and Susan Hemmings, Eds., *Radical Records: Thirty Years of Lesbian & Gay History,* London: Routledge, 1988.

Cook, Matt, Ed., with H.G. Cocks, Robert Mills & Randolph Trumbach, *A Gay History of Britain,* Oxford/Westport, CT: Greenwood World Publishing, 2007.

Crisp, Quentin, *How To Become a Virgin,* London: Fontana Paperbacks, 1981.

Debord, Guy, Trans., Ken Knabb, *Society of the Spectacle,* London: Rebel Press. First English publication, Detroit: Black & Red, 1970.

D'Emilio, John, *Sexual Politics, Sexual Communities: The Making of a Homosexual minority in the USA 1940-1970,* Univ., of Chicago Press: 1993.

Duberman, Martin, *Stonewall,* New York, London: Dutton, 1993.

Edgley, Roy & Richard Osborne, Eds., *Radical Philosophy Reader,* Jacques Ranciere, Theory of Ideology, London: Verso, 1985.

Firestone, Shulamith, *The Dialectic of Sex: The Case for Feminist Revolution,* Frogmore, St. Albans, Herts: UK., Paladin, 1972.

Foucault, Michel, *The History of Sexuality,* New York: Pantheon Books, 1978.

Gay Left Collective, Eds., *Homosexuality: Power & Politics,* London: Allison & Busby, 1980.

Hall Carpenter Archives Lesbian Oral History Group, *Inventing Ourselves: Lesbian Life Stories,* London: Routledge, 1989.

Hall Carpenter Archives Gay Men's Oral History Group, *Walking After Midnight: Gay Men's Life Stories,* London: Routledge, 1989.

Hamer, Emily, *Britannia's Glory: A History of Twentieth-Century Lesbians,* London: Cassell, 1996.

Hanscombe, Gillian E., and Andrew Lumsden, *Title Fight: The Battle for GAY NEWS,* London: Brilliance Books, 1983.

Lesbian History Group 1989 & 1993, *Not a Passing Phase,* London: The Women's Press Ltd., 1989.

Jeffrey-Poulter, Stephen, *Peers, Queers & Commons: The Struggle for Gay Law Reform from 1950 to the Present,* London: Routledge, 1991.

Kilmister, Lemmy with Garza Janis, *White Line Fever,* London: Simon & Schuster, 2002.

Marotta, Toby, *The Politics of Homosexuality,* Boston: Houghton Mifflin Co., 1981.

Mellors, Bob, *"Homosexuality," Androgyny & Evolution, A Simple Introduction,* London: Quantum Jump, Another Orbit Press, 1978.

Mellors, Bob, *We Are All Androgynous Yellow,* London: Quantum Jump, Another Orbit Press, 1980.

Mieli, Mario, Trans., David Fernbach, *Homosexuality & Liberation: Elements of a Gay Critique,* London: Gay Men's Press, 1980.

Mitchell, Larry, and Ned Asta, *The Faggots & Their Friends Between Revolutions,* New York: Cadmus Books, 1977.

Morgan, Elaine, *The Descent of Woman,* London: Souvenir Press, 1972.

Norton, Rictor, *Mother Clap's Molly House,* London: Gay Men's Press, 1992.

O'Malley, Jan, *The Politics of Community Action: A Decade of*

Struggle in Notting Hill, Nottingham: Russell Foundation, 1977.

Palmer, Tony, *The Trials of Oz,* London: Blond & Briggs, 1971.

Porter, Kevin and Jeffrey Weeks, Eds., *Between the Acts: Lives of Homosexual Men 1885 – 1967,* London: Routledge, 1991.

Power, Lisa, *No Bath But Plenty Of Bubbles: An Oral History of the Gay Liberation Front 1970-73,* London: Cassell, 1995.

Proudhon, Pierre-Joseph, Tran., John Beverley Robinson, *General Idea of the Revolution in the Nineteenth Century,* London: Pluto Press, 1989.

Reed, Leonard with James Morton, *Nipper Read: The Man Who Nicked the Krays,* London: Macdonald & Co (Publishers) Ltd., 1991.

Reich, Wilhelm, *Sex-Pol Essays, The Imposition of Sexual Morality* 1929-1934, London: Verso, 2012.

Reich, Wilhelm, *The Sexual Revolution,* London: Vision Press, 1972.

Rocke, Michael, *Forbidden Friendships: Homosexuality & Male Culture in Renaissance Florence,* Oxford University Press: 1996.

Saunders, Nicholas, *Alternative London,* London: Nicholas Saunders, 1971.

Sedgwick, Eve Kossofsky, *Between Men: English Literature and Male Homosocial Desire,* Columbia University Press: 1985.

Sontag, Susan, *Against Interpretation and Other Essays,* London: Penguin Classics, 2009.

Tolstoy, Leo, *Government is Violence,* London: Phoenix Press, 1990.

Vaneigem, Raul, Tran., Donald Nicholson Smith, *The Revolution of Everyday Life,* London: Left Bank Books & Rebel Press, 1983, Original title: *Traité de savoir-vivre à l'usage des jeunes générations*. Paris: Gallimard, 1967.

Vienet, Rene, *Enrages and Situationists in the Occupation Movement, France, May '68,* Brooklyn, New York: Autonomedia, 1992.

Walter, Aubrey, Ed., & Intro., *Come Together – the years of gay liber-*

ation 1970-73, London: Gay Men's Press, 1980.

Weeks, Jeffrey, *Coming Out: Homosexual Politics in Britain, from the Nineteenth Century to the Present,* London: Quartet Book, 1977.

Wheen, Francis, *Who Was Dr. Charlotte Bach,* London: Short Books, 2002.

Wilde, Oscar Fingal O'Flahertie Wills, *The Works of Oscar Wilde,* London: Spring Books, 1963.

Wolff, Charlotte, Dr., *Love Between Women,* London: Duckworth, 1973.

Index of Names

Contemporary culture has eliminated both the concept of the public and the figure of the intellectual. Former public spaces – both physical and cultural – are now either derelict or colonized by advertising. A cretinous anti-intellectualism presides, cheerled by expensively educated hacks in the pay of multinational corporations who reassure their bored readers that there is no need to rouse themselves from their interpassive stupor. The informal censorship internalized and propagated by the cultural workers of late capitalism generates a banal conformity that the propaganda chiefs of Stalinism could only ever have dreamt of imposing. Zer0 Books knows that another kind of discourse – intellectual without being academic, popular without being populist – is not only possible: it is already flourishing, in the regions beyond the striplit malls of so-called mass media and the neurotically bureaucratic halls of the academy. Zer0 is committed to the idea of publishing as a making public of the intellectual. It is convinced that in the unthinking, blandly consensual culture in which we live, critical and engaged theoretical reflection is more important than ever before.